NON-LEAGUE FOOTBALL TABLES OF NORTH EAST ENGLAND 1889-2018

EDITOR
Michael Robinson

FOREWORD

Following the success of our 'Non-League Football Tables' series of books, the first of which was published in 2002, we long considered introducing a number of regionalised titles about various football leagues both past and present.

The first book in the eventual series, 'Non-League Football Tables of South West England 1892-2015' was published in 2015 and 'Non-League Football Tables of North West England 1889-2016' and 'Non-League Football Tables of South East England 1894-2017' were published in subsequent years. All of these books are available for purchase at our address shown below, each priced £11.99.

This fourth book, of a planned series of six, covers seven football leagues from the North East of England. The earliest of these commenced in 1889 and still (along with a number of the other leagues included) continues to operate to this day.

The Leagues which currently form the apex of the 'Non-League Pyramid', namely the National League (formerly the Football Conference) and its three feeder leagues (Northern Premier, Southern Premier & Isthmian) will continue to be covered by our yearly National League and Non-League Football Tables books.

As always, we are indebted to Mick Blakeman for providing tables for the various Leagues included in this book.

British Library Cataloguing in Publication Data
A catalogue record for this book is available from the British Library

ISBN: 978-1-86223-388-1

Copyright © 2018   Soccer Books Limited, 72 St. Peters Avenue,
Cleethorpes, DN35 8HU, United Kingdom   (01472 696226)

All rights are reserved. No part of this publication may be reproduced, stored into a retrieval system or transmitted, in any form or by any means, electronic, mechanical, photocopying, recording, or otherwise, without the prior written permission of Soccer Books Limited.

Printed in the UK by 4edge Ltd.

CONTENTS

Northern League 1889-2018 .... Pages 4-33

Northern Alliance 1890-2018 .... Pages 34-63

Tyneside League 1891-1939 .... Pages 64-70

Wearside League 1892-2018 .... Pages 71-95

North-Eastern League 1906-1964 .... Pages 96-108

Midland League 1958-1960 .... Pages 107-108

Northern Counties League 1960-1962 .... Page 108

Palatine League 1920-1926 .... Pages 109

North Regional League 1958-1969 .... Pages 110-112

NORTHERN LEAGUE 1889-2018

The Football League, founded in 1888 and the first competition of its type in the world, was an instant success. The format of 12 clubs, playing each other home and away, with a simple points system to decide their relative positions, was hugely attractive to supporters who turned out for league matches in numbers rarely experienced for the programme of friendlies that had been replaced.

If it worked at a national level, then surely it would work in the North-East as well and on Tuesday 26th March 1889, a meeting was held at the Three Tuns Hotel, Durham City to discuss the possibility of a Northern League. The meeting was called by the secretary of Darlington F.C., Charles S. Craven, who invited 19 clubs to the meeting but only 6 of those – Middlesbrough, Morpeth Harriers, Newcastle West End, Stockton, Sunderland and Sunderland Albion – actually attended.

Even so, the meeting resolved to form the league with 9 invited clubs. Morpeth Harriers excluded themselves because of "the town not being handy for clubs in the South" but Bishop Auckland Town, Elswick Rangers and Newcastle East End were added to those present. Darlington St. Augustine's were chosen to replace any club who declined the invitation.

Sunderland Albion declined and joined the Football Alliance instead while Sunderland decided to continue with cup-ties and friendlies. St. Augustine's were duly elected as one of the replacements and the number of clubs was increased to 10 as Birtley and South Bank were also voted in as founder members of the new league.

1889-90

Darlington St. Augustine's	18	12	2	4	39	17	26
Newcastle West End	18	12	2	4	44	24	26
Stockton	18	10	4	4	41	18	24
Newcastle East End	18	9	3	6	32	28	21
Darlington	18	7	6	5	46	20	20
Middlesbrough	18	8	3	7	42	37	19
South Bank	18	6	2	10	33	60	14
Bishop Auckland Town	18	4	4	10	41	49	12
Birtley	18	3	3	12	28	48	9
Elswick Rangers	18	2	5	11	21	66	9

Darlington St. Augustine's won the championship on goal average. Birtley, Bishop Auckland Town and Elswick Rangers left to become founder members of the Northern Alliance. South Bank also resigned from the league and reverted to playing a programme of friendlies and cup-ties. Middlesbrough Ironopolis joined as a newly formed club and Sunderland Albion joined while continuing to play in the Football Alliance.

1890-91

Middlesbrough Ironopolis	14	9	2	3	37	24	20
Middlesbrough	14	8	3	3	33	17	19
Sunderland Albion	14	7	3	4	33	16	17
Stockton	14	8	1	5	38	19	17
Darlington	14	7	0	7	25	29	14
Newcastle East End	14	5	2	7	25	39	12
Newcastle West End	14	3	4	7	21	38	10
Darlington St. Augustine's	14	0	3	11	14	44	3

Darlington St. Augustine's left the league and reverted to playing just friendlies and cup-ties. Sheffield United joined from the Midland League and South Bank joined having not played in a league in 1890-91.

1891-92

Middlesbrough Ironopolis	16	14	1	1	49	13	29
Middlesbrough	16	13	0	3	33	13	26
Sheffield United	16	10	2	4	49	21	22
Newcastle East End	16	9	2	5	37	20	20
Stockton	16	6	2	8	31	34	14
Sunderland Albion	16	5	0	11	36	38	10
South Bank	16	3	2	11	21	50	8
Newcastle West End	16	4	0	12	21	56	8
Darlington	16	2	3	11	17	49	7

Newcastle West End and Sunderland Albion both disbanded at the end of the season. South Bank resigned in August 1892, reverted to being an amateur club and joined the Teesside League. Sheffield United continued to play in the league despite having also joined the Football League – Division Two.

1892-93

Middlesbrough Ironopolis	10	9	1	0	22	6	19
Newcastle East End / United	10	5	1	4	30	19	11
Sheffield United	10	4	2	4	18	16	10
Middlesbrough	10	4	0	6	17	17	8
Stockton	10	3	1	6	24	27	7
Darlington	10	2	1	7	11	37	5

Newcastle East End officially changed their name to Newcastle United on 9th December 1892.

Middlesbrough Ironopolis and Newcastle United both left the league after being elected to the Football League – Division Two and Sheffield United left after winning promotion from the Football League – Division Two to Division One. North Skelton Rovers and Whitby joined from the Cleveland Amateur League, South Bank joined from the Teesside League and Bishop Auckland and Darlington St. Augustine's both joined, having played only friendlies and cup-ties in 1892-93.

Northern League 1893-1899

1893-94

	P	W	D	L	F	A	Pts
Middlesbrough	14	11	1	2	51	16	23
Stockton	14	10	1	3	41	23	21
South Bank	14	8	0	6	36	34	16
Darlington	14	7	1	6	30	25	15
Bishop Auckland	14	6	0	8	41	39	12
Whitby	14	5	2	7	45	43	12
North Skelton Rovers	14	3	1	10	25	52	7
Darlington St. Augustine's	14	3	0	11	25	62	6

Howden Rangers and Tow Law both joined from the Bishop Auckland & District League.

1894-95

	P	W	D	L	F	A	Pts
Middlesbrough	18	12	5	1	58	17	29
South Bank	18	11	4	3	64	23	26
Tow Law	18	10	3	5	59	30	23
Darlington	18	11	0	7	56	30	22
Whitby	18	8	2	8	43	45	18
Stockton	18	8	1	9	44	37	17
Bishop Auckland	18	7	2	9	42	39	16
Howden Rangers	18	6	1	11	40	56	13
Darlington St. Augustine's	18	5	3	10	38	66	13
North Skelton Rovers	18	1	1	16	16	117	3

North Skelton Rovers moved to the Cleveland Amateur League as North Skelton and Darlington St. Augustine's reverted to playing just cup-ties and friendlies. Saltburn Swifts joined from the Cleveland Amateur League. Howden Rangers changed their name to Howden-le-Wear.

1895-96

	P	W	D	L	F	A	Pts
Darlington	16	10	4	2	53	24	24
South Bank	16	9	2	5	44	20	20
Middlesbrough	16	8	4	4	28	22	20
Bishop Auckland	16	7	3	6	42	32	17
Tow Law	16	5	5	6	23	28	15
Whitby	16	6	3	7	23	38	15
Stockton	16	5	3	8	26	30	13
Howden-le-Wear	16	4	3	9	19	36	11
Saltburn Swifts	16	4	1	11	12	40	9

Howden-le-Wear moved to the Wear Valley League and Whitby moved to the Cleveland Amateur League. Leadgate Park joined from the Tyneside League, Crook Town joined from the Bishop Auckland & District League and Darlington St. Augustine's joined after a year not playing in a league.

1896-97

	P	W	D	L	F	A	Pts
Middlesbrough	16	11	4	1	36	15	26
Darlington	16	10	2	4	54	35	22
South Bank	16	10	1	5	32	25	21
Stockton	16	7	3	6	37	24	17
Tow Law	16	7	1	8	29	25	15
Bishop Auckland	16	6	3	7	23	34	15
Crook Town	16	4	2	10	35	42	10
Leadgate Park	16	4	1	11	27	45	9
Darlington St. Augustine's	16	2	5	9	26	54	7

Darlington St. Augustine's had 2 points deducted.
Saltburn Swifts resigned and disbanded on 3rd April 1897 and their record was deleted when it stood as: 13 3 4 6 21 33 10

A Second Division was formed containing 7 clubs. Brotton and Loftus both joined from the Cleveland Amateur League, Howden-le-Wear and Shildon United both joined from the Wear Valley League and Darlington Rise Carr Rangers joined from the Teesside League. The other two members were Leadgate Exiles and Britannia Rovers, a newly re-formed club who had also entered the Middlesbrough League.

1897-98

Promoted clubs in bold, relegated clubs in bold italics

Division One

	P	W	D	L	F	A	Pts
Stockton	16	11	2	3	37	20	24
Middlesbrough	16	9	4	3	42	22	22
Darlington	16	8	2	6	41	31	18
Bishop Auckland	16	6	4	6	33	35	16
Darlington St. Augustine's	16	7	2	7	29	32	16
Leadgate Park	16	5	4	7	23	34	14
South Bank	16	5	3	8	34	38	13
Tow Law	16	4	4	8	16	24	12
Crook Town	16	3	3	10	17	36	9

Due to a smallpox epidemic in the area, Middlesbrough could not complete their fixtures until the following season. The last of their three outstanding games was played on 8th October 1898. Promotion and relegation was supposed to have been decided by a series of Test Matches but with 3 games still to be played in Division One and various other fixture problems, it was decided to scrap the test matches and no clubs were either promoted or relegated.

Division Two

	P	W	D	L	F	A	Pts
Howden-le-Wear	10	5	2	3	17	14	12
Darlington Rise Carr Rangers	10	5	1	4	22	18	11
Loftus	10	5	1	4	18	17	11
Leadgate Exiles	10	5	0	5	17	17	10
Shildon United	10	4	1	5	15	17	9
Brotton	10	3	1	6	14	20	7

Britannia Rovers "were struck out of the competition" on 31st March 1898 as they had not played a league game since 18th December. Their record was deleted when it stood as: 6 0 1 5 6 25 1
Britannia Rovers subsequently disbanded.
Leadgate Exiles moved to the North-West Durham Alliance and Darlington Rise Carr Rangers disbanded. Stockton St. John's, Thornaby and Thornaby Utopians all joined from the Teesside League and West Hartlepool joined as a newly formed club. Stockton Vulcan and Scarborough also joined.

1898-99

Division One

	P	W	D	L	F	A	Pts
Bishop Auckland	16	9	7	0	35	16	25
Darlington	16	10	3	3	50	29	23
Middlesbrough	16	7	4	5	29	27	18
South Bank	16	6	6	4	20	21	18
Darlington St. Augustine's	16	5	5	6	19	23	15
Leadgate Park	16	4	4	8	25	30	12
Stockton	16	4	4	8	25	31	12
Tow Law	16	3	6	7	18	25	12
Crook Town	16	4	1	11	25	44	9

Middlesbrough left the league after being elected to the Football League – Division Two while Leadgate Park moved to the Northern Alliance.

Division Two

	P	W	D	L	F	A	Pts
Stockton St. John's	18	11	5	2	38	11	27
Thornaby Utopians	18	10	4	4	45	21	24
Thornaby	18	10	1	7	42	28	21
Brotton	17	9	2	6	33	22	20
Stockton Vulcan	17	10	0	7	29	30	20
Shildon United	16	7	1	8	21	20	15
West Hartlepool	18	6	1	11	23	48	13
Scarborough	16	5	1	10	21	37	11
Loftus	17	4	3	10	18	41	11
Howden-le-Wear	17	4	2	11	21	33	10

Neither of the two games between Scarborough and Shildon United were played nor were Stockton Vulcan vs Loftus or Howden-le-Wear vs Brotton. Howden-le-Wear moved to the Wear Valley League. Grangetown Athletic joined from the Teesside League, Whitby joined after playing just cup-ties and friendlies in 1898-99 and Dorman, Long & Co. joined as a recently formed club.

1899-1900

Division One

	P	W	D	L	F	A	Pts
Darlington	16	12	3	1	42	16	27
Stockton St. John's	16	10	3	3	32	17	23
Bishop Auckland	16	9	2	5	41	21	20
Darlington St. Augustine's	16	7	4	5	34	27	18
South Bank	16	7	3	6	18	26	17
Crook Town	16	3	7	6	14	24	13
Thornaby Utopians	16	3	6	7	14	25	12
Tow Law	16	3	3	10	23	43	9
Stockton	16	2	1	13	25	44	5

Tow Law moved to the South Durham Alliance.

Division Two

	P	W	D	L	F	A	Pts
Whitby	14	9	3	2	49	23	21
Thornaby	14	8	3	3	29	15	19
Grangetown Athletic	14	7	5	2	36	24	19
Loftus	14	6	2	6	23	24	14
West Hartlepool	14	6	0	8	28	28	12
Scarborough	14	4	3	7	27	34	11
Stockton Vulcan	14	4	2	8	20	36	10
Brotton	14	3	0	11	20	48	6

Dorman, Long & Co. resigned on 15th November 1899 and their record was deleted when it stood as: 8 1 1 6 8 26 3
Shildon United resigned and disbanded on 13th January 1900 and their record at the time deleted: 5 3 1 1 13 5 7

Division Two closed down at the end of the season.

Brotton, Grangetown Athletic and Loftus became founder members of the newly formed Cleveland Alliance while Thornaby moved to the Teesside League. However a vacancy occurred in the Northern Alliance at the start of December and Thornaby were elected to fill it. Stockton Vulcan are thought to have disbanded in 1900 but to have then re-formed and joined the Teesside League in 1901-02. However they failed to complete the season and may have merged with another club.

1900-01

	P	W	D	L	F	A	Pts
Bishop Auckland	20	12	5	3	61	22	29
Darlington St. Augustine's	20	10	5	5	37	25	25
Darlington	20	11	2	7	55	37	24
Stockton	20	8	5	7	34	25	21
Crook Town	20	7	7	6	38	30	21
Scarborough	20	9	3	8	25	28	21
South Bank	20	9	3	8	35	45	21
Thornaby Utopians	20	8	2	10	30	37	18
Stockton St. John's	20	7	3	10	23	35	17
West Hartlepool	20	5	5	10	31	37	15
Whitby	20	2	4	14	17	65	8

Whitby moved to the Cleveland Alliance and Thornaby Utopians disbanded. Grangetown Athletic joined from the Cleveland Alliance.

1901-02

	P	W	D	L	F	A	Pts
Bishop Auckland	18	12	3	3	48	22	27
Grangetown Athletic	18	9	8	1	34	14	26
Darlington	18	9	4	5	37	22	22
South Bank	18	7	6	5	32	23	20
Darlington St. Augustine's	18	7	5	6	31	22	19
Stockton	18	6	7	5	25	25	19
Crook Town	18	5	3	10	29	41	13
West Hartlepool	18	5	3	10	24	48	13
Scarborough	18	5	3	10	20	35	13
Stockton St. John's	18	2	4	12	13	41	8

Middlesbrough Reserves, Newcastle United Reserves and Sunderland Reserves all joined from the Northern Alliance. These reserve teams were described as "A" teams at the time but are described as Reserves here for clarity.

1902-03

	P	W	D	L	F	A	Pts
Newcastle United Reserves	24	22	0	2	100	14	42
Sunderland Reserves	24	18	4	2	93	22	40
Middlesbrough Reserves	24	13	7	4	66	30	33
Bishop Auckland	24	13	3	8	57	35	29
Stockton	24	9	5	10	35	38	23
Darlington	24	10	3	11	34	50	23
South Bank	24	8	6	10	30	44	22
Crook Town	24	9	4	11	27	41	22
Grangetown Athletic	24	8	4	12	34	47	20
Stockton St. John's	24	6	5	13	24	52	15
Scarborough	24	5	4	15	23	69	14
Darlington St. Augustine's	24	4	5	15	21	58	13
West Hartlepool	24	3	6	15	27	71	12

Newcastle United Reserves and Stockton St. John's each had 2 points deducted.

1903-04

	P	W	D	L	F	A	Pts
Newcastle United Reserves	24	19	1	4	97	23	39
Bishop Auckland	24	17	2	5	55	27	36
Sunderland Reserves	24	14	6	4	66	32	34
Middlesbrough Reserves	24	12	5	7	56	32	29
Stockton	24	13	2	9	36	34	28
Darlington	24	11	3	10	48	49	25
Grangetown Athletic	24	10	3	11	50	49	23
South Bank	24	9	1	14	42	56	19
Darlington St. Augustine's	24	8	2	14	30	58	18
# Shildon Athletic	24	8	2	14	28	54	18
Scarborough	24	7	2	15	36	70	16
Crook Town	24	5	4	15	33	62	14
West Hartlepool	24	5	3	16	31	62	13

Stockton St. John's resigned and disbanded on 8th October 1903 and Shildon Athletic moved from the South Durham Alliance to take over their fixtures. Stockton St. John's record when it was transferred to Shildon Athletic stood as follows: 3 0 0 3 2 7 0

1904-05

	P	W	D	L	F	A	Pts
Newcastle United Reserves	24	22	0	2	83	12	44
Sunderland Reserves	24	16	3	5	59	29	33
Middlesbrough Reserves	24	13	6	5	69	35	32
Darlington	24	9	6	9	38	38	24
Shildon Athletic	24	8	7	9	48	48	23
South Bank	24	9	5	10	42	44	23
West Hartlepool	24	10	3	11	35	44	23
Bishop Auckland	24	10	2	12	51	49	22
Stockton	24	8	6	10	32	37	22
Darlington St. Augustine's	24	9	4	11	34	43	22
Grangetown Athletic	24	8	4	12	36	52	20
Scarborough	24	4	5	15	22	60	13
Crook Town	24	4	1	19	23	81	9

Sunderland Reserves had 2 points deducted.
Spennymoor United joined from the Mid-Durham League.

1905-06

	P	W	D	L	F	A	Pts
Sunderland Reserves	26	21	3	2	90	21	45
Newcastle United Reserves	26	19	4	3	92	14	42
Bishop Auckland	26	15	3	8	45	39	33
Darlington	26	12	7	7	47	47	31
Middlesbrough Reserves	26	12	5	9	59	30	29
South Bank	26	13	2	11	49	35	28
Shildon Athletic	26	11	6	9	40	45	28
Spennymoor United	26	8	6	12	34	34	22
Grangetown Athletic	26	9	2	15	37	43	20
Stockton	26	7	5	14	32	54	19
Crook Town	26	7	5	14	33	57	19
West Hartlepool	26	7	5	14	49	65	17
Scarborough	26	7	2	17	24	93	16
Darlington St. Augustine's	26	3	7	16	16	70	13

West Hartlepool had 2 points deducted.

Northern League 1906-1913

Middlesbrough Reserves, Newcastle United Reserves and Sunderland Reserves all left to become founder members of the newly formed North-Eastern League. Leadgate Park joined from the Northern Alliance.

1906-07

Stockton	22	17	2	3	44	16	36
South Bank	22	14	3	5	46	24	31
Crook Town	22	12	1	9	41	33	25
Leadgate Park	22	11	2	9	40	34	24
Bishop Auckland	22	10	3	9	40	33	23
Spennymoor United	22	9	5	8	28	30	23
Darlington	22	9	2	11	30	37	20
Shildon Athletic	22	8	3	11	30	38	19
Grangetown Athletic	22	8	1	13	24	39	17
West Hartlepool	22	7	2	13	33	44	16
Darlington St. Augustine's	22	6	3	13	32	44	15
Scarborough	22	7	1	14	34	50	15

Shildon Athletic moved to the North-Eastern League.
Saltburn joined from the Cleveland Alliance.

1907-08

Stockton	22	13	7	2	49	21	33
South Bank	22	15	3	4	53	26	33
Crook Town	22	12	4	6	40	33	28
West Hartlepool	22	10	4	8	40	32	24
Spennymoor United	22	11	2	9	39	36	24
Bishop Auckland	22	9	4	9	40	36	22
Darlington St. Augustine's	22	9	3	10	32	39	21
Saltburn	22	9	2	11	46	47	20
Darlington	22	9	2	11	39	41	20
Leadgate Park	22	6	4	12	33	43	16
Grangetown Athletic	22	3	7	12	21	52	13
Scarborough	22	5	0	17	44	70	10

South Bank were declared champions on 19th September 1908 after winning the championship play-off 2-0 against Stockton on Darlington St. Augustine's Chesnut Grove ground.
Darlington and Spennymoor United both moved to the North-Eastern League. West Auckland joined having been playing cup-ties and friendlies in 1907-08 and York City joined as a newly formed club.

1908-09

Bishop Auckland	22	14	5	3	67	29	33
South Bank	22	15	3	4	61	34	33
Stockton	22	10	6	6	46	29	26
Crook Town	22	10	6	6	49	40	26
West Hartlepool	22	11	2	9	50	35	24
Grangetown Athletic	22	9	3	10	47	53	21
Darlington St. Augustine's	22	8	4	10	48	52	20
Scarborough	22	9	1	12	45	56	19
Saltburn	22	6	6	10	33	42	18
West Auckland	22	6	4	12	32	46	16
York City	22	6	3	13	31	73	15
Leadgate Park	22	6	1	15	30	50	13

Bishop Auckland were declared champions after beating South Bank 4-2 in the championship play-off at Darlington St. Augustine's Chesnut Grove ground on 27th November, 1909.
Leadgate Park moved to the Chester-le-Street & District League.
Knaresborough joined from the York & District League.

1909-10

Bishop Auckland	22	15	3	4	67	37	33
South Bank	22	13	4	5	50	26	30
Stockton	22	13	3	6	68	34	29
Darlington St. Augustine's	22	12	2	8	41	35	26
West Auckland	22	9	4	9	35	35	22
Crook Town	22	8	4	10	45	43	20
Scarborough	22	8	4	10	43	49	20
West Hartlepool	22	8	4	10	32	40	20
Knaresborough	22	8	4	10	43	58	20
Saltburn	22	7	4	11	28	46	18
Grangetown Athletic	22	6	2	14	30	44	14
York City	22	4	4	14	36	71	12

Scarborough and York City both left to become founder members of the newly formed Yorkshire Combination while West Hartlepool disbanded.
Eston United joined from the Teesside League, Leadgate Park joined from the Chester-le-Street & District League and Stanley United joined having played just friendlies and cup-ties in 1909-10.

1910-11

Eston United	22	15	4	3	56	24	34
South Bank	22	14	4	4	50	23	32
Bishop Auckland	22	13	5	4	67	30	31
Stockton	22	10	6	6	43	27	26
West Auckland	22	10	6	6	39	27	26
Darlington St. Augustine's	22	9	4	9	40	41	22
Crook Town	22	8	4	10	40	48	20
Leadgate Park	22	8	3	11	38	43	19
Stanley United	22	6	6	10	29	41	18
Saltburn	22	5	5	12	35	51	15
Grangetown Athletic	22	4	7	11	13	33	15
Knaresborough	22	2	2	18	27	89	6

Knaresborough were also playing in the Yorkshire Combination and they left to concentrate on that competition. Willington joined from the Auckland & District League.

1911-12

Bishop Auckland	22	14	6	2	60	28	34
South Bank	22	12	5	5	33	18	29
Crook Town	22	13	3	6	37	24	29
Leadgate Park	22	11	3	8	36	32	25
Willington	22	10	3	9	42	36	23
Stockton	22	8	5	9	46	34	21
Darlington St. Augustine's	22	8	5	9	44	36	21
Grangetown Athletic	22	7	6	9	25	32	20
Stanley United	22	8	3	11	27	35	19
Eston United	22	7	3	12	33	40	17
West Auckland	22	6	2	14	29	52	14
Saltburn	22	4	4	14	20	65	12

Saltburn moved to the Teesside League and West Auckland disbanded.
Craghead United joined from the Chester-le-Street & District League and Esh Winning Rangers joined, having been playing just friendlies and cup-ties in 1911-12.

1912-13

Esh Winning Rangers	22	13	6	3	40	22	32
Willington	22	12	4	6	43	26	28
South Bank	22	12	4	6	36	23	28
Crook Town	22	11	5	6	33	23	27
Craghead United	22	11	3	8	51	26	25
Stockton	22	10	4	8	34	27	24
Darlington St. Augustine's	22	9	5	8	33	28	23
Eston United	22	9	5	8	44	43	23
Stanley United	22	6	4	12	29	54	16
Bishop Auckland	22	5	5	12	37	52	15
Grangetown Athletic	22	5	2	15	29	57	12
Leadgate Park	22	3	5	14	32	60	11

Esh Winning Rangers changed their name to Esh Winning. Redcar joined as a newly formed club.

1913-14

Willington	24	20	2	2	52	17	42
South Bank	24	16	4	4	47	22	36
Crook Town	24	11	5	8	41	27	27
Darlington St. Augustine's	24	11	5	8	35	29	27
Craghead United	24	11	3	10	42	36	25
Stockton	24	8	8	8	41	35	24
Bishop Auckland	24	9	4	11	38	35	22
Stanley United	24	7	7	10	33	36	21
Eston United	24	8	5	11	31	38	21
Leadgate Park	24	6	7	11	30	46	19
Esh Winning	24	5	8	11	27	42	18
Grangetown Athletic	24	5	7	12	26	52	17
Redcar	24	4	5	15	30	58	13

Craghead United moved to the Northern Combination. Scarborough joined from the Yorkshire Combination and Harrogate joined as a new football club, having just converted from rugby union.

1914-15

Crook Town	16	12	1	3	36	10	25
Bishop Auckland	16	10	4	2	42	13	24
Willington	16	8	2	6	37	23	18
Leadgate Park	16	7	4	5	33	22	18
Stanley United	16	7	2	7	31	25	16
Esh Winning	15	6	2	7	25	30	14
Scarborough	16	6	1	9	23	49	13
Darlington St. Augustine's	16	3	1	12	22	51	7
Stockton	15	3	1	11	17	43	7

Stockton vs Esh Winning was not played.
Redcar resigned as soon as war was declared because their ground was needed for military purposes. Harrogate resigned on 5th September before playing a game because almost all of their players had joined The Army.
Eston United resigned on 12th December for the same reason and their record was deleted: 3 1 1 1 5 5 3
Grangetown Athletic resigned on 12th December, due to financial issues and their record was deleted: 6 0 1 5 8 17 1
South Bank resigned on 29th January because of a lack of players and their record was deleted: 12 4 2 6 28 33 10

At the end of the season, the Northern League closed down completely for the duration of the war.

1919

Of the pre-war members, Darlington St. Augustine's and Grangetown Athletic had disbanded and Leadgate Park moved to the North-Eastern League. Harrogate re-formed after the war but did not play in a league until the 1920-21 season when they joined the Yorkshire League. The remaining 10 pre-war members all rejoined the league.
There were four new members. Grangetown St. Mary's and West Hartlepool St. Joseph's joined, both having played in the Teesside League before the war. Auckland St. Helen's United were formed in 1919 and took over the ground of the pre-war West Auckland club. Darlington Railway Athletic had been formed in 1918 and played in the Darlington & District League in 1918-19.

1919-20

Bishop Auckland	26	16	6	4	76	23	38
South Bank	26	16	6	4	78	27	38
Crook Town	26	17	4	5	57	24	38
Stanley United	26	13	5	8	52	39	31
Grangetown St. Mary's	26	11	9	6	51	41	31
Willington	26	11	7	8	43	36	29
Esh Winning	26	11	4	11	48	34	26
Eston United	26	9	6	11	48	51	24
Darlington Railway Athletic	26	10	4	12	45	58	24
Redcar	26	9	4	13	38	55	22
West Hartlepool St. Joseph's	26	7	6	13	34	51	20
Stockton	26	5	5	16	44	70	15
Auckland St. Helen's United	26	5	5	16	26	67	15
Scarborough	26	5	3	18	30	94	13

South Bank were declared champions after winning the 3-way championship play-offs in September 1920 on goal average. Bishop Auckland beat South Bank 4-2 at Stockton on 4th September, Crook Town beat Bishop Auckland 2-1 at Willington on 11th September and South Bank beat Crook Town 4-0 at Bishop Auckland on 18th September.
Auckland St. Helen's United changed their name to West Auckland and left to become founder members of the newly formed Palatine League. West Hartlepool St. Joseph's also moved to the Palatine League. Tow Law Town joined from the Auckland & District League and Langley Park joined from the Durham Central League.

1920-21

Bishop Auckland	26	19	5	2	71	24	43
Stockton	26	18	3	5	57	43	39
Crook Town	26	15	4	7	58	39	34
South Bank	26	14	6	6	48	38	34
Willington	26	14	3	9	52	43	31
Darlington Railway Athletic	26	13	2	11	43	39	28
Tow Law Town	26	11	7	8	50	32	27
Langley Park	26	8	7	11	53	48	23
Esh Winning	26	9	5	12	39	39	23
Eston United	26	7	8	11	43	51	22
Stanley United	26	8	3	15	51	56	19
Grangetown St. Mary's	26	6	2	18	30	75	14
Redcar	26	5	4	17	22	58	14
Scarborough	26	4	3	19	28	60	11

Tow Law Town had 2 points deducted.
Grangetown St. Mary's left the league.
Cockfield joined from the Auckland & District League.

1921-22

South Bank	26	18	6	2	59	23	42
Bishop Auckland	26	15	8	3	53	22	38
Crook Town	26	16	6	4	58	31	38
Stockton	26	13	4	9	59	41	30
Cockfield	26	12	6	8	52	37	30
Tow Law Town	26	13	4	9	52	38	30
Esh Winning	26	12	3	11	39	41	27
Willington	26	9	6	11	55	57	24
Eston United	26	10	3	13	40	52	23
Langley Park	26	8	5	13	34	52	21
Darlington Railway Athletic	26	7	6	13	45	58	20
Scarborough	26	4	8	14	39	71	16
Stanley United	26	5	3	18	36	64	13
Redcar	26	3	6	17	20	53	12

Redcar disbanded and Loftus Albion joined the league.

1922-23

Eston United	26	17	3	6	60	41	37
Bishop Auckland	26	16	4	6	54	35	36
Cockfield	26	13	4	9	56	40	30
Crook Town	26	10	8	8	41	43	28
Esh Winning	26	12	3	11	48	47	27
Loftus Albion	26	10	7	9	41	41	27
Stockton	26	11	3	12	49	35	25
Tow Law Town	26	8	8	10	36	39	24
Darlington Railway Athletic	26	10	3	13	35	40	23
Stanley United	26	8	7	11	44	57	23
Langley Park	26	11	0	15	45	60	22
Scarborough	26	10	1	15	51	52	21
Willington	26	9	3	14	37	47	21
South Bank	26	9	2	15	36	56	20

Ferryhill Athletic joined from the Palatine League.

Northern League 1923-1930

1923-24

Tow Law Town	28	17	6	5	61	34	40
Ferryhill Athletic	28	15	9	4	69	36	39
Bishop Auckland	28	17	3	8	53	33	37
Stockton	28	16	4	8	79	52	36
Crook Town	28	14	8	6	66	50	36
South Bank	28	13	7	8	49	31	33
Cockfield	28	12	5	11	50	43	29
Loftus Albion	28	11	4	13	42	47	26
Eston United	28	9	7	12	56	53	25
Scarborough	28	8	9	11	55	55	25
Stanley United	28	8	7	13	44	65	23
Darlington Railway Athletic	28	8	6	14	45	69	22
Esh Winning	28	6	6	16	36	69	18
Langley Park	28	6	4	18	36	69	16
Willington	28	5	5	18	33	68	15

1924-25

Tow Law Town	28	20	3	5	73	27	43
Crook Town	28	19	4	5	70	29	42
Stockton	28	15	7	6	54	33	37
Bishop Auckland	28	14	4	10	58	37	32
Cockfield	28	10	11	7	50	42	31
Willington	28	12	3	13	67	57	27
Ferryhill Athletic	28	12	3	13	70	60	27
South Bank	28	11	5	12	44	42	27
Loftus Albion	28	12	3	13	50	72	27
Scarborough	28	11	2	15	50	45	24
Stanley United	28	10	4	14	33	60	24
Langley Park	28	9	5	14	31	49	23
Esh Winning	28	8	5	15	42	63	21
Darlington Railway Athletic	28	7	6	15	32	71	20
Eston United	28	6	3	19	32	69	15

Darlington Railway Athletic moved to the Darlington & District League.

1925-26

Willington	26	19	3	4	84	44	41
Stockton	26	17	2	7	79	39	36
Esh Winning	26	17	2	7	76	41	36
Ferryhill Athletic	26	14	4	8	62	42	32
Bishop Auckland	26	13	5	8	64	50	31
Cockfield	26	13	3	10	59	51	29
Tow Law Town	26	11	4	11	58	54	26
Crook Town	26	10	5	11	48	48	25
South Bank	26	10	4	12	37	47	24
Langley Park	26	10	4	12	40	53	24
Scarborough	26	10	2	14	53	72	22
Stanley United	26	5	5	16	49	61	15
Loftus Albion	26	3	7	16	27	87	13
Eston United	26	3	4	19	36	83	10

Scarborough moved to the Yorkshire League. Whitby United joined as a new club, having been formed by a merger of Whitby Town and Whitby Whitehall Swifts on 6th March 1926.

1926-27

Crook Town	26	18	7	1	79	32	43
South Bank	26	17	4	5	74	43	38
Ferryhill Athletic	26	16	3	7	76	37	35
Tow Law Town	26	15	4	7	74	46	34
Stockton	26	15	3	8	66	42	33
Bishop Auckland	26	14	3	9	68	42	31
Whitby United	26	13	2	11	69	57	28
Willington	26	10	7	9	68	58	27
Cockfield	26	10	4	12	64	55	24
Loftus Albion	26	9	4	13	55	70	22
Langley Park	26	7	2	17	46	84	16
Stanley United	26	3	5	18	40	77	11
Eston United	26	4	3	19	42	106	11
Esh Winning	26	4	3	19	32	104	11

Eston United moved to the Teesside League. Chilton Colliery Recreation Athletic joined from the North-Eastern League.

1927-28

Chilton Colliery Recreation Athletic	24	16	5	3	71	35	37
Whitby United	24	14	4	6	63	58	32
Stockton	24	13	4	7	62	42	30
Cockfield	24	10	8	6	50	40	28
Willington	24	11	3	10	78	57	25
Esh Winning	24	10	4	10	58	58	24
South Bank	24	8	7	9	60	63	23
Tow Law Town	24	10	2	12	58	53	22
Ferryhill Athletic	24	7	5	12	52	73	19
Stanley United	24	7	4	13	57	71	18
Loftus Albion	24	7	4	13	48	64	18
Bishop Auckland	24	7	4	13	43	65	18
Langley Park	24	7	4	13	41	62	18

Crook Town were suspended by the Durham F.A. on 7th January 1928 for making illegal payments and their record was deleted on 9th February when it stood as follows: 13 11 0 2 40 14 22
They subsequently played in the Durham Central League in 1928-29.

1928-29

Stockton	24	13	8	3	73	46	34
Tow Law Town	24	15	3	6	70	40	33
Whitby United	24	14	4	6	72	47	32
Willington	24	13	4	7	63	49	30
Langley Park	24	9	8	7	50	44	26
Chilton Colliery Recreation Athletic	24	11	3	10	54	55	25
Ferryhill Athletic	24	10	4	10	47	55	24
South Bank	24	6	10	8	44	50	22
Stanley United	24	7	6	11	45	55	20
Bishop Auckland	24	7	6	11	45	58	20
Cockfield	24	6	6	12	41	50	18
Esh Winning	24	7	2	15	40	54	16
Loftus Albion	24	5	2	17	34	75	12

Loftus Albion moved to the Teesside League. Crook Town joined from the Durham Central League and Eden Colliery Welfare joined as a newly re-formed club.

1929-30

Willington	24	16	3	5	71	41	35
Stockton	24	16	1	7	72	36	33
Bishop Auckland	24	11	5	8	58	47	27
Eden Colliery Welfare	24	11	4	9	53	51	26
South Bank	24	9	7	8	60	53	25
Whitby United	24	10	5	9	69	76	25
Ferryhill Athletic	24	11	2	11	53	59	24
Esh Winning	24	11	2	11	56	64	24
Chilton Colliery Recreation Athletic	24	10	2	12	58	54	22
Crook Town	24	9	2	13	40	53	20
Cockfield	24	9	3	12	43	59	19
Tow Law Town	24	6	4	14	49	62	16
Stanley United	24	6	2	16	44	71	14

Cockfield had 2 points deducted.
Langley Park resigned and disbanded on 11th December and their record was deleted when it stood as follows: 7 2 0 5 14 26 4
Crook Town moved to the North-Eastern League. Trimdon Grange Colliery joined from the Mid-Durham League.

1930-31

Bishop Auckland	24	17	3	4	75	36	37
Stockton	24	15	5	4	90	35	35
South Bank	24	13	4	7	56	42	30
Tow Law Town	24	12	4	8	43	50	28
Stanley United	24	13	1	10	70	48	27
Cockfield	24	10	7	7	52	65	27
Willington	24	10	5	9	54	47	25
Whitby United	24	8	6	10	56	53	22
Eden Colliery Welfare	24	8	6	10	37	53	22
Trimdon Grange Colliery	24	7	6	11	60	76	20
Esh Winning	24	5	5	14	44	73	15
Chilton Colliery Recreation Athletic	24	5	3	16	44	78	13
Ferryhill Athletic	24	4	3	17	41	66	11

Eden Colliery Welfare moved to the North-Eastern League. Evenwood Town joined from the Auckland & District League and Harrogate joined from the Yorkshire League.

1931-32

Stockton	26	20	2	4	91	32	42
Trimdon Grange Colliery	26	13	5	8	63	48	31
South Bank	26	13	4	9	60	55	30
Bishop Auckland	26	13	3	10	67	49	29
Cockfield	26	10	9	7	69	55	29
Tow Law Town	26	11	6	9	46	45	28
Ferryhill Athletic	26	12	3	11	66	63	27
Whitby United	26	12	3	11	67	66	27
Evenwood Town	26	12	3	11	61	61	27
Chilton Colliery Recreation Athletic	26	11	3	12	59	61	25
Willington	26	10	4	12	55	62	24
Stanley United	26	6	4	16	43	65	16
Harrogate	26	6	3	17	45	79	15
Esh Winning	26	5	4	17	42	93	14

Harrogate resigned from the league and disbanded. Leeds United used Harrogate's ground for their "A" team games in the Yorkshire League in 1932-33. Shildon joined from the North-Eastern League.

1932-33

Stockton	26	20	1	5	77	34	41
Shildon	26	16	4	6	63	38	36
South Bank	26	14	5	7	59	45	33
Willington	26	14	5	7	68	56	33
Ferryhill Athletic	26	12	4	10	64	51	28
Bishop Auckland	26	11	5	10	67	67	27
Trimdon Grange Colliery	26	11	4	11	62	63	26
Whitby United	26	9	6	11	85	65	24
Cockfield	26	9	5	12	57	64	23
Esh Winning	26	8	7	11	48	57	23
Stanley United	26	8	6	12	53	65	22
Evenwood Town	26	8	5	13	46	60	21
Tow Law Town	26	6	4	16	51	90	16
Chilton Colliery Recreation Athletic	26	4	3	19	42	87	11

1933-34

Shildon	26	16	5	5	81	41	37
Whitby United	26	14	7	5	67	53	35
South Bank	26	12	4	10	48	43	28
Ferryhill Athletic	26	12	4	10	63	61	28
Stockton	26	12	3	11	59	60	27
Willington	26	10	6	10	59	48	26
Cockfield	26	10	6	10	58	49	26
Evenwood Town	26	11	4	11	54	60	26
Trimdon Grange Colliery	26	10	4	12	59	56	24
Bishop Auckland	26	8	8	10	63	61	24
Tow Law Town	26	8	7	11	51	67	23
Chilton Colliery Recreation Athletic	26	9	3	14	47	65	21
Stanley United	26	5	10	11	47	66	20
Esh Winning	26	7	5	14	39	65	19

1934-35

Shildon	26	19	5	2	86	23	43
Stockton	26	17	2	7	88	55	36
Ferryhill Athletic	26	16	3	7	69	43	35
Tow Law Town	26	14	4	8	54	46	32
South Bank	26	14	3	9	49	33	31
Bishop Auckland	26	12	4	10	73	59	28
Willington	26	12	2	12	53	57	26
Cockfield	26	11	3	12	69	73	25
# West Auckland Town	26	9	5	12	59	69	23
Trimdon Grange Colliery	26	8	6	12	51	75	22
Whitby United	26	7	5	14	52	65	19
Chilton Colliery Recreation Athletic	26	6	5	15	56	87	17
Stanley United	26	5	5	16	44	80	15
Evenwood Town	26	5	2	19	41	79	12

Esh Winning resigned from the league and disbanded on 5th October and West Auckland Town moved from the Auckland & District League to take over their fixtures. Esh Winning's record as inherited by West Auckland Town was as follows: 4 0 1 3 5 13 1
Trimdon Grange Colliery changed their name to Trimdon Grange.

1935-36

Shildon	26	20	4	2	81	27	44
South Bank	26	19	1	6	86	43	39
Stockton	26	14	5	7	93	64	33
Willington	26	14	5	7	64	47	33
Bishop Auckland	26	10	7	9	66	65	27
Evenwood Town	26	11	5	10	59	63	27
West Auckland Town	26	9	7	10	54	52	25
Ferryhill Athletic	26	9	7	10	65	64	25
Cockfield	26	8	6	12	59	53	22
Chilton Colliery Recreation Athletic	26	8	5	13	62	93	21
Trimdon Grange	26	8	3	15	41	67	19
Whitby United	26	7	4	15	62	83	18
Stanley United	26	6	6	14	53	73	18
Tow Law Town	26	5	3	18	47	98	13

Stanley United moved to the Durham Central League. Crook Town joined from the North-Eastern League.

1936-37

Shildon	26	20	6	0	80	25	46
Bishop Auckland	26	19	2	5	70	37	40
South Bank	26	15	4	7	72	49	34
Cockfield	26	15	2	9	67	49	32
Whitby United	26	14	1	11	72	60	29
Stockton	26	12	3	11	77	52	27
West Auckland Town	26	11	5	10	68	58	27
Ferryhill Athletic	26	11	3	12	62	66	25
Evenwood Town	26	10	2	14	58	75	22
Willington	26	10	1	15	63	74	21
Crook Town	26	9	3	14	58	77	21
Chilton Colliery Recreation Athletic	26	7	3	16	53	67	17
Trimdon Grange	26	6	1	19	38	86	13
Tow Law Town	26	4	2	20	39	102	10

Trimdon Grange moved to the Durham Central League. Billingham South joined from the Stockton & District League.

1937-38

Ferryhill Athletic	26	21	0	5	81	36	42
Bishop Auckland	26	16	4	6	70	38	36
Shildon	26	16	2	8	72	39	34
Cockfield	26	14	6	6	44	31	34
Stockton	26	14	5	7	69	48	33
Chilton Colliery Recreation Athletic	26	11	6	9	44	45	28
Billingham South	26	11	4	11	59	56	26
Evenwood Town	26	9	4	13	45	55	22
Whitby United	26	8	6	12	47	78	22
South Bank	26	8	4	14	49	56	20
Willington	26	9	2	15	55	66	20
Crook Town	26	9	2	15	41	56	20
West Auckland Town	26	7	3	16	52	68	17
Tow Law Town	26	2	6	18	44	100	10

Billingham South changed their name to Billingham.

1938-39

Bishop Auckland	26	21	3	2	94	27	45
Shildon	26	21	2	3	92	27	44
Stockton	26	17	3	6	88	44	37
Billingham	26	15	1	10	76	57	31
Willington	26	13	4	9	75	62	30
Whitby United	26	12	1	13	51	64	25
Cockfield	26	9	6	11	53	55	24
West Auckland Town	26	11	2	13	50	56	24
Ferryhill Athletic	26	9	4	13	62	65	22
Tow Law Town	26	8	3	15	39	81	19
South Bank	26	5	8	13	43	69	18
Evenwood Town	26	7	2	17	43	70	16
Chilton Colliery Recreation Athletic	26	6	3	17	47	95	15
Crook Town	26	4	6	16	52	93	14

Stockton moved to the Northern League and Chilton Colliery Recreation Athletic moved to the Durham Central League. Brandon Social Club joined from the Wearside League and Heaton Stannington joined from the Tyneside League.

1939-45

When war was declared on 3rd September, 1939 the league suspended all activity. It was able to restart on 7th October but in the meantime, Whitby United had resigned from the league due transport difficulties. Evenwood Town resigned on 25th October because many of their players had joined the Armed Forces and they too cited transport difficulties. Next to resign because of war-time difficulties were Brandon Social Club on 1st November, followed by Billingham and Cockfield, both on 29th November. Ferryhill Athletic resigned on 16th December, the same day that the league decided to abandon the existing fixture programme and start a new fixture programme on 1st January 1940 with the remaining 8 clubs.

NORTHERN LEAGUE 1939

Table of results of games played between 26th August and 31st December.

	Resignation date							
Willington		11	8	1	2	37	22	17
Ferryhill Athletic	16 Dec	10	7	2	1	31	18	16
Bishop Auckland		9	6	1	2	36	13	13
Crook Town		9	5	3	1	28	22	13
Shildon		8	6	0	2	32	10	12
South Bank		11	5	0	6	35	32	10
Tow Law Town		11	2	2	7	29	34	6
West Auckland Town		8	2	2	4	11	15	6
Billingham	29 Nov	7	2	2	3	13	21	6
Heaton Stannington		11	2	1	8	24	38	5
Evenwood Town	25 Oct	4	2	0	2	4	12	4
Cockfield	29 Nov	9	2	0	7	8	34	4
Brandon Social	01 Nov	4	0	2	2	6	16	2
Whitby United	30 Sep	2	0	0	2	1	8	0

The competition was eventually abandoned on 16th December 1939.

NORTHERN LEAGUE 1940

Shildon	10	9	0	1	47	19	18
Bishop Auckland	10	5	2	3	33	27	12
Crook Town	10	5	1	4	29	24	11
Heaton Stannington	10	3	1	6	26	29	7
South Bank	10	3	1	6	20	34	7
West Auckland Town	10	2	1	7	18	40	5

Tow Law Town resigned on 20th March and their record was deleted when it stood as follows: 4 1 0 3 6 16 2
Willington also resigned on 20th March and their record was deleted when it stood as follows: 3 1 1 1 5 5 3

At the A.G.M. on 29th June 1940, it was decided to suspend the league for the duration of the war. This decision was reviewed in July 1944 but it was agreed that there was no consensus amongst the clubs to restart the competition before the war ended.

When the war in Europe ended on 8th May 1945, the league prepared to restart in the 1945-46 season. Of the pre-war members, Whitby United and Heaton Stannington were unable to resume as their grounds were still in use for military purposes while Crook Town had closed down in 1940. However, they were replaced by Crook Colliery Welfare who were formed in 1943 by a merger of Peases West Welfare and Hole-in-the-Wall Colliery. Billingham did not re-form but were replaced by Billingham Synthonia who had been playing in the Teesside League before the war. Brandon Social Club rejoined under their new name of Brandon Welfare. Cockfield had not re-formed and were replaced by Stanley United who had been playing in the Durham Central League before the war. The remaining pre-war members all rejoined.

1945-46

Stanley United	22	20	0	2	101	29	40
South Bank	22	16	1	5	61	41	33
Billingham Synthonia	22	13	0	9	70	57	26
Shildon	22	12	2	8	57	48	26
Bishop Auckland	22	12	1	9	83	46	25
Evenwood Town	22	9	3	10	45	57	21
Tow Law Town	22	8	4	10	55	59	20
Willington	22	7	5	10	37	52	19
Brandon Welfare	22	7	5	10	42	64	19
Crook Colliery Welfare	22	7	2	13	51	60	16
Ferryhill Athletic	22	5	3	14	44	76	13
West Auckland Town	22	2	2	18	29	89	6

Whitby United and Heaton Stannington were able to resume playing and re-joined the league, Whitby United after changing their name to Whitby Town.

1946-47

Bishop Auckland	26	18	2	6	81	47	38
Crook Colliery Welfare	26	18	2	6	85	50	38
Stanley United	26	15	5	6	81	49	35
Shildon	26	15	5	6	72	45	35
Willington	26	13	5	8	69	53	31
Ferryhill Athletic	26	13	3	10	77	66	29
Evenwood Town	26	10	6	10	65	72	26
Heaton Stannington	26	11	2	13	58	68	24
Billingham Synthonia	26	9	3	14	58	60	21
Tow Law Town	26	9	3	14	59	68	21
West Auckland Town	26	7	5	14	39	62	19
South Bank	26	7	4	15	65	61	18
Whitby Town	26	7	4	15	46	75	18
Brandon Welfare	26	4	3	19	38	117	11

Bishop Auckland were declared champions after beating Crook Colliery Welfare 5-1 in the championship play-off at Willington's Hall Lane ground on 7th June 1947.
Brandon Welfare moved to the Durham Central League.
East Tanfield Colliery Welfare joined from the Northern Combination.

1947-48

	P	W	D	L	F	A	Pts
Ferryhill Athletic	26	20	4	2	90	40	44
Bishop Auckland	26	17	3	6	90	41	37
South Bank	26	13	7	6	61	40	33
Shildon	26	15	0	11	52	51	30
Evenwood Town	26	12	5	9	53	44	29
Stanley United	26	10	7	9	60	62	27
Tow Law Town	26	12	3	11	58	61	27
Crook Colliery Welfare	26	12	3	11	53	58	27
Willington	26	11	3	12	53	54	25
West Auckland Town	26	8	5	13	57	73	21
East Tanfield Colliery Welfare	26	7	5	14	52	67	19
Whitby Town	26	8	3	15	52	76	19
Heaton Stannington	26	4	7	15	47	66	15
Billingham Synthonia	26	5	1	20	51	96	11

Penrith joined from the Carlisle & District League. East Tanfield Colliery Welfare also left and subsequently joined the Northern Alliance in 1949.

1948-49

	P	W	D	L	F	A	Pts
Evenwood Town	26	19	4	3	64	33	42
Bishop Auckland	26	19	3	4	79	38	41
Billingham Synthonia	26	16	5	5	69	41	37
Ferryhill Athletic	26	14	3	9	53	49	31
Willington	26	13	4	9	79	55	30
Penrith	26	14	1	11	66	60	29
Crook Colliery Welfare	26	9	7	10	61	66	25
South Bank	26	9	6	11	54	63	24
Shildon	26	9	5	12	59	57	23
West Auckland Town	26	11	1	14	53	63	23
Stanley United	26	7	4	15	47	66	18
Whitby Town	26	7	3	16	39	68	17
Tow Law Town	26	4	5	17	52	79	13
Heaton Stannington	26	3	5	18	41	78	11

Crook Colliery Welfare changed their name to Crook Town.

1949-50

	P	W	D	L	F	A	Pts
Bishop Auckland	26	21	1	4	81	28	43
Billingham Synthonia	26	17	3	6	77	46	37
Whitby Town	26	16	3	7	67	42	35
Willington	26	16	1	9	76	46	33
Evenwood Town	26	14	2	10	70	59	30
Tow Law Town	26	12	4	10	63	52	28
Ferryhill Athletic	26	11	5	10	64	67	27
Shildon	26	10	5	11	56	52	25
Crook Town	26	10	3	13	61	58	23
Penrith	26	9	2	15	54	74	20
South Bank	26	8	3	15	46	78	19
West Auckland Town	26	8	2	16	45	89	18
Stanley United	26	5	6	15	46	74	16
Heaton Stannington	26	4	2	20	34	75	10

1950-51

	P	W	D	L	F	A	Pts
Bishop Auckland	26	20	2	4	101	34	42
Billingham Synthonia	26	17	3	6	70	24	37
Whitby Town	26	15	6	5	75	42	36
Willington	26	14	4	8	81	46	32
Evenwood Town	26	14	3	9	76	58	29
Shildon	26	13	3	10	57	49	29
Crook Town	26	12	2	12	56	66	26
South Bank	26	11	2	13	54	58	24
Stanley United	26	9	4	13	60	64	22
Ferryhill Athletic	26	9	3	14	53	79	21
Penrith	26	7	7	12	43	76	21
Heaton Stannington	26	9	2	15	48	68	20
Tow Law Town	26	4	4	18	41	95	12
West Auckland Town	26	4	3	19	31	87	11

Evenwood Town had 2 points deducted.

1951-52

	P	W	D	L	F	A	Pts
Bishop Auckland	26	20	5	1	89	26	45
Billingham Synthonia	26	17	3	6	67	35	37
Willington	26	17	2	7	79	49	36
Tow Law Town	26	16	1	9	68	45	33
Whitby Town	26	12	6	8	71	49	30
South Bank	26	12	5	9	64	68	29
Evenwood Town	26	10	7	9	53	47	27
Ferryhill Athletic	26	10	6	10	60	67	26
Crook Town	26	9	6	11	49	59	24
Shildon	26	9	3	14	54	62	21
West Auckland Town	26	7	4	15	43	61	18
Heaton Stannington	26	8	2	16	55	87	18
Stanley United	26	7	1	18	38	81	15
Penrith	26	1	3	22	32	86	5

Heaton Stannington moved to the Northern Alliance.
Durham City joined from the Wearside League.

1952-53

	P	W	D	L	F	A	Pts
Crook Town	26	19	5	2	106	38	43
Bishop Auckland	26	14	9	3	79	38	37
Whitby Town	26	15	5	6	71	45	35
Shildon	26	12	9	5	60	40	33
Tow Law Town	26	13	5	8	56	54	31
Ferryhill Athletic	26	11	7	8	51	43	29
Billingham Synthonia	26	11	6	9	59	56	28
Willington	26	10	6	10	53	57	26
Penrith	26	9	7	10	58	64	25
Evenwood Town	26	6	8	12	50	56	20
Stanley United	26	8	2	16	49	72	18
Durham City	26	7	4	15	41	69	18
West Auckland Town	26	4	5	17	37	72	13
South Bank	26	2	4	20	37	103	8

1953-54

	P	W	D	L	F	A	Pts
Bishop Auckland	26	19	4	3	97	34	42
Crook Town	26	19	2	5	95	38	40
Ferryhill Athletic	26	17	5	4	56	27	39
Billingham Synthonia	26	15	2	9	61	44	32
West Auckland Town	26	15	2	9	58	48	32
Durham City	26	15	2	9	62	52	32
Whitby Town	26	9	6	11	58	56	24
Willington	26	11	1	14	48	51	23
Evenwood Town	26	9	3	14	57	65	21
Tow Law Town	26	10	0	16	43	64	20
Penrith	26	8	1	17	39	81	17
Shildon	26	11	2	13	74	68	16
Stanley United	26	3	5	18	33	84	11
South Bank	26	3	1	22	36	105	7

Shildon had 8 points deducted.

1954-55

	P	W	D	L	F	A	Pts
Bishop Auckland	26	19	3	4	87	44	41
Crook Town	26	16	2	8	93	40	34
Shildon	26	11	8	7	65	47	30
Billingham Synthonia	26	12	6	8	62	49	30
Evenwood Town	26	12	6	8	67	59	30
Stanley United	26	13	4	9	45	64	30
Whitby Town	26	10	7	9	65	58	27
Ferryhill Athletic	26	9	8	9	58	57	26
Willington	26	11	3	12	42	46	25
West Auckland Town	26	8	7	11	58	67	23
Tow Law Town	26	8	5	13	45	72	21
South Bank	26	5	7	14	36	63	17
Penrith	26	5	6	15	38	66	16
Durham City	26	4	6	16	47	79	14

Northern League 1955-1962

1955-56

Team	P	W	D	L	F	A	Pts
Bishop Auckland	26	18	2	6	85	54	38
Crook Town	26	17	3	6	92	44	37
Durham City	26	17	1	8	82	40	35
South Bank	26	12	6	8	51	37	30
Evenwood Town	26	12	5	9	58	49	29
West Auckland Town	26	13	2	11	66	51	28
Billingham Synthonia	26	12	3	11	58	63	27
Shildon	26	10	6	10	70	52	26
Willington	26	10	4	12	58	71	24
Stanley United	26	9	6	11	53	66	24
Ferryhill Athletic	26	8	5	13	42	62	21
Tow Law Town	26	6	7	13	55	80	19
Penrith	26	6	3	17	38	81	15
Whitby Town	26	4	3	19	39	97	11

1956-57

Team	P	W	D	L	F	A	Pts
Billingham Synthonia	26	20	2	4	66	37	42
West Auckland Town	26	16	2	8	79	52	34
Bishop Auckland	26	13	7	6	76	48	33
Ferryhill Athletic	26	14	4	8	63	48	32
Willington	26	13	6	7	60	48	32
Crook Town	26	13	5	8	67	62	31
Durham City	26	12	5	9	58	50	29
Shildon	26	11	3	12	60	56	25
Stanley United	26	9	6	11	48	54	24
Evenwood Town	26	8	5	13	58	78	21
Penrith	26	8	3	15	41	65	19
South Bank	26	8	2	16	49	57	18
Whitby Town	26	5	4	17	54	84	14
Tow Law Town	26	3	4	19	37	77	10

1957-58

Team	P	W	D	L	F	A	Pts
Ferryhill Athletic	26	20	3	3	90	41	43
Willington	26	16	5	5	66	41	37
Crook Town	26	16	4	6	95	35	36
Bishop Auckland	26	14	6	6	75	49	34
Evenwood Town	26	12	5	9	62	58	29
Durham City	26	11	5	10	57	45	27
Stanley United	26	10	3	13	59	58	23
Tow Law Town	26	10	3	13	57	57	23
West Auckland Town	26	9	5	12	68	72	23
Billingham Synthonia	26	6	10	10	54	61	22
Penrith	26	9	3	14	45	79	21
Whitby Town	26	7	5	14	58	69	19
Shildon	26	7	4	15	51	73	18
South Bank	26	4	1	21	30	129	9

Whitley Bay joined from the North-Eastern League, having changed their name from Whitley Bay Athletic.

1958-59

Team	P	W	D	L	F	A	Pts
Crook Town	28	19	4	5	89	51	42
West Auckland Town	28	16	4	8	80	51	36
Willington	28	15	6	7	65	48	36
Durham City	28	14	5	9	63	52	33
Bishop Auckland	28	13	5	10	76	56	31
Whitby Town	28	13	5	10	70	61	31
Stanley United	28	12	4	12	57	68	28
Evenwood Town	28	13	1	14	54	59	27
Ferryhill Athletic	28	10	5	13	60	72	25
Billingham Synthonia	28	9	6	13	66	70	24
Tow Law Town	28	10	4	14	58	70	24
South Bank	28	7	9	12	48	64	23
Shildon	28	9	4	15	67	83	22
Whitley Bay	28	8	5	15	52	64	21
Penrith	28	7	3	18	43	79	17

1959-60

Team	P	W	D	L	F	A	Pts
West Auckland Town	28	19	4	5	63	40	42
Whitley Bay	28	17	6	5	76	37	40
Crook Town	28	18	3	7	84	50	39
Shildon	28	15	4	9	75	50	34
Bishop Auckland	28	15	4	9	55	45	34
Ferryhill Athletic	28	13	4	11	76	46	30
Tow Law Town	28	10	7	11	50	58	27
Stanley United	28	10	6	12	57	69	26
Whitby Town	28	10	5	13	61	62	25
Evenwood Town	28	12	3	13	65	67	25
South Bank	28	11	3	14	55	63	25
Penrith	28	9	5	14	52	66	23
Willington	28	8	6	14	49	64	22
Durham City	28	4	7	17	35	84	15
Billingham Synthonia	28	4	3	21	34	86	11

Evenwood Town had 2 points deducted.
Spennymoor United joined from the Midland League.

1960-61

Team	P	W	D	L	F	A	Pts
West Auckland Town	30	18	8	4	77	36	44
Bishop Auckland	30	19	2	9	85	46	40
Ferryhill Athletic	30	18	4	8	80	56	40
Crook Town	30	15	8	7	79	51	38
Whitley Bay	30	15	8	7	81	57	38
Spennymoor United	30	14	8	8	62	37	36
Stanley United	30	14	7	9	61	56	35
South Bank	30	15	2	13	67	62	32
Penrith	30	11	8	11	53	63	30
Evenwood Town	30	8	9	13	59	59	25
Shildon	30	11	2	17	66	73	24
Billingham Synthonia	30	7	8	15	52	86	22
Willington	30	9	3	18	59	80	21
Tow Law Town	30	8	5	17	54	88	21
Whitby Town	30	7	6	17	52	84	18
Durham City	30	5	4	21	52	105	14

Whitby Town had 2 points deducted.

1961-62

Team	P	W	D	L	F	A	Pts
Stanley United	30	22	4	4	91	52	48
Penrith	30	16	8	6	55	31	40
West Auckland Town	30	19	2	9	80	50	40
Whitley Bay	30	18	4	8	95	61	40
Crook Town	30	14	7	9	54	31	35
Spennymoor United	30	15	2	13	71	52	32
Billingham Synthonia	30	13	5	12	83	66	31
Durham City	30	14	3	13	49	49	31
Ferryhill Athletic	30	13	3	14	66	68	29
Bishop Auckland	30	10	7	13	71	69	27
South Bank	30	10	5	15	52	68	25
Shildon	30	10	4	16	58	82	24
Whitby Town	30	9	6	15	61	87	24
Tow Law Town	30	9	3	18	56	82	21
Willington	30	6	7	17	44	90	19
Evenwood Town	30	6	2	22	39	87	14

1962-63

Team	P	W	D	L	F	A	Pts
Crook Town	30	21	6	3	82	30	48
Stanley United	30	20	4	6	78	45	44
Penrith	30	17	7	6	60	31	41
Spennymoor United	30	13	12	5	62	45	38
Whitley Bay	30	12	10	8	69	46	34
Billingham Synthonia	30	14	5	11	58	49	33
West Auckland Town	30	13	7	10	66	65	33
Bishop Auckland	30	11	6	13	68	68	28
Tow Law Town	30	12	3	15	62	71	27
Whitby Town	30	12	2	16	62	65	26
Durham City	30	10	6	14	49	55	26
Ferryhill Athletic	30	6	14	10	51	59	26
South Bank	30	9	5	16	46	63	23
Shildon	30	6	9	15	52	87	21
Evenwood Town	30	7	5	18	30	62	19
Willington	30	5	3	22	35	89	13

1963-64

Team	P	W	D	L	F	A	Pts
Stanley United	30	18	7	5	94	47	43
Crook Town	30	17	8	5	67	28	42
West Auckland Town	30	15	7	8	67	44	37
Evenwood Town	30	13	7	10	42	38	33
Ferryhill Athletic	30	13	7	10	64	60	33
Penrith	30	14	4	12	69	54	32
Whitley Bay	30	14	4	12	66	52	32
Bishop Auckland	30	13	6	11	62	61	32
Whitby Town	30	13	3	14	57	52	29
Tow Law Town	30	12	5	13	63	60	29
Willington	30	11	7	12	57	73	29
Spennymoor United	30	11	6	13	38	51	28
Billingham Synthonia	30	9	7	14	25	43	25
Shildon	30	10	4	16	55	70	24
South Bank	30	9	6	15	47	78	24
Durham City	30	2	4	24	35	97	6

Durham City had 2 points deducted.
Blyth Spartans and North Shields joined from the North-Eastern League.

1964-65

Team	P	W	D	L	F	A	Pts
Whitley Bay	34	24	5	5	112	45	53
Crook Town	34	22	8	4	86	32	52
North Shields	34	18	8	8	99	60	44
Whitby Town	34	19	4	11	74	52	42
Tow Law Town	34	15	10	9	72	56	40
Willington	34	18	4	12	72	61	40
Spennymoor United	34	16	7	11	53	53	39
Ferryhill Athletic	34	15	7	12	79	62	37
Stanley United	34	16	3	15	86	84	35
West Auckland Town	34	14	6	14	66	54	34
Billingham Synthonia	34	13	6	15	51	79	32
Penrith	34	10	10	14	57	64	30
Bishop Auckland	34	11	6	17	58	73	28
Durham City	34	10	6	18	49	78	26
South Bank	34	9	6	19	67	97	24
Evenwood Town	34	9	5	20	51	80	23
Shildon	34	8	7	19	51	89	23
Blyth Spartans	34	4	2	28	38	105	10

1965-66

Team	P	W	D	L	F	A	Pts
Whitley Bay	34	25	2	7	89	46	52
North Shields	34	22	5	7	109	51	49
Bishop Auckland	34	20	8	6	75	33	48
Spennymoor United	34	15	10	9	70	62	40
Tow Law Town	34	14	11	9	66	39	39
Evenwood Town	34	17	5	12	79	56	37
Whitby Town	34	15	6	13	63	57	36
Crook Town	34	14	7	13	82	66	35
Billingham Synthonia	34	14	7	13	59	51	35
Blyth Spartans	34	13	7	14	87	81	33
Ferryhill Athletic	34	13	7	14	57	88	33
Willington	34	12	7	15	64	79	31
Penrith	34	12	5	17	54	62	29
Stanley United	34	13	3	18	78	90	29
West Auckland Town	34	9	9	16	47	66	27
Shildon	34	8	6	20	66	112	22
South Bank	34	8	4	22	56	106	20
Durham City	34	5	5	24	48	104	15

Evenwood Town had 2 points deducted.

1966-67

Team	P	W	D	L	F	A	Pts
Bishop Auckland	34	23	8	3	85	34	54
Whitley Bay	34	19	10	5	72	37	48
North Shields	34	20	6	8	90	43	46
Tow Law Town	34	20	4	10	76	42	44
Spennymoor United	34	15	10	9	65	52	40
Crook Town	34	15	9	10	74	62	39
Billingham Synthonia	34	15	8	11	61	46	38
West Auckland Town	34	17	3	14	59	54	37
Blyth Spartans	34	16	4	14	69	63	36
Whitby Town	34	16	4	14	85	75	34
Penrith	34	11	9	14	71	72	31
Stanley United	34	13	5	16	62	70	31
Evenwood Town	34	13	5	16	57	58	27
Ferryhill Athletic	34	10	7	17	56	75	27
Shildon	34	12	3	19	65	88	27
Willington	34	6	8	20	45	77	20
Durham City	34	5	4	25	48	128	14
South Bank	34	4	5	25	44	108	13

Whitby Town had 2 points deducted.
Evenwood Town had 4 points deducted.

1967-68

Team	P	W	D	L	F	A	Pts
Spennymoor United	34	28	5	1	99	37	61
Whitby Town	34	24	6	4	107	41	54
Tow Law Town	34	22	5	7	103	57	49
Whitley Bay	34	21	5	8	93	41	47
Crook Town	34	15	8	11	71	67	38
North Shields	34	14	9	11	75	56	37
Durham City	34	15	5	14	83	71	35
Blyth Spartans	34	14	7	13	80	71	35
South Bank	34	12	10	12	58	56	34
Billingham Synthonia	34	13	8	13	63	62	34
Bishop Auckland	34	13	6	15	62	67	32
West Auckland Town	34	12	5	17	57	72	29
Evenwood Town	34	11	7	16	61	86	29
Stanley United	34	10	6	18	53	88	26
Shildon	34	11	2	21	58	81	24
Ferryhill Athletic	34	6	7	21	57	94	19
Penrith	34	4	7	23	47	96	15
Willington	34	4	6	24	45	129	14

Northern League 1968-1973

1968-69

North Shields	34	26	2	6	106	29	54
Whitley Bay	34	22	9	3	86	37	53
Tow Law Town	34	23	4	7	110	61	50
Evenwood Town	34	22	4	8	81	50	48
Blyth Spartans	34	18	9	7	76	36	45
Whitby Town	34	20	5	9	71	55	45
Spennymoor United	34	15	9	10	73	52	39
Billingham Synthonia	34	16	5	13	76	61	37
South Bank	34	14	9	11	58	51	37
Shildon	34	16	4	14	61	58	36
Crook Town	34	14	7	13	59	59	35
West Auckland Town	34	10	6	18	55	69	26
Durham City	34	9	4	21	49	81	22
Penrith	34	8	6	20	37	68	22
Bishop Auckland	34	8	2	24	43	98	18
Willington	34	6	5	23	33	94	17
Ferryhill Athletic	34	3	9	22	33	83	15
Stanley United	34	5	3	26	50	113	13

1969-70

Evenwood Town	34	26	5	3	83	34	57
Whitley Bay	34	23	6	5	78	26	52
Blyth Spartans	34	23	6	5	92	34	52
Spennymoor United	34	20	5	9	80	48	45
Durham City	34	15	9	10	53	40	39
North Shields	34	18	5	11	71	57	39
South Bank	34	14	7	13	55	51	35
Billingham Synthonia	34	12	10	12	61	62	34
Tow Law Town	34	13	8	13	55	51	32
Whitby Town	34	11	10	13	45	49	32
Shildon	34	10	12	12	53	59	32
Bishop Auckland	34	6	14	14	43	68	26
West Auckland Town	34	7	11	16	37	43	25
Penrith	34	7	11	16	47	72	25
Stanley United	34	10	4	20	37	86	24
Willington	34	8	6	20	45	76	22
Crook Town	34	6	9	19	45	73	21
Ferryhill Athletic	34	5	6	23	32	83	14

North Shields, Tow Law Town and Ferryhill Athletic each had 2 points deducted.
Ashington joined from the Northern Alliance and Consett joined from the Wearside League.

1970-71

Evenwood Town	38	25	7	6	94	36	57
Durham City	38	24	6	8	79	52	54
Ferryhill Athletic	38	22	6	10	75	58	50
Whitby Town	38	19	11	8	82	51	49
Blyth Spartans	38	19	7	12	74	49	45
Whitley Bay	38	18	8	12	65	44	44
North Shields	38	19	6	13	80	64	44
Spennymoor United	38	16	10	12	66	50	42
Tow Law Town	38	18	8	12	58	52	42
South Bank	38	17	7	14	72	63	41
Ashington	38	14	10	14	71	72	38
Shildon	38	13	11	14	76	74	37
Stanley United	38	13	8	17	50	86	34
Consett	38	12	9	17	69	83	33
West Auckland Town	38	9	13	16	41	65	31
Billingham Synthonia	38	9	10	19	45	65	28
Bishop Auckland	38	11	3	24	62	86	25
Crook Town	38	8	9	21	45	66	25
Penrith	38	6	8	24	45	87	20
Willington	38	6	7	25	47	93	19

Tow Law Town had 2 points deducted.

1971-72

Spennymoor United	38	29	6	3	103	26	64
Blyth Spartans	38	24	7	7	85	42	55
Whitley Bay	38	20	10	8	66	29	48
Durham City	38	20	8	10	78	51	48
Consett	38	20	6	12	78	58	46
Shildon	38	18	9	11	98	69	45
Whitby Town	38	18	8	12	75	59	44
Tow Law Town	38	17	10	11	83	72	44
Evenwood Town	38	17	9	12	65	57	43
North Shields	38	14	12	12	61	51	40
Ferryhill Athletic	38	16	8	14	60	58	40
Willington	38	15	8	15	72	59	38
South Bank	38	13	7	18	54	76	33
Penrith	38	13	6	19	52	69	32
Billingham Synthonia	38	11	8	19	55	75	30
Crook Town	38	5	16	17	50	81	26
Bishop Auckland	38	8	9	21	42	72	25
Ashington	38	8	8	22	47	68	24
West Auckland Town	38	6	8	24	45	102	20
Stanley United	38	3	7	28	32	127	11

Whitley Bay and Stanley United each had 2 points deducted.

1972-73

Blyth Spartans	38	28	3	7	102	39	59
Bishop Auckland	38	25	7	6	76	40	57
Willington	38	24	5	9	83	36	53
Billingham Synthonia	38	21	7	10	76	49	49
Spennymoor United	38	20	7	11	70	50	47
Ferryhill Athletic	38	21	4	13	60	56	46
Whitley Bay	38	18	8	12	67	46	42
Shildon	38	17	5	16	72	62	39
Ashington	38	14	10	14	51	45	38
Durham City	38	14	8	16	58	60	36
Consett	38	12	12	14	53	57	36
Evenwood Town	38	15	5	18	52	66	35
Whitby Town	38	13	7	18	58	72	31
Penrith	38	12	7	19	53	80	31
Tow Law Town	38	11	8	19	51	68	30
West Auckland Town	38	12	3	23	39	76	27
Crook Town	38	9	8	21	48	67	26
Stanley United	38	11	4	23	49	88	26
North Shields	38	10	7	21	37	62	25
South Bank	38	9	3	26	49	85	21

Whitley Bay, Whitby Town and North Shields each had 2 points deducted.

1973-74

Team	P	W	D	L	F	A	Pts
Blyth Spartans	38	30	4	4	95	32	64
Spennymoor United	38	30	4	4	87	37	64
Willington	38	21	6	11	87	60	48
Bishop Auckland	38	19	9	10	68	43	47
Billingham Synthonia	38	20	7	11	67	50	47
North Shields	38	17	8	13	68	52	42
Tow Law Town	38	18	4	16	62	63	40
Ashington	38	16	6	16	60	56	38
Penrith	38	15	8	15	56	62	38
Durham City	38	16	5	17	74	60	37
Whitley Bay	38	14	8	16	48	48	36
Evenwood Town	38	13	10	15	63	65	36
Consett	38	14	7	17	61	63	35
Ferryhill Athletic	38	14	7	17	47	69	35
Shildon	38	12	9	17	59	62	33
Whitby Town	38	11	9	18	52	76	31
Crook Town	38	9	9	20	44	75	27
South Bank	38	8	7	23	43	77	23
West Auckland Town	38	5	11	22	37	83	21
Stanley United	38	4	10	24	41	86	18

Spennymoor United were declared champions after beating Blyth Spartans 2-1 at Portland Park, Ashington in the championship play-off on 7th May. Stanley United resigned from the league shortly before the start of the 1974-75 season due to financial reasons and joined the Durham City & District League instead.

3 points were awarded for a win from the next season.

1974-75

Team	P	W	D	L	F	A	Pts
Blyth Spartans	36	30	6	0	105	38	96
Spennymoor United	36	27	5	4	100	38	86
Bishop Auckland	36	23	5	8	81	33	74
Willington	36	19	12	5	91	53	69
Whitby Town	36	16	8	12	60	53	56
Consett	36	14	11	11	72	72	53
Durham City	36	14	11	11	60	68	53
Tow Law Town	36	14	10	12	59	58	52
Ashington	36	13	11	12	73	61	50
South Bank	36	12	8	16	65	75	44
North Shields	36	9	15	12	58	55	42
Whitley Bay	36	11	8	17	52	65	41
Ferryhill Athletic	36	9	12	15	52	72	39
Billingham Synthonia	36	9	9	18	55	74	36
Evenwood Town	36	9	7	20	40	59	34
Crook Town	36	9	7	20	39	72	34
Penrith	36	9	6	21	47	71	33
Shildon	36	7	9	20	50	79	30
West Auckland Town	36	4	8	24	29	92	20

Horden Colliery Welfare joined from the Wearside League.

1975-76

Team	P	W	D	L	F	A	Pts
Blyth Spartans	38	28	4	6	88	36	88
Willington	38	27	6	5	102	43	87
Spennymoor United	38	27	6	5	90	43	87
Bishop Auckland	38	25	8	5	75	32	83
Tow Law Town	38	22	8	8	102	60	74
Whitby Town	38	21	11	6	76	36	72
Ashington	38	18	4	16	60	52	58
North Shields	38	15	7	16	57	49	52
Consett	38	15	6	17	53	56	51
Evenwood Town	38	11	11	16	50	58	44
Horden Colliery Welfare	38	11	10	17	42	62	43
Penrith	38	11	10	17	49	89	43
Durham City	38	10	10	18	36	57	40
Billingham Synthonia	38	10	8	20	39	67	38
Crook Town	38	9	10	19	55	68	37
Shildon	38	9	10	19	43	61	37
Whitley Bay	38	8	11	19	41	74	35
Ferryhill Athletic	38	8	9	21	51	73	33
South Bank	38	7	8	23	41	80	29
West Auckland Town	38	7	5	26	44	98	26

Whitby Town had 2 points deducted.

1976-77

Team	P	W	D	L	F	A	Pts
Spennymoor United	38	22	10	6	72	38	76
Consett	38	22	10	6	71	45	76
Whitby Town	38	21	8	9	97	62	71
Crook Town	38	19	11	8	63	40	68
Blyth Spartans	38	19	9	10	80	49	66
North Shields	38	19	8	11	62	51	65
Whitley Bay	38	19	8	11	73	62	65
Bishop Auckland	38	17	9	12	67	47	60
Ashington	38	17	8	13	84	61	57
South Bank	38	15	5	18	53	58	50
Willington	38	13	10	15	66	68	49
Durham City	38	12	11	15	44	53	47
Horden Colliery Welfare	38	12	10	16	59	65	46
Ferryhill Athletic	38	12	10	16	42	58	46
Evenwood Town	38	13	4	21	54	72	43
West Auckland Town	38	12	7	19	45	69	43
Tow Law Town	38	11	8	19	55	73	41
Billingham Synthonia	38	9	6	23	37	64	33
Shildon	38	6	9	23	32	75	27
Penrith	38	4	11	23	49	95	23

Ashington had 2 points deducted. Spennymoor United were declared champions on 9th May after beating Consett 3-0 in the championship play-off at Willington's Hall Lane Ground.

1977-78

Team	P	W	D	L	F	A	Pts
Spennymoor United	38	30	5	3	103	36	95
Blyth Spartans	38	27	8	3	107	37	89
Whitby Town	38	22	7	9	84	61	73
Bishop Auckland	38	22	6	10	82	44	72
Consett	38	19	7	12	78	49	64
Horden Colliery Welfare	38	19	6	13	53	44	63
North Shields	38	16	10	12	55	39	55
Durham City	38	15	9	14	55	51	54
Willington	38	16	6	16	53	62	54
Crook Town	38	12	17	9	56	47	53
West Auckland Town	38	12	15	11	49	51	51
Billingham Synthonia	38	17	8	16	65	64	50
South Bank	38	12	13	13	40	43	49
Whitley Bay	38	13	7	18	46	66	46
Ashington	38	15	7	16	56	54	43
Shildon	38	11	8	19	55	64	41
Tow Law Town	38	9	5	24	59	103	32
Ferryhill Athletic	38	8	8	22	30	69	32
Evenwood Town	38	4	5	29	36	90	17
Penrith	38	3	5	30	25	113	14

North Shields had 3 points deducted. Ashington had 9 points deducted.

Northern League 1978-1983

1978-79

Team	P	W	D	L	F	A	Pts
Spennymoor United	38	25	6	7	96	43	81
Bishop Auckland	38	25	5	8	96	38	80
Ashington	38	23	7	8	79	47	76
Crook Town	38	21	10	7	63	38	73
Blyth Spartans	38	19	12	7	81	39	69
Consett	38	21	9	8	84	52	69
North Shields	38	21	4	13	76	55	67
South Bank	38	16	11	11	58	47	59
Horden Colliery Welfare	38	17	8	13	64	56	59
Durham City	38	15	9	14	63	62	54
Billingham Synthonia	38	12	12	14	60	55	48
Tow Law Town	38	12	8	18	54	63	44
Shildon	38	11	10	17	52	69	43
Whitby Town	38	11	12	15	55	68	42
Whitley Bay	38	9	9	20	54	77	36
West Auckland Town	38	9	9	20	54	87	36
Ferryhill Athletic	38	10	5	23	43	74	35
Willington	38	7	10	21	41	75	31
Penrith	38	8	7	23	35	82	31
Evenwood Town	38	4	5	29	31	112	14

Consett, Whitby Town and Evenwood Town each had 3 points deducted.

1979-80

Team	P	W	D	L	F	A	Pts
Blyth Spartans	38	29	5	4	93	28	92
Spennymoor United	38	26	7	5	83	40	85
Horden Colliery Welfare	38	24	6	8	73	32	78
Ashington	38	21	8	9	88	53	71
Crook Town	38	21	8	9	77	51	71
Bishop Auckland	38	18	9	11	64	54	63
Consett	38	19	4	15	78	59	61
South Bank	38	16	7	15	68	52	55
Shildon	38	16	7	15	70	71	55
West Auckland Town	38	16	6	16	57	52	54
Whitby Town	38	14	10	14	72	62	52
Tow Law Town	38	16	4	18	50	56	52
Evenwood Town	38	14	9	15	49	55	51
Penrith	38	13	5	20	54	72	44
Billingham Synthonia	38	10	12	16	44	72	42
North Shields	38	12	3	23	62	81	39
Ferryhill Athletic	38	9	7	22	38	60	34
Durham City	38	7	9	22	30	63	30
Willington	38	6	5	27	27	105	23
Whitley Bay	38	4	7	27	31	90	16

Whitley Bay had 3 points deducted.

1980-81

Team	P	W	D	L	F	A	Pts
Blyth Spartans	38	27	5	6	89	35	86
Spennymoor United	38	26	7	5	82	38	85
Bishop Auckland	38	22	7	9	68	36	73
Tow Law Town	38	18	13	7	83	54	67
Ashington	38	17	12	9	95	66	63
Ferryhill Athletic	38	17	10	11	71	49	61
Shildon	38	17	8	13	56	54	59
South Bank	38	16	9	13	55	44	57
Billingham Synthonia	38	13	15	10	52	51	54
Penrith	38	15	8	15	75	66	53
Whitby Town	38	15	7	16	55	59	52
Horden Colliery Welfare	38	12	9	17	48	65	45
Consett	38	12	6	20	49	54	42
North Shields	38	10	10	18	56	71	40
Evenwood Town	38	10	10	18	41	66	40
West Auckland Town	38	10	10	18	40	67	40
Durham City	38	9	11	18	46	74	38
Crook Town	38	10	8	20	47	79	38
Whitley Bay	38	9	7	22	53	72	34
Willington	38	6	6	26	41	102	24

1981-82

Team	P	W	D	L	F	A	Pts
Blyth Spartans	38	25	8	5	77	31	83
Whitby Town	38	23	11	4	64	21	80
South Bank	38	20	7	11	72	44	67
Tow Law Town	38	18	8	12	76	58	62
Spennymoor United	38	16	13	9	59	37	61
Billingham Synthonia	38	17	9	12	57	46	60
Bishop Auckland	38	17	8	13	63	51	59
Durham City	38	17	5	16	75	67	56
Shildon	38	16	8	14	57	53	56
North Shields	38	14	13	11	67	61	55
Ferryhill Athletic	38	16	6	16	57	59	54
Horden Colliery Welfare	38	15	6	17	55	58	51
Crook Town	38	15	6	17	60	69	51
Evenwood Town	38	13	9	16	57	66	48
Penrith	38	13	10	15	63	66	46
Consett	38	10	18	18	46	64	40
West Auckland Town	38	9	10	19	42	67	37
Ashington	38	9	8	21	50	87	35
Whitley Bay	38	8	7	23	47	83	31
Willington	38	3	10	25	46	102	19

Penrith had 3 points deducted.
Penrith moved to the North-West Counties League.

A new Division Two was formed containing 11 clubs.
Alnwick Town, Bedlington Terriers, Ryhope Community Association and Esh Winning all joined from the Northern Alliance, Esh Winning having changed their name from Esh Winning Pineapple; Norton and Stockton Ancients and Billingham Town both joined from the Teesside League, Billingham Town having changed their name from Billingham Social; Hartlepool United Reserves and Peterlee Newtown both joined from the Wearside League; Gretna joined from the Carlisle & District League; Northallerton Town joined from the Harrogate & District League and Darlington Reserves also joined.

Promoted clubs are shown in bold, relegated clubs in bold italics.

1982-83

Division One

Team	P	W	D	L	F	A	Pts
Blyth Spartans	36	23	11	2	92	31	80
Whitby Town	36	23	9	4	80	34	78
Horden Colliery Welfare	36	21	5	10	65	35	68
Bishop Auckland	36	17	13	6	69	34	64
Spennymoor United	36	17	10	9	70	53	61
Billingham Synthonia	36	16	12	8	71	43	60
North Shields	36	17	7	12	73	46	58
Tow Law Town	36	16	10	10	71	63	58
Consett	36	15	10	11	53	37	55
Crook Town	36	16	7	13	54	47	55
South Bank	36	14	12	10	56	32	54
Ferryhill Athletic	36	14	12	10	53	42	54
Whitley Bay	36	13	8	15	56	50	47
Shildon	36	9	11	16	48	71	38
Evenwood Town	36	9	8	19	49	67	35
Ashington	36	9	6	21	36	73	33
Durham City	*36*	*4*	*8*	*24*	*32*	*83*	*20*
West Auckland Town	*36*	*5*	*3*	*28*	*37*	*110*	*18*
Willington	*36*	*2*	*2*	*32*	*26*	*140*	*8*

Division Two (Clubs played each other 3 times)

Peterlee Newtown	30	18	9	3	67	33	63
Gretna	30	18	6	6	63	29	60
Darlington Reserves	30	15	7	8	55	36	52
Hartlepool United Reserves	30	16	4	10	69	46	46
Ryhope Community Association	30	14	6	10	61	55	45
Esh Winning	30	10	7	13	42	60	37
Billingham Town	30	8	11	11	36	47	35
Northallerton Town	30	10	4	16	41	61	34
Norton and Stockton Ancients	30	7	6	17	35	61	27
Bedlington Terriers	30	5	9	16	33	48	24
Alnwick Town	30	5	9	16	31	57	24

Ryhope Community Association had 3 points deducted.
Hartlepool United Reserves had 6 points deducted.
Brandon United, Chester-le-Street Town and Seaham Colliery Welfare Red Star all joined from the Wearside League, Darlington Cleveland Bridge and Shotton Comrades joined from the Northern Alliance and Langley Park Welfare joined from the Durham & District League, having changed their name from Rams Head.

1983-84

Division One

Blyth Spartans	34	23	9	2	74	22	78
North Shields	34	21	6	7	81	51	69
Whitby Town	34	20	7	7	79	33	67
Tow Law Town	34	19	8	7	72	44	65
Bishop Auckland	34	19	7	8	80	39	64
South Bank	34	18	7	9	62	35	61
Billingham Synthonia	34	14	8	12	56	54	50
Gretna	34	15	7	12	65	58	49
Whitley Bay	34	14	5	15	39	60	47
Horden Colliery Welfare	34	12	7	15	48	59	43
Spennymoor United	34	10	9	15	41	57	39
Consett	34	10	8	16	43	58	38
Peterlee Newtown	34	11	5	18	50	78	38
Crook Town	34	9	10	15	38	50	37
Shildon	34	10	6	18	50	66	36
Ferryhill Athletic	34	9	6	19	47	61	33
Ashington	**34**	**7**	**8**	**19**	**39**	**71**	**26**
Evenwood Town	**34**	**1**	**5**	**28**	**27**	**95**	**8**

Gretna and Ashington each had 3 points deducted.

Division Two

Chester-le-Street Town	**34**	**25**	**7**	**2**	**84**	**21**	**82**
Ryhope Community Association	**34**	**23**	**6**	**5**	**66**	**33**	**75**
Seaham Colliery Welfare Red Star	34	23	5	6	69	30	74
Brandon United	34	20	6	8	67	37	66
Durham City	34	16	11	7	61	38	59
Darlington Cleveland Bridge	34	15	9	10	60	52	54
Hartlepool United Reserves	34	18	5	11	73	52	53
Bedlington Terriers	34	14	7	13	52	41	49
Esh Winning	34	13	10	11	49	55	49
Billingham Town	34	13	6	15	63	51	45
Darlington Reserves	34	12	4	18	47	69	40
Northallerton Town	34	12	6	16	48	52	39
Langley Park Welfare	34	9	8	17	46	76	35
Alnwick Town	34	7	12	15	49	53	33
Shotton Comrades	34	9	5	20	55	76	32
Norton and Stockton Ancients	34	6	10	18	30	55	28
West Auckland Town	34	7	3	24	36	83	24
Willington	34	2	4	28	27	108	10

Northallerton Town had 3 points deducted.
Hartlepool United Reserves had 6 points deducted.

1984-85

Division One

Bishop Auckland	34	26	4	4	92	26	82
Blyth Spartans	34	24	3	7	86	36	75
South Bank	34	19	10	5	62	30	67
Tow Law Town	34	18	10	6	57	45	64
North Shields	34	19	5	10	62	49	62
Gretna	34	17	8	9	56	39	59
Whitby Town	34	17	7	10	61	44	58
Chester-le-Street Town	34	15	6	13	54	44	51
Peterlee Newtown	34	13	7	14	51	44	46
Ryhope Community Association	34	13	6	15	49	55	45
Spennymoor United	34	11	8	15	63	56	41
Billingham Synthonia	34	11	5	18	39	65	38
Whitley Bay	34	8	11	15	51	55	32
Ferryhill Athletic	34	8	8	18	39	70	32
Consett	34	8	3	23	42	95	27
Crook Town	34	6	8	20	32	66	26
Horden Colliery Welfare	**34**	**5**	**10**	**19**	**36**	**67**	**25**
Shildon	**34**	**5**	**7**	**22**	**41**	**87**	**22**

Whitley Bay had 3 points deducted.

Division Two

Brandon United	**34**	**27**	**2**	**5**	**102**	**38**	**83**
Bedlington Terriers	**34**	**25**	**5**	**4**	**77**	**28**	**80**
Hartlepool United Reserves	**34**	**25**	**2**	**7**	**86**	**37**	**77**
Billingham Town	**34**	**22**	**6**	**6**	**74**	**32**	**72**
Durham City	34	21	9	4	73	36	72
Seaham Colliery Welfare Red Star	34	19	7	8	76	41	64
Willington	34	17	5	12	59	57	56
Darlington Cleveland Bridge	34	14	6	14	57	64	48
Langley Park Welfare	34	11	9	14	53	62	42
Ashington	34	11	7	16	59	58	40
Esh Winning	34	12	6	16	46	64	39
Northallerton Town	34	11	5	18	44	71	38
Norton and Stockton Ancients	34	7	7	20	34	69	28
Alnwick Town	34	6	8	20	42	78	26
Evenwood Town	34	7	5	22	41	78	26
Darlington Reserves	34	6	7	21	49	81	25
West Auckland Town	34	7	3	24	47	88	24
Shotton Comrades	34	4	9	21	37	74	21

Esh Winning had 3 points deducted.
Blue Star, Easington Colliery and Stockton joined from the Wearside League and Guisborough Town joined from the Northern Counties (East) League.

1985-86

Division One

Bishop Auckland	38	21	10	7	79	45	73
Bedlington Terriers	38	19	10	9	65	44	67
South Bank	38	18	12	8	66	36	66
Blyth Spartans	38	19	9	10	79	52	66
Tow Law Town	38	18	10	10	72	47	64
Peterlee Newtown	38	19	6	13	66	56	63
Chester-le-Street Town	38	18	7	13	62	53	61
Brandon United	38	16	10	12	72	68	58
Crook Town	38	15	8	15	73	70	53
Hartlepool United Reserves	38	14	10	14	65	69	52
Gretna	38	13	11	14	70	69	50
North Shields	38	14	8	16	65	72	50
Consett	38	13	9	16	44	58	48
Spennymoor United	38	12	11	15	51	54	47
Ryhope Community Association	38	13	7	18	50	69	46
Whitby Town	38	12	9	17	59	74	45
Whitley Bay	38	11	8	19	65	73	41
Ferryhill Athletic	38	11	6	21	62	94	39
Billingham Synthonia	**38**	**8**	**11**	**19**	**47**	**66**	**35**
Billingham Town	**38**	**6**	**8**	**24**	**46**	**89**	**26**

Northern League 1986-1989

Division Two

Blue Star	38	36	1	1	133	15	109
Easington Colliery	38	27	7	4	101	36	88
Guisborough Town	38	25	7	6	88	36	82
Durham City	38	22	9	7	89	48	75
West Auckland Town	38	19	7	12	64	61	64
Seaham Colliery Welfare Red Star	38	17	7	14	63	56	58
Stockton	38	15	9	14	62	56	54
Ashington	38	15	9	14	81	85	54
Norton and Stockton Ancients	38	16	5	17	67	72	53
Alnwick Town	38	13	12	13	62	56	51
Willington	38	15	5	18	53	65	50
Langley Park Welfare	38	11	11	16	43	57	44
Horden Colliery Welfare	38	12	8	18	54	85	44
Shotton Comrades	38	9	12	17	56	82	39
Darlington Reserves	38	9	9	20	45	86	36
Northallerton Town	38	10	5	23	54	83	35
Evenwood Town	38	9	7	22	51	79	34
Darlington Cleveland Bridge	38	10	4	24	55	89	34
Shildon	38	6	15	17	42	66	33
Esh Winning	38	5	9	24	49	99	24

Darlington Reserves moved to the Central League.
Blue Star changed their name to Newcastle Blue Star.

1986-87

Division One

Blyth Spartans	38	29	7	2	87	36	94
Bishop Auckland	38	26	2	10	96	42	80
Spennymoor United	38	20	13	5	89	41	73
Newcastle Blue Star	38	20	11	7	74	34	71
Whitley Bay	38	19	9	10	74	53	66
North Shields	38	18	10	10	65	47	64
Gretna	38	17	10	11	73	57	61
South Bank	38	16	12	10	59	36	60
Tow Law Town	38	15	10	13	50	57	55
Easington Colliery	38	16	5	17	59	59	53
Whitby Town	38	13	13	12	56	63	52
Brandon United	38	12	11	15	55	64	47
Consett	38	14	5	19	46	72	47
Ryhope Community Association	38	11	9	18	47	64	42
Hartlepool United Reserves	38	10	10	18	41	59	40
Chester-le-Street Town	38	7	14	17	37	66	35
Crook Town	38	9	5	24	47	85	22
Ferryhill Athletic	38	7	9	22	42	80	30
Peterlee Newtown	**38**	**7**	**7**	**24**	**31**	**66**	**28**
Bedlington Terriers	**38**	**6**	**4**	**28**	**40**	**87**	**22**

Hartlepool United withdrew their reserve side from the league.

Division Two

Billingham Synthonia	**36**	**26**	**9**	**1**	**83**	**34**	**87**
Guisborough Town	**36**	**24**	**7**	**5**	**87**	**33**	**79**
Shildon	**36**	**19**	**8**	**9**	**77**	**47**	**65**
Billingham Town	36	17	9	10	70	43	60
West Auckland Town	36	15	13	8	56	46	58
Alnwick Town	36	15	11	10	45	30	56
Stockton	36	15	11	10	65	51	56
Norton and Stockton Ancients	36	16	6	14	64	47	54
Seaham Colliery Welfare Red Star	36	16	6	14	60	53	54
Ashington	36	14	6	16	67	73	48
Northallerton Town	36	13	6	17	74	74	45
Durham City	36	12	8	16	52	63	44
Willington	36	12	10	14	53	52	43
Shotton Comrades	36	8	16	12	52	64	37
Evenwood Town	36	10	7	19	58	70	37
Darlington Cleveland Bridge	36	8	10	18	45	81	34
Esh Winning	36	8	7	21	44	81	31
Horden Colliery Welfare	36	8	6	22	39	79	30
Langley Park Welfare	36	5	6	25	41	98	21

Willington and Shotton Comrades each had 3 points deducted.
Seaham Colliery Welfare Red Star changed their name to Seaham Red Star.

1987-88

Division One

Blyth Spartans	38	28	8	2	106	36	92
Newcastle Blue Star	38	28	3	7	79	33	87
Billingham Synthonia	38	23	8	7	76	41	77
Whitley Bay	38	22	9	7	60	27	75
Guisborough Town	38	18	12	8	63	41	66
Bishop Auckland	38	19	7	12	70	48	64
Gretna	38	17	6	15	69	46	57
Tow Law Town	38	16	6	16	65	72	54
North Shields	38	16	5	17	62	59	53
Brandon United	38	15	7	16	64	61	52
Spennymoor United	38	15	7	16	57	57	52
Shildon	38	14	7	17	61	59	49
Whitby Town	38	12	10	16	57	74	46
Ferryhill Athletic	38	12	7	19	58	75	43
Easington Colliery	38	12	6	20	65	85	42
South Bank	38	10	11	17	34	48	41
Crook Town	38	8	9	21	45	84	33
Chester-le-Street Town	38	7	9	22	38	73	30
Ryhope Community Association	**38**	**5**	**10**	**23**	**40**	**89**	**25**
Consett	**38**	**5**	**9**	**24**	**44**	**105**	**24**

Bishop Auckland and Whitley Bay both moved to the Northern Premier League – Division One.

Division Two

Stockton	34	21	10	3	78	31	73
Seaham Red Star	34	21	8	5	63	32	71
Durham City	34	19	6	9	55	37	63
Billingham Town	**34**	**14**	**13**	**7**	**60**	**43**	**55**
Esh Winning	34	14	7	13	47	49	49
Alnwick Town	34	12	9	13	53	47	45
Bedlington Terriers	34	11	11	12	49	46	44
Peterlee Newtown	34	11	11	12	37	34	44
Northallerton Town	34	13	5	16	49	49	44
Norton and Stockton Ancients	34	11	10	13	49	58	43
Horden Colliery Welfare	34	10	13	11	48	65	43
Langley Park Welfare	34	11	9	14	52	57	42
Willington	34	11	7	16	44	53	40
Darlington Cleveland Bridge	34	11	7	16	45	57	40
Ashington	34	10	9	15	45	62	39
Evenwood Town	34	10	8	16	42	56	38
West Auckland Town	34	9	8	17	46	62	35
Shotton Comrades	34	7	9	18	33	57	30

Murton, Washington and Whickham all joined from the Wearside League and Prudhoe East End joined from the Northern Alliance.

1988-89

Division One

Billingham Synthonia	38	26	6	6	83	34	84
Tow Law Town	38	23	8	7	74	45	77
Gretna	38	22	7	9	80	37	73
Guisborough Town	38	21	9	8	74	37	72
Billingham Town	38	20	4	14	59	47	64
Newcastle Blue Star	38	17	10	11	61	38	61
Brandon United	38	15	8	15	50	60	53
Ferryhill Athletic	38	15	7	16	72	65	52
Blyth Spartans	38	13	13	12	51	50	52
Stockton	38	15	7	16	58	63	52
Spennymoor United	38	14	9	15	47	60	51
Whitby Town	38	13	9	16	56	52	48
Easington Colliery	38	12	11	15	51	57	47
Durham City	38	11	13	14	41	42	46
South Bank	38	12	10	16	46	58	46
Seaham Red Star	38	12	8	18	50	67	44
Shildon	38	9	11	18	50	88	38
North Shields	38	10	6	22	56	77	36
Chester-le-Street Town	**38**	**6**	**14**	**18**	**35**	**60**	**32**
Crook Town	**38**	**5**	**8**	**25**	**32**	**89**	**20**

Crook Town had 3 points deducted.
North Shields moved to the Northern Counties (East) League – Premier Division.

Division Two

Consett	38	30	3	5	89	32	93
Alnwick Town	38	25	9	4	92	36	84
Whickham	38	26	6	6	88	38	84
Prudhoe East End	38	24	6	8	68	32	78
Ashington	38	21	5	12	79	52	68
Peterlee Newtown	38	20	7	11	70	53	67
Bedlington Terriers	38	16	7	15	63	50	55
Horden Colliery Welfare	38	15	10	13	57	58	55
Northallerton Town	38	13	15	10	62	38	51
Ryhope Community Association	38	13	11	14	67	60	50
Murton	38	14	8	16	65	62	50
West Auckland Town	38	12	11	15	66	72	47
Langley Park Welfare	38	13	6	19	58	72	42
Norton and Stockton Ancients	38	11	7	20	52	72	40
Esh Winning	38	10	8	20	42	68	38
Darlington Cleveland Bridge	38	10	8	20	49	83	38
Evenwood Town	38	8	8	22	53	100	32
Washington	38	8	6	24	50	87	30
Willington	38	8	6	24	43	97	30
Shotton Comrades	38	5	9	24	32	83	24

Northallerton Town and Langley Park Welfare each had 3 points deducted. Hebburn joined from the Wearside League.

1989-90

Division One

Billingham Synthonia	38	29	4	5	87	35	91
Gretna	38	23	6	9	79	44	75
Tow Law Town	38	22	7	9	78	57	73
Newcastle Blue Star	38	19	10	9	77	48	67
Stockton	38	18	8	12	73	64	62
Consett	38	16	9	13	57	61	57
Guisborough Town	38	16	8	14	59	46	56
Alnwick Town	38	16	6	16	59	54	54
Blyth Spartans	38	15	8	15	58	58	53
Seaham Red Star	38	15	7	16	62	66	52
Spennymoor United	38	14	8	16	58	53	50
Whitby Town	38	15	8	15	74	73	50
Ferryhill Athletic	38	14	4	20	63	79	46
Shildon	38	12	10	16	58	75	46
Whickham	38	11	7	20	48	69	40
South Bank	38	10	10	18	40	65	40
Durham City	38	9	12	17	64	77	39
Brandon United	38	9	12	17	46	60	39
Billingham Town	**38**	**10**	**9**	**19**	**52**	**67**	**39**
Easington Colliery	**38**	**6**	**9**	**23**	**29**	**70**	**27**

Whitby Town had 3 points deducted.
Spennymoor United moved to the Northern Counties (East) League – Premier Division.

Division Two

Murton	38	27	8	3	86	33	89
Northallerton Town	38	26	9	3	82	32	87
Peterlee Newtown	38	24	10	4	71	24	82
Langley Park Welfare	38	24	8	6	67	35	80
Chester-le-Street	38	23	8	7	62	34	77
Crook Town	38	20	7	11	70	45	67
Evenwood Town	38	19	8	11	77	52	65
Prudhoe East End	38	17	10	11	63	49	61
Bedlington Terriers	38	17	5	16	67	72	56
Washington	38	16	4	18	50	58	52
Ryhope Community Association	38	14	6	18	68	67	48
Darlington Cleveland Bridge	38	13	7	18	45	72	43
Ashington	38	10	6	22	62	85	36
Willington	38	10	5	23	51	86	35
Hebburn	38	8	8	22	56	76	32
Horden Colliery Welfare	38	8	8	22	34	66	32
Shotton Comrades	38	8	10	20	51	69	31
Norton and Stockton Ancients	38	7	9	22	43	71	30
West Auckland Town	38	5	13	20	43	72	28
Esh Winning	38	7	5	26	41	91	23

Darlington Cleveland Bridge, Shotton Comrades and Esh Winning each had 3 points deducted.
Langley Park Welfare changed their name to Langley Park.

1990-91

Division One

Gretna	38	30	5	3	86	23	95
Guisborough Town	38	21	12	5	79	43	75
Blyth Spartans	38	20	8	10	80	50	68
Billingham Synthonia	38	20	8	10	72	43	68
Consett	38	19	11	8	67	43	68
Whitby Town	38	16	13	9	66	49	61
Tow Law Town	38	16	10	12	65	64	58
Ferryhill Athletic	38	16	9	13	55	50	54
Northallerton Town	38	14	11	13	50	46	53
Newcastle Blue Star	38	13	13	12	59	48	52
Seaham Red Star	38	12	12	14	44	46	48
South Bank	38	9	16	13	40	43	43
Murton	38	10	11	17	47	59	41
Shildon	38	10	9	19	49	75	39
Whickham	38	10	9	19	44	71	39
Peterlee Newtown	38	7	17	14	57	65	38
Brandon United	38	9	11	18	44	70	38
Stockton	**38**	**10**	**6**	**22**	**40**	**79**	**36**
Alnwick Town	**38**	**7**	**10**	**21**	**40**	**78**	**31**
Durham City	**38**	**6**	**9**	**23**	**47**	**86**	**27**

Ferryhill Athletic had 3 points deducted.

Division Two

West Auckland Town	36	24	7	5	72	39	79
Langley Park	36	24	4	8	83	40	76
Easington Colliery	36	20	8	8	80	42	68
Hebburn	36	22	5	9	89	56	68
Billingham Town	36	21	5	10	69	39	68
Evenwood Town	36	20	8	8	69	40	65
Esh Winning	36	19	6	11	77	57	63
Prudhoe East End	36	16	10	10	71	46	58
Norton and Stockton Ancients	36	16	3	17	60	67	51
Darlington Cleveland Bridge	36	14	7	15	53	60	49
Bedlington Terriers	36	14	6	16	60	73	48
Ashington	36	14	6	16	47	68	48
Crook Town	36	13	8	15	57	64	47
Ryhope Community Association	36	13	4	19	54	57	43
Shotton Comrades	36	7	9	20	43	73	30
Chester-le-Street Town	36	6	11	19	45	68	29
Washington	36	7	6	23	44	79	27
Willington	36	4	9	23	34	77	21
Horden Colliery Welfare	36	2	10	24	37	99	16

Hebburn and Evenwood Town each had 3 points deducted.
Dunston Federation Brewery joined from the Wearside League.

1991-92

Division One

Team	P	W	D	L	F	A	Pts
Gretna	38	25	10	3	81	33	85
Murton	38	23	9	6	83	36	78
Whitby Town	38	23	9	6	74	41	78
Guisborough Town	38	22	10	6	81	36	76
Billingham Synthonia	38	21	6	11	70	44	69
Blyth Spartans	38	19	8	11	63	44	65
South Bank	38	18	9	11	68	50	63
Northallerton Town	38	18	8	12	63	53	62
Consett	38	15	5	18	59	59	50
Tow Law Town	38	13	11	14	60	73	50
Seaham Red Star	38	13	9	16	50	57	48
Peterlee Newtown	38	14	3	21	47	70	45
Newcastle Blue Star	38	14	5	19	49	52	44
West Auckland Town	38	11	8	19	45	68	41
Brandon United	38	10	10	18	61	75	40
Ferryhill Athletic	38	10	10	18	45	60	40
Easington Colliery	38	11	7	20	42	61	40
Shildon	**38**	**11**	**7**	**20**	**47**	**83**	**40**
Langley Park	**38**	**7**	**7**	**24**	**51**	**89**	**28**
Whickham	**38**	**4**	**5**	**29**	**38**	**93**	**17**

Newcastle Blue Star had 3 points deducted.
Gretna were promoted to the Northern Premier League – Division One.

Division Two

Team	P	W	D	L	F	A	Pts
Stockton	**38**	**27**	**7**	**4**	**102**	**35**	**88**
Durham City	**38**	**26**	**9**	**3**	**82**	**24**	**87**
Chester-le-Street Town	**38**	**26**	**8**	**4**	**80**	**36**	**86**
Hebburn	**38**	**27**	**4**	**7**	**101**	**44**	**85**
Dunston Federation Brewery	38	26	6	6	104	33	84
Prudhoe East End	38	22	4	12	61	36	70
Billingham Town	38	18	7	13	60	47	61
Crook Town	38	16	9	13	54	53	57
Alnwick Town	38	15	12	11	54	60	57
Ryhope Community Association	38	17	5	16	77	59	56
Esh Winning	38	13	9	16	76	74	48
Ashington	38	13	9	16	50	69	48
Norton and Stockton Ancients	38	11	10	17	61	69	43
Shotton Comrades	38	11	6	21	52	66	39
Horden Colliery Welfare	38	10	6	22	52	76	36
Washington	38	8	9	21	36	63	33
Evenwood Town	38	8	7	23	42	105	31
Darlington Cleveland Bridge	38	7	4	27	47	97	25
Bedlington Terriers	38	7	2	29	38	97	20
Willington	38	4	3	31	33	119	15

Bedlington Terriers had 3 points deducted.
Eppleton Colliery Welfare joined from the Wearside League.

1992-93

Division One

Team	P	W	D	L	F	A	Pts
Whitby Town	38	26	10	2	104	30	88
Billingham Synthonia	38	25	10	3	98	41	85
Guisborough Town	38	25	9	4	91	35	84
Blyth Spartans	38	26	4	8	83	35	82
Seaham Red Star	38	21	10	7	76	45	73
Durham City	38	21	10	7	73	51	73
Stockton	38	14	15	9	65	59	57
Murton	38	14	12	12	72	65	54
Chester-le-Street Town	38	15	8	15	82	82	53
Consett	38	15	7	16	54	56	52
Northallerton Town	38	13	14	11	54	47	50
West Auckland Town	38	12	9	17	64	76	45
Newcastle Blue Star	38	12	6	20	64	81	42
Tow Law Town	38	11	8	19	65	73	41
Brandon United	38	11	5	22	47	81	38
Hebburn	38	8	11	19	74	94	29
Ferryhill Athletic	38	6	10	22	51	97	28
Easington Colliery	**38**	**6**	**8**	**24**	**51**	**94**	**26**
Peterlee Newtown	**38**	**3**	**9**	**26**	**40**	**105**	**18**
South Bank	38	3	11	24	34	95	17

Northallerton Town and South Bank each had 3 points deducted.
Hebburn had 6 points deducted.
South Bank were forced to suspend playing after losing their ground.
They subsequently re-formed and joined the Wearside League in 1995.

Division Two

Team	P	W	D	L	F	A	Pts
Dunston Federation Brewery	**38**	**30**	**5**	**3**	**139**	**34**	**95**
Eppleton Colliery Welfare	**38**	**27**	**7**	**4**	**116**	**51**	**88**
Shildon	**38**	**25**	**6**	**7**	**93**	**24**	**81**
Billingham Town	38	24	8	6	89	36	80
Prudhoe East End	38	18	7	13	65	53	61
Evenwood Town	38	18	7	13	75	68	61
Whickham	38	19	3	16	71	62	60
Ashington	38	17	5	16	77	70	56
Alnwick Town	38	16	7	15	51	61	55
Ryhope Community Association	38	16	8	14	67	61	53
Darlington Cleveland Bridge	38	14	11	13	48	53	50
Norton and Stockton Ancients	38	13	5	20	54	79	44
Esh Winning	38	13	4	21	70	82	43
Shotton Comrades	38	11	10	17	53	74	43
Washington	38	10	9	19	54	74	39
Willington	38	12	3	23	61	106	39
Bedlington Terriers	38	11	3	24	64	86	33
Crook Town	38	9	9	20	45	78	33
Horden Colliery Welfare	38	6	8	24	48	99	26
Langley Park	38	5	7	26	52	141	22

Bedlington Terriers, Crook Town, Ryhope Community Association and Darlington Cleveland Bridge each had 3 points deducted.
Darlington Cleveland Bridge changed their name to Darlington Cleveland Social and Langley Park changed their name to Langley Park S. & S. United.

1993-94

Division One

Durham City	38	23	11	4	88	39	80
Blyth Spartans	38	22	7	9	81	37	73
Seaham Red Star	38	20	10	8	70	40	70
Whitby Town	38	17	14	7	90	57	65
Guisborough Town	38	17	12	9	71	41	63
Northallerton Town	38	18	7	13	68	39	61
Tow Law Town	38	18	6	14	70	58	60
Murton	38	17	8	13	63	65	59
Shildon	38	17	6	15	59	54	57
Billingham Synthonia	38	15	9	14	57	45	54
Dunston Federation Brewery	38	15	9	14	72	69	54
Consett	38	15	6	17	67	70	48
Ferryhill Athletic	38	11	8	19	61	81	41
Newcastle Blue Star	38	11	8	19	44	65	41
Hebburn	38	12	5	21	55	93	41
Eppleton Colliery Welfare	38	11	7	20	52	76	40
Chester-le-Street Town	38	13	5	20	64	74	38
West Auckland Town	38	10	8	20	49	89	38
Brandon United	**38**	**9**	**6**	**23**	**45**	**94**	**33**
Stockton	**38**	**9**	**8**	**21**	**46**	**86**	**32**

Consett had 3 points deducted.
Chester-le-Street Town had 6 points deducted.
Blyth Spartans were promoted to the Northern Premier League – Division One. Northallerton Town disbanded but were quickly re-formed as Northallerton and continued in the Northern League. Newcastle Blue Star changed their name to R.T.M. Newcastle.

Division Two

Bedlington Terriers	36	28	5	3	114	36	89
Peterlee Newtown	36	23	9	4	77	27	78
Prudhoe East End	36	21	9	6	72	36	72
Evenwood Town	36	22	4	10	78	47	70
Easington Colliery	36	20	7	9	77	40	67
Billingham Town	36	21	3	12	88	49	66
Crook Town	36	18	8	10	80	58	62
Norton and Stockton Ancients	36	18	7	11	72	70	61
Darlington Cleveland Social	36	18	2	16	65	68	56
Whickham	36	16	7	13	71	64	52
Washington	36	14	5	17	67	72	47
Esh Winning	36	12	7	17	50	72	43
Langley Park S. & S. United	36	12	5	19	55	67	41
Shotton Comrades	36	9	9	18	61	84	36
Alnwick Town	36	10	7	19	50	69	34
Willington	36	9	3	24	48	90	30
Ashington	36	8	3	25	46	100	24
Ryhope Community Association	36	7	3	26	37	94	18
Horden Colliery Welfare	36	3	3	30	35	100	12

Whickham, Alnwick Town and Ashington each had 3 points deducted.
Ryhope Community Association had 6 points deducted.
Hartlepool Town joined from the Wearside League and Morpeth Town joined from the Northern Alliance. Prudhoe East End changed their name to Prudhoe Town.

1994-95

Division One

Tow Law Town	38	28	6	4	105	39	90
Billingham Synthonia	38	23	7	8	99	35	76
Whitby Town	38	22	10	6	88	45	76
Bedlington Terriers	38	21	12	5	72	35	75
R.T.M. Newcastle	38	21	9	8	93	42	72
Guisborough Town	38	19	11	8	79	48	68
Durham City	38	17	12	9	75	45	63
Dunston Federation Brewery	38	16	12	10	70	62	60
Consett	38	15	11	12	74	55	56
Shildon	38	12	13	13	57	63	49
Hebburn	**38**	**14**	**9**	**15**	**57**	**68**	**48**
West Auckland Town	38	13	8	17	47	61	47
Seaham Red Star	38	14	6	18	72	72	45
Peterlee Newtown	38	12	9	17	62	80	45
Murton	38	10	5	23	48	89	35
Chester-le-Street Town	38	8	7	23	57	99	31
Ferryhill Athletic	38	9	6	23	34	80	30
Eppleton Colliery Welfare	38	8	4	26	38	97	28
Northallerton	**38**	**9**	**3**	**26**	**35**	**93**	**27**
Prudhoe Town	**38**	**6**	**6**	**26**	**39**	**93**	**24**

Seaham Red Star, Ferryhill Athletic and Northallerton each had 3 points deducted.
Hebburn had 3 points deducted. They were relegated at the end of the season because their ground did not meet all grading requirements.

Division Two

Whickham	38	26	10	2	103	37	88
Crook Town	38	26	6	6	102	40	84
Stockton	38	26	5	7	116	49	77
Brandon United	38	21	9	8	77	39	72
Billingham Town	38	23	4	11	95	50	70
Hartlepool Town	38	22	9	7	91	50	69
Ashington	38	19	2	17	77	66	59
Evenwood Town	38	17	8	13	72	63	59
Washington	38	17	9	12	74	55	57
Easington Colliery	38	15	10	13	55	51	55
Willington	38	17	3	18	62	61	54
Shotton Comrades	38	15	8	15	86	83	53
Esh Winning	38	15	7	16	78	88	52
Morpeth Town	38	13	6	19	69	67	45
Ryhope Community Association	38	12	9	17	55	62	45
Norton and Stockton Ancients	38	13	4	21	71	83	43
Alnwick Town	38	10	6	22	61	88	33
Darlington Cleveland Social	38	4	5	29	37	140	17
Horden Colliery Welfare	38	3	3	32	42	151	12
Langley Park S. & S. United	38	3	3	32	40	140	9

Billingham Town, Washington and Alnwick Town each had 3 points deducted.
Stockton and Hartlepool Town each had 6 points deducted.
Hartlepool Town and Langley Park S. & S. United both left. South Shields joined from the Wearside League.

Northern League 1995-1998

1995-96
Division One

Billingham Synthonia	38	24	8	6	78	34	80
Bedlington Terriers	38	22	12	4	90	37	78
Durham City	38	24	6	8	85	35	78
Tow Law Town	38	23	9	6	82	43	78
Whitby Town	38	21	7	10	100	59	70
Guisborough Town	38	20	8	10	80	54	68
Dunston Federation Brewery	38	20	8	10	75	52	68
West Auckland Town	38	19	5	14	66	57	62
Crook Town	38	17	9	12	59	41	60
Consett	38	17	7	14	76	64	58
Stockton	38	16	8	14	88	71	56
Shildon	38	16	3	19	74	74	51
Seaham Red Star	38	13	11	14	62	66	50
Murton	38	12	11	15	57	53	47
R.T.M. Newcastle	38	13	7	18	68	58	46
Chester-le-Street Town	38	11	9	18	72	78	42
Whickham	38	11	8	19	43	77	41
Peterlee Newtown	*38*	*5*	*4*	*29*	*40*	*96*	*19*
Eppleton Colliery Welfare	*38*	*2*	*3*	*33*	*26*	*153*	*9*
Ferryhill Athletic	*38*	*0*	*5*	*33*	*27*	*146*	*5*

Division Two

Morpeth Town	36	27	5	4	104	40	86
South Shields	36	25	4	7	89	34	79
Easington Colliery	36	23	7	6	86	40	76
Shotton Comrades	36	22	7	7	72	42	73
Northallerton	36	18	9	9	70	45	63
Ashington	36	18	9	9	66	48	63
Billingham Town	36	18	6	12	73	51	60
Evenwood Town	36	16	8	12	70	61	56
Prudhoe Town	36	17	4	15	75	69	55
Brandon United	36	16	6	14	59	55	54
Esh Winning	36	13	7	16	80	75	46
Hebburn	36	13	5	18	50	56	44
Washington	36	14	4	18	71	73	43
Horden Colliery Welfare	36	13	3	20	64	74	42
Willington	36	11	8	17	53	75	41
Alnwick Town	36	10	6	20	47	65	36
Ryhope Community Association	36	6	5	25	41	82	23
Norton and Stockton Ancients	36	6	5	25	53	120	17
Darlington Cleveland Social	36	0	4	32	33	151	4

Washington had 3 points deducted.
Norton and Stockton Ancients had 6 points deducted.
Jarrow Roofing Boldon C.A. joined from the Wearside League.

1996-97
Division One

Whitby Town	38	32	3	3	131	37	99
Billingham Synthonia	38	28	6	4	109	46	90
Bedlington Terriers	38	28	5	5	113	37	86
Durham City	38	19	11	8	69	50	68
Crook Town	38	19	9	10	88	56	66
Morpeth Town	38	20	6	12	73	56	66
Guisborough Town	38	17	9	12	68	54	60
Tow Law Town	38	14	11	13	76	70	53
South Shields	38	13	11	14	52	63	50
Murton	38	15	5	18	58	80	50
Consett	38	12	11	15	65	59	47
Dunston Federation Brewery	38	12	10	16	64	70	46
Shildon	38	13	7	18	72	86	46
Easington Colliery	38	12	8	18	56	72	44
R.T.M. Newcastle	38	13	3	22	66	87	42
Seaham Red Star	38	7	14	17	50	83	35
Stockton	38	8	10	20	70	105	34
Chester-le-Street Town	*38*	*7*	*12*	*19*	*53*	*86*	*33*
Whickham	*38*	*5*	*6*	*27*	*38*	*98*	*21*
West Auckland Town	*38*	*6*	*3*	*29*	*41*	*117*	*21*

Bedlington Terriers had 3 points deducted.
Whitby Town were promoted to the Northern Premier League – Division One. Penrith joined from the North-West Counties League.

Division Two

Northallerton	**36**	**25**	**6**	**5**	**98**	**41**	**81**
Billingham Town	**36**	**24**	**6**	**6**	**111**	**39**	**75**
Jarrow Roofing Boldon C.A.	**36**	**23**	**6**	**7**	**88**	**34**	**75**
Ashington	36	22	5	9	71	38	71
Evenwood Town	36	21	4	11	84	46	67
Horden Colliery Welfare	36	20	7	9	67	37	64
Prudhoe Town	36	18	10	8	73	48	64
Shotton Comrades	36	20	6	10	91	43	63
Willington	36	18	7	11	78	54	61
Peterlee Newtown	36	16	8	12	56	56	56
Hebburn	36	16	3	17	66	61	51
Ryhope Community Association	36	12	5	19	50	70	41
Norton and Stockton Ancients	36	11	7	18	47	58	37
Brandon United	36	10	7	19	64	76	37
Alnwick Town	36	11	4	21	55	79	34
Eppleton Colliery Welfare	36	6	7	23	44	110	25
Washington	36	6	7	23	43	79	22
Esh Winning	36	7	3	26	44	100	21
Ferryhill Athletic	36	1	2	33	16	177	5

Billingham Town, Horden Colliery Welfare, Shotton Comrades, Norton and Stockton Ancients, Alnwick Town, Washington and Esh Winning all had 3 points deducted
Darlington Cleveland Social resigned and disbanded and their record was deleted when it stood as: 9 0 1 8 5 43 1

1997-98
Division One

Bedlington Terriers	38	29	3	6	120	32	90
Billingham Synthonia	38	23	9	6	81	36	78
Guisborough Town	38	23	6	9	84	53	75
Dunston Federation Brewery	38	21	10	7	69	35	73
R.T.M. Newcastle	38	20	5	13	92	70	65
Penrith	38	19	8	11	81	62	65
Morpeth Town	38	16	14	8	75	48	62
South Shields	38	15	19	4	65	38	61
Shildon	38	16	7	15	77	87	55
Billingham Town	38	17	2	19	72	79	53
Tow Law Town	38	16	7	15	78	61	52
Consett	38	13	11	14	60	62	50
Jarrow Roofing Boldon C.A.	38	11	12	15	64	70	45
Crook Town	38	12	7	19	58	67	43
Seaham Red Star	38	12	7	19	60	83	43
Easington Colliery	38	13	6	19	77	97	42
Stockton	38	10	10	18	54	65	37
Durham City	*38*	*10*	*7*	*21*	*55*	*67*	*37*
Northallerton	*38*	*4*	*6*	*28*	*39*	*102*	*18*
Murton	*38*	*2*	*0*	*36*	*23*	*170*	*3*

South Shields, Tow Law Town, Easington Colliery, Stockton and Murton all had 3 points deducted.
R.T.M. Newcastle changed their name to Newcastle Blue Star and Northallerton changed their name to Northallerton Town.

Division Two

Chester-le-Street Town	36	29	3	4	105	27	90
West Auckland Town	36	24	8	4	85	36	80
Marske United	36	24	5	7	78	30	77
Prudhoe Town	36	20	5	11	87	58	62
Ashington	36	18	7	11	76	52	61
Willington	36	16	6	14	87	65	54
Peterlee Newtown	36	16	7	13	60	55	52
Evenwood Town	36	14	9	13	62	62	51
Alnwick Town	36	15	5	16	68	64	50
Norton and Stockton Ancients	36	14	7	15	58	57	49
Shotton Comrades	36	13	8	15	66	61	47
Hebburn	36	12	10	14	57	43	46
Ryhope Community Association	36	12	10	14	60	63	46
Horden Colliery Welfare	36	12	8	16	58	67	44
Whickham	36	14	7	15	51	66	43
Esh Winning	36	11	9	16	58	79	42
Brandon United	36	11	6	19	59	87	39
Eppleton Colliery Welfare	36	4	4	28	29	103	16
Washington	36	1	0	35	24	153	0

Prudhoe Town, Peterlee Newtown and Washington each had 3 points deducted. Whickham had 6 points deducted.

1998-99

Division One

Bedlington Terriers	38	33	2	3	128	37	101
Tow Law Town	38	23	6	9	80	49	75
Chester-le-Street Town	38	17	14	7	71	46	65
West Auckland Town	38	19	8	11	65	57	65
Dunston Federation Brewery	38	18	10	10	73	51	64
Guisborough Town	38	18	5	15	68	65	59
Seaham Red Star	38	16	7	15	62	59	55
Consett	38	15	7	16	72	64	52
Morpeth Town	38	15	6	17	54	60	51
Stockton	38	15	6	17	68	76	51
Billingham Synthonia	38	15	7	16	60	56	49
Marske United	38	13	9	16	58	63	48
Crook Town	38	13	7	18	51	60	46
Billingham Town	38	13	9	16	66	81	45
South Shields	38	9	16	13	54	66	43
Jarrow Roofing Boldon C.A.	38	11	10	17	62	85	43
Easington Colliery	38	11	6	21	67	78	39
Newcastle Blue Star	*38*	*12*	*5*	*21*	*59*	*83*	*38*
Penrith	*38*	*10*	*8*	*20*	*59*	*82*	*35*
Shildon	*38*	*6*	*8*	*24*	*48*	*107*	*26*

Billingham Synthonia, Billingham Town, Newcastle Blue Star and Penrith all had 3 points deducted.
Stockton changed their name to Thornaby-on-Tees.

Division Two

Durham City	36	29	4	3	101	28	91
Shotton Comrades	36	22	7	7	89	44	73
Peterlee Newtown	36	21	8	7	80	43	71
Northallerton Town	36	20	6	10	73	33	66
Norton and Stockton Ancients	36	20	6	10	73	43	66
Brandon United	36	17	8	11	87	49	59
Hebburn	36	18	4	14	66	54	58
Evenwood Town	36	15	10	11	82	63	55
Whickham	36	15	8	13	51	43	53
Prudhoe Town	36	14	10	12	70	61	52
Ashington	36	14	9	13	64	47	51
Alnwick Town	36	15	5	16	63	66	50
Horden Colliery Welfare	36	13	11	12	53	56	50
Willington	36	13	10	13	58	53	49
Esh Winning	36	9	10	17	59	73	37
Washington	36	10	6	20	55	79	36
Ryhope Community Association	36	5	3	28	29	90	18
Murton	36	4	2	30	33	167	14
Eppleton Colliery Welfare	36	4	1	31	26	120	7

Eppleton Colliery Welfare had 6 points deducted.

Washington changed their name to Washington Ikeda Hoover and Ryhope Community Association changed their name to Kennek Ryhope Community Association.

1999-2000

Division One

Bedlington Terriers	38	25	8	5	89	26	83
Seaham Red Star	38	23	5	10	64	49	74
Dunston Federation Brewery	38	20	7	11	73	41	67
Marske United	38	19	8	11	67	45	65
West Auckland Town	38	17	14	7	65	43	65
Billingham Synthonia	38	17	6	15	72	64	57
Jarrow Roofing Boldon C.A.	38	15	12	11	64	61	57
Morpeth Town	38	14	15	9	55	56	57
Consett	38	12	18	8	57	43	54
Tow Law Town	38	15	8	15	65	55	53
Billingham Town	38	13	13	12	58	47	52
Guisborough Town	38	15	7	16	57	62	52
Chester-le-Street Town	38	14	9	15	57	67	51
Crook Town	38	13	11	14	55	57	50
Durham City	38	11	13	14	50	61	46
Peterlee Newtown	38	13	7	18	56	76	46
Easington Colliery	38	10	11	17	57	74	41
Thornaby-on-Tees	*38*	*7*	*12*	*19*	*47*	*68*	*33*
Shotton Comrades	*38*	*4*	*9*	*25*	*37*	*88*	*21*
South Shields	*38*	*3*	*7*	*28*	*33*	*95*	*16*

Whitley Bay joined following relegation from the Northern Premier League. Thornaby-on-Tees changed their name to Thornaby.

Division Two

Brandon United	36	25	9	2	82	24	84
Newcastle Blue Star	36	24	5	7	94	43	77
Hebburn	36	22	4	10	72	35	70
Northallerton Town	36	21	5	10	76	48	68
Shildon	36	20	7	9	62	44	67
Willington	36	21	3	12	81	41	66
Washington Ikeda Hoover	36	19	7	10	95	57	64
Norton and Stockton Ancients	36	18	8	10	70	51	62
Ashington	36	17	10	9	92	36	61
Penrith	36	15	11	10	69	40	56
Alnwick Town	36	16	7	13	78	58	55
Horden Colliery Welfare	36	13	10	13	53	57	49
Prudhoe Town	36	11	9	16	59	74	39
Evenwood Town	36	11	6	19	57	100	39
Esh Winning	36	11	2	23	59	81	35
Kennek Ryhope C.A.	36	9	7	20	49	70	34
Whickham	36	6	7	23	27	70	25
Murton	36	1	4	31	21	133	7
Eppleton Colliery Welfare	36	0	3	33	22	156	3

Prudhoe Town had 3 points deducted.
Hebburn changed their name to Hebburn Town.

2000-01

Division One

Bedlington Terriers	40	28	5	7	108	31	89
Dunston Federation Brewery	40	26	7	7	93	49	85
Marske United	40	24	7	9	82	35	79
Durham City	40	24	6	10	95	42	78
Brandon United	40	23	8	9	86	53	77
Peterlee Newtown	40	22	9	9	75	55	75
Tow Law Town	40	20	7	13	90	64	67
Billingham Synthonia	40	18	11	11	81	58	65
Billingham Town	40	19	7	14	74	59	64
Consett	40	17	8	15	63	60	59
Whitley Bay	40	15	10	15	69	61	55
West Auckland Town	40	16	7	17	65	68	55
Jarrow Roofing Boldon C.A.	40	12	12	16	63	71	48
Guisborough Town	40	13	8	19	53	60	47
Chester-le-Street Town	40	13	5	22	61	64	44
Newcastle Blue Star	40	12	8	20	53	83	44
Seaham Red Star	40	14	2	24	59	111	44
Morpeth Town	40	12	6	22	63	78	36
Easington Colliery	*40*	*10*	*6*	*24*	*57*	*86*	*36*
Hebburn Town	*40*	*5*	*7*	*28*	*33*	*113*	*22*
Crook Town	*40*	*2*	*4*	*34*	*33*	*155*	*10*

Morpeth Town had 6 points deducted.

Division Two

Ashington	**36**	**25**	**5**	**6**	**100**	**41**	**80**
Washington Ikeda Hoover	**36**	**23**	**10**	**3**	**83**	**35**	**79**
Thornaby	**36**	**23**	**7**	**6**	**85**	**50**	**76**
Horden Colliery Welfare	36	20	7	9	53	35	67
Esh Winning	36	19	7	10	79	44	64
Northallerton Town	36	16	12	8	75	45	60
Penrith	36	14	12	10	60	52	54
Norton and Stockton Ancients	36	16	9	11	51	51	54
Willington	36	12	12	12	52	46	48
Kennek Ryhope C.A.	36	12	10	14	46	53	46
South Shields	36	12	9	15	71	81	45
Prudhoe Town	36	13	5	18	69	66	44
Shildon	36	12	8	16	62	58	44
Alnwick Town	36	9	12	15	53	61	39
Evenwood Town	36	10	5	21	50	97	35
Shotton Comrades	36	8	10	18	49	85	34
Murton	36	9	8	19	53	76	32
Whickham	36	6	11	19	43	68	29
Eppleton Colliery Welfare	36	1	5	30	29	99	8

Norton and Stockton Ancients and Murton each had 3 points deducted.
Washington Nissan joined from the Wearside League.

2001-02

Division One

Bedlington Terriers	40	28	8	4	103	34	92
Tow Law Town	40	26	7	7	89	43	85
Dunston Federation Brewery	40	22	9	9	86	53	75
Marske United	40	21	8	11	56	48	71
Whitley Bay	40	20	8	12	78	49	68
Durham City	40	19	11	10	87	62	68
West Auckland Town	40	19	11	10	80	57	68
Billingham Town	40	16	9	15	67	66	57
Brandon United	40	17	8	15	68	53	56
Billingham Synthonia	40	15	10	15	79	75	55
Guisborough Town	40	16	9	15	68	63	54
Jarrow Roofing Boldon C.A.	40	15	8	17	62	74	53
Peterlee Newtown	40	14	10	16	54	60	52
Chester-le-Street Town	40	14	7	19	63	68	49
Washington Ikeda Hoover	40	13	5	22	54	74	44
Consett	40	11	10	19	60	65	43
Newcastle Blue Star	40	13	6	21	56	80	42
Morpeth Town	40	10	10	20	48	70	40
Ashington	*40*	*11*	*8*	*21*	*62*	*98*	*38*
Thornaby	*40*	*8*	*5*	*27*	*48*	*96*	*29*
Seaham Red Star	*40*	*6*	*5*	*29*	*38*	*118*	*20*

Brandon United, Guisborough Town, Newcastle Blue Star, Ashington and Seaham Red Star all had 3 points deducted.
Washington Ikeda Hoover changed their name to Washington.

Division Two

Shildon	**38**	**28**	**4**	**6**	**135**	**51**	**88**
Prudhoe Town	**38**	**26**	**7**	**5**	**104**	**32**	**85**
Esh Winning	**38**	**27**	**4**	**7**	**93**	**39**	**85**
Penrith	38	26	4	8	101	42	82
Easington Colliery	38	24	5	9	87	47	77
Horden Colliery Welfare	38	21	9	8	87	55	72
Washington Nissan	38	23	3	12	95	68	72
South Shields	38	18	8	12	62	41	62
Northallerton Town	38	17	10	11	59	52	61
Kennek Ryhope C.A.	38	17	8	13	65	47	59
Crook Town	38	16	6	16	53	60	51
Norton and Stockton Ancients	38	14	7	17	66	71	49
Alnwick Town	38	12	12	14	63	74	48
Hebburn Town	38	12	6	20	52	97	42
Evenwood Town	38	8	5	25	46	96	29
Whickham	38	7	5	26	50	90	26
Willington	38	6	6	26	52	114	24
Murton	38	5	7	26	34	108	22
Eppleton Colliery Welfare	38	6	6	26	42	91	18
Shotton Comrades	38	4	4	30	45	116	16

Crook Town had 3 points deducted.
Eppleton Colliery Welfare had 6 points deducted.

2002-03

Division One

Brandon United	40	26	10	4	77	28	88
Bedlington Terriers	40	24	9	7	96	42	81
Billingham Town	40	23	6	11	100	53	72
Billingham Synthonia	40	21	8	11	73	47	71
Durham City	40	21	5	14	77	54	68
Shildon	40	19	7	14	83	74	64
Guisborough Town	40	19	6	15	58	43	63
Dunston Federation Brewery	40	17	11	12	52	43	62
Jarrow Roofing Boldon C.A.	40	17	7	16	64	67	58
Whitley Bay	40	17	8	15	68	62	56
Morpeth Town	40	15	11	14	67	67	56
Washington	40	16	8	16	52	60	56
West Auckland Town	40	16	9	15	87	74	54
Chester-le-Street Town	40	14	11	15	60	63	53
Tow Law Town	40	14	8	18	58	63	50
Marske United	40	13	10	17	64	74	49
Esh Winning	40	14	8	18	51	84	47
Peterlee Newtown	40	8	9	23	44	89	33
Prudhoe Town	**40**	**7**	**10**	**23**	**52**	**89**	**31**
Consett	**40**	**7**	**8**	**25**	**44**	**83**	**29**
Newcastle Blue Star	**40**	**3**	**9**	**28**	**37**	**105**	**18**

Billingham Town, Whitley Bay, West Auckland Town and Esh Winning each had 3 points deducted.

Division Two

Penrith	**38**	**26**	**10**	**2**	**102**	**28**	**88**
Horden Colliery Welfare	**38**	**26**	**7**	**5**	**83**	**38**	**85**
Thornaby	**38**	**25**	**8**	**5**	**84**	**32**	**83**
Seaham Red Star	38	26	4	8	91	45	82
Ashington	38	22	13	3	101	37	79
Washington Nissan	38	21	5	12	102	57	68
Easington Colliery	38	19	5	14	83	72	62
South Shields	38	16	11	11	86	70	59
Northallerton Town	38	17	5	16	72	58	56
Whickham	38	14	9	15	68	72	51
Kennek Ryhope C.A.	38	12	9	17	63	67	45
Hebburn Town	38	13	5	20	55	66	44
Evenwood Town	38	12	6	20	58	95	42
Murton	38	10	8	20	55	95	38
Alnwick Town	38	10	8	20	50	69	35
Crook Town	38	11	8	19	64	92	35
Shotton Comrades	38	8	5	25	46	103	29
Norton and Stockton Ancients	38	5	9	24	38	81	24
Willington	38	6	5	27	50	132	23
Eppleton Colliery Welfare	38	8	6	24	45	87	15

Alnwick Town had 3 points deducted.
Crook Town had 6 points deducted.
Eppleton Colliery Welfare had 15 points deducted.
Eppleton Colliery Welfare moved to the Northern Alliance.
Newcastle Benfield Saints joined from the Northern Alliance.

2003-04

Division One

Dunston Federation Brewery	40	25	9	6	76	32	84
Durham City	40	23	9	8	90	53	78
Bedlington Terriers	40	25	5	10	104	58	77
Shildon	40	21	11	8	82	52	71
Billingham Town	40	20	10	10	83	62	70
Jarrow Roofing Boldon C.A.	40	19	6	15	98	90	63
Peterlee Newtown	40	17	9	14	82	67	60
Brandon United	40	17	7	16	71	77	58
Billingham Synthonia	40	16	9	15	75	65	57
Whitley Bay	40	16	6	18	71	76	54
Morpeth Town	40	16	8	16	70	59	53
Thornaby	40	14	12	14	56	61	51
West Auckland Town	40	14	8	18	63	96	50
Guisborough Town	40	13	10	17	59	57	49
Esh Winning	40	13	9	18	52	68	48
Tow Law Town	40	13	8	19	63	78	47
Chester-le-Street Town	40	14	4	22	74	85	46
Horden Colliery Welfare	40	11	11	18	58	81	44
Washington	**40**	**10**	**6**	**24**	**55**	**97**	**36**
Marske United	**40**	**8**	**9**	**23**	**46**	**76**	**33**
Penrith	**40**	**8**	**8**	**24**	**45**	**83**	**32**

Bedlington Terriers, Shildon, Morpeth Town and Thornaby each had 3 points deducted.

Division Two

Ashington	38	27	7	4	91	28	88
Newcastle Benfield Saints	38	26	7	5	106	42	85
Consett	38	25	8	5	84	32	83
Newcastle Blue Star	38	24	6	8	87	53	75
Washington Nissan	38	21	6	11	81	47	69
Prudhoe Town	38	18	4	16	73	70	58
Northallerton Town	38	15	12	11	73	57	57
Hebburn Town	38	16	6	16	64	58	54
Kennek Ryhope C.A.	38	15	8	15	65	55	53
Whickham	38	14	10	14	66	57	52
Alnwick Town	38	15	6	17	50	59	51
South Shields	38	14	8	16	61	68	50
Seaham Red Star	38	11	10	17	73	78	43
Evenwood Town	38	13	4	21	43	58	43
Murton	38	11	9	18	58	68	42
Crook Town	38	11	8	19	61	79	41
Willington	38	11	5	22	50	104	38
Norton and Stockton Ancients	38	10	5	23	49	89	35
Easington Colliery	38	8	3	27	41	119	27
Shotton Comrades	38	6	6	26	47	99	24

Newcastle Blue Star had 3 points deducted.
Murton moved to the Northern Alliance and Shotton Comrades moved to the Wearside League. West Allotment Celtic joined from the Northern Alliance and North Shields joined from the Wearside League.

2004-05

Division One

Dunston Federation Brewery	40	28	11	1	83	25	95
Billingham Synthonia	40	21	12	7	71	41	75
Bedlington Terriers	40	20	11	9	73	40	71
Newcastle Benfield Saints	40	19	12	9	85	52	69
Whitley Bay	40	20	8	12	80	62	68
Durham City	40	19	6	15	67	53	63
Billingham Town	40	17	9	14	79	53	60
Chester-le-Street Town	40	15	15	10	69	61	60
Horden Colliery Welfare	40	16	9	15	68	63	57
Ashington	40	15	10	15	75	67	55
Shildon	40	16	7	17	73	71	55
Jarrow Roofing Boldon C.A.	40	15	8	17	84	75	53
Morpeth Town	40	15	8	17	62	69	53
Esh Winning	40	12	14	14	58	52	50
Thornaby	40	14	10	16	57	69	49
Tow Law Town	40	13	4	23	53	87	43
West Auckland Town	40	10	9	21	66	98	39
Brandon United	40	10	9	21	67	101	39
Consett	**40**	**9**	**9**	**22**	**40**	**68**	**36**
Peterlee Newtown	**40**	**8**	**7**	**25**	**53**	**136**	**31**
Guisborough Town	**40**	**8**	**12**	**20**	**49**	**69**	**30**

Thornaby had 3 points deducted.
Guisborough Town had 6 points deducted.
Newcastle Benfield Saints changed their name to Newcastle Benfield Bay Plastics.

Division Two

West Allotment Celtic	**38**	**29**	**5**	**4**	**121**	**41**	**92**
Washington Nissan	**38**	**28**	**5**	**5**	**121**	**41**	**86**
Newcastle Blue Star	**38**	**27**	**5**	**6**	**95**	**39**	**86**
Prudhoe Town	38	24	7	7	91	45	79
Northallerton Town	38	25	4	9	87	43	79
Norton and Stockton Ancients	38	20	6	12	72	65	63
Crook Town	38	19	5	14	80	65	62
Penrith	38	18	7	13	80	51	61
Whickham	38	17	3	18	83	78	54
Seaham Red Star	38	15	6	17	59	67	51
North Shields	38	14	8	16	55	54	50
Alnwick Town	38	13	9	16	65	64	48
South Shields	38	13	8	17	73	66	44
Washington	38	11	6	21	47	71	39
Marske United	38	11	5	22	50	78	38
Evenwood Town	38	11	5	22	52	94	35
Kennek Ryhope C.A.	38	9	7	22	59	93	34
Hebburn Town	38	8	7	23	50	94	31
Easington Colliery	38	7	7	24	49	97	28
Willington	38	2	3	33	24	167	9

Washington Nissan, Norton and Stockton Ancients, South Shields and Evenwood Town each had 3 points deducted.
Easington Colliery moved to the Northern Alliance and Willington moved to the Wearside League. Ryton joined from the Northern Alliance and Darlington Railway Athletic joined from the Wearside League.
Washington Nissan changed their name to Sunderland Nissan.
Evenwood Town moved into the defunct Spennymoor United's ground and changed their name to Spennymoor Town.

2005-06

Division One

Newcastle Blue Star	40	28	6	6	87	34	90
Bedlington Terriers	40	22	8	10	86	61	74
Dunston Federation Brewery	40	20	11	9	82	45	71
Billingham Town	40	18	13	9	81	54	67
West Auckland Town	40	20	7	13	76	53	67
Morpeth Town	40	19	10	11	68	50	67
Billingham Synthonia	40	17	12	11	65	58	63
Chester-le-Street Town	40	18	9	13	64	64	63
Newcastle Benfield Bay Plastics	40	18	8	14	81	62	62
Whitley Bay	40	17	9	14	68	51	60
Durham City	40	15	13	12	58	44	58
Tow Law Town	40	15	9	16	63	65	54
West Allotment Celtic	40	14	8	18	77	83	50
Sunderland Nissan	40	14	8	18	64	73	50
Jarrow Roofing Boldon C.A.	40	14	7	19	65	76	49
Ashington	40	13	9	18	64	60	48
Thornaby	**40**	**14**	**6**	**20**	**72**	**85**	**48**
Horden Colliery Welfare	40	12	11	17	55	65	47
Shildon	40	11	14	15	55	65	47
Esh Winning	**40**	**3**	**7**	**30**	**32**	**103**	**16**
Brandon United	**40**	**4**	**3**	**33**	**35**	**147**	**15**

Thornaby were relegated as their ground did not meet the required standards. Bishop Auckland joined following relegation from the Northern Premier League – Division One.

Division Two

Consett	**38**	**33**	**3**	**2**	**134**	**31**	**102**
Northallerton Town	**38**	**25**	**8**	**5**	**86**	**30**	**83**
Darlington Railway Athletic	**38**	**23**	**5**	**10**	**83**	**46**	**74**
Penrith	38	20	10	8	73	46	70
Crook Town	38	19	11	8	95	43	68
Washington	38	17	10	11	68	54	61
Norton and Stockton Ancients	38	17	9	12	83	73	60
Spennymoor Town	38	16	11	11	70	66	59
Whickham	38	16	10	12	84	64	58
Marske United	38	12	13	13	62	69	49
Ryton	38	13	9	16	51	65	48
North Shields	38	13	8	17	57	67	47
Prudhoe Town	38	12	10	16	45	49	46
Seaham Red Star	38	11	12	15	60	59	45
Hebburn Town	38	12	9	17	46	67	45
Alnwick Town	38	12	1	25	62	93	34
Kennek Ryhope C.A.	38	5	13	20	41	76	28
South Shields	38	10	4	24	51	95	28
Guisborough Town	38	7	7	24	35	86	28
Peterlee Newtown	38	5	1	32	48	155	16

Alnwick Town had 3 points deducted.
South Shields had 6 points deducted.
Stokesley Sports Club joined from the Wearside League and Team Northumbria joined from the Northern Alliance. Peterlee Newtown changed their name to Peterlee Town and joined the Northern Alliance.
Kennek Ryhope Community Association changed their name to Sunderland Ryhope Community Association.

2006-07

Division One

Team	P	W	D	L	F	A	Pts
Whitley Bay	42	28	8	6	104	45	92
Billingham Town	42	28	8	6	98	47	92
Sunderland Nissan	42	28	6	8	96	41	90
Consett	42	23	10	9	89	51	79
Newcastle Benfield Bay Plastics	42	21	11	10	79	45	74
West Auckland Town	42	22	8	12	88	61	74
Dunston Federation Brewery	42	19	16	7	67	48	73
Durham City	42	20	12	10	87	62	72
Shildon	42	21	9	12	80	57	72
Morpeth Town	42	19	9	14	87	70	66
Newcastle Blue Star	42	17	7	18	71	60	58
Tow Law Town	42	15	11	16	68	72	56
Northallerton Town	42	16	6	20	76	82	54
Billingham Synthonia	42	13	14	15	61	71	53
Jarrow Roofing Boldon C.A.	42	13	7	22	68	101	46
Bishop Auckland	42	11	10	21	59	86	43
Chester-le-Street Town	42	10	9	23	51	80	39
West Allotment Celtic	42	9	11	22	62	80	38
Ashington	42	9	7	26	46	87	34
Bedlington Terriers	42	7	8	27	47	99	26
Horden Colliery Welfare	**42**	**6**	**10**	**26**	**46**	**107**	**25**
Darlington Railway Athletic	*42*	*6*	*5*	*31*	*41*	*119*	*23*

Bedlington Terriers and Horden Colliery Welfare each had 3 points deducted.
Newcastle Blue Star moved to the Northern Premier League – Division One (North). Dunston Federation Brewery changed their name to Dunston Federation. Newcastle Benfield Bay Plastics changed their name to Newcastle Benfield.

Division Two

Team	P	W	D	L	F	A	Pts
Spennymoor Town	**40**	**29**	**9**	**2**	**85**	**33**	**96**
Seaham Red Star	**40**	**26**	**8**	**6**	**99**	**52**	**86**
Washington	**40**	**24**	**9**	**7**	**78**	**36**	**81**
South Shields	40	23	7	10	89	58	76
Marske United	40	20	13	7	68	44	73
Norton and Stockton Ancients	40	21	5	14	86	58	68
Penrith	40	18	10	12	81	52	64
Stokesley Sports Club	40	18	8	14	83	70	62
Guisborough Town	40	17	4	19	65	71	55
Hebburn Town	40	15	9	16	68	71	54
Team Northumbria	40	16	5	19	57	70	53
Ryton	40	12	14	14	71	60	50
Thornaby	40	13	9	18	60	69	48
Crook Town	40	13	7	20	72	88	46
Whickham	40	12	9	19	71	76	45
Esh Winning	40	12	7	21	63	83	43
Brandon United	40	12	7	21	64	87	43
North Shields	40	13	4	23	49	72	43
Sunderland Ryhope C.A.	40	12	4	24	50	85	37
Prudhoe Town	40	8	4	28	48	104	28
Alnwick Town	40	8	4	28	50	118	28

Sunderland Ryhope Community Association had 3 points deducted.
Alnwick Town moved to the Northern Alliance. Birtley Town joined from the Wearside League. Penrith changed their name to Penrith Town.

2007-08

Division One

Team	P	W	D	L	F	A	Pts
Durham City	42	32	6	4	106	42	102
Consett	42	26	8	8	105	43	86
Whitley Bay	42	26	7	9	99	55	85
Newcastle Benfield	42	22	7	13	67	51	73
Shildon	42	22	6	14	80	53	72
Dunston Federation	42	19	11	12	67	59	68
Tow Law Town	42	21	5	16	70	63	68
Morpeth Town	42	18	10	14	78	64	64
Billingham Synthonia	42	19	7	16	63	63	64
Billingham Town	42	19	6	17	80	73	63
Sunderland Nissan	42	17	12	13	70	64	63
Spennymoor Town	42	14	14	14	68	52	56
West Allotment Celtic	42	16	8	18	75	80	56
Seaham Red Star	42	14	10	18	78	83	52
Bedlington Terriers	42	12	10	20	60	80	46
West Auckland Town	42	12	9	21	65	81	45
Ashington	42	12	9	21	50	77	45
Chester-le-Street Town	42	12	9	21	51	86	45
Northallerton Town	42	13	4	25	53	85	43
Bishop Auckland	42	12	6	24	55	82	42
Washington	**42**	**12**	**5**	**25**	**53**	**97**	**41**
Jarrow Roofing Boldon C.A.	*42*	*4*	*7*	*31*	*36*	*96*	*19*

Durham City were promoted to the Northern Premier League – Division One (North).

Division Two

Team	P	W	D	L	F	A	Pts
Penrith Town	38	24	7	7	78	40	79
South Shields	38	24	5	9	98	52	77
Ryton	38	24	3	11	83	41	75
Sunderland Ryhope C.A.	38	22	4	12	83	54	70
Horden Colliery Welfare	38	21	5	12	71	57	68
Whickham	38	20	6	12	87	73	66
Thornaby	38	18	7	13	78	64	61
Marske United	38	17	8	13	69	43	59
Stokesley Sports Club	38	17	5	16	68	71	56
Norton and Stockton Ancients	38	17	3	18	66	46	54
Birtley Town	38	16	6	16	57	66	54
Guisborough Town	38	16	5	17	73	64	53
Esh Winning	38	15	7	16	73	58	52
Crook Town	38	14	9	15	60	74	51
Hebburn Town	38	14	7	17	55	72	49
Prudhoe Town	38	13	9	16	61	68	48
North Shields	38	11	4	23	50	87	37
Darlington Railway Athletic	38	10	6	22	51	78	36
Team Northumbria	38	6	8	24	43	90	23
Brandon United	38	2	4	32	26	132	10

Team Northumbria had 3 points deducted.
Whitehaven Amateurs joined from the Wearside League. Penrith Town merged with Penrith United of the Northern Alliance to form Penrith.

Northern League 2008-2010

2008-09

Division One

Newcastle Benfield	42	25	9	8	78	42	84
Consett	42	25	8	9	91	51	83
Whitley Bay	42	25	7	10	108	58	82
Spennymoor Town	42	24	10	8	78	49	82
Sunderland Nissan	42	23	9	10	93	57	78
Dunston Federation	42	20	13	9	77	48	73
Penrith	42	21	8	13	90	62	71
Shildon	42	18	15	9	84	58	69
West Allotment Celtic	42	19	11	12	66	60	68
Ryton	42	18	8	16	81	77	62
Tow Law Town	42	17	11	14	73	69	62
Morpeth Town	42	19	4	19	64	68	61
Chester-le-Street Town	42	17	7	18	74	72	58
Bedlington Terriers	42	15	9	18	66	76	54
Billingham Synthonia	42	12	11	19	68	75	47
Ashington	42	13	8	21	63	83	47
Billingham Town	42	11	8	23	64	96	41
Bishop Auckland	42	9	11	22	56	85	38
South Shields	42	9	10	23	52	79	37
West Auckland Town	42	8	7	27	50	99	31
Seaham Red Star	**42**	**8**	**7**	**27**	**42**	**94**	**31**
Northallerton Town	**42**	**8**	**5**	**29**	**50**	**110**	**29**

Sunderland Nissan disbanded. Dunston Federation changed their name to Dunston U.T.S..

Division Two

Horden Colliery Welfare	**38**	**24**	**8**	**6**	**92**	**44**	**80**
Norton and Stockton Ancients	**38**	**24**	**8**	**6**	**79**	**36**	**80**
Esh Winning	**38**	**23**	**8**	**7**	**89**	**59**	**77**
Sunderland Ryhope C.A.	38	21	8	9	88	46	71
Marske United	38	18	8	12	63	59	62
Brandon United	38	18	7	13	85	67	61
Guisborough Town	38	18	7	13	71	53	61
Birtley Town	38	18	7	13	73	62	61
Crook Town	38	17	7	14	68	71	58
Hebburn Town	38	15	10	13	71	83	55
Whitehaven Amateurs	38	15	8	15	57	52	53
Team Northumbria	38	13	12	13	75	66	51
Stokesley Sports Club	38	14	7	17	63	67	49
Whickham	38	14	7	17	55	73	49
North Shields	38	13	6	19	53	76	45
Jarrow Roofing Boldon C.A.	38	11	4	23	50	78	37
Washington	38	10	6	22	44	61	33
Darlington Railway Athletic	38	10	2	26	45	80	32
Prudhoe Town	38	5	11	22	47	88	26
Thornaby	38	5	7	26	50	97	22

Washington had 3 points deducted.
Prudhoe Town disbanded. They subsequently re-formed and joined the Wearside League in 2010. Gillford Park joined from the Northern Alliance and Newton Aycliffe joined from the Wearside League. Stokesley Sports Club changed their name to Stokesley.

2009-10

Division One

Spennymoor Town	42	31	7	4	118	33	100
Shildon	42	27	6	9	102	60	87
Whitley Bay	42	25	8	9	111	48	83
Dunston U.T.S.	42	24	10	8	96	41	82
Newcastle Benfield	42	23	9	10	89	45	78
Ashington	42	22	8	12	79	59	74
Bedlington Terriers	42	21	8	13	71	51	71
Norton and Stockton Ancients	42	20	7	15	82	84	67
Tow Law Town	42	20	6	16	80	85	66
Consett	42	19	7	16	71	73	64
South Shields	42	19	6	17	83	87	63
Billingham Synthonia	42	17	8	17	76	75	59
Bishop Auckland	42	17	7	18	81	89	58
Penrith	42	17	7	18	75	71	55
West Allotment Celtic	42	16	6	20	68	84	54
West Auckland Town	42	15	5	22	83	92	50
Ryton	42	13	5	24	62	86	44
Esh Winning	42	11	6	25	57	94	39
Billingham Town	42	10	5	27	54	110	35
Chester-le-Street Town	**42**	**10**	**3**	**29**	**68**	**115**	**33**
Morpeth Town	**42**	**7**	**6**	**29**	**49**	**110**	**27**
Horden Colliery Welfare	**42**	**6**	**4**	**32**	**48**	**111**	**22**

Penrith had 3 points deducted.

Division Two

Stokesley	**38**	**29**	**4**	**5**	**121**	**45**	**91**
Sunderland Ryhope C.A.	**38**	**24**	**8**	**6**	**85**	**29**	**80**
Jarrow Roofing Boldon C.A.	**38**	**25**	**5**	**8**	**107**	**60**	**80**
Marske United	38	22	9	7	77	34	75
Guisborough Town	38	21	9	8	76	43	72
North Shields	38	17	12	9	66	52	63
Whitehaven Amateurs	38	17	9	12	80	60	60
Northallerton Town	38	16	9	13	74	63	57
Newton Aycliffe	38	15	12	11	64	53	57
Whickham	38	17	7	14	51	51	55
Gillford Park	38	15	5	18	67	74	50
Seaham Red Star	38	15	4	19	70	72	49
Crook Town	38	12	9	17	63	90	45
Team Northumbria	38	12	6	20	58	64	42
Brandon United	38	12	6	20	64	92	42
Hebburn Town	38	11	8	19	61	98	41
Thornaby	38	8	10	20	52	80	34
Washington	38	9	6	23	44	77	33
Darlington Railway Athletic	38	4	8	26	46	115	20
Birtley Town	38	4	4	30	41	115	16

Whickham had 3 points deducted.

2010-11

Division One

Spennymoor Town	42	33	4	5	116	31	103
Consett	42	29	6	7	103	51	93
Whitley Bay	42	28	9	5	73	32	93
Newcastle Benfield	42	27	6	9	94	53	87
Shildon	42	26	5	11	114	46	83
West Auckland Town	42	26	4	12	96	62	82
Dunston U.T.S.	42	24	8	10	84	49	80
Ashington	42	21	5	16	83	65	68
Bedlington Terriers	42	20	7	15	94	62	67
Norton and Stockton Ancients	42	19	9	14	66	45	66
South Shields	42	17	7	18	61	66	58
Billingham Synthonia	42	16	9	17	63	65	57
Sunderland Ryhope C.A.	42	15	6	21	67	80	51
Bishop Auckland	42	15	6	21	75	93	51
Billingham Town	42	13	7	22	58	88	46
Stokesley	42	12	9	21	61	85	45
Penrith	42	12	10	20	65	76	43
Tow Law Town	42	12	7	23	49	77	43
Jarrow Roofing Boldon C.A.	42	10	9	23	50	98	39
West Allotment Celtic	*42*	*9*	*5*	*28*	*51*	*82*	*32*
Esh Winning	*42*	*4*	*4*	*34*	*40*	*121*	*16*
Ryton	*42*	*2*	*2*	*38*	*34*	*170*	*8*

Penrith had 3 points deducted.
Stokesley changed their name to Stokesley Sports Club and Ryton changed their name to Ryton & Crawcrook Albion.

Division Two

Newton Aycliffe	38	30	5	3	116	38	95
Guisborough Town	38	28	4	6	110	52	88
Marske United	38	25	7	6	95	41	82
North Shields	38	24	8	6	98	36	80
Team Northumbria	38	24	1	13	88	45	73
Whickham	38	21	5	12	70	51	68
Whitehaven Amateurs	38	18	8	12	104	85	62
Chester-le-Street Town	38	18	5	15	78	63	59
Northallerton Town	38	17	7	14	80	58	58
Hebburn Town	38	17	5	16	76	72	53
Gillford Park	38	14	9	15	63	59	51
Crook Town	38	15	5	18	77	80	50
Birtley Town	38	13	10	15	70	89	49
Thornaby	38	12	6	20	53	84	42
Darlington Railway Athletic	38	12	3	23	54	92	39
Washington	38	9	7	22	46	95	34
Seaham Red Star	38	9	4	25	66	118	31
Horden Colliery Welfare	38	8	4	26	52	95	28
Brandon United	38	5	8	25	41	86	23
Morpeth Town	38	4	3	31	47	145	15

Hebburn Town had 3 points deducted.
Alnwick Town joined from the Northern Alliance and Easington Colliery joined from the Wearside League.

2011-12

Division One

Spennymoor Town	42	30	7	5	86	31	97
West Auckland Town	42	29	8	5	117	58	95
Dunston U.T.S.	42	27	9	6	85	34	90
Sunderland Ryhope C.A.	42	27	7	8	106	54	88
Ashington	42	23	8	11	91	58	77
Whitley Bay	42	23	7	12	90	54	76
Bedlington Terriers	42	20	10	12	97	49	70
Bishop Auckland	42	20	9	13	87	69	69
Newton Aycliffe	42	18	11	13	70	52	65
Shildon	42	18	5	19	83	63	59
Billingham Synthonia	42	18	5	19	74	77	59
Newcastle Benfield	42	16	7	19	73	65	55
South Shields	42	15	6	21	81	92	51
Norton and Stockton Ancients	42	14	8	20	54	60	50
Consett	42	13	11	18	71	78	50
Guisborough Town	42	13	11	18	67	97	50
Billingham Town	42	15	4	23	72	95	49
Marske United	42	11	11	20	61	89	44
Penrith	42	11	7	24	59	97	40
Jarrow Roofing Boldon C.A.	*42*	*12*	*4*	*26*	*65*	*114*	*40*
Tow Law Town	*42*	*9*	*1*	*32*	*44*	*102*	*28*
Stokesley Sports Club	*42*	*0*	*4*	*38*	*31*	*176*	*4*

Darlington 1883 joined as a club that was newly formed by fans of Darlington F.C. of the Conference – National Division who had been wound up in the summer of 2012. Durham City joined from the Northern Premier League – Division One (North).

Division Two

Team Northumbria	42	28	5	9	112	49	89
Gillford Park	42	27	8	7	125	62	86
Hebburn Town	42	26	4	12	110	73	82
Morpeth Town	42	22	10	10	78	54	76
Darlington Railway Athletic	42	22	7	13	84	68	73
Birtley Town	42	21	9	12	100	77	72
West Allotment Celtic	42	21	8	13	90	72	71
North Shields	42	19	11	12	77	51	68
Northallerton Town	42	19	11	12	99	74	68
Crook Town	42	18	13	11	99	69	67
Esh Winning	42	20	6	16	95	74	66
Chester-le-Street Town	42	16	8	18	70	63	56
Whitehaven Amateurs	42	15	9	18	71	79	54
Washington	42	16	5	21	69	97	53
Whickham	42	13	10	19	76	82	49
Alnwick Town	42	13	10	19	56	86	49
Brandon United	42	13	7	22	70	94	46
Ryton & Crawcrook Albion	42	13	5	24	68	117	44
Thornaby	42	11	8	23	78	110	41
Seaham Red Star	42	8	7	27	61	113	31
Horden Colliery Welfare	42	8	6	28	44	92	30
Easington Colliery	42	6	7	29	60	136	22

Gilford Park and Easington Colliery each had 3 points deducted.
Easington Colliery moved to the Wearside League while Ryhope Colliery Welfare joined from the Wearside League. Gillford Park changed their name to Celtic Nation.

Northern League 2012-2014

2012-13

Division One

Team	P	W	D	L	F	A	Pts
Darlington 1883	46	40	2	4	145	35	122
Spennymoor Town	46	33	10	3	108	34	109
Whitley Bay	46	27	7	12	110	62	88
West Auckland Town	46	25	9	12	112	75	84
Dunston U.T.S.	46	23	10	13	74	50	79
Bishop Auckland	46	24	7	15	95	77	79
Ashington	46	21	13	12	106	68	76
Shildon	46	19	12	15	83	69	69
Consett	46	19	11	16	68	63	68
Celtic Nation	46	19	10	17	80	79	67
Guisborough Town	46	20	6	20	78	87	66
Billingham Synthonia	46	17	10	19	79	83	61
Penrith	46	17	9	20	92	96	60
Durham City	46	17	8	21	90	90	59
Bedlington Terriers	46	18	7	21	90	83	58
Team Northumbria	46	14	14	18	63	80	56
Newton Aycliffe	46	16	5	25	71	89	53
Hebburn Town	46	15	8	23	81	109	53
Marske United	46	15	4	27	66	91	49
Billingham Town	46	13	8	25	84	125	47
Newcastle Benfield	46	14	4	28	51	88	46
Sunderland Ryhope C.A.	46	12	8	26	62	103	41
South Shields	**46**	**11**	**5**	**30**	**54**	**117**	**38**
Norton and Stockton Ancients	**46**	**6**	**7**	**33**	**39**	**128**	**25**

Bedlington Terriers and Sunderland Ryhope C.A. each had 3 points deducted.
Darlington 1883 were promoted to the Northern Premier League – Division One (North).

Division Two

Team	P	W	D	L	F	A	Pts
Crook Town	**42**	**32**	**5**	**5**	**123**	**60**	**101**
Ryhope Colliery Welfare	42	30	8	4	147	52	98
Morpeth Town	**42**	**25**	**10**	**7**	**108**	**51**	**85**
Jarrow Roofing Boldon C.A.	42	26	7	9	100	46	85
Darlington Railway Athletic	42	22	12	8	82	57	78
Northallerton Town	42	23	8	11	101	63	77
West Allotment Celtic	42	23	8	11	95	66	77
North Shields	42	21	7	14	72	54	70
Whitehaven Amateurs	42	20	8	14	97	74	65
Seaham Red Star	42	19	8	15	86	85	65
Tow Law Town	42	19	7	16	83	66	64
Washington	42	16	4	22	72	93	52
Chester-le-Street Town	42	13	10	19	51	73	49
Ryton & Crawcrook Albion	42	15	4	23	56	82	49
Stokesley Sports Club	42	12	8	22	60	93	44
Whickham	42	11	8	23	57	86	41
Birtley Town	42	10	8	24	47	83	38
Brandon United	42	10	11	21	55	93	38
Thornaby	42	9	5	28	59	106	32
Esh Winning	42	10	3	29	49	108	30
Alnwick Town	42	8	8	26	63	100	29
Horden Colliery Welfare	42	7	5	30	43	115	26

Whitehaven Amateurs, Brandon United, Esh Winning and Alnwick Town all had 3 points deducted.
Ryhope Colliery Welfare moved to the Wearside League because their ground did not satisfy grading requirements. Horden Colliery Welfare also moved to the Wearside League. Willington joined from the Wearside League and Heaton Stannington joined from the Northern Alliance.

2013-14

Division One

Team	P	W	D	L	F	A	Pts
Spennymoor Town	44	30	10	4	117	38	100
Celtic Nation	44	28	11	5	107	41	95
Shildon	44	27	10	7	109	45	91
Guisborough Town	44	26	7	11	100	61	85
West Auckland Town	44	23	15	6	86	58	84
Ashington	44	24	5	15	94	60	77
Dunston U.T.S.	44	20	13	11	84	55	73
Bishop Auckland	44	18	14	12	82	54	68
Durham City	44	18	14	12	85	59	68
Whitley Bay	44	21	4	19	92	73	67
Consett	44	19	9	16	110	83	66
Billingham Synthonia	44	20	5	19	86	83	65
Penrith	44	17	10	17	90	88	61
Newcastle Benfield	44	14	14	16	85	59	56
Crook Town	44	16	8	20	90	111	56
Marske United	44	14	10	20	64	88	52
Morpeth Town	44	13	10	21	73	78	49
Newton Aycliffe	44	14	7	23	80	106	49
Sunderland Ryhope C.A.	44	12	8	24	57	93	44
Bedlington Terriers	44	11	10	23	52	99	43
Team Northumbria	**44**	**10**	**7**	**27**	**60**	**109**	**37**
Hebburn Town	**44**	**4**	**7**	**33**	**43**	**124**	**19**
Billingham Town	**44**	**2**	**2**	**40**	**26**	**207**	**8**

Spennymoor Town were promoted to the Northern Premier League – Division One (North).

Division Two

Team	P	W	D	L	F	A	Pts
North Shields	42	31	7	4	141	33	100
West Allotment Celtic	**42**	**27**	**9**	**6**	**96**	**58**	**90**
Jarrow Roofing Boldon C.A.	42	26	8	8	118	63	86
Seaham Red Star	42	27	7	8	99	45	85
Heaton Stannington	42	25	6	11	88	59	81
Norton and Stockton Ancients	42	20	9	13	83	66	69
Northallerton Town	42	19	9	14	84	67	66
Whickham	42	19	7	16	86	63	64
Washington	42	19	5	18	92	98	62
Tow Law Town	42	17	8	17	91	82	59
Chester-le-Street Town	42	15	13	14	66	72	58
Darlington Railway Athletic	42	15	11	16	81	76	56
Birtley Town	42	16	8	18	64	74	56
Thornaby	42	16	6	20	85	84	54
Willington	42	14	8	20	64	86	50
Whitehaven Amateurs	42	14	7	21	69	94	49
South Shields	42	11	15	16	62	88	48
Alnwick Town	42	10	9	23	65	99	39
Brandon United	42	9	7	26	61	101	34
Stokesley Sports Club	42	8	9	25	61	99	33
Ryton & Crawcrook Albion	42	7	7	28	45	106	28
Esh Winning	42	8	3	31	50	138	27

Whitehaven Amateurs moved to the Wearside League because their ground did not satisfy grading standards. Ryhope Colliery Welfare joined from the Wearside League.

2014-15

Division One

Team	P	W	D	L	F	A	Pts
Marske United	42	27	9	6	118	54	90
Shildon	42	28	5	9	109	48	89
Guisborough Town	42	26	8	8	101	50	86
North Shields	42	26	7	9	87	49	85
West Auckland Town	42	25	7	10	106	58	82
Dunston U.T.S.	42	23	7	12	75	51	76
Jarrow Roofing Boldon C.A.	42	21	7	14	84	61	70
Morpeth Town	42	19	13	10	90	70	70
Consett	42	20	9	13	110	85	69
Newcastle Benfield	42	18	8	16	92	73	62
Bishop Auckland	42	20	2	20	75	75	62
Durham City	42	17	7	18	76	76	58
Ashington	42	17	5	20	77	77	56
Penrith	42	15	11	16	68	74	56
Whitley Bay	42	17	5	20	81	97	56
Sunderland Ryhope C.A.	42	13	8	21	66	87	47
Bedlington Terriers	42	13	5	24	75	97	44
Newton Aycliffe	42	13	3	26	57	78	42
West Allotment Celtic	42	12	4	26	59	101	40
Billingham Synthonia	*42*	*11*	*4*	*27*	*69*	*102*	*37*
Celtic Nation	42	7	7	28	52	121	28
Crook Town	*42*	*1*	*5*	*36*	*39*	*182*	*5*

Crook Town had 3 points deducted.
Celtic Nation disbanded.

Division Two

Team	P	W	D	L	F	A	Pts
Seaham Red Star	42	31	5	6	134	54	98
Washington	42	28	5	9	123	66	89
Norton and Stockton Ancients	42	25	10	7	98	49	85
Team Northumbria	42	25	8	9	102	44	83
Hebburn Town	42	24	9	9	100	60	81
Ryhope Colliery Welfare	42	21	11	10	93	57	74
Thornaby	42	21	10	11	84	66	73
Whickham	42	20	10	12	80	60	70
Heaton Stannington	42	23	4	15	95	69	69
Northallerton Town	42	18	9	15	93	64	63
Willington	42	17	9	16	78	77	60
Ryton & Crawcrook Albion	42	17	7	18	75	94	58
Chester-le-Street Town	42	15	12	15	70	60	57
Darlington Railway Athletic	42	17	6	19	81	87	57
South Shields	42	16	5	21	78	74	53
Alnwick Town	42	15	5	22	85	121	50
Birtley Town	42	13	3	26	67	112	42
Billingham Town	42	9	11	22	59	75	38
Stokesley Sports Club	42	10	3	29	72	120	33
Esh Winning	42	9	4	29	47	135	31
Tow Law Town	42	5	8	29	37	114	23
Brandon United	42	4	4	34	38	131	16

Heaton Stannington had 4 points deducted.
Easington Colliery joined from the Wearside League.

2015-16

Division One

Team	P	W	D	L	F	A	Pts
Shildon	42	31	3	8	135	37	96
Marske United	42	26	3	13	86	60	81
Guisborough Town	42	22	11	9	95	55	77
Morpeth Town	42	24	5	13	89	64	77
North Shields	42	21	9	12	77	48	72
Newton Aycliffe	42	21	9	12	76	61	72
Consett	42	21	8	13	92	76	71
Bishop Auckland	42	20	7	15	80	79	67
Seaham Red Star	42	18	11	13	90	85	65
Washington	42	20	5	17	82	85	65
Dunston U.T.S.	42	18	8	16	78	64	62
Ashington	42	18	6	18	85	76	60
Sunderland Ryhope C.A.	42	15	9	18	73	89	54
Penrith	42	14	10	18	67	75	52
Jarrow Roofing Boldon C.A.	42	15	6	21	90	102	51
Whitley Bay	42	15	5	22	75	70	50
West Auckland Town	42	15	5	22	56	84	50
Newcastle Benfield	42	11	11	20	79	96	44
West Allotment Celtic	42	11	7	24	50	105	40
Durham City	*42*	*9*	*9*	*24*	*59*	*95*	*36*
Norton and Stockton Ancients	*42*	*8*	*8*	*26*	*67*	*120*	*32*
Bedlington Terriers	*42*	*8*	*7*	*27*	*57*	*112*	*31*

Division Two

Team	P	W	D	L	F	A	Pts
South Shields	42	35	2	5	122	31	107
Ryhope Colliery Welfare	42	30	4	8	121	65	94
Chester-le-Street Town	42	28	6	8	106	44	90
Team Northumbria	42	26	11	5	101	41	89
Billingham Synthonia	42	25	8	9	81	37	83
Easington Colliery	42	22	10	10	106	59	76
Thornaby	42	23	6	13	93	65	75
Northallerton Town	42	21	10	11	81	48	73
Heaton Stannington	42	21	8	13	92	59	71
Hebburn Town	42	17	10	15	78	54	61
Billingham Town	42	18	7	17	80	67	61
Whickham	42	17	8	17	57	68	59
Darlington Railway Athletic	42	18	4	20	86	89	58
Tow Law Town	42	14	11	17	75	82	53
Brandon United	42	14	4	24	77	98	46
Ryton & Crawcrook Albion	42	11	11	20	58	79	44
Alnwick Town	42	12	6	24	66	113	42
Crook Town	42	10	5	27	53	99	35
Willington	42	9	5	28	45	98	32
Esh Winning	42	7	6	29	46	127	27
Birtley Town	42	5	6	31	50	117	21
Stokesley Sports Club	42	4	2	36	33	167	14

Birtley Town moved to the Northern Alliance and Stokesley Sports Club moved to the Wearside League. Stockton Town joined from the Wearside League and Blyth Town joined from the Northern Alliance.

Northern League 2016-2018

2016-17

Division One

Team	P	W	D	L	F	A	Pts
South Shields	42	34	6	2	127	35	108
Morpeth Town	42	32	5	5	136	56	101
North Shields	42	32	5	5	107	39	101
Shildon	42	29	7	6	112	52	94
Marske United	42	22	6	14	103	75	72
Whitley Bay	42	19	13	10	88	70	70
Consett	42	19	8	15	105	81	65
Bishop Auckland	42	18	10	14	88	67	64
Newton Aycliffe	42	19	7	16	78	76	64
Newcastle Benfield	42	16	10	16	101	71	58
Sunderland Ryhope C.A.	42	16	9	17	85	79	57
Penrith	42	17	6	19	67	89	57
Jarrow Roofing Boldon C.A.	42	14	12	16	83	90	54
Seaham Red Star	42	15	6	21	78	81	51
Dunston U.T.S.	42	14	6	22	77	96	48
Ashington	42	13	8	21	73	90	47
Ryhope Colliery Welfare	42	11	10	21	82	129	43
West Auckland Town	42	11	3	28	60	120	36
Washington	42	10	5	27	67	111	35
Guisborough Town	42	10	7	25	70	124	34
Chester-le-Street Town	**42**	**6**	**5**	**31**	**51**	**127**	**23**
West Allotment Celtic	**42**	**6**	**4**	**32**	**42**	**122**	**22**

Guisborough Town had 3 points deducted.
South Shields were promoted to the Northern Premier League – Division One (North).

2017-18

Division One

Team	P	W	D	L	F	A	Pts
Marske United	42	32	6	4	102	31	102
Morpeth Town	42	30	7	5	117	52	97
Shildon	42	24	8	10	93	55	80
Sunderland Ryhope C.A.	42	24	7	11	96	54	79
West Auckland Town	42	23	9	10	107	64	78
Stockton Town	42	23	2	17	91	72	71
Newcastle Benfield	42	22	5	15	90	71	71
North Shields	42	21	6	15	103	73	69
Consett	42	21	5	16	93	83	68
Dunston U.T.S.	42	19	6	17	77	68	63
Ryhope Colliery Welfare	42	19	3	20	85	87	60
Ashington	42	16	11	15	80	67	59
Team Northumbria	42	17	5	20	64	70	56
Newton Aycliffe	42	13	13	16	53	58	52
Guisborough Town	42	15	10	17	70	82	52
Whitley Bay	42	15	6	21	73	91	51
Penrith	42	15	3	24	71	85	48
Seaham Red Star	42	12	7	23	57	90	43
Bishop Auckland	42	13	4	25	68	112	43
Jarrow Roofing Boldon C.A.	42	11	6	25	70	102	39
Washington	**42**	**4**	**6**	**32**	**39**	**132**	**18**
Billingham Synthonia	**42**	**2**	**7**	**33**	**28**	**128**	**13**

Guisborough Town had 3 points deducted.
Marske United and Morpeth Town were both promoted to the Northern Premier League – Division One (East). Jarrow Roofing Boldon Community Association disbanded at the end of the season. Team Northumbria left shortly before the start of the 2018-19 season but continued to play in University and College competitions.

2016-17

Division Two

Team	P	W	D	L	F	A	Pts
Stockton Town	**40**	**28**	**9**	**3**	**111**	**37**	**93**
Team Northumbria	**40**	**28**	**5**	**7**	**98**	**37**	**89**
Billingham Synthonia	**40**	**26**	**8**	**6**	**89**	**37**	**86**
Heaton Stannington	40	25	4	11	87	44	79
Billingham Town	40	23	9	8	109	42	78
Whickham	40	20	9	11	83	51	69
Easington Colliery	40	20	9	11	84	61	69
Blyth Town	40	20	8	12	96	56	68
Northallerton Town	40	17	11	12	90	68	62
Durham City	40	18	7	15	73	63	61
Hebburn Town	40	18	7	15	57	59	61
Bedlington Terriers	40	16	6	18	76	90	54
Tow Law Town	40	15	8	17	68	66	53
Brandon United	40	9	10	21	46	89	37
Alnwick Town	40	10	6	24	72	113	36
Thornaby	40	9	7	24	55	102	34
Crook Town	40	10	4	26	60	115	34
Willington	40	9	5	26	40	94	32
Darlington Railway Athletic	40	9	4	27	61	126	31
Ryton & Crawcrook Albion	40	7	9	24	46	93	30
Esh Winning	40	7	7	26	53	111	28

Norton and Stockton Ancients resigned on 9th December and their record was deleted when it was: 18 9 1 8 38 33 28
They then left senior football.
Jarrow joined from the Wearside League.
Blyth Town changed their name to Blyth.

2017-18

Division Two

Team	P	W	D	L	F	A	Pts
Blyth	**40**	**26**	**8**	**6**	**95**	**39**	**86**
Hebburn Town	**40**	**24**	**9**	**7**	**85**	**37**	**81**
Whickham	**40**	**25**	**5**	**10**	**80**	**52**	**80**
Northallerton Town	40	25	4	11	99	64	79
Heaton Stannington	40	21	9	10	86	57	72
Thornaby	40	21	5	14	85	53	68
Willington	40	20	7	13	65	49	67
Tow Law Town	40	19	7	14	88	70	64
Billingham Town	40	17	10	13	81	60	61
Easington Colliery	40	16	9	15	78	75	57
Durham City	40	14	9	17	73	79	51
Jarrow	40	13	11	16	56	69	50
Esh Winning	40	14	8	18	76	90	50
Chester-le-Street Town	40	13	10	17	58	71	49
West Allotment Celtic	40	13	6	21	64	86	45
Bedlington Terriers	40	14	5	21	63	70	44
Ryton & Crawcrook Albion	40	12	8	20	53	76	44
Crook Town	40	12	6	22	62	104	42
Brandon United	40	8	9	23	56	88	33
Darlington Railway Athletic	40	9	4	27	41	90	31
Alnwick Town	40	6	7	27	51	116	25

Bedlington Terriers had 3 points deducted.
Alnwick Town moved to the Northern Alliance and Darlington Railway Athletic moved to the Wearside League. Redcar Athletic joined from the Wearside League and Birtley Town joined from the Northern Alliance.

NORTHERN ALLIANCE 1890-2018

Following the formation of the Northern League in 1889, those clubs who had not been included, quickly got together and formed a second competition, the North-Eastern Counties League. It began operating in the 1889-90 season but was not a success. There was very little publicity for the league and no final table has been found. The 10 clubs who formed it were Barnard Castle, Bishop Auckland Church Institute, Gateshead North Eastern Railway, Morpeth Harriers, Port Clarence, Rendel, Redcar, Shankhouse, West Hartlepool and Whitburn.

A second attempt was made to form the league a year later and this time, it was successful, albeit with a different title, the Northern Alliance. The 7 clubs who formed the league at the Neville Hotel in North Road, Durham on 9th July 1890 were Bishop Auckland Town, Birtley, Elswick Rangers, Gateshead North Eastern Railway, Rendel, Sunderland "A" (as Sunderland Reserves were known at the time) and Whitburn. Of these 7, Bishop Auckland Town, Birtley and Elswick Rangers had been members of the Northern League in 1889-90.

Note: Reserve teams were often referred to as "A" teams at the time. For consistency and clarity, they are always referred to as Reserves below.

1890-91

Sunderland Reserves	12	10	0	2	53	13	20
Gateshead N.E.R.	12	6	2	4	29	23	14
Rendel	12	6	0	6	29	26	12
Bishop Auckland	11	5	1	5	20	27	11
Birtley	12	3	3	6	23	31	9
Elswick Rangers	11	4	1	6	25	36	9
Whitburn	10	2	1	7	14	37	5

Two games were not played.
Birtley, Bishop Auckland and Elswick Rangers left the league and Mickley, Shankhouse, Southwick, Sunderland Olympic and Willington Athletic all joined.

1891-92

Shankhouse	16	14	0	2	46	14	28
Sunderland Reserves	15	11	0	4	47	19	22
Southwick	16	8	2	6	39	29	18
Gateshead N.E.R.	16	7	1	8	45	43	15
Whitburn	16	7	1	8	37	62	15
Willington Athletic	16	6	2	8	29	31	14
Rendel	16	5	2	9	23	30	12
Sunderland Olympic	16	4	2	10	23	45	10
Mickley	15	4	0	11	21	37	8

One game was not played.
Sunderland Olympic left the league and Ashington, Blyth, Newcastle United Reserves and Seaham Harbour all joined.

1892-93

Sunderland Reserves	21	16	3	2	73	24	35
Blyth	22	15	1	6	81	36	29
Willington Athletic	20	13	2	5	59	33	28
Southwick	18	13	1	4	56	26	27
Rendel	18	10	3	5	64	28	23
Shankhouse	18	10	2	6	58	34	22
Gateshead N.E.R.	21	6	2	13	49	55	14
Newcastle United Reserves	20	6	2	12	39	55	14
Mickley	21	5	3	13	31	72	13
Seaham Harbour	19	4	3	12	29	74	11
Ashington	18	3	2	13	35	76	8
Whitburn	18	3	2	13	18	78	8

Blyth had 2 points deducted.
15 games were not played.
Ashington ceased activity until 1895 when they joined the East Northumberland League. Mickley, Seaham Harbour and Whitburn also left the league. Hebburn Argyle joined from the Tyneside League and Dipton Wanderers also joined.

1893-94

Sunderland Reserves	18	13	1	4	50	25	27
Gateshead N.E.R.	18	10	3	5	53	32	23
Hebburn Argyle	18	10	2	6	48	31	22
Rendel	18	8	6	4	52	30	22
Willington Athletic	18	8	6	4	33	27	22
Blyth	18	9	2	7	41	29	20
Shankhouse	18	6	5	7	35	42	17
Newcastle United Reserves	18	5	5	8	35	44	15
Dipton Wanderers	18	4	2	12	29	52	10
Southwick	18	1	2	15	22	72	4

Jarrow joined as a club newly formed to replace Jarrow Rangers who had recently disbanded. Trafalgar also joined the league.

1894-95

Sunderland Reserves	22	16	2	4	65	28	34
Blyth	22	16	2	4	70	33	34
Shankhouse	22	14	1	7	51	30	29
Willington Athletic	22	13	2	7	54	36	28
Jarrow	22	12	3	7	46	40	27
Gateshead N.E.R.	22	12	2	8	58	33	26
Dipton Wanderers	21	8	2	11	49	75	18
Hebburn Argyle	21	7	4	10	30	42	16
Trafalgar	22	8	0	14	44	57	16
Rendel	22	5	4	13	30	43	12
Newcastle United Reserves	22	4	5	13	32	57	9
Southwick	22	2	1	19	21	89	5

Hebburn Argyle and Rendel each had 2 points deducted.
Newcastle United Reserves had 4 points deducted.
One game was unplayed.
Trafalgar changed their name to Newcastle East End.
Axwell Rovers joined from the Tyneside League and Birtley also joined.

Northern Alliance 1895-1901

1895-96

Sunderland Reserves	26	19	3	4	68	27	41
Shankhouse	26	17	3	6	84	22	37
Blyth	26	17	2	7	79	39	36
Newcastle United Reserves	26	15	5	6	74	36	35
Willington Athletic	26	15	5	6	80	42	35
Jarrow	26	15	5	6	54	31	35
Gateshead N.E.R.	26	11	8	7	61	36	30
Southwick	26	9	6	11	40	59	24
Hebburn Argyle	26	8	5	13	39	51	21
Rendel	26	8	4	14	29	43	20
Dipton Wanderers	26	8	3	15	46	74	19
Birtley	26	5	5	16	28	84	15
Axwell Rovers	26	3	5	18	27	89	11
Newcastle East End	26	2	1	23	16	90	5

Sunderland Reserves and Newcastle East End left the league.
St. Peter's Albion joined from the Tyneside League and Stanley also joined.

1896-97

Hebburn Argyle	24	17	4	3	68	19	38
Newcastle United Reserves	24	17	4	3	74	22	38
Shankhouse	24	14	3	7	67	36	31
Gateshead N.E.R.	24	14	3	7	60	38	31
Jarrow	24	14	2	8	52	24	30
Blyth	23	10	4	9	55	37	24
Stanley	24	12	0	12	55	59	24
Willington Athletic	24	9	6	9	39	47	24
Birtley	24	10	4	10	42	55	24
Southwick	24	6	5	13	44	46	17
Rendel	24	6	4	14	32	64	16
St. Peter's Albion	24	4	2	18	25	83	10
Dipton Wanderers	23	1	1	21	19	106	3

Dipton Wanderers vs Blyth was not played.
Axwell Park Rovers resigned after 15 games and their record was deleted.
Dipton Wanderers moved to the Tyneside League and Southwick also left.
Wallsend Park Villa joined from the Tyneside League, South Shields joined as a newly formed club and Sunderland Reserves also joined.

1897-98

Newcastle United Reserves	26	21	3	2	73	23	45
Jarrow	26	15	5	6	53	26	35
Wallsend Park Villa	26	13	5	8	41	42	31
South Shields	26	9	11	6	47	44	29
Hebburn Argyle	26	10	8	8	50	34	28
Willington Athletic	26	9	7	10	44	44	25
Stanley	26	9	6	11	56	55	24
Gateshead N.E.R.	26	9	5	12	47	50	23
Shankhouse	26	9	4	13	50	60	22
St. Peter's Albion	26	9	4	13	37	70	22
Rendel	26	9	3	14	42	48	21
Sunderland Reserves	26	8	5	13	42	48	21
Blyth	26	8	4	14	35	63	20
Birtley	26	7	4	15	28	47	18

Rendel left the league.
Sunderland Nomads joined from the Wearside League.

1898-99

Jarrow	26	19	4	3	73	24	42
Newcastle United Reserves	26	18	4	4	62	32	38
Hebburn Argyle	26	15	5	6	62	29	35
Willington Athletic	26	15	4	7	58	36	34
South Shields	26	13	5	8	60	37	31
Sunderland Reserves	25	11	8	6	74	29	28
Stanley	25	10	6	9	50	41	26
Wallsend Park Villa	26	9	5	12	59	60	23
Gateshead N.E.R.	25	9	3	13	36	56	21
Shankhouse	24	8	3	13	32	65	19
Birtley	24	7	4	13	40	60	18
Blyth	20	5	5	10	31	50	15
Sunderland Nomads	23	2	5	16	22	63	9
St. Peter's Albion	26	1	4	21	19	100	6

Blyth resigned during the season but their record was allowed to stand.
Two other games were also not played.
Newcastle United Reserves and Sunderland Reserves each had 2 points deducted.
Sunderland Nomads left the league, Leadgate Park joined from the Northern League and Middlesbrough Reserves also joined.

1899-1900

Willington Athletic	26	20	2	4	73	28	42
Newcastle United Reserves	26	16	8	2	49	17	40
Sunderland Reserves	26	15	6	5	56	25	36
Middlesbrough Reserves	26	13	3	10	56	39	29
Wallsend Park Villa	26	10	7	9	45	44	27
South Shields	26	11	6	9	43	35	26
Hebburn Argyle	25	9	7	9	48	41	25
Leadgate Park	25	9	6	10	50	33	24
Stanley	26	9	6	11	37	46	24
Jarrow	26	8	8	10	39	32	22
Birtley	25	7	4	14	27	62	16
Gateshead N.E.R.	26	6	6	14	30	60	14
St. Peter's Albion	25	4	4	17	21	71	12
Shankhouse	26	2	3	19	36	77	11

Birtley, Gateshead N.E.R., Jarrow and South Shields each had 2 points deducted. Two games were not played.
South Shields disbanded but a new club called South Shields Athletic was quickly formed and this replaced the old club in the Northern Alliance for the 1900-01 season.

1900-01

Newcastle United Reserves	26	20	5	1	83	23	45
Sunderland Reserves	26	17	6	3	86	21	40
Wallsend Park Villa	26	16	4	6	51	29	36
Middlesbrough Reserves	26	14	4	8	58	41	32
Willington Athletic	26	11	5	10	47	38	27
Jarrow	26	9	7	10	28	36	25
# St. Peter's Albion / Thornaby	26	10	4	12	45	52	24
Leadgate Park	26	10	3	13	52	49	23
Gateshead N.E.R.	26	8	5	13	31	44	21
South Shields Athletic	26	8	4	14	38	57	20
Hebburn Argyle	26	7	6	13	30	51	20
Birtley / Morpeth Harriers	26	9	2	15	33	65	20
Stanley	26	6	5	15	28	54	17
Shankhouse	26	5	4	17	25	75	14

St. Peter's Albion disbanded at the start of December and their record and fixtures were taken over by Thornaby who moved from the Teesside League. This record was: 8 2 1 5 14 23 5)
Birtley resigned during October and their record and fixtures were taken over by Morpeth Harriers who moved from the Northumberland League. This record was: 4 0 0 4 1 15 0
Stanley moved to the Chester-le-Street & District League and Prudhoe joined from the Northern Combination.

1901-02

	P	W	D	L	F	A	Pts
Newcastle United Reserves	26	22	3	1	84	16	47
Sunderland Reserves	26	17	3	6	71	33	37
Middlesbrough Reserves	26	13	7	6	55	32	33
Morpeth Harriers	26	12	6	8	40	37	30
Wallsend Park Villa	26	12	5	9	45	34	29
Leadgate Park	26	10	7	9	48	44	27
Thornaby	26	8	8	10	54	48	24
Willington Athletic	26	9	6	11	28	39	24
Shankhouse	26	11	2	13	51	69	24
Prudhoe	26	8	6	12	40	48	22
Gateshead N.E.R.	26	9	3	14	35	46	21
Hebburn Argyle	26	5	7	14	29	56	17
Jarrow	26	7	3	16	25	57	17
South Shields Athletic	26	3	6	17	25	71	12

Middlesbrough Reserves, Newcastle United Reserves and Sunderland Reserves all moved to the Northern League. South Shields Athletic disbanded after losing their Mowbray Road ground, Thornaby disbanded for financial reasons and so Stockton St. John's of the Northern League moved into Thornaby's cycle track ground just to the north of Lanehouse Road. Jarrow also disbanded for financial reasons.
Annfield Plain Celtic, Consett Town Swifts and Stanley all joined from the Chester-le-Street & District League, Ashington and Dudley Wanderers joined from the Northumberland League and Mickley also joined.

1902-03

	P	W	D	L	F	A	Pts
Morpeth Harriers	26	24	1	1	77	21	49
Wallsend Park Villa	26	19	3	4	59	23	41
Mickley	26	14	5	7	44	30	33
Leadgate Park	26	11	5	10	49	34	27
Willington Athletic	26	10	5	11	41	48	25
Stanley	26	9	6	11	45	53	24
Gateshead N.E.R.	26	10	3	13	36	41	23
Hebburn Argyle	26	7	8	11	27	30	22
Shankhouse	26	10	3	13	50	59	21
Prudhoe	26	9	3	14	39	64	21
Annfield Plain Celtic	26	9	4	13	40	51	20
Consett Town Swifts	26	8	4	14	35	54	20
Ashington	26	8	5	13	30	39	19
Dudley Wanderers	26	5	3	18	22	47	13

Annfield Plain Celtic, Ashington and Shankhouse each had 2 points deducted.
Gateshead N.E.R. disbanded. New Delaval joined from the East Northumberland League, Burradon Athletic joined as a newly formed club and Jarrow joined as a newly re-formed club.

1903-04

	P	W	D	L	F	A	Pts
Wallsend Park Villa	28	21	2	5	81	28	44
Annfield Plain Celtic	28	15	7	6	59	35	37
Willington Athletic	28	17	3	8	58	36	37
Stanley	28	16	4	8	69	33	36
Morpeth Harriers	28	16	3	9	58	29	35
Jarrow	27	13	2	12	44	44	28
Ashington	28	12	3	13	45	43	27
Mickley	28	11	4	13	44	37	26
Hebburn Argyle	28	12	2	14	41	37	26
Leadgate Park	28	9	7	12	42	47	23
New Delaval	28	10	3	15	24	62	23
Shankhouse	27	10	3	14	30	46	23
Burradon Athletic	28	10	4	14	43	61	22
Consett Town Swifts	28	6	3	19	26	75	13
Dudley Wanderers	28	5	2	21	16	67	12

Prudhoe resigned in the first half of December and their record was deleted when it stood as follows: 6 1 0 5 7 21 2
Jarrow vs Shankhouse was not played.
Burradon Athletic, Consett Town Swifts and Leadgate Park each had 2 points deducted.
New Delaval resigned from the league. North Shields Athletic joined from the Northern Combination and Gateshead Town joined as a newly formed club.

1904-05

	P	W	D	L	F	A	Pts
Willington Athletic	28	20	4	4	60	23	44
Leadgate Park	28	15	6	7	54	33	36
Stanley	28	14	7	7	53	33	35
Wallsend Park Villa	27	16	2	9	43	31	34
Jarrow	27	15	3	9	46	42	33
Ashington	27	10	8	9	42	33	28
Gateshead Town	28	9	10	9	43	41	28
Hebburn Argyle	28	12	6	10	49	49	28
Morpeth Harriers	28	10	8	10	49	54	28
North Shields Athletic	28	11	4	13	43	40	26
Mickley	28	11	4	13	43	42	26
Annfield Plain Celtic	28	10	3	15	49	54	23
Shankhouse	28	5	8	15	32	67	18
Dudley Wanderers	28	4	8	16	27	54	16
Consett Town Swifts	27	3	5	19	25	62	9

Burradon Athletic resigned from the league and their record was deleted when it stood as follows: 14 2 5 7 13 26 9
Two other games were not played.
Hebburn Argyle and Consett Town Swifts each had 2 points deducted.
Dudley Wanderers moved to the East Northumberland League. Newcastle East End and Walker Parish both joined from the Northern Combination.

1905-06

	P	W	D	L	F	A	Pts
Willington Athletic	30	21	4	5	58	35	46
Ashington	30	19	7	4	78	33	45
Stanley	30	16	10	4	72	32	42
Hebburn Argyle	30	18	3	9	47	33	39
North Shields Athletic	30	15	2	13	50	44	32
Leadgate Park	30	13	5	12	50	45	31
Newcastle East End	30	14	3	13	56	59	31
Morpeth Harriers	29	12	5	12	48	54	29
Gateshead Town	30	11	5	14	39	48	27
Jarrow	28	9	8	11	44	40	26
Walker Parish	30	7	11	12	39	48	25
Mickley	30	8	9	13	42	53	25
Annfield Plain Celtic	30	10	4	16	56	58	24
Wallsend Park Villa	30	7	7	16	50	68	21
Consett Town Swifts	29	7	3	19	38	68	17
Shankhouse	30	7	2	21	31	80	16

2 games involving Jarrow were not played.
Stanley changed their name to West Stanley and joined the newly formed North-Eastern League and Hebburn Argyle also moved to the North-Eastern League. Leadgate Park moved to the Northern League.
Shankhouse were not re-elected and later merged with Shankhouse Albion. They then joined the Blyth & District League as Shankhouse.
Consett Town Swifts were also not re-elected and ceased activity.
Scotswood and Rutherford College both joined.

1906-07

	P	W	D	L	F	A	Pts
North Shields Athletic	24	19	3	2	61	23	41
Wallsend Park Villa	24	16	2	6	61	31	34
Annfield Plain Celtic	24	14	3	7	60	38	31
Scotswood	24	13	5	6	51	30	31
Ashington	24	13	3	8	52	38	29
Walker Parish	24	12	5	7	47	39	29
Willington Athletic	24	12	3	9	39	37	27
Mickley	24	10	5	9	34	34	25
Gateshead Town	24	7	5	12	35	43	19
Morpeth Harriers	24	4	6	14	31	52	14
Newcastle East End	24	5	1	18	31	56	11
Jarrow	24	3	5	16	27	69	11
Rutherford College	24	4	2	18	35	74	10

South Shields Adelaide joined from the Tyneside League, Blyth Spartans joined from the East Northumberland League and Kingston Villa joined from the Wearside League.

Northern Alliance 1907-1913

1907-08

North Shields Athletic	30	25	3	2	81	27	53
Scotswood	30	17	8	5	72	39	42
Wallsend Park Villa	30	17	8	5	65	38	42
South Shields Adelaide	30	19	3	8	81	38	41
Blyth Spartans	30	16	8	6	81	47	40
Ashington	30	13	8	9	58	44	34
Willington Athletic	30	10	11	9	55	42	31
Jarrow	30	11	7	12	48	45	29
Walker Parish	30	10	8	12	49	55	28
Annfield Plain Celtic	29	9	8	12	51	49	26
Kingston Villa	30	10	5	15	39	58	25
Morpeth Harriers	28	10	4	14	54	63	24
Gateshead Town	30	7	2	21	35	73	16
Mickley	30	7	3	20	31	75	15
Newcastle East End	30	4	7	19	33	83	15
Rutherford College	27	5	1	21	32	89	11

Mickley had 2 points deducted.
Rutherford College did not play their 3 outstanding games.
North Shields Athletic, South Shields Adelaide and Wallsend Park Villa all moved to the North-Eastern League and Rutherford College moved to the Newcastle & District League. Byker East End and Newburn both joined from the Tyneside Combination, Bedlington United joined from the East Northumberland League and Blaydon United also joined.

1908-09

Blyth Spartans	28	17	8	3	70	21	42
Byker East End	28	17	3	8	60	35	37
Blaydon United	28	14	8	6	53	31	36
Newburn	28	13	8	7	58	40	34
Mickley	28	13	6	9	43	38	32
Ashington	28	12	6	10	56	50	30
Bedlington United	28	11	8	9	42	50	30
Walker Parish	28	10	9	9	46	42	29
Annfield Plain Celtic	28	12	3	13	42	49	27
Willington Athletic	28	8	10	10	37	43	26
Morpeth Harriers	27	8	7	12	42	52	23
Newcastle East End	28	9	2	17	32	53	20
Scotswood	28	8	3	17	43	63	19
Kingston Villa	28	8	2	18	38	66	18
Gateshead Town	27	5	5	17	39	68	15

One game remained unplayed.
Jarrow resigned and disbanded at the end of February and their record was deleted when it was: 12 4 3 5 16 19 11
Gateshead Town disbanded. Jarrow Caledonians joined from the Tyneside League and Birtley also joined. Byker East End changed their name to Newcastle City.

1909-10

Willington Athletic	28	18	6	4	51	21	42
Newburn	28	16	6	6	57	29	38
Blaydon United	28	15	6	7	52	49	36
Annfield Plain Celtic	28	15	5	8	51	26	35
Ashington	28	14	4	10	57	41	32
Scotswood	28	13	6	9	62	46	32
Blyth Spartans	28	11	9	8	55	39	31
Bedlington United	28	10	10	8	55	39	30
Jarrow Caledonians	28	11	7	10	44	43	29
Mickley	28	11	6	11	37	36	28
Newcastle City	28	7	8	13	37	51	22
Birtley	28	8	4	16	44	66	20
Newcastle East End	28	5	9	14	31	65	19
Kingston Villa	28	5	5	18	40	69	15
Morpeth Harriers	28	4	3	21	23	76	9

Morpeth Harriers had 2 points deducted.
Walker Parish resigned late in the season and their record was deleted.
Morpeth Harriers ceased activity as they had lost their ground. South Shields Parkside joined from the Tyneside League and New Hartley Rovers joined from the Blyth & District League. Kingston Villa changed their name to Harton Colliery.

1910-11

Newburn	30	19	7	4	56	19	45
Ashington	30	19	4	7	63	33	42
Annfield Plain Celtic	30	17	7	6	52	24	41
Scotswood	30	18	4	8	55	33	40
Jarrow Caledonians	30	16	7	7	65	45	39
Blyth Spartans	30	14	6	10	43	32	34
Mickley	30	13	7	10	47	39	33
Newcastle City	30	14	4	12	49	38	32
Bedlington United	30	12	7	11	57	33	31
Willington Athletic	30	8	11	11	36	41	27
South Shields Parkside	30	10	6	14	47	54	26
Blaydon United	29	7	8	14	35	51	22
New Hartley Rovers	30	6	8	16	36	66	20
Birtley	30	5	9	16	25	52	19
Harton Colliery	29	5	6	18	30	85	16
Newcastle East End	30	4	3	23	27	78	11

Harton Colliery resigned before playing their final game against Blaydon United but their record was allowed to stand.
Newcastle City moved to the North-Eastern League. Benwell Adelaide joined from the Northern Combination and Choppington joined from the Wansbeck League.

1911-12

Newburn	30	18	7	5	55	25	43
Ashington	30	17	7	6	55	29	41
Jarrow Caledonians	30	17	7	6	50	28	41
Bedlington United	30	15	9	6	52	23	39
Scotswood	30	15	7	8	45	22	37
South Shields Parkside	30	13	9	8	58	35	35
Blyth Spartans	30	13	8	9	52	46	34
New Hartley Rovers	30	15	4	11	40	32	34
Choppington	30	14	3	13	46	42	31
Blaydon United	30	11	8	11	42	52	30
Annfield Plain Celtic	30	11	6	13	37	38	28
Mickley	30	8	10	12	30	38	26
Birtley	30	9	7	14	52	49	25
Benwell Adelaide	30	5	9	16	36	69	19
Willington Athletic	30	3	4	23	29	78	10
Newcastle East End	30	2	3	25	18	91	7

Seaton Delaval joined from the Blyth & District League and Hexham Athletic also joined.

1912-13

Blyth Spartans	32	20	10	2	72	24	50
Newburn	32	19	5	8	56	33	43
Seaton Delaval	32	18	6	8	57	38	42
Choppington	32	17	6	9	69	29	40
Ashington	32	17	5	10	73	43	39
Bedlington United	32	17	4	11	62	44	38
Mickley	32	17	3	12	61	38	37
Scotswood	32	15	5	12	71	39	35
Birtley	32	15	5	12	66	40	35
Jarrow Caledonians	32	14	5	13	49	58	33
Hexham Athletic	32	14	3	15	62	56	31
Annfield Plain Celtic	32	11	4	17	44	80	26
Benwell Adelaide	32	7	7	18	35	73	21
Willington Athletic	32	7	6	19	49	81	20
Newcastle East End	32	8	4	20	35	86	20
New Hartley Rovers	32	9	3	20	37	77	19
South Shields Parkside	32	5	3	24	26	84	13

New Hartley Rovers had 2 points deducted.
Blaydon United resigned in early January and their record was deleted when it stood as follows: 10 0 1 9 6 21 1
Blyth Spartans moved to the North-Eastern League and Jarrow Caledonians disbanded. Spen Black & White joined.

1913-14

Ashington	30	22	3	5	74	21	47
Birtley	30	18	9	3	58	27	45
Seaton Delaval	30	13	11	6	58	40	37
Newcastle East End	30	13	10	7	58	42	36
Spen Black & White	30	13	8	9	61	40	34
Annfield Plain Celtic	30	13	6	11	66	53	32
Bedlington United	30	10	11	9	40	35	31
Hexham Athletic	30	13	5	12	48	46	31
Newburn	30	9	11	10	47	49	29
Scotswood	30	11	7	12	53	61	29
Mickley	30	9	9	12	33	37	27
Benwell Adelaide	30	9	9	12	41	48	27
New Hartley Rovers	30	10	6	14	35	60	26
Willington Athletic	30	7	9	14	43	76	23
Choppington	30	8	3	19	46	67	19
South Shields Parkside	30	2	3	25	21	80	7

Ashington moved to the North-Eastern League, South Shields Parkside moved to the Tyneside League and Choppington also left. Newbiggin Athletic joined from the Wansbeck League while Gateshead Rodsley and Windy Nook Albion both joined from the Tyneside League but following the outbreak of war, Windy Nook Albion resigned and ceased activity before playing any games. New Hartley Rovers disbanded just before the start of the new season, leaving the league with 14 members for 1914-15.

1914-15

Spen Black & White	18	12	4	2	52	20	28
Scotswood	18	11	3	4	46	23	25
Willington Athletic	18	10	2	6	32	20	22
Mickley	18	5	8	5	25	25	18
Annfield Plain Celtic	17	6	4	7	33	32	16
Newbiggin Athletic	16	4	7	5	32	32	15
Gateshead Rodsley	18	5	5	8	23	30	15
Hexham Athletic	16	5	4	7	20	27	14
Bedlington United	17	4	5	8	24	45	13
Newcastle East End	18	2	4	12	19	52	8

3 games were not played.

Four clubs resigned after the start of the season because they found it increasingly difficult to field a side with many players having joined the Army. In all cases, the clubs' records were deleted. The records of those clubs are shown below with the approximate date of withdrawal in brackets:

Seaton Delaval (mid-November)	5	1	2	2	11	7	4
Birtley (early March)	12	3	3	6	21	34	9
Benwell Adelaide (early March)	18	6	2	10	20	39	14
Newburn (mid-March)	14	7	1	6	28	27	15

1915-18

At the end of the 1914-15 season, the Northern Alliance closed down. However, a temporary competition was set up for 1915-16 which was operated by the officials of the North-Eastern League and called the "North-Eastern League – Tyneside Combination". There were 8 clubs competing in this league, 7 of which came from the North-Eastern League but the other club was Scotswood of the Northern Alliance.

This temporary league also operated in 1916-17 with 7 clubs, and again Scotswood were one of those who competed but this too closed down at the end of the season.

The information found about this competition has been included with the North-Eastern League tables.

1919

The Northern Alliance was revived in 1919 and 8 of the pre-war members rejoined the competition: Annfield Plain Celtic, Bedlington United, Birtley, Mickley, Newbiggin Athletic, Newburn, Seaton Delaval and Spen Black & White.
Scotswood moved to the North-Eastern League while Benwell Adelaide, Gateshead Rodsley, Hexham Athletic, New Hartley Rovers, Newcastle East End, Willington Athletic and Windy Nook Albion did not rejoin.
There were 8 new members: Chopwell Institute and Lintz Institute were pre-war members of the Northern Combination while Close Works (Gateshead), Consett Celtic, Felling Colliery, Hebburn Colliery, Prudhoe Castle and Walker Celtic also joined.

1919-20

Annfield Plain Celtic	30	20	5	5	71	32	45
Chopwell Institute	30	17	4	9	64	32	38
Walker Celtic	30	15	8	7	59	37	38
Mickley	30	16	5	9	48	29	37
Consett Celtic	30	16	4	10	55	50	36
Felling Colliery	30	14	7	9	55	52	35
Seaton Delaval	30	15	3	12	57	55	33
Bedlington United	30	15	3	12	51	51	33
Newburn	30	13	6	11	47	42	32
Spen Black & White	30	14	4	12	39	37	32
Birtley	30	8	10	12	46	45	26
Newbiggin Athletic	30	8	5	17	41	68	21
Lintz Institute	30	9	2	19	35	51	20
Close Works (Gateshead)	30	7	6	17	39	63	20
Hebburn Colliery	30	6	8	16	29	52	20
Prudhoe Castle	30	5	4	21	25	65	14

Bedlington United moved to the North-Eastern League.
Preston Colliery joined from the Tyneside League.

1920-21

Chopwell Institute	30	19	7	4	66	35	45
Seaton Delaval	30	18	3	9	52	37	39
Lintz Institute	30	16	6	8	48	27	38
Spen Black & White	30	14	9	7	46	35	35
Hebburn Colliery	30	14	5	11	64	46	33
Mickley	30	13	6	11	45	44	32
Annfield Plain Celtic	30	12	7	11	57	46	31
Consett Celtic	30	12	7	11	56	55	31
Birtley	30	11	8	11	52	46	30
Prudhoe Castle	30	11	7	12	36	37	29
Newburn	30	10	6	14	42	50	26
Walker Celtic	30	12	2	16	51	63	26
Felling Colliery	30	8	6	14	38	53	22
Close Works (Gateshead)	30	7	10	13	39	55	22
Preston Colliery	30	7	7	16	40	54	21
Newbiggin Athletic	30	3	8	19	35	79	14

Close Works (Gateshead) and Spen Black & White each had 2 points deducted.
Preston Colliery and Seaton Delaval both moved to the North-Eastern League. Newbiggin Athletic also left the league. Ashington Reserves joined from the Ashington & District League, Backworth United joined from the Blyth & District League, Craghead United joined from the Northern Combination and Durham City Reserves joined from the Palatine League. Hexham Town also joined, having changed their name from Hexham Comrades.

Northern Alliance 1921-1935

1921-22

Felling Colliery	34	20	7	7	57	29	47
Mickley	34	18	10	6	52	27	46
Chopwell Institute	34	20	5	9	69	39	45
Ashington Reserves	34	18	6	10	77	45	42
Craghead United	34	15	11	8	47	33	41
Prudhoe Castle	34	16	7	11	44	31	39
Hebburn Colliery	34	14	8	12	54	59	36
Hexham Town	34	14	7	13	55	48	35
Newburn	34	13	6	15	54	49	32
Lintz Institute	34	12	8	14	35	50	32
Close Works (Gateshead)	34	12	7	15	48	53	31
Consett Celtic	34	11	9	14	55	68	31
Annfield Plain Celtic	34	12	6	16	40	54	30
Durham City Reserves	34	11	7	16	52	50	29
Birtley	34	12	4	18	39	53	28
Spen Black & White	34	10	6	18	54	70	26
Backworth United	34	10	5	19	43	67	25
Walker Celtic	34	7	3	24	38	88	17

Close Works (Gateshead) changed their name to Gateshead Town and Consett Celtic changed their name to Consett.

1922-23

Annfield Plain Celtic	34	21	7	6	66	32	49
Ashington Reserves	34	21	6	7	64	24	48
Newburn	34	21	5	8	75	38	47
Craghead United	34	15	11	8	59	41	41
Durham City Reserves	34	16	9	9	60	42	41
Walker Celtic	34	18	4	12	64	56	40
Mickley	34	15	9	10	54	40	39
Hebburn Colliery	34	14	9	11	63	48	37
Felling Colliery	34	13	8	13	49	41	34
Gateshead Town	34	12	7	15	40	46	31
Hexham Town	34	10	10	14	54	67	30
Lintz Institute	34	11	8	15	35	52	30
Chopwell Institute	34	12	5	17	53	49	29
Prudhoe Castle	34	11	8	15	47	63	28
Birtley	34	10	7	17	45	65	27
Backworth United	34	10	7	17	49	81	27
Spen Black & White	34	7	6	21	38	59	20
Consett	34	3	6	25	28	99	12

Prudhoe Castle had 2 points deducted.
Backworth United and Lintz Institute left the league. Percy Main Amateurs joined from the Northern Amateur League and Ouston Rovers also joined.
Annfield Plain Celtic changed their name to Annfield Plain.

1923-24

Birtley	34	19	9	6	68	40	47
Spen Black & White	34	18	9	7	52	32	45
Chopwell Institute	34	20	3	11	67	36	43
Craghead United	34	16	11	7	70	40	43
Durham City Reserves	34	17	8	9	64	45	42
Ashington Reserves	34	13	11	10	60	44	37
Mickley	34	14	6	14	50	55	34
Ouston Rovers	34	13	7	14	52	59	33
Felling Colliery	34	13	6	15	48	46	32
Annfield Plain	34	13	6	15	55	54	32
Gateshead Town	34	13	6	15	49	50	32
Prudhoe Castle	34	12	8	14	48	49	30
Walker Celtic	34	11	8	15	43	58	30
Consett	34	11	8	15	54	79	30
Hebburn Colliery	34	11	7	16	49	57	29
Hexham Town	34	9	9	16	51	62	27
Percy Main Amateurs	34	10	2	22	53	85	22
Newburn	34	7	8	19	43	85	22

Prudhoe Castle had 2 points deducted.
Percy Main Amateurs returned to the Northern Amateur League and Gateshead Town also left. High Fell and Crawcrook Albion joined.

1924-25

Ashington Reserves	34	23	7	4	94	31	53
Durham City Reserves	34	21	8	5	78	38	50
Annfield Plain	34	18	8	8	74	57	44
Craghead United	34	18	6	10	60	39	42
Mickley	34	16	10	8	53	39	42
Consett	34	17	6	11	73	58	40
High Fell	34	15	8	11	65	60	38
Chopwell Institute	34	13	8	13	58	48	34
Crawcrook Albion	34	12	10	12	59	54	32
Newburn	34	12	6	16	59	56	30
Ouston Rovers	34	11	7	16	53	70	29
Spen Black & White	34	10	8	16	45	59	28
Felling Colliery	34	10	8	16	39	63	28
Walker Celtic	34	10	7	17	55	74	27
Hebburn Colliery	34	10	7	17	52	70	27
Birtley	34	10	6	18	38	62	26
Hexham Town	34	8	8	18	42	58	24
Prudhoe Castle	34	5	6	23	32	89	14

Crawcrook Albion and Prudhoe Castle each had 2 points deducted.
Annfield Plain and Durham City Reserves both moved to the North-Eastern League while Hebburn Colliery, Hexham Town and Prudhoe Castle also left. Wallsend joined from the North-Eastern League and Chilton Colliery Recreation Athletic joined from the Palatine League. Washington Colliery also joined.

1925-26

Chilton Colliery Recreation Athletic	30	19	5	6	88	38	43
Consett	30	20	2	8	80	59	42
Wallsend	30	18	4	8	83	46	40
Walker Celtic	30	15	6	9	66	47	36
Crawcrook Albion	30	15	5	10	64	35	35
Newburn	30	16	1	13	76	70	33
Craghead United	30	14	4	12	67	66	32
Mickley	30	13	6	11	56	57	32
Ashington Reserves	30	13	5	12	52	56	31
Washington Colliery	30	11	5	14	51	59	27
Ouston Rovers	30	12	3	15	67	85	27
Chopwell Institute	30	10	5	15	56	66	25
High Fell	30	9	5	16	53	65	23
Birtley	30	8	7	15	53	78	23
Spen Black & White	30	9	2	19	62	96	20
Felling Colliery	30	2	7	21	40	91	11

The Northern Alliance amalgamated with the North-Eastern League and all 16 Northern Alliance clubs became members of the North-Eastern League's new Division Two. These 16 were joined by Dipton United from the Northern Combination and Seaham Harbour from the Wearside League, both of whom had been elected to the Northern Alliance for 1926-27 prior to the amalgamation.
The Northern Alliance then ceased to exist as a separate competition.

1926-35

The Northern Alliance did not exist again as a separate competition until March 1935 when the North-Eastern League decided to scrap its second division and revert to a single division.

The 13 second division clubs then decided to re-form the Northern Alliance but 4 of the 13 – Birtley, Chester-le-Street, Usworth Colliery and Washington Colliery moved to the Wearside League instead. The remaining 9 clubs – Bedlington United, Hexham, Mickley, Newbiggin West End, Pegswood United, Scotswood, Stakeford Albion, Wallsend Town and West Wylam Colliery Welfare became founder members of the re-formed Northern Alliance. The league was made up to 12 by Amble from the North-East Alliance, Consett from the North-Eastern League – Division One and Whitley & Monkseaton who were a newly formed club.

1935-36

	P	W	D	L	F	A	Pts
Hexham	22	11	8	3	85	37	30
Newbiggin West End	22	12	3	7	62	51	27
Stakeford Albion	22	10	5	7	66	49	25
Whitley & Monkseaton	22	10	5	7	45	41	25
Bedlington United	22	11	1	10	44	52	23
Scotswood	22	7	8	7	50	50	22
West Wylam Colliery Welfare	22	10	1	11	53	52	21
Consett	22	11	1	10	30	46	21
Mickley	22	7	5	10	41	55	19
Wallsend Town	22	8	3	11	51	60	19
Amble	22	8	1	13	47	61	17
Pegswood United	22	5	3	14	45	65	13

Consett had 2 points deducted.
Hexham moved to the North-Eastern League and Wallsend Town also left. Ashington Reserves and Morpeth Town both joined from the North-Eastern Alliance and Blyth Spartans Reserves joined from the Tyneside League. Alnwick Town joined as a club recently formed by a merger between Alnwick United of the North Northumberland League and Aindales of the North-Eastern Alliance while Chopwell Colliery Welfare joined as a newly formed club. Crookhall Colliery Welfare also joined.

1936-37

	P	W	D	L	F	A	Pts
Stakeford Albion	30	22	4	4	96	36	48
Blyth Spartans Reserves	30	22	3	5	109	45	47
West Wylam Colliery Welfare	30	20	4	6	84	46	44
Morpeth Town	30	17	7	6	89	54	41
Alnwick Town	30	18	4	8	88	52	40
Crookhall Colliery Welfare	30	15	5	10	71	70	35
Amble	30	14	2	14	94	93	30
Chopwell Colliery Welfare	30	13	3	14	52	58	29
Scotswood	30	10	6	14	55	58	26
Ashington Reserves	30	9	8	13	63	79	26
Bedlington United	30	10	3	17	61	85	23
Pegswood United	30	9	3	18	62	78	21
Consett	30	8	5	17	54	72	21
Newbiggin West End	30	8	3	19	71	95	19
Whitley & Monkseaton	30	7	4	19	62	118	18
Mickley	30	5	2	23	45	117	12

Consett moved to the North-Eastern League. Newcastle United "A" and South Shields Reserves both joined from the Tyneside League and Hexham Reserves also joined. Mickley changed their name to Mickley Colliery Welfare.

1937-38

	P	W	D	L	F	A	Pts
Alnwick Town	32	25	4	3	102	29	54
Morpeth Town	32	24	4	4	103	44	52
South Shields Reserves	32	22	3	7	109	53	47
Newcastle United "A"	32	22	1	9	131	55	45
Blyth Spartans Reserves	32	17	4	11	79	75	38
Crookhall Colliery Welfare	32	12	7	13	65	72	31
Hexham Reserves	32	13	3	16	72	88	29
Amble	32	13	2	17	76	66	28
Ashington Reserves	32	10	6	16	57	67	26
Scotswood	32	10	6	16	57	76	26
Mickley Colliery Welfare	32	12	2	18	57	92	26
Chopwell Colliery Welfare	32	10	5	17	58	75	25
Stakeford Albion	32	10	5	17	57	74	25
Newbiggin West End	32	9	6	17	64	76	24
Whitley & Monkseaton	32	9	5	18	52	89	23
Pegswood United	32	10	3	19	52	100	23
Bedlington United	32	9	4	19	48	108	22

West Wylam Colliery Welfare resigned early in April and their record was deleted when it stood as: 26 6 3 17 32 94 15
Bedlington United and Stakeford Albion both disbanded. Newburn and North Shields Reserves both joined from the Tyneside League. Three clubs playing in the Cramlington & District League – East Cramlington Black Watch, Cramlington Village and Cramlington Welfare – merged and joined the league as East Cramlington Black Watch. Newbiggin West End changed their name to Newbiggin Colliery Welfare.

1938-39

	P	W	D	L	F	A	Pts
Newcastle United "A"	34	23	6	5	125	58	52
East Cramlington Black Watch	34	24	4	6	89	56	52
Newburn	34	22	5	7	97	51	49
Morpeth Town	34	20	5	9	115	55	45
Amble	34	20	4	10	118	71	44
North Shields Reserves	34	19	4	11	109	73	42
Alnwick Town	34	19	3	12	100	79	41
Ashington Reserves	34	17	5	12	92	60	39
South Shields Reserves	34	16	5	13	102	81	37
Newbiggin Colliery Welfare	34	15	5	14	79	88	35
Pegswood United	34	13	3	18	85	119	29
Whitley & Monkseaton	34	10	6	18	85	105	26
Blyth Spartans Reserves	34	11	3	20	60	105	25
Chopwell Colliery Welfare	34	10	4	20	69	98	24
Scotswood	34	8	6	20	57	88	22
Crookhall Colliery Welfare	34	8	6	20	49	118	22
Mickley Colliery Welfare	34	5	6	23	56	108	16
Hexham Reserves	34	5	2	27	61	135	10

Hexham Reserves had 2 points deducted.

Championship Play-Off
Newcastle United "A" v East Cramlington Black Watch   3-1
(Played on Friday 5th May at St. James' Park, Newcastle)

South Shields Reserves moved to the Wearside League, Hexham Reserves moved to the West Tyne League, Crookhall Colliery Welfare moved to the Durham Central League and Pegswood United disbanded. Crawcrook Albion and Newcastle West End both joined from the Tyneside League and Walker Celtic joined from the North-Eastern League.

1939-40 (Pre-war competition)

War was declared on 3rd September and the competition was immediately suspended. 16 games had been played and the table stood as follows:

	P	W	D	L	F	A	Pts
Newcastle United "A"	2	2	0	0	8	1	4
Morpeth Town	2	2	0	0	8	2	4
Whitley & Monkseaton	2	2	0	0	7	2	4
Walker Celtic	2	2	0	0	9	3	4
East Cramlington Black Watch	2	1	1	0	5	3	3
Ashington Reserves	2	1	1	0	9	8	3
Crawcrook Albion	1	1	0	0	5	1	2
North Shields Reserves	3	1	0	2	6	7	2
Scotswood	2	1	0	1	3	4	2
Amble	1	0	1	0	2	2	1
Chopwell Colliery Welfare	1	0	1	0	3	3	1
Mickley Colliery Welfare	2	0	1	1	4	5	1
Blyth Spartans Reserves	2	0	1	1	3	5	1
Alnwick Town	2	0	0	2	5	10	0
Newburn	2	0	0	2	2	8	0
Newcastle West End	2	0	0	2	3	12	0
Newbiggin Colliery Welfare	2	0	0	2	1	7	0

1939-40 (War-time competitions)

The government soon issued regulations under which football could continue and the league was then organised into two geographical divisions. Allocated to the North Division were Alnwick Town, Amble, Ashington Reserves, Blyth Spartans Reserves, East Cramlington Black Watch, Morpeth Town, Newbiggin Colliery Welfare, North Shields Reserves and Whitley & Monkseaton. Allocated to the South Division were Chopwell Colliery Welfare, Crawcrook Albion, Mickley Colliery Welfare, Newburn, Newcastle United "A", Newcastle West End, Scotswood and Walker Celtic. Games were planned to commence on 7th October.

Northern Alliance 1939-1947

However North Shields soon stated their intention not to run a reserve side as did Blyth Spartans while Newcastle United "A" and Scotswood also decided they were unable to take part.

Newcastle West End lost their ground and decided in mid-November to cease activity until the end of the war while Whitley & Monkseaton resigned in mid-December as support was insufficient to meet costs. Alnwick Town and Newbiggin Colliery Welfare had to resign early in 1940 and Amble followed them at the start of February when they decided to cease activity for the duration of the war because so many players had joined the armed forces.

These resignations left just 3 clubs in the North Division and 5 in the South with the fixtures dribbling to an end several weeks before the end of the season. It was then decided to run a second competition but of the 8 remaining clubs, Walker Celtic had already been unable to raise a team to complete their South Division fixtures and Crawcrook Albion were also unable to continue.

There were then just 6 clubs still active and the subsidiary competition was completed at the end of May.

North Division 1939-40

East Cramlington Black Watch	4	2	1	1	10	8	5
Morpeth Town	4	1	2	1	9	9	4
Ashington Reserves	4	1	1	2	11	13	3

South Division 1939-40

Chopwell Colliery Welfare	8	5	1	2	31	17	11
Newburn	7	4	1	2	25	24	9
Walker Celtic	7	3	2	2	19	16	8
Mickley Colliery Welfare	7	3	2	2	17	15	8
Crawcrook Albion	7	0	0	7	11	31	0

Two games remained unplayed.

Subsidiary League 1939-40

Ashington Reserves	10	8	0	2	49	34	16
East Cramlington Black Watch	10	7	1	2	33	25	15
Morpeth Town	10	6	0	4	22	30	12
Chopwell Colliery Welfare	10	4	1	5	29	34	9
Newburn	10	2	1	7	28	36	5
Mickley Colliery Welfare	10	1	1	8	21	43	3

1940-45

At the end of the 1939-40 season, Morpeth Town resigned, leaving just 5 clubs able to continue. With wartime conditions getting ever more difficult, a meeting was held at the County Hotel, Newcastle on 10th August 1940 at which the decision was taken "that the Northern Football Alliance should suspend its operations during hostilities".

1945-46

With the war in Europe finally over, a notice was placed in the Newcastle Evening Chronicle on 7th June 1945, inviting clubs to apply for membership of the league for the 1945-46 season. However, the response was insufficient to allow the league to be revived and it was not until 25th May 1946 that the league was revived.
A meeting was held that day at the County Hotel, Newcastle and it was decided that the league would restart in 1946-47 with 18 clubs. Of those 18, there were 8 clubs who had been members in September 1939 when normal operations ceased upon the outbreak of war.

The 8 pre-war members who rejoined the league were Alnwick Town, Amble, Ashington Reserves, Cramlington Welfare (who had changed their name from East Cramlington Black Watch), Morpeth Town, Newburn, Newbiggin Colliery Welfare and North Shields Reserves.
Of these clubs, Alnwick Town, Amble and Newbiggin Colliery Welfare had all played in the North-East Alliance in 1945-46 while Newburn and North Shields Reserves had both played in the Northern Combination.

The 10 new members of the league were:
Blyth Spartans – pre-war members of the North-Eastern League who disbanded during the war and re-formed in 1946. Their reserves were pre-war members of the Northern Alliance.
Burradon Welfare – pre-war members of the Cramlington & District League and had been playing in the Northern Combination in 1945-46.
Gosforth & Coxlodge Welfare – moved from the Tyneside League to the Cramlington & District League in the summer of 1939 and had been playing in the Northern Combination in 1945-46.
Hexham Hearts – formed after the war to replace the pre-war North-Eastern League club called Hexham who had disbanded during the war. Hexham Hearts played in the Ryton-West Tyne League in 1945-46.
Jarrow – formed after the war as Bedewell and playing in the Northern Combination in 1945-46, changing their name to Jarrow during the season.
Lynemouth Welfare – pre-war members of the Ashington Collieries Welfare League who did not compete in a league in 1945-46.
Prudhoe East Park – formed after the war and played in the Ryton-West Tyne League in 1945-46.
Seaton Burn Welfare – pre-war members of the Cramlington & District League who did not compete in a league in 1945-46.
Shilbottle C.W.S. Welfare – members of the North Northumberland League before the war who played in the North-East Alliance in 1945-46.
West Sleekburn Welfare – champions of the Cramlington & District League in 1938-39 but did not compete in a league in 1945-46.

There were 9 pre-war members of the Northern Alliance who did not rejoin the league in 1946. Of these, Mickley Colliery Welfare, Newcastle West End, Scotswood, Walker Celtic and Whitley & Monkseaton had not reformed as football clubs while Newcastle United were not running their "A" team and Blyth Spartans entered their first (and only) team in the league instead of their reserves. Crawcrook Albion had been playing in the Northern Combination during the war but left and ceased activity in 1945 while Chopwell Colliery Welfare were playing in the Newcastle & District Welfare League.

1946-47

Newburn	30	21	6	3	110	40	48
Blyth Spartans	30	19	6	5	102	49	44
Jarrow	30	20	2	8	97	59	42
West Sleekburn Welfare	30	17	5	8	93	60	39
Cramlington Welfare	30	18	2	10	83	67	38
Alnwick Town	30	16	4	10	89	74	36
Hexham Hearts	30	15	3	12	80	82	33
Ashington Reserves	30	15	3	12	69	80	33
Newbiggin Colliery Welfare	30	12	5	13	61	62	29
Seaton Burn Welfare	30	12	2	16	63	65	24
Amble	30	13	3	14	69	78	23
Morpeth Town	30	10	2	18	74	106	22
Gosforth & Coxlodge Welfare	30	9	2	19	67	96	20
Shilbottle C.W.S. Welfare	30	5	5	20	44	99	15
North Shields Reserves	30	3	8	19	60	107	14
Lynemouth Welfare	30	3	6	21	60	97	12

Seaton Burn Welfare had 2 points deducted.
Amble had 6 points deducted.
Burradon Welfare resigned early in December and their record was deleted when it stood as follows: 9 1 0 8 20 42 2
Prudhoe East Park resigned early in January and their record was deleted when it stood as follows: 13 3 0 10 26 68 6
Blyth Spartans moved to the North-Eastern League and were replaced by their reserves. Newcastle United "A" joined the league. Shankhouse joined having only just been reformed after the war. They were pre-war members of the Cramlington & District League. Shilbottle C.W.S. Welfare changed their name to Shilbottle Colliery Welfare following nationalisation of the coal industry.

1947-48

Team	P	W	D	L	F	A	Pts
Hexham Hearts	34	25	6	3	112	37	56
Newcastle United "A"	34	26	3	5	133	52	55
Newburn	34	21	8	5	97	51	50
West Sleekburn Welfare	34	21	6	7	104	54	48
Cramlington Welfare	34	17	8	9	104	74	42
Alnwick Town	34	15	7	12	94	75	37
Ashington Reserves	34	17	2	15	84	77	36
North Shields Reserves	34	15	4	15	86	83	34
Blyth Spartans Reserves	34	12	8	14	67	70	32
Seaton Burn Welfare	34	13	6	15	68	75	32
Gosforth & Coxlodge Welfare	34	14	3	17	78	87	31
Lynemouth Welfare	34	10	7	17	64	101	27
Shankhouse	34	11	5	18	68	94	25
Morpeth Town	34	9	7	18	74	108	25
Jarrow	34	9	4	21	73	107	22
Shilbottle Colliery Welfare	34	8	5	21	54	101	21
Newbiggin Colliery Welfare	34	8	4	22	52	107	20
Amble	34	6	5	23	55	114	17

Shankhouse had 2 points deducted.

1948-49

Team	P	W	D	L	F	A	Pts
Cramlington Welfare	32	25	4	3	98	34	54
West Sleekburn Welfare	32	23	4	5	103	43	50
Hexham Hearts	32	20	2	10	91	50	42
Newbiggin Colliery Welfare	32	17	4	11	80	68	38
Newburn	32	14	7	11	83	78	35
Newcastle United "A"	32	14	6	12	67	53	34
North Shields Reserves	32	15	4	13	76	81	34
Blyth Spartans Reserves	32	12	5	15	61	74	29
Seaton Burn Welfare	32	11	7	14	67	82	29
Morpeth Town	32	11	6	15	73	79	28
Alnwick Town	32	13	1	18	76	83	27
Gosforth & Coxlodge Welfare	32	11	5	16	65	90	27
Ashington Reserves	32	10	6	16	88	91	26
Lynemouth Welfare	32	11	3	18	52	92	25
Shankhouse	32	11	2	19	71	91	24
Amble	32	10	4	18	62	85	24
Shilbottle Colliery Welfare	32	7	4	21	61	100	18

Jarrow resigned on 16th March due to financial problems and their record at the time was deleted: 23 6 3 14 37 73 15
Seaton Burn Welfare resigned from the league and disbanded.
Barrington United joined from the Northern Combination and East Tanfield Colliery Welfare also joined.

1949-50

Team	P	W	D	L	F	A	Pts
West Sleekburn Welfare	34	25	5	4	119	60	55
Cramlington Welfare	34	25	3	6	95	46	53
Hexham Hearts	34	25	2	7	114	55	52
Newburn	34	21	5	8	134	79	47
Gosforth & Coxlodge Welfare	34	21	4	9	88	58	46
Blyth Spartans Reserves	34	17	4	13	74	54	38
Barrington United	34	17	3	14	97	84	37
Newcastle United "A"	34	14	8	12	79	66	36
North Shields Reserves	34	14	6	14	72	73	34
Ashington Reserves	34	12	6	16	76	88	30
Alnwick Town	34	11	7	16	83	86	29
Newbiggin Colliery Welfare	34	11	7	16	64	84	29
East Tanfield Colliery Welfare	34	11	6	17	82	104	28
Shankhouse	34	9	8	17	69	101	26
Lynemouth Welfare	34	9	6	19	74	116	24
Amble	34	7	6	21	68	106	20
Shilbottle Colliery Welfare	34	5	4	25	62	124	14
Morpeth Town	34	4	6	24	45	112	14

East Tanfield Colliery Welfare moved to the Northern Combination.
Whitley Bay Athletic joined from the Northern Combination having changed their name from Monkseaton.

1950-51

Team	P	W	D	L	F	A	Pts
Cramlington Welfare	34	25	5	4	135	43	55
Newburn	34	25	2	7	128	64	52
Gosforth & Coxlodge Welfare	34	21	7	6	93	56	49
Hexham Hearts	34	20	8	6	89	60	48
Blyth Spartans Reserves	34	19	4	11	92	64	42
Barrington United	34	20	1	13	86	70	41
Shankhouse	34	16	8	10	72	70	40
North Shields Reserves	34	18	3	13	93	70	39
Alnwick Town	34	16	6	12	107	83	38
Ashington Reserves	34	16	3	15	88	75	35
Amble	34	12	10	12	82	89	34
Whitley Bay Athletic	34	14	5	15	82	86	33
Newcastle United "A"	34	13	6	15	89	59	32
West Sleekburn Welfare	34	12	3	19	78	94	27
Shilbottle Colliery Welfare	34	5	6	23	54	105	16
Morpeth Town	34	5	4	25	40	121	14
Newbiggin Colliery Welfare	34	3	6	25	58	140	12
Lynemouth Welfare	34	2	1	31	48	165	5

Newbiggin Colliery Welfare moved to the Northumberland Miners Welfare League.

1951-52

Team	P	W	D	L	F	A	Pts
Newburn	32	20	7	5	104	51	47
North Shields Reserves	32	19	6	7	84	54	44
Ashington Reserves	32	18	6	8	84	69	42
Gosforth & Coxlodge Welfare	32	16	9	7	81	55	41
Whitley Bay Athletic	32	17	7	8	100	68	41
Newcastle United "A"	32	15	8	9	87	54	38
West Sleekburn Welfare	32	14	7	11	76	62	35
Shankhouse	32	14	4	14	74	74	32
Hexham Hearts	32	13	5	14	86	70	31
Cramlington Welfare	32	13	4	15	77	84	30
Amble	32	11	8	13	66	77	30
Alnwick Town	32	12	5	15	94	90	29
Blyth Spartans Reserves	32	7	10	15	63	86	24
Barrington United	32	8	8	16	56	84	24
Lynemouth Welfare	32	8	7	17	68	93	23
Shilbottle Colliery Welfare	32	6	9	17	58	86	21
Morpeth Town	32	3	6	23	49	150	12

Barrington United moved to the Northumberland Miners Welfare League.
Heaton Stannington joined from the Northern League and South Shields Reserves also joined.

1952-53

Team	P	W	D	L	F	A	Pts
Whitley Bay Athletic	34	27	4	3	107	31	58
Newburn	34	26	5	3	113	50	57
Newcastle United "A"	34	20	6	8	85	37	46
Amble	34	18	7	9	82	53	43
Ashington Reserves	34	18	4	12	80	49	40
Shankhouse	34	15	9	10	67	45	39
Hexham Hearts	34	17	5	12	86	78	39
Alnwick Town	34	17	4	13	74	70	38
Cramlington Welfare	34	15	5	14	91	87	35
North Shields Reserves	34	14	6	14	77	77	34
Blyth Spartans Reserves	34	13	2	19	67	81	28
Heaton Stannington	34	12	4	18	66	82	28
West Sleekburn Welfare	34	9	8	17	54	90	26
Gosforth & Coxlodge Welfare	34	11	3	20	58	79	25
South Shields Reserves	34	8	6	20	69	91	22
Morpeth Town	34	9	3	22	65	107	21
Shilbottle Colliery Welfare	34	6	5	23	58	129	17
Lynemouth Welfare	34	5	6	23	59	122	16

Northern Alliance 1953-1959

1953-54

Whitley Bay Athletic	34	29	3	2	115	31	61
Newcastle United "A"	34	29	2	3	145	45	60
Blyth Spartans Reserves	34	22	5	7	87	52	49
Newburn	34	18	6	10	105	69	42
Alnwick Town	34	17	5	12	104	68	39
Hexham Hearts	34	16	7	11	89	64	39
Ashington Reserves	34	16	5	13	82	71	37
South Shields Reserves	34	17	3	14	84	80	37
Lynemouth Welfare	34	14	7	13	94	94	35
West Sleekburn Welfare	34	15	3	16	77	84	33
Gosforth & Coxlodge Welfare	34	12	7	15	85	99	31
North Shields Reserves	34	11	6	17	82	96	28
Amble	34	12	2	20	93	120	26
Heaton Stannington	34	9	8	17	82	107	26
Cramlington Welfare	34	10	3	21	81	82	23
Shankhouse	34	9	3	22	62	131	21
Shilbottle Colliery Welfare	34	6	4	24	70	124	16
Morpeth Town	34	3	3	28	53	173	9

Shilbottle Colliery Welfare moved to the Northumberland Miners Welfare League.

1954-55

Amble	32	22	6	4	85	31	50
Ashington Reserves	32	23	4	5	112	49	50
Newburn	32	21	4	7	85	50	46
Whitley Bay Athletic	32	19	5	8	90	33	43
Newcastle United "A"	32	18	6	8	95	43	42
Cramlington Welfare	32	15	5	12	75	73	35
South Shields Reserves	32	11	9	12	78	82	31
Blyth Spartans Reserves	32	12	6	14	60	70	30
North Shields Reserves	32	12	5	15	65	71	29
Morpeth Town	32	12	5	15	70	90	29
Heaton Stannington	32	12	4	16	70	73	28
Hexham Hearts	32	12	3	17	66	81	27
West Sleekburn Welfare	32	10	6	16	50	73	26
Gosforth & Coxlodge Welfare	32	8	8	16	51	89	24
Alnwick Town	32	9	3	20	70	85	21
Lynemouth Welfare	32	8	5	19	49	101	21
Shankhouse	32	5	2	25	50	127	12

Whitley Bay Athletic moved to the North-Eastern League.
Bedlington Mechanics joined from the East Northumberland League and Seaton Delaval joined from the Northern Amateur League.

1955-56

Ashington Reserves	34	26	4	4	123	42	56
Cramlington Welfare	34	23	2	9	90	43	48
Newcastle United "A"	34	21	1	12	91	56	43
Amble	34	19	4	11	87	56	42
Newburn	34	19	4	11	84	55	42
Morpeth Town	34	18	4	12	89	64	40
Bedlington Mechanics	34	17	4	13	100	67	38
North Shields Reserves	34	16	5	13	89	71	37
Blyth Spartans Reserves	34	16	5	13	79	91	37
South Shields Reserves	34	15	5	14	92	85	35
Shankhouse	34	15	5	14	69	84	35
Alnwick Town	34	13	8	13	65	62	34
Hexham Hearts	34	11	8	15	69	97	30
Seaton Delaval	34	9	10	15	53	84	28
Heaton Stannington	34	11	5	18	84	95	27
West Sleekburn Welfare	34	6	5	23	47	105	17
Lynemouth Welfare	34	5	3	26	57	134	13
Gosforth & Coxlodge Welfare	34	4	2	28	59	136	10

Heaton Stannington moved to the Northern Amateur League and Lynemouth Welfare also left. Craghead Colliery Welfare joined from the Durham Central League and Whitley Bay Athletic Reserves joined from the Tynemouth & District League.

1956-57

Amble	34	27	5	2	127	38	59
Ashington Reserves	34	24	6	4	105	47	54
Alnwick Town	34	19	5	10	106	53	43
North Shields Reserves	34	18	6	10	82	64	42
South Shields Reserves	34	19	4	11	100	80	42
Bedlington Mechanics	34	17	7	10	81	57	41
Newcastle United "A"	34	17	5	12	76	49	39
Morpeth Town	34	15	9	10	83	59	39
Newburn	34	18	3	13	90	80	39
Cramlington Welfare	34	16	6	12	73	62	38
Craghead Colliery Welfare	34	15	3	16	110	89	33
Blyth Spartans Reserves	34	13	7	14	72	75	33
Seaton Delaval	34	13	5	16	80	82	31
Gosforth & Coxlodge Welfare	34	7	5	22	51	119	19
Whitley Bay Athletic Reserves	34	8	2	24	58	110	18
West Sleekburn Welfare	34	5	7	22	43	123	17
Hexham Hearts	34	7	1	26	66	119	15
Shankhouse	34	3	4	27	45	142	10

Shankhouse moved to the Tynemouth & District League.
Crawcrook Albion joined from the Northern Combination.

1957-58

Newcastle United "A"	32	26	3	3	115	25	55
Crawcrook Albion	32	21	4	7	103	54	46
Amble	32	21	2	9	76	35	44
Ashington Reserves	32	19	3	10	113	49	41
North Shields Reserves	32	19	3	10	89	52	41
Craghead Colliery Welfare	32	18	5	9	83	58	41
Alnwick Town	32	18	4	10	83	50	40
Seaton Delaval	32	12	8	12	60	62	32
Bedlington Mechanics	32	13	5	14	67	64	31
South Shields Reserves	32	14	2	16	72	70	30
Cramlington Welfare	32	12	6	14	47	58	30
Newburn	32	10	6	16	63	91	26
Morpeth Town	32	10	4	18	62	102	24
Blyth Spartans Reserves	32	6	8	18	46	73	20
West Sleekburn Welfare	32	7	5	20	59	110	19
Whitley Bay Athletic Reserves	32	5	7	20	46	108	17
Gosforth & Coxlodge Welfare	32	2	3	27	36	159	7

Hexham Hearts resigned and disbanded due to financial problems on 23rd September. Their record was deleted when it stood as:
                                        5   0   0   5   3   55   0
Whitley Bay Athletic Reserves and Gosforth & Coxlodge Welfare both left the league. Annfield Plain and West Stanley joined from the North-Eastern League and Wallsend Rising Sun Colliery Welfare joined from the Northern Amateur League.

1958-59

Amble	34	27	4	3	113	39	58
Ashington Reserves	34	27	2	5	118	38	56
Crawcrook Albion	34	23	3	8	117	73	49
Bedlington Mechanics	34	24	0	10	94	50	48
Craghead Colliery Welfare	34	17	10	7	96	62	44
Newcastle United "A"	34	17	7	10	74	62	41
South Shields Reserves	34	15	7	12	64	66	37
Newburn	34	14	3	17	84	91	31
Wallsend Rising Sun Coll. Welfare	34	14	3	17	71	83	31
Seaton Delaval	34	12	5	17	61	74	29
Alnwick Town	34	11	6	17	73	83	28
Annfield Plain	34	11	5	18	68	88	27
West Stanley	34	10	7	17	65	98	27
North Shields Reserves	34	8	10	16	59	74	26
Blyth Spartans Reserves	34	9	5	20	66	103	23
Morpeth Town	34	10	0	24	68	112	20
Cramlington Welfare	34	7	5	22	79	105	19
West Sleekburn Welfare	34	7	4	23	49	118	18

South Shields Reserves moved to the re-formed North-Eastern League.
West Stanley disbanded and West Sleekburn Welfare also left the league. Highfield joined.

1959-60

Amble	30	20	6	4	76	34	46
Alnwick Town	30	19	5	6	85	40	43
Ashington Reserves	30	18	6	6	70	45	42
Bedlington Mechanics	30	17	7	6	72	47	41
Craghead Colliery Welfare	30	17	4	9	68	45	38
Newcastle United "A"	30	13	8	9	77	60	34
North Shields Reserves	30	16	1	13	70	58	33
Crawcrook Albion	30	12	6	12	77	80	30
Blyth Spartans Reserves	30	11	7	12	70	74	29
Annfield Plain	30	8	12	10	58	63	28
Newburn	30	9	5	16	54	71	23
Highfield	30	10	2	18	54	81	22
Morpeth Town	30	9	3	18	59	91	21
Wallsend Rising Sun Coll. Welfare	30	6	5	19	43	61	17
Seaton Delaval	30	6	5	19	53	91	17
Cramlington Welfare	30	5	6	19	51	96	16

Annfield Plain moved to the newly formed Northern Counties League and Cramlington Welfare also left. Gateshead Reserves joined from the North Regional League while Blaydon Casuals, Consett Reserves and Dudley Welfare also joined.

1960-61

A Final table has not been found for this season and only the top two placings are known:

Amble	34	24	4	6	76	50	52
Newburn	34	22	5	7	71	36	49

The 16 other clubs which played this season were Alnwick Town, Ashington Reserves, Bedlington Mechanics, Blaydon Casuals, Blyth Spartans Reserves, Consett Reserves, Craghead Colliery Welfare, Crawcrook Albion, Dudley Welfare, Gateshead Reserves, Highfield, Morpeth Town, Newcastle United "A", North Shields Reserves, Seaton Delaval and Wallsend Rising Sun Colliery Welfare.
Ashington disbanded its reserve side and Newcastle United disbanded its "A" team. Kibblesworth Colliery Welfare joined the league.

1961-62

Newburn	32	23	5	4	78	31	51
Alnwick Town	32	21	6	5	93	46	48
Amble	32	19	4	9	77	49	42
Bedlington Mechanics	32	17	5	10	83	57	39
Highfield	32	14	9	9	85	75	37
Crawcrook Albion	32	16	4	12	73	61	36
Consett Reserves	32	14	4	14	77	72	32
North Shields Reserves	32	15	2	15	74	72	32
Blaydon Casuals	32	13	5	14	59	68	31
Craghead Colliery Welfare	32	11	7	14	65	56	29
Kibblesworth Colliery Welfare	32	11	6	15	57	90	28
Wallsend Rising Sun Coll. Welfare	32	12	2	18	55	60	26
Morpeth Town	32	9	8	15	52	75	26
Dudley Welfare	32	9	6	17	60	89	24
Seaton Delaval	32	8	5	19	43	65	21
Blyth Spartans Reserves	32	7	7	18	51	83	21
Gateshead Reserves	32	7	7	18	43	76	21

North Shields disbanded their reserve side while Newburn and Wallsend Rising Star Colliery Welfare also left. Newcastle United "A" joined.

1962-63

Alnwick Town	26	21	3	2	77	24	45
Gateshead Reserves	26	19	3	4	62	27	41
Bedlington Mechanics	26	20	0	6	72	31	40
Dudley Welfare	26	15	2	9	67	42	32
Morpeth Town	26	15	2	9	60	42	32
Newcastle United "A"	26	11	7	8	61	41	29
Consett Reserves	26	11	5	10	59	50	27
Highfield	26	11	3	12	58	68	25
Amble	26	8	4	14	42	57	20
Seaton Delaval	26	9	2	15	42	61	20
Blyth Spartans Reserves	26	8	2	16	46	57	18
Crawcrook Albion	26	8	2	16	49	72	18
Kibblesworth Colliery Welfare	26	5	1	20	36	93	11
Blaydon Casuals	26	2	2	22	26	92	6

Craghead Colliery Welfare resigned and their record was deleted when it stood as follows: 15 10 1 4 43 20 21
Bedlington Mechanics disbanded. Blaydon Casuals and Consett Reserves also left the league.

1963-64

Alnwick Town	20	14	4	2	62	33	32
Gateshead Reserves	20	13	3	4	65	30	29
Morpeth Town	20	13	2	5	62	27	28
Highfield	20	12	3	5	63	27	27
Newcastle United "A"	20	9	5	6	46	29	23
Amble	20	7	5	8	45	51	19
Dudley Welfare	20	7	4	9	51	52	18
Crawcrook Albion	20	5	6	9	43	57	16
Blyth Spartans Reserves	20	5	5	10	39	47	15
Seaton Delaval	20	3	1	16	35	98	7
Kibblesworth Colliery Welfare	20	2	2	16	25	85	6

1964-65

The league did not operate.

Dudley Welfare and Seaton Delaval resigned at the end of the 1963-64 season, leaving just 9 clubs as members. As this was too few to continue, the league closed down for the 1964-65 season. Alnwick Town, Crawcrook Albion, Gateshead Reserves, Highfield and Kibblesworth Colliery Welfare all moved to the Durham Central League, Blyth Spartans Reserves, Morpeth Town and Newcastle United "A" all moved to the Northern Combination and Amble moved to the Northumberland Miners Welfare League.

The league was re-formed for the 1965-66 season with 14 members: Alnwick Town, Bradley's Social Club, Crawcrook Albion, Dipton St. Patrick's, Gateshead Reserves, Highfield and Sacriston Welfare all joined from the Durham Central League, Morpeth Town joined from the Northern Combination and Amble joined from the Northumberland Miners Welfare League. Bedlington Colliery Welfare joined as a newly formed club and Morrison Busty Colliery Welfare, North Walbottle Welfare and Wallington also joined.

1965-66

Alnwick Town	26	21	3	2	103	31	45
Morpeth Town	26	18	4	4	96	52	40
Bedlington Colliery Welfare	26	16	5	5	92	35	37
Amble	26	14	4	8	75	48	32
Bradleys Social Club	26	11	6	9	57	49	28
Gateshead Reserves	26	12	3	11	59	43	27
Wallington	26	13	0	13	72	69	26
Sacriston Welfare	26	10	4	12	50	70	24
North Walbottle Welfare	26	10	3	13	58	67	23
Crawcrook Albion	26	7	8	11	43	50	22
Highfield	26	6	7	13	46	72	19
Dipton St. Patrick's	26	8	3	15	41	83	19
Morrison Busty Colliery Welfare	26	3	7	16	30	80	13
Kibblesworth Colliery Welfare	26	3	3	20	32	109	9

Wallsend Athletic joined from the Tyneside Amateur League and Ashington Reserves also joined.

Northern Alliance 1966-1973

1966-67

Compiled from the latest table found, dated 6th May 1967, with some later results added, leaving 8 games outstanding:

Bedlington Colliery Welfare	30	25	4	1	138	22	54
Alnwick Town	30	22	3	5	104	36	47
Morpeth Town	30	12	12	6	75	58	36
Amble	29	15	5	9	68	47	35
Sacriston Welfare	29	13	7	9	63	49	33
Morrison Busty Colliery Welfare	30	13	6	11	68	66	32
Bradleys Social Club	29	13	6	10	61	62	32
Wallington	30	12	7	11	66	66	31
Wallsend Athletic	30	13	4	13	52	61	30
Gateshead Reserves	29	9	10	10	56	55	28
Ashington Reserves	29	10	6	13	55	72	26
Crawcrook Albion	28	9	5	14	55	73	23
Highfield	26	8	3	15	45	77	19
Dipton St. Patrick's	27	4	7	16	35	82	15
North Walbottle Welfare	30	5	4	21	46	82	14
Kibblesworth Colliery Welfare	28	3	3	22	49	128	9

Gateshead Reserves moved to the Wearside League and Dipton St. Patrick's also left. Newcastle University, Washington Colliery and Washington Mechanics joined.

1967-68

Alnwick Town	26	21	3	2	101	24	45
Bedlington Colliery Welfare	26	18	5	3	71	27	41
Wallsend Athletic	26	15	5	6	62	36	35
Amble	26	14	5	7	59	51	33
Morrison Busty Colliery Welfare	26	13	4	9	70	55	30
Wallington	26	13	3	10	60	47	29
Washington Mechanics	26	13	3	10	58	47	29
Newcastle University	26	9	4	13	60	63	22
Crawcrook Albion	26	8	6	12	46	54	22
Morpeth Town	26	9	2	15	63	83	20
Sacriston Welfare	26	5	8	13	47	62	18
Ashington Reserves	26	7	4	15	46	73	18
Bradleys Social Club	26	5	3	18	32	86	13
Washington Colliery	26	2	5	19	42	109	9

Kibblesworth Colliery Welfare, North Walbottle Welfare and Highfield all resigned during the season and their records were deleted.
At the time of their resignation, Kibblesworth Colliery Welfare's record stood as follows: 14 1 2 11 24 63 4
At the time of their resignation, North Walbottle Welfare's record stood as follows 18 1 5 12 35 79 7
At the time of their resignation, Highfield's record stood as follows: 19 4 2 13 31 97 10
Washington Mechanics changed their name to Washington and moved to the Wearside League. Morrison Busty Colliery Welfare also moved to the Wearside League. Ashington Reserves, Sacriston Welfare and Washington Colliery also left. Chopwell St. John's, Marine Park, Percy Main Amateurs, Wallsend Gordon United and Winlaton Mill Athletic all joined.

1968-69

Alnwick Town	22	15	5	2	70	21	35
Wallsend Athletic	22	16	3	3	78	26	35
Percy Main Amateurs	21	13	2	6	65	39	28
Bedlington Colliery Welfare	22	12	4	6	64	44	28
Marine Park	21	9	6	6	47	31	24
Chopwell St. John's	22	9	2	11	58	66	20
Morpeth Town	21	8	3	10	63	55	19
Bradleys Social Club	20	7	4	9	34	47	18
Newcastle University	22	6	5	11	43	62	17
Wallington	21	6	3	12	38	55	15
Amble	22	5	3	14	39	65	13
Winlaton Mill Athletic	22	2	2	18	31	119	6

Wallsend Gordon United resigned during the season and their record was deleted when it stood as follows: 13 2 1 10 19 43 5
Crawcrook Albion also resigned during the season and their record was deleted when it stood as follows: 17 3 4 10 28 56 10
3 games appear not to have been played.
Bradleys Social Club left the league and Ashington joined from the Northern Premier League.

1969-70

Alnwick Town	22	21	1	0	85	15	43
Bedlington Colliery Welfare	22	17	2	3	72	21	36
Ashington	22	14	3	5	70	31	31
Marine Park	22	13	5	4	57	31	31
Percy Main Amateurs	22	12	3	7	64	29	27
Morpeth Town	22	9	3	10	56	48	21
Wallsend Athletic	22	8	3	11	43	43	19
Newcastle University	22	7	2	13	46	64	16
Chopwell St. John's	22	6	1	15	49	84	13
Wallington	22	3	4	15	19	73	10
Amble	22	3	3	16	13	54	9
Winlaton Mill Athletic	22	4	0	18	19	100	8

Ashington moved to the Northern League and Amble disbanded. Winlaton Mill Athletic changed their name to Spen Black & White but resigned shortly before the start of the 1970-71 season because they had lost their ground. Alston joined from the Carlisle & District League and Workington Reserves also joined.

1970-71

Alnwick Town	20	16	2	2	68	29	34
Workington Reserves	20	12	5	3	38	21	29
Percy Main Amateurs	20	13	2	5	53	30	28
Bedlington Colliery Welfare	20	13	1	6	49	32	27
Alston	20	10	4	6	63	42	24
Chopwell St. John's	20	8	3	9	42	51	19
Newcastle University	19	7	2	10	28	39	16
Wallsend Athletic	19	5	4	10	27	39	14
Morpeth Town	20	6	2	12	40	60	14
Marine Park	20	3	2	13	20	46	8
Wallington	20	0	5	15	19	58	5

One game was not played.
Chopwell St. John's left the league and Throckley Welfare joined.

1971-72

Alnwick Town	20	14	3	3	69	26	31
Bedlington Colliery Welfare	20	13	4	3	50	23	30
Marine Park	20	12	2	6	34	17	26
Percy Main Amateurs	20	11	4	5	54	38	26
Morpeth Town	20	10	1	9	58	60	21
Workington Reserves	20	8	4	8	43	26	20
Newcastle University	20	7	1	12	46	48	15
Alston	20	5	5	10	36	53	15
Wallsend Athletic	20	6	3	11	29	52	15
Throckley Welfare	20	5	2	13	29	54	12
Wallington	20	3	3	14	27	78	9

Bede College, Belford and Northumberland College all joined the league.

1972-73

Marine Park	26	20	3	3	70	21	43
Alnwick Town	26	19	3	4	86	42	41
Percy Main Amateurs	26	17	3	6	62	31	37
Bedlington Colliery Welfare	26	13	7	6	56	28	33
Belford	26	14	4	8	74	57	32
Morpeth Town	26	12	6	8	74	58	30
Newcastle University	26	13	3	10	64	59	29
Throckley Welfare	26	12	4	10	67	48	28
Workington Reserves	26	9	7	10	51	44	25
Alston	26	9	4	13	60	57	22
Wallington	26	4	5	17	39	67	13
Bede College	26	3	7	16	41	81	13
Northumberland College	26	5	2	19	30	95	12
Wallsend Athletic	26	2	2	22	22	108	6

Stockton joined from the Midland League.

1973-74

Marine Park	28	18	4	6	70	44	40
Morpeth Town	28	xx	x	x	xx	xx	39
Stockton	28	16	6	6	67	35	38
Bedlington Colliery Welfare	28	18	1	9	57	26	37
Alnwick Town	28	16	5	7	62	39	37
Percy Main Amateurs	28	14	8	6	62	38	36
Belford	28	15	2	11	63	47	32
Throckley Welfare	28	10	9	9	58	49	29
Workington Reserves	28	12	5	11	42	38	29
Alston	28	12	5	11	56	55	29
Newcastle University	28	7	8	13	54	68	22
Wallington	28	10	2	16	42	66	22
Bede College	28	3	6	19	35	72	12
Wallsend Athletic	28	3	4	21	24	99	10
Northumberland College	28	2	4	22	25	89	8

Northumberland College left the league. South Shields Mariners joined as a newly formed club. Seaham Colliery Welfare Red Star and Sunderland Greenwells also joined.

1974-75

South Shields Mariners	32	26	4	2	118	29	56
Marine Park	32	22	6	4	69	21	50
Morpeth Town	32	19	6	7	91	50	44
Percy Main Amateurs	31	12	9	10	74	58	35
Alnwick Town	32	13	9	10	67	57	35
Alston	32	16	2	14	70	77	34
Seaham Colliery Welfare Red Star	32	15	3	14	55	39	33
Wallington	32	14	5	13	59	56	33
Belford	32	12	8	12	84	74	32
Wallsend Athletic	32	12	7	13	57	64	31
Workington Reserves	32	10	10	12	57	58	30
Newcastle University	32	12	5	15	47	61	29
Bede College	32	11	6	15	36	51	28
Bedlington Colliery Welfare	32	10	3	19	48	84	23
Throckley Welfare	32	6	8	18	59	89	20
Stockton	31	6	7	18	43	92	19
Sunderland Greenwells	32	4	4	24	37	111	12

Percy Main Amateurs were awarded 2 points after Stockton did not turn up for their scheduled game.
Stockton disbanded and Alston also left the league. Carlisle City joined as a newly formed club and Durham University also joined.

1975-76

South Shields Mariners	30	24	3	3	102	29	51
Carlisle City	30	20	2	8	60	25	42
Percy Main Amateurs	30	19	4	7	71	44	42
Seaham Colliery Welfare Red Star	30	17	7	6	60	36	41
Marine Park	30	19	2	9	67	36	40
Wallington	30	17	5	8	63	40	39
Belford	30	15	6	9	57	45	36
Alnwick Town	30	12	5	13	51	42	29
Durham University	30	9	8	13	40	51	26
Workington Reserves	30	7	9	14	40	57	23
Morpeth Town	30	9	5	16	50	75	23
Newcastle University	30	7	6	17	30	59	20
Bedlington Colliery Welfare	30	8	2	20	40	101	18
Bede College	30	7	4	19	34	67	18
Sunderland Greenwells	30	8	1	21	54	68	17
Wallsend Athletic	30	-	—	—	—	—	15

The published table mistakenly omitted the bottom club, Wallsend Athletic. It is known that Wallsend Athletic finished the season with 15 points, but a more detailed playing record for them is not recorded.

Throckley Welfare were expelled from the league at the end of March 1976 and Wallsend Athletic were not re-elected. South Shields Mariners changed their name to South Shields and moved to the Wearside League. Peterlee Newtown joined as a newly formed club and Sunderland Pyrex also joined.

1976-77

Wallington	30	24	4	2	85	27	52
Carlisle City	30	24	3	3	90	23	51
Marine Park	30	20	5	5	72	30	45
Peterlee Newtown	30	20	4	6	75	43	44
Seaham Colliery Welfare Red Star	30	16	5	9	70	42	37
Percy Main Amateurs	30	14	7	9	73	45	35
Workington Reserves	30	14	5	11	54	52	33
Alnwick Town	30	10	9	11	54	61	29
Sunderland Greenwells	30	10	6	14	61	70	26
Belford	30	9	8	13	61	80	26
Morpeth Town	30	8	4	18	48	93	20
Newcastle University	30	7	4	19	38	66	18
Bedlington Colliery Welfare	30	6	5	19	46	67	17
Bede College	30	6	5	19	34	85	17
Durham University	30	4	7	19	30	60	15
Sunderland Pyrex	30	5	5	20	40	87	15

Bede College, Sunderland Greenwells and Workington Reserves all left. Brandon United joined from the Durham & District Sunday League, Guisborough Town joined from the South Bank & District League, while Cramlington New Town and Stobswood Welfare also joined.

1977-78

Brandon United	32	26	3	3	120	39	55
Carlisle City	32	25	4	3	101	25	54
Guisborough Town	32	19	7	6	80	39	45
Wallington	32	18	8	6	74	43	44
Seaham Colliery Welfare Red Star	32	20	3	9	73	50	43
Peterlee Newtown	32	17	8	7	70	33	42
Percy Main Amateurs	32	12	9	11	64	59	33
Marine Park	32	13	6	13	65	59	32
Belford	32	10	7	15	59	66	27
Alnwick Town	32	9	8	15	63	85	26
Cramlington New Town	32	8	9	15	59	74	25
Morpeth Town	32	8	8	16	58	74	24
Bedlington Colliery Welfare	32	8	7	17	46	82	23
Stobswood Welfare	32	8	6	18	48	92	22
Sunderland Pyrex	32	6	6	20	36	80	18
Durham University	32	6	5	21	34	93	17
Newcastle University	32	6	2	24	38	95	14

Newcastle University moved to the Northern Combination.
Ryhope Community Association joined as a newly re-formed club and Newcastle United "A" also joined.

1978-79

Brandon United	34	27	4	3	105	35	58
Guisborough Town	34	25	7	2	107	24	57
Seaham Colliery Welfare Red Star	34	23	7	4	111	33	53
Ryhope Community Association	34	16	10	8	67	46	42
Peterlee Newtown	34	19	2	13	63	50	40
Wallington	34	18	3	13	73	49	39
Carlisle City	34	15	8	11	60	45	38
Newcastle United "A"	34	15	7	12	82	53	37
Marine Park	34	13	9	12	59	50	35
Morpeth Town	34	13	7	14	69	68	33
Stobswood Welfare	34	14	5	15	46	74	33
Percy Main Amateurs	34	11	7	16	47	74	29
Belford	34	11	4	19	46	82	26
Alnwick Town	34	10	6	18	49	88	26
Cramlington New Town	34	10	5	19	54	83	25
Sunderland Pyrex	34	8	5	21	31	63	21
Bedlington Colliery Welfare	34	6	5	23	51	97	17
Durham University	34	1	1	32	24	130	3

Peterlee Newtown and Seaham Colliery Welfare Red Star both moved to the Wearside League and Bedlington Colliery Welfare moved to the Tyneside Amateur League, changing their name to Bedlington United. Forest Hall joined from the Northern Amateur League.

Northern Alliance 1979-1985

1979-80

Guisborough Town	28	21	7	0	83	21	49
Carlisle City	28	18	8	2	79	20	44
Percy Main Amateurs	28	19	5	4	76	30	43
Brandon United	28	16	4	8	50	31	36
Ryhope Community Association	28	14	6	8	68	39	34
Forest Hall	28	14	4	10	53	35	32
Newcastle United "A"	28	13	4	11	54	46	30
Morpeth Town	28	11	5	12	59	58	27
Cramlington New Town	28	9	6	13	41	47	24
Sunderland Pyrex	28	9	5	14	51	54	23
Stobswood Welfare	28	6	9	13	32	50	21
Belford	28	8	3	17	38	83	19
Wallington	28	6	6	16	47	72	18
Alnwick Town	28	4	8	16	33	72	16
Durham University	28	1	2	25	19	125	4

Marine Park resigned from the league and disbanded in October and their record was deleted.
Guisborough Town moved to the Midland League and Brandon United moved to the Northern Amateur League. Belford, Durham University and Newcastle United "A" also left. Dudley Welfare joined from the Northern Combination, Stockton Buffs joined from the Teesside League, Wigton joined from the Carlisle & District League and Bedlington United joined from the Tyneside Amateur League, changing their name to Bedlington Terriers. Cramlington High Pit and Shotton Comrades also joined.

1980-81

Percy Main Amateurs	30	23	6	1	97	38	52
Ryhope Community Association	30	20	4	6	67	38	44
Bedlington Terriers	30	18	7	5	70	26	43
Forest Hall	30	19	5	6	67	33	43
Stockton Buffs	30	14	10	6	49	30	38
Dudley Welfare	30	13	9	8	58	48	35
Carlisle City	30	14	7	9	50	48	35
Wigton	30	11	8	11	46	37	30
Cramlington High Pit	30	11	4	15	54	57	26
Stobswood Welfare	30	9	8	13	41	54	26
Sunderland Pyrex	30	6	10	14	40	62	22
Shotton Comrades	30	8	4	18	37	55	20
Cramlington New Town	30	8	4	18	33	75	20
Alnwick Town	30	3	12	15	44	66	18
Wallington	30	4	7	19	44	78	15
Morpeth Town	30	5	3	22	41	93	13

Sunderland Pyrex left the league. Wallsend Town joined from the Wearside League, Darlington Cleveland Bridge joined from the Darlington & District League and Esh Winning Pineapple joined from the Durham & District Sunday League. Cramlington High Pit changed their name to High Pit Social.

1981-82

Percy Main Amateurs	34	23	5	6	77	38	51
Morpeth Town	34	21	6	7	74	49	48
Bedlington Terriers	34	19	6	9	81	37	44
Forest Hall	34	18	8	8	68	33	44
High Pit Social	34	18	8	8	63	47	44
Esh Winning Pineapple	34	17	7	10	58	41	41
Darlington Cleveland Bridge	34	15	8	11	52	42	38
Dudley Welfare	34	15	8	11	44	42	38
Ryhope Community Association	34	16	5	13	52	46	37
Carlisle City	34	13	6	15	47	58	32
Wigton	34	11	9	14	50	50	31
Shotton Comrades	34	10	10	14	42	50	30
Cramlington New Town	34	14	2	18	49	64	30
Stockton Buffs	34	10	7	17	40	55	27
Wallsend Town	34	7	6	21	43	68	20
Stobswood Welfare	34	7	6	21	36	82	20
Alnwick Town	34	7	5	22	59	90	19
Wallington	34	6	6	22	34	77	18

Stockton Buffs changed their name to Stockton Town during the season. Alnwick Town, Bedlington Terriers, Esh Winning Pineapple and Ryhope Community Association all left to become founder members of the Northern League's new Division Two. Wallington and Cramlington New Town also left. High Pit Social disbanded but were replaced by a new club called Seaton Terrace who took over their ground and signed most of their players. Prudhoe joined from the Newcastle & District Welfare League.

1982-83

Darlington Cleveland Bridge	24	14	7	3	55	27	35
Percy Main Amateurs	24	14	4	6	52	29	32
Dudley Welfare	24	13	6	5	48	33	32
Seaton Terrace	24	12	7	5	52	32	31
Stobswood Welfare	24	11	8	5	54	38	30
Wallsend Town	24	12	5	7	30	32	29
Prudhoe	24	9	6	9	51	50	24
Shotton Comrades	24	8	6	10	51	44	22
Wigton	24	7	4	13	32	40	18
Carlisle City	24	5	6	13	43	64	16
Morpeth Town	24	4	9	11	40	51	15
Forest Hall	24	4	5	15	27	58	13
Stockton Town	24	4	5	15	27	64	13

Morpeth Town had 2 points deducted.
Darlington Cleveland Bridge and Shotton Comrades both moved to the Northern League. Stockton Town also left. West Allotment Celtic joined from the Northern Amateur League and Haltwhistle Crown Paints joined as a new club formed by a merger of Haltwhistle United and Hadrian Paints. Ponteland United and Seaton Delaval Amateurs also joined.

1983-84

Morpeth Town	26	16	6	4	63	32	38
Dudley Welfare	26	13	6	7	49	34	32
Stobswood Welfare	26	12	7	7	63	42	31
Seaton Terrace	26	11	9	6	49	39	31
West Allotment Celtic	26	10	10	6	41	34	30
Prudhoe	26	12	5	9	45	42	29
Wigton	26	10	8	8	51	45	28
Seaton Delaval Amateurs	26	8	7	11	37	34	23
Ponteland United	26	7	9	10	38	38	23
Wallsend Town	26	8	7	11	40	50	23
Haltwhistle Crown Paints	26	8	5	13	44	58	21
Forest Hall	26	6	8	12	32	51	20
Percy Main Amateurs	26	7	5	14	33	66	19
Carlisle City	26	4	8	14	27	47	16

Prudhoe disbanded. Gosforth St. Nicholas and Prudhoe East End both joined from the Northern Combination.

1984-85

Dudley Welfare	28	19	3	6	58	28	41
Morpeth Town	28	16	7	5	49	30	39
Prudhoe East End	28	15	8	5	70	37	38
Ponteland United	28	15	5	8	60	29	35
Seaton Delaval Amateurs	28	14	7	7	46	40	35
West Allotment Celtic	28	10	9	9	56	42	29
Seaton Terrace	28	11	7	10	48	43	29
Forest Hall	28	11	7	10	44	44	29
Wallsend Town	28	11	6	11	51	58	28
Stobswood Welfare	28	9	9	10	40	49	27
Wigton	28	9	6	13	46	49	24
Percy Main Amateurs	28	9	3	16	50	57	21
Carlisle City	28	7	5	16	43	73	19
Gosforth St. Nicholas	28	7	1	20	39	85	15
Haltwhistle Crown Paints	28	2	7	19	28	64	11

Haltwhistle Crown Paints moved to the Northern Combination. Winlaton Queens Head joined from the Northern Amateur League and Gateshead Tyne Sports also joined. Seaton Terrace changed their name to Seaton Delaval Seaton Terrace.

1985-86

Gateshead Tyne Sports	30	21	6	3	80	37	48
Prudhoe East End	30	17	9	4	68	38	43
Morpeth Town	30	16	6	8	51	39	38
Winlaton Queen's Head	30	12	11	7	53	40	35
West Allotment Celtic	30	12	8	10	48	36	32
Wigton	30	10	12	8	58	48	32
Seaton Delaval Seaton Terrace	30	11	9	10	56	54	31
Seaton Delaval Amateurs	30	12	6	12	54	61	30
Carlisle City	30	13	3	14	50	56	29
Ponteland United	30	11	6	13	48	49	28
Dudley Welfare	30	11	6	13	52	57	28
Forest Hall	30	9	8	13	56	55	26
Percy Main Amateurs	30	10	5	15	68	69	25
Gosforth St. Nicholas	30	7	10	13	42	51	24
Wallsend Town	30	4	8	18	40	81	16
Stobswood Welfare	30	4	7	19	37	90	15

Wallsend Town moved to the Northern Amateur League and Stobswood Welfare moved to the Northern Combination. Heaton Stannington joined from the Northern Amateur League and Swalwell joined from the Northern Combination. Gateshead Tyne Sports changed their name to Dunston Tyne Sports.

1986-87

West Allotment Celtic	30	15	10	5	61	40	40
Dunston Tyne Sports	30	16	8	6	63	38	40
Morpeth Town	30	16	5	9	73	51	37
Gosforth St. Nicholas	30	12	10	8	45	37	34
Ponteland United	30	14	6	10	46	43	34
Winlaton Queen's Head	30	11	10	9	53	49	32
Prudhoe East End	30	10	11	9	43	40	31
Forest Hall	30	9	11	10	52	43	29
Wigton	30	13	3	14	66	70	29
Seaton Delaval Seaton Terrace	30	12	5	13	47	57	29
Percy Main Amateurs	30	10	8	12	59	65	28
Dudley Welfare	30	9	10	11	44	52	28
Heaton Stannington	30	7	11	12	50	53	25
Swalwell	30	10	5	15	48	64	25
Seaton Delaval Amateurs	30	8	5	17	44	60	21
Carlisle City	30	6	6	18	38	70	18

Carlisle City moved to the Northern Combination and Newbiggin Central Welfare joined from the Northern Amateur League.

1987-88

Seaton Delaval Seaton Terrace	28	20	3	5	66	35	43
Prudhoe East End	28	18	3	7	81	45	39
Gosforth St. Nicholas	28	16	7	5	61	30	39
West Allotment Celtic	28	17	5	6	75	49	39
Forest Hall	28	11	7	10	55	53	29
Dudley Welfare	28	12	5	11	58	57	29
Heaton Stannington	28	12	4	12	42	43	28
Seaton Delaval Amateurs	28	10	7	11	50	56	27
Morpeth Town	28	11	4	13	51	52	26
Wigton	28	11	3	14	48	52	25
Percy Main Amateurs	28	8	6	14	42	54	22
Newbiggin Central Welfare	28	8	5	15	65	86	21
Ponteland United	28	9	2	17	41	67	20
Swalwell	28	7	4	17	39	62	18
Dunston Tyne Sports	28	6	3	19	37	70	15

Winlaton Queen's Head resigned during the second week of September and their record was deleted.
Prudhoe East End moved to the Northern League.

The league expanded to 3 divisions following amalgamation with the Northern Combination and the Northern Amateur League. The existing division became the Premier Division and there were new divisions, One and Two.

The Premier Division consisted of the 14 remaining clubs from the existing division plus Wark and Stobswood Welfare who both joined from the Northern Combination.

The new Division One consisted of Carlisle City, Haltwhistle Crown Paints, Heddon Institute, Lynemouth Alcan, New York Bay Plastics, Newcastle University, Ryton, Seaton Sluice, Wallsend Rising Sun and Winlaton Hallgarth who all joined from the disbanded Northern Combination; Ashington Premier, Gosforth Bohemian, Hexham Swinton, Gateshead Northern Counties and Westerhope Hillheads who all joined from the disbanded Northern Amateur League, plus newly formed Walker Central.

The new Division Two consisted of Belford, Longbenton, Monkseaton K.O.S.A., Northern Electric ERC, Procter & Gamble and Whitley Bay Athletic who all joined from the disbanded Northern Amateur League; Norgas United and Ryton Adult Association who all joined from the Tyneside Amateur League; Brunswick Village and Woolsington Athletic who both joined from the Newcastle & District Welfare League; Gosforth Brandling Arms and Highfields United who joined from the North-West Durham Combination; plus Blyth Kitty Brewster, South Shields BCA, Stobswood United and Walker Stack.

Promoted clubs are shown in bold type, relegated clubs in bold italics.

Three points for a win was introduced.

1988-89

Premier Division

Seaton Delaval Seaton Terrace	28	22	3	3	72	25	69
West Allotment Celtic	28	20	2	6	84	38	62
Seaton Delaval Amateurs	28	18	4	6	57	32	58
Dunston Tyne Sports	28	12	6	10	52	48	42
Newbiggin Central Welfare	28	12	5	11	51	51	41
Heaton Stannington	28	12	5	11	38	42	41
Swalwell	28	11	6	11	61	57	39
Ponteland United	28	10	5	13	55	54	35
Morpeth Town	28	9	8	11	54	62	35
Forest Hall	28	11	3	14	47	48	33
Wark	28	9	6	13	52	56	33
Dudley Welfare	28	8	7	13	57	64	31
Percy Main Amateurs	28	9	4	15	50	66	31
Wigton	28	6	5	17	46	78	23
Stobswood Welfare	**28**	**5**	**3**	**20**	**56**	**111**	**15**

Forest Hall and Stobswood Welfare each had 3 points deducted.
Gosforth St. Nicholas resigned and disbanded early in the season and their record was deleted.
Stobswood Welfare merged with Stobswood United of Division Two and were placed in Division One as Stobswood Welfare.

Northern Alliance 1989-1990

1989-90

Division One

Ashington Premier	30	20	3	7	76	45	63
Haltwhistle Crown Paints	30	17	10	3	69	31	61
Westerhope Hillheads	30	17	8	5	82	41	59
Carlisle City	30	17	6	7	77	55	57
Hexham Swinton	30	17	5	8	63	49	56
Ryton	30	15	8	7	66	37	53
Gateshead Northern Counties	30	15	8	7	53	29	53
Winlaton Hallgarth	30	13	11	6	55	38	50
Walker Central	30	11	4	15	57	67	37
Gosforth Bohemian	30	10	3	17	57	70	33
Newcastle University	30	10	2	18	56	68	32
Lynemouth Alcan	30	9	4	17	42	81	31
New York Bay Plastics	30	8	4	18	56	58	28
Heddon Institute	30	7	7	16	52	68	28
Seaton Sluice	30	7	3	20	36	95	24
Wallsend Rising Sun	30	2	4	24	29	94	19

Lynemouth Alcan and Seaton Sluice left the league and Pegswood joined.
Ashington Premier changed their name to Ashington & Pegswood.

Division Two

Blyth Kitty Brewster	30	20	5	5	84	35	65
Stobswood United	30	21	2	7	77	40	65
Walker Stack	30	19	6	5	73	42	63
Northern Electric ERC	30	18	4	8	71	29	58
Belford	30	15	4	11	62	48	49
Longbenton	30	16	3	11	73	54	48
South Shields BCA	30	13	8	9	55	41	47
Monkseaton K.O.S.A.	30	11	9	10	42	46	42
Highfields United	30	11	6	13	54	53	39
Brunswick Village	30	11	2	17	53	63	35
Ryton Adult Association	30	9	7	14	41	73	34
Norgas United	30	7	8	15	58	80	29
Procter & Gamble	30	6	11	13	44	66	29
Woolsington Athletic	30	9	6	15	61	87	27
Gosforth Brandling Arms	30	5	5	20	46	85	20
Whitley Bay Athletic	30	4	4	22	44	96	16

Longbenton had 3 points deducted.
Woolsington Athletic had 6 points deducted.

Division Two Championship play-off

Blyth Kitty Brewster vs Stobswood United	2-1

Stobswood United merged with Stobswood Welfare of the Premier Division and were placed in Division One as Stobswood Welfare. Belford, South Shields BCA, Walker Stack, Whitley Bay Athletic and Woolsington Athletic all left. Ashington Hirst Progressive, Berwick Spittal Rovers, Brinkburn, North Shields St. Columba's, Percy Rovers Alnwick, Portland Arms, Shankhouse and Swalwell Cricket Club all joined. Brunswick Village changed their name to Heaton Corner House and Gosforth Brandling Arms changed their name to Gosforth Victoria. Ryton Adult Association merged with Newburn to form Newburn & Ryton Adult Association who continued in Division Two.

1989-90

Premier Division

Seaton Delaval Amateurs	28	18	5	5	63	39	59
West Allotment Celtic	28	17	7	4	72	34	58
Forest Hall	28	17	6	5	79	28	57
Newbiggin Central Welfare	28	17	3	8	70	43	54
Ponteland United	28	17	3	8	62	35	54
Percy Main Amateurs	28	14	3	11	53	39	45
Wigton	28	12	5	11	56	55	41
Heaton Stannington	28	11	7	10	39	41	40
Seaton Delaval Seaton Terrace	28	9	8	11	46	44	35
Morpeth Town	28	11	2	15	55	70	35
Swalwell	28	9	5	14	50	52	32
Haltwhistle Crown Paints	28	6	7	15	27	51	25
Dunston Tyne Sports	28	9	1	18	44	74	25
Wark	28	8	1	19	44	72	22
Dudley Welfare	**28**	**1**	**5**	**22**	**23**	**106**	**8**

Dunston Tyne Sports and Wark each had 3 points deducted.
Ashington & Pegswood resigned mid-season and their record was deleted.
Dunston Tyne Sports and Wigton left the league and Carlisle Gilford Park joined. Walker Central changed their name following their promotion from Division One and joined the Premier Division as Walker while Westerhope Hillheads joined the Premier Division as Westerhope.

Division One

Westerhope Hillheads	30	22	7	1	87	23	73
Walker Central	30	19	5	7	93	47	62
Hexham Swinton	30	18	7	5	62	35	61
Carlisle City	30	18	4	8	89	44	58
Blyth Kitty Brewster	30	17	7	6	93	52	58
Ryton	30	16	7	7	65	37	55
Stobswood Welfare	30	15	2	13	55	58	47
Gateshead Northern Counties	30	13	5	12	71	57	44
Northern Electric E.R.C.	30	13	4	13	67	59	43
Winlaton Hallgarth	30	12	4	14	52	50	40
New York Bay Plastics	30	9	3	18	59	65	30
Wallsend Rising Sun	30	9	3	18	38	83	30
Newcastle University	30	8	4	18	42	66	28
Heddon Institute	**30**	**8**	**4**	**18**	**45**	**86**	**19**
Gosforth Bohemian	**30**	**5**	**2**	**23**	**37**	**93**	**17**
Pegswood	30	2	4	23	26	114	10

Heddon Institute had 9 points deducted.
Pegswood left the league. Walker Central changed their name to Walker and Westerhope Hillheads changed their name to Westerhope.

Division Two

Heaton Corner House	**28**	**21**	**3**	**4**	**79**	**32**	**66**
Longbenton	**28**	**19**	**4**	**5**	**74**	**41**	**61**
Berwick Spittal Rovers	**28**	**18**	**4**	**6**	**79**	**34**	**58**
Portland Arms	28	18	2	8	80	40	56
Shankhouse	28	15	7	6	70	43	52
Swalwell Cricket Club	28	13	3	12	70	53	42
Brinkburn	28	12	4	12	50	44	40
Ashington Hirst Progressive	28	10	7	11	49	47	37
North Shields St. Columba's	28	10	6	12	55	70	36
Highfields United	28	9	8	11	43	47	35
Percy Rovers Alnwick	28	11	4	13	50	67	34
Monkseaton K.O.S.A.	28	9	5	14	48	66	32
Procter & Gamble	28	5	6	17	31	64	21
Norgas United	28	2	5	21	28	96	11
Gosforth Victoria	28	2	4	22	40	108	10

Percy Rovers Alnwick had 3 points deducted.
Newburn & Ryton Adult Association resigned mid-season and their record was deleted.
Gosforth Victoria and Portland Arms both left the league.
Hebburn N.E.I. Reyrolle, Newsham B.D. and Wylam Home Service joined.
Brinkburn changed their name to South Shields W.R.S. Brinkburn.

1990-91

Premier Division

West Allotment Celtic	28	20	2	6	82	35	62
Seaton Delaval Seaton Terrace	28	17	3	8	65	34	54
Heaton Stannington	28	13	10	5	57	37	49
Seaton Delaval Amateurs	28	13	7	8	50	42	46
Forest Hall	28	13	4	11	50	44	43
Swalwell	28	11	9	8	56	54	42
Walker	28	10	9	9	47	43	39
Newbiggin Central Welfare	28	12	3	13	52	65	39
Ponteland United	28	10	7	11	44	47	37
Westerhope Hillheads	28	9	6	13	52	53	33
Carlisle Gillford Park	28	9	6	13	59	64	33
Morpeth Town	28	10	2	16	49	70	32
Haltwhistle Crown Paints	28	8	6	14	38	55	30
Wark	28	8	5	15	43	68	29
Percy Main Amateurs	**28**	**3**	**9**	**16**	**33**	**66**	**18**

Division One

Blyth Kitty Brewster	**28**	**21**	**1**	**6**	**84**	**39**	**64**
Berwick Spittal Rovers	**28**	**18**	**6**	**4**	**95**	**39**	**60**
Heaton Corner House	28	17	5	6	80	36	56
Winlaton Hallgarth	28	17	5	6	62	32	56
Longbenton	28	15	5	8	64	40	50
Carlisle City	28	15	5	8	73	51	50
Dudley Welfare	28	13	6	9	56	51	45
Hexham Swinton	28	12	3	13	64	61	39
Ryton	28	11	6	11	51	56	39
Gateshead Northern Counties	28	10	4	14	51	63	31
Newcastle University	28	8	3	17	50	62	27
New York Bay Plastics	28	8	2	18	43	88	26
Northern Electric ERC	28	5	6	17	37	68	21
Wallsend Rising Sun	28	4	4	20	23	85	16
Stobswood Welfare	**28**	**4**	**3**	**21**	**40**	**102**	**15**

Gateshead Northern Counties had 3 points deducted.
Heaton Corner House changed their name to Newcastle Benfield Park.
New York Bay Plastics changed their name to New York United.
Northern Electric E.R.C. changed their name to Northern Electric (Wallsend). Wylam Home Service changed their name following their promotion and joined Division One as Wylam.

Division Two

Procter & Gamble	**28**	**18**	**4**	**6**	**82**	**54**	**58**
Wylam Home Service	**28**	**17**	**6**	**5**	**77**	**40**	**57**
Hebburn N.E.I. Reyrolle	**28**	**16**	**5**	**7**	**71**	**36**	**53**
Percy Rovers Alnwick	28	15	7	6	79	45	52
Ashington Hirst Progressive	28	16	4	8	80	47	52
North Shields St. Columba's	28	15	3	10	80	55	48
Monkseaton K.O.S.A.	28	14	6	8	54	48	48
Swalwell Cricket Club	28	14	4	10	64	59	46
South Shields W.R.S. Brinkburn	28	14	2	12	76	63	44
Shankhouse	28	13	2	13	57	55	41
Norgas United	28	10	4	14	65	66	34
Newsham B.D.	28	8	3	17	63	78	27
Gosforth Bohemian	28	6	3	19	31	74	21
Heddon Institute	28	2	6	20	35	114	12
Highfields United	28	1	3	24	24	104	6

Newsham B.D. left the league. Amble Town, Marden Athletic and Spartan Blyth all joined. Wylam Home Service changed their name to Wylam.

1991-92

Premier Division

West Allotment Celtic	30	20	4	6	77	26	64
Walker	30	18	4	8	63	35	58
Carlisle Gillford Park	30	17	5	8	77	35	56
Seaton Delaval Amateurs	30	15	9	6	62	35	54
Berwick Spittal Rovers	30	16	4	10	56	32	52
Seaton Delaval Seaton Terrace	30	15	6	9	65	45	51
Westerhope	30	13	6	11	48	46	45
Wark	30	12	7	11	62	58	43
Haltwhistle Crown Paints	30	13	5	12	39	38	41
Ponteland United	30	11	7	12	55	46	40
Blyth Kitty Brewster	30	11	7	12	48	54	40
Forest Hall	30	9	8	13	38	55	35
Morpeth Town	30	8	8	14	38	61	32
Heaton Stannington	30	7	10	13	42	39	31
Swalwell	**30**	**3**	**7**	**20**	**33**	**72**	**16**
Newbiggin Central Welfare	**30**	**2**	**3**	**25**	**31**	**157**	**6**

Haltwhistle Crown Paints and Newbiggin Central Welfare each had 3 points deducted.

Division One

Carlisle City	**30**	**24**	**3**	**3**	**121**	**32**	**75**
Winlaton Hallgarth	**30**	**19**	**8**	**3**	**75**	**38**	**65**
Longbenton	30	18	7	5	69	49	61
Newcastle Benfield Park	30	15	8	7	69	44	53
Percy Main Amateurs	30	14	5	11	60	53	47
Hebburn N.E.I. Reyrolle	30	12	7	11	61	56	43
Wylam	30	11	9	10	58	56	42
Ryton	30	11	9	10	56	57	42
Procter & Gamble	30	12	5	13	71	71	41
Northern Electric (Wallsend)	30	10	6	14	53	69	36
Gateshead Northern Counties	30	9	8	13	51	66	35
New York United	30	8	9	13	48	63	33
Dudley Welfare	30	7	9	14	52	72	30
Hexham Swinton	30	10	2	18	46	68	29
Newcastle University	**30**	**5**	**6**	**19**	**33**	**69**	**21**
Wallsend Rising Sun	**30**	**3**	**3**	**24**	**34**	**95**	**12**

Hexham Swinton had 3 points deducted.

Division Two

North Shields St. Columba's	**28**	**22**	**4**	**2**	**64**	**25**	**70**
Percy Rovers Alnwick	**28**	**20**	**4**	**4**	**76**	**32**	**64**
South Shields W.R.S. Brinkburn	28	16	7	5	103	50	52
Shankhouse	28	14	9	5	82	42	51
Ashington Hirst Progressive	28	15	6	7	74	54	51
Amble Town	28	15	5	8	75	49	50
Marden Athletic	28	12	7	9	57	57	43
Gosforth Bohemian	28	11	6	11	63	54	39
Swalwell Cricket Club	28	9	8	11	69	70	35
Norgas United	28	9	4	15	62	65	31
Monkseaton K.O.S.A.	28	7	6	15	40	77	27
Highfields United	28	6	4	18	53	90	22
Stobswood Welfare	28	4	9	15	48	72	21
Heddon Institute	28	5	4	19	34	79	19
Swinton Brinkburn	28	1	5	22	15	99	8

Swinton Brinkburn left the league. New Winning joined from the South-East Northumberland League and Newcastle D.H.S.S. joined from the Tyneside Amateur League. Swalwell Cricket Club changed their name to Swalwell Crowley and South Shields W.R.S. Brinkburn changed their name to County Kitchens Brinkburn.

Northern Alliance 1992-1994

1992-93

Premier Division

Seaton Delaval Amateurs	30	20	6	4	79	34	66
West Allotment Celtic	30	21	3	6	86	35	66
Carlisle City	30	19	6	5	80	41	63
Morpeth Town	30	20	3	7	67	37	63
Seaton Delaval Seaton Terrace	30	18	1	11	74	46	55
Walker	30	15	5	10	75	52	50
Carlisle Gillford Park	30	13	9	8	72	56	48
Ponteland United	30	13	6	11	71	59	45
Haltwhistle Crown Paints	30	12	5	13	43	41	41
Winlaton Hallgarth	30	12	4	14	58	64	40
Berwick Spittal Rovers	30	12	3	15	55	54	39
Heaton Stannington	30	9	4	17	49	68	31
Wark	30	8	2	20	45	79	26
Blyth Kitty Brewster	30	7	5	18	50	100	26
Westerhope	30	5	7	18	36	66	22
Forest Hall	**30**	**1**	**1**	**28**	**24**	**132**	**4**

Division One

Longbenton	**30**	**21**	**4**	**5**	**105**	**38**	**67**
Newbiggin Central Welfare	30	21	2	7	80	36	65
Newcastle Benfield Park	30	19	3	8	84	42	60
North Shields St. Columba's	30	16	6	8	63	50	54
Hebburn N.E.I. Reyrolle	30	14	7	9	76	60	49
Wylam	30	14	7	9	66	50	49
Swalwell	30	12	7	11	53	48	43
Procter & Gamble	30	11	8	11	61	59	41
Dudley Welfare	30	10	8	12	60	69	38
Percy Rovers Alnwick	30	11	5	14	57	68	38
Gateshead Northern Counties	30	10	6	14	52	74	36
New York United	30	8	8	14	49	62	32
Percy Main Amateurs	30	9	5	16	52	70	32
Ryton	30	7	7	16	41	69	28
Hexham Swinton	30	5	6	19	36	94	21
Northern Electric (Wallsend)	**30**	**5**	**5**	**20**	**48**	**94**	**20**

New York United left the league. Hebburn N.E.I. Reyrolle changed their name to Hebburn Reyrolle. Percy Rovers Alnwick changed their name to Percy Rovers.

Division Two

Amble Town	**30**	**24**	**3**	**3**	**132**	**42**	**75**
Gosforth Bohemian	**30**	**23**	**3**	**4**	**101**	**43**	**72**
Ashington Hirst Progressive	30	23	3	4	104	52	72
Shankhouse	30	20	2	8	92	46	62
County Kitchens Brinkburn	30	18	3	9	119	68	57
Marden Athletic	30	16	6	8	69	48	54
Highfields United	30	13	3	14	73	76	42
Monkseaton K.O.S.A.	30	12	7	11	58	69	40
Swalwell Crowley	30	12	3	15	70	74	39
Newcastle D.H.S.S.	30	10	5	15	58	87	34
Newcastle University	30	9	6	15	58	57	33
Norgas United	30	8	4	18	79	100	28
Stobswood Welfare	30	7	5	18	52	106	26
Heddon Institute	30	6	7	17	43	74	25
New Winning	30	5	3	22	73	127	18
Wallsend Rising Sun	30	2	1	27	32	144	7

Monkseaton K.O.S.A. had 3 points deducted.
County Kitchens Brinkburn moved to the Wearside League, changing their name to South Shields County Kitchens. Swalwell Crowley resigned just before the start of the 1993-94 season. Gateshead Durham Rangers joined from South-East Northumberland League and Shilbottle Colliery Welfare joined from the North Northumberland League.

1993-94

Premier Division

Morpeth Town	30	25	2	3	86	27	77
Carlisle City	30	22	3	5	73	33	69
Ponteland United	30	18	5	7	80	43	59
Seaton Delaval Amateurs	30	16	7	7	61	37	55
West Allotment Celtic	30	17	3	10	74	48	54
Carlisle Gillford Park	30	13	7	10	56	31	46
Walker	30	14	3	13	64	57	45
Berwick Spittal Rovers	30	13	5	12	40	44	44
Winlaton Hallgarth	30	12	6	12	58	50	42
Seaton Delaval Seaton Terrace	30	12	6	12	49	47	42
Longbenton	30	11	6	13	60	53	39
Westerhope	30	11	3	16	40	55	36
Blyth Kitty Brewster	30	8	3	19	39	76	27
Haltwhistle Crown Paints	30	6	5	19	38	51	20
Heaton Stannington	30	4	4	22	38	117	16
Wark	30	2	4	24	31	118	10

Haltwhistle Crown Paints had 3 points deducted.
Morpeth Town moved to the Northern League. Seaton Delaval Seaton Terrace merged with Seaton Delaval Amateurs, continuing in the Premier Division as Seaton Delaval Amateurs. Blyth Kitty Brewster changed their name to Blyth Seahorse and Winlaton Hallgarth changed their name to Winlaton.

Division One

Amble Town	28	21	4	3	100	29	67
Newcastle Benfield Park	**28**	**19**	**6**	**3**	**84**	**20**	**63**
Hebburn Reyrolle	28	20	3	5	84	34	63
Swalwell	28	16	6	6	67	40	54
Dudley Welfare	28	12	7	9	51	55	43
Ryton	28	13	4	11	45	52	43
North Shields St. Columba's	28	13	6	9	62	47	42
Hexham Swinton	28	10	7	11	48	46	37
Newbiggin Central Welfare	28	9	9	10	57	49	36
Percy Main Amateurs	28	11	2	15	53	80	35
Gosforth Bohemian	28	9	4	15	51	67	31
Procter & Gamble	28	7	4	17	34	76	25
Gateshead Northern Counties	28	7	4	17	45	72	22
Wylam	28	6	1	21	35	86	19
Forest Hall	28	2	3	23	20	83	9

Percy Rovers failed to complete their fixtures and their record was deleted. North Shields St. Columba's and Gateshead Northern Counties each had 3 points deducted. New Winning changed their name following their promotion and joined Division One as Orwin Rosehill.

Division Two

Ashington Hirst Progressive	**28**	**23**	**4**	**1**	**126**	**38**	**73**
New Winning	**28**	**20**	**4**	**4**	**91**	**49**	**64**
Shankhouse	28	18	4	6	93	25	58
Heddon Institute	28	17	2	9	73	41	53
Newcastle University	28	15	2	11	56	58	47
Marden Athletic	28	16	1	11	70	56	46
Highfields United	28	14	3	11	67	47	45
Stobswood Welfare	28	14	2	12	68	48	44
Newcastle D.H.S.S.	28	14	5	9	60	62	44
Norgas United	28	11	2	15	52	83	35
Monkseaton K.O.S.A.	28	7	6	15	45	59	27
Durham Rangers	28	8	3	17	53	83	27
Shilbottle Colliery Welfare	28	6	4	18	32	62	22
Northern Electric (Wallsend)	28	5	1	22	36	82	16
Wallsend Rising Sun	28	0	1	27	19	148	1

Marden Athletic and Newcastle D.H.S.S. each had 3 points deducted. Wallsend Rising Sun moved to the South-East Northumberland League and Northern Electric (Wallsend) also left. Otterburn and Rutherford Newcastle both joined from the North-East Amateur League, Walker Ledwood Fosse joined from the Tyneside Amateur League, Hexham Border Counties joined from the Hexham & North Tyne League, Throckley & District Social Club joined from the Newcastle & District Welfare League and Alnwick Aydon Forest joined from the North Northumberland League. New Winning changed their name to Orwin Rosehill, Highfields United changed their name to Highfields United Berwick and Durham Rangers changed their name to Wheelcroft.

1994-95
Premier Division

Newcastle Benfield Park	28	20	4	4	76	32	64
West Allotment Celtic	28	20	2	6	78	34	62
Carlisle Gillford Park	28	19	4	5	74	30	61
Seaton Delaval Amateurs	28	18	6	4	72	38	60
Carlisle City	28	18	5	5	93	39	59
Ponteland United	28	15	6	7	64	43	51
Westerhope	28	11	9	8	61	53	42
Winlaton	28	13	5	10	69	55	41
Blyth Seahorse	28	9	7	12	53	60	34
Berwick Spittal Rovers	28	9	6	13	54	47	33
Heaton Stannington	28	7	2	19	46	80	23
Walker	28	8	3	17	57	72	21
Longbenton	28	5	4	19	40	92	16
Haltwhistle Crown Paints	28	2	3	23	21	102	9
Wark	**28**	**2**	**2**	**24**	**20**	**101**	**8**

Winlaton and Longbenton each had 3 points deducted.
Walker had 6 points deducted. Middlesbrough "A" joined the league.
Walker changed their name to Walker Central.

Division One

Amble Town	**30**	**24**	**0**	**6**	**108**	**45**	**72**
North Shields St. Columba's	**30**	**19**	**4**	**7**	**77**	**46**	**61**
Hexham Swinton	30	17	8	5	59	40	59
Orwin Rosehill	30	18	4	8	96	51	58
Ashington Hirst Progressive	30	16	4	10	98	64	52
Percy Main Amateurs	30	13	9	8	60	37	48
Newbiggin Central Welfare	30	14	4	12	70	72	46
Hebburn Reyrolle	30	13	6	11	90	64	45
Dudley Welfare	30	13	4	13	64	75	43
Forest Hall	30	12	6	12	49	52	42
Gosforth Bohemian	30	10	5	15	55	68	35
Swalwell	30	8	10	12	63	76	31
Procter & Gamble	30	8	2	20	54	90	26
Ryton	30	6	6	18	51	86	24
Gateshead Northern Counties	30	5	5	20	46	122	20
Wylam	30	4	3	23	52	104	15

Gateshead Northern Counties left the league.
Orwin Rosehill changed their name to Orwin.

Division Two

Walker Ledwood Fosse	**30**	**24**	**2**	**4**	**118**	**43**	**74**
Shankhouse	**30**	**21**	**1**	**8**	**108**	**45**	**64**
Rutherford Newcastle	30	20	3	7	98	42	63
Newcastle University	30	18	5	7	77	57	59
Monkseaton K.O.S.A.	30	13	6	11	66	65	45
Otterburn	30	12	8	10	51	43	44
Highfields United Berwick	30	13	2	15	71	65	41
Heddon Institute	30	11	7	12	67	68	40
Hexham Border Counties	30	12	4	14	66	91	40
Wheelcroft	30	11	5	14	57	71	38
Throckley & District Social Club	30	16	1	13	82	65	37
Stobswood Welfare	30	11	4	15	55	71	37
Marden Athletic	30	10	4	16	66	78	34
Aydon Park	30	9	4	17	63	83	31
Shilbottle Colliery Welfare	30	7	5	18	52	87	26
Norgas United	30	0	3	27	29	152	0

Norgas United had 3 points deducted.
Throckley & District Social Club had 12 points deducted.
Newcastle D.H.S. withdrew during the season and their record was deleted.
Norgas United, Stobswood Welfare, Throckley & District Social Club and Wheelcroft all left the league. Wallington joined from the North Northumberland League, Walbottle Masons joined from the South-East Northumberland League and Newcastle B.T. and Northbank also joined.
Aydon Park changed their name to Aydon Forest.

1995-96
Premier Division

Seaton Delaval Amateurs	32	23	4	5	97	39	73
Carlisle City	32	19	10	3	85	23	67
Carlisle Gillford Park	32	20	6	6	62	23	66
Newcastle Benfield Park	32	21	3	8	73	41	66
Middlesbrough "A"	32	17	7	8	79	37	58
West Allotment Celtic	32	18	4	10	79	49	58
Ponteland United	32	15	7	10	73	39	52
Amble Town	32	15	6	11	81	58	51
Haltwhistle Crown Paints	32	14	5	13	52	58	47
Walker Central	32	13	5	14	59	62	44
North Shields St. Columba's	32	12	7	13	56	55	43
Westerhope	32	13	4	15	58	68	43
Winlaton	32	9	9	14	59	56	36
Blyth Seahorse	32	7	2	23	32	86	20
Berwick Spittal Rovers	32	5	6	21	27	71	18
Longbenton	**32**	**4**	**1**	**27**	**29**	**156**	**13**
Heaton Stannington	**32**	**3**	**2**	**27**	**34**	**114**	**11**

Blyth Seahorse and Berwick Spittal Rovers each had 3 points deducted.
Blyth Seahorse left the league and Hartlepool United "A" joined.
Westerhope changed their name to Lemington United S&S, Haltwhistle Crown Paints changed their name to Haltwhistle and Winlaton changed their name to Winlaton Hallgarth.

Division One

Gosforth Bohemian	**30**	**25**	**3**	**2**	**100**	**28**	**78**
Walker Ledwood Fosse	**30**	**21**	**5**	**4**	**73**	**33**	**68**
Newbiggin Central Welfare	30	20	4	6	84	41	64
Ryton	30	18	3	9	82	47	57
Orwin	30	14	7	9	83	50	55
Percy Main Amateurs	30	15	5	10	75	55	50
Forest Hall	30	14	5	11	75	62	47
Shankhouse	30	14	5	11	78	70	47
Hebburn Reyrolle	30	13	5	12	68	49	44
Swalwell	30	13	3	14	61	58	42
Dudley Welfare	30	10	5	15	67	79	35
Ashington Hirst Progressive	30	9	4	17	56	79	31
Procter & Gamble	30	7	4	19	42	81	25
Hexham Swinton	30	7	3	20	37	63	24
Wark	**30**	**3**	**4**	**23**	**36**	**110**	**13**
Wylam	30	3	0	27	26	138	9

Dudley Welfare, Forest Hall and Wylam all left the league.

Division Two

Walbottle Masons	**26**	**17**	**3**	**6**	**98**	**51**	**54**
Heddon Institute	**26**	**17**	**2**	**7**	**84**	**41**	**53**
Highfields United Berwick	26	14	7	5	75	37	49
Newcastle B.T.	26	14	6	6	68	44	48
Northbank	26	15	2	9	100	60	47
Rutherford Newcastle	26	12	6	8	72	44	42
Monkseaton K.O.S.A.	26	12	5	9	74	54	41
Newcastle University	26	12	8	6	62	50	38
Otterburn	26	11	5	10	39	39	38
Wallington	26	6	6	14	42	68	24
Aydon Forest	26	5	8	13	37	66	23
Shilbottle Colliery Welfare	26	5	4	17	27	78	17
Hexham Border Counties	26	4	4	18	60	115	16
Marden Athletic	26	5	1	20	46	137	16

Newcastle University had 6 points deducted.
Aydon Forest, Monkseaton K.O.S.A. and Shilbottle Colliery Welfare all left the league. Coxlodge Social Club, Morpeth Town "A", Northern Social Club and Shieldfield Social Club all joined. Marden Athletic changed their name to Whitley Lodge Snooker.

Northern Alliance 1996-1998

1996-97

Premier Division

Lemington United S&S	32	25	4	3	84	25	79
Ponteland United	32	25	3	4	109	30	78
Middlesbrough "A"	32	21	6	5	89	44	69
West Allotment Celtic	32	21	3	8	78	44	66
Carlisle City	32	19	5	8	71	41	59
North Shields St. Columba's	32	14	4	14	60	59	46
Hartlepool United "A"	32	13	6	13	56	56	45
Walker Ledwood Fosse	32	12	6	14	47	71	42
Seaton Delaval Amateurs	32	11	8	13	43	51	41
Berwick Spittal Rovers	32	11	7	14	36	53	40
Carlisle Gillford Park	32	10	5	17	57	65	35
Newcastle Benfield Park	32	10	5	17	52	63	35
Winlaton Hallgarth	32	8	9	15	44	59	33
Walker Central	32	10	3	19	44	67	30
Haltwhistle	32	8	6	18	40	76	30
Amble Town	*32*	*5*	*6*	*21*	*46*	*82*	*21*
Gosforth Bohemian	*32*	*3*	*6*	*23*	*32*	*102*	*15*

Carlisle City and Walker Central each had 3 points deducted.
Haltwhistle and Middlesbrough "A" both left the league.

Division One

Ryton	26	21	1	4	84	27	64
Hebburn Reyrolle	26	19	3	4	65	23	60
Newbiggin Central Welfare	26	17	4	5	68	26	55
Shankhouse	26	16	3	7	65	38	51
Heddon Institute	26	14	4	8	72	49	46
Walbottle Masons	26	14	4	8	77	53	43
Percy Main Amateurs	26	12	5	9	60	40	41
Hexham Swinton	26	10	3	13	38	61	33
Longbenton	26	6	3	17	46	75	21
Heaton Stannington	26	8	3	15	42	79	21
Swalwell	26	4	7	15	45	68	19
Procter & Gamble	26	4	6	16	33	61	18
Ashington Hirst Progressive	26	4	6	16	45	86	18
Orwin	26	4	6	16	32	86	18

Walbottle Masons had 3 points deducted.
Heaton Stannington had 6 points deducted.
Orwin and Walbottle Masons both left the league.

Division Two

Northbank	26	20	4	2	107	23	64
Newcastle University	26	20	3	3	101	25	63
Coxlodge Social	26	18	3	5	108	45	57
Wallington	26	12	9	5	80	54	45
Newcastle B.T.	26	11	6	9	63	49	39
Highfields United Berwick	26	12	3	11	56	56	39
Rutherford Newcastle	26	9	10	7	48	44	37
Shieldfield Social Club	26	11	2	13	57	66	35
Morpeth Town "A"	26	8	7	11	73	58	31
Hexham Border Counties	26	10	1	15	61	97	31
Northern Social Club	26	8	6	12	56	61	30
Otterburn	26	8	4	14	49	55	28
Whitley Lodge Snooker	26	1	5	20	22	169	8
Wark	26	1	3	22	37	116	6

Cullercoats, Gateshead Schooner and Stobhill Rangers joined the league.

1997-98

Premier Division

West Allotment Celtic	28	24	3	1	80	30	75
Lemington United S&S	28	21	3	4	79	31	66
Ponteland United	28	19	2	7	87	41	59
Hartlepool United "A"	28	15	6	7	72	45	51
Carlisle City	28	13	8	7	51	29	47
Ryton	28	11	3	14	56	69	36
Newcastle Benfield Park	28	10	4	14	39	61	34
Winlaton Hallgarth	28	8	7	13	37	57	31
Walker Ledwood Fosse	28	7	9	12	35	43	30
North Shields St. Columba's	28	8	6	14	42	76	30
Hebburn Reyrolle	28	8	7	13	54	53	28
Seaton Delaval Amateurs	28	7	6	15	43	60	27
Carlisle Gillford Park	28	7	6	15	34	52	27
Walker Central	28	5	10	13	33	51	19
Berwick Spittal Rovers	28	5	4	19	31	75	19

Hebburn Reyrolle had 3 points deducted.
Walker Central had 6 points deducted.
Carlisle Gillford Park and Hartlepool United "A" both left the league.

Division One

Shankhouse	26	22	1	3	100	28	67
Northbank	26	21	2	3	113	28	65
Heaton Stannington	26	20	1	5	99	31	61
Heddon Institute	26	16	3	7	82	47	48
Amble Town	26	15	3	8	78	51	48
Newcastle University	26	13	3	10	61	47	42
Newbiggin Central Welfare	26	14	1	11	72	65	40
Percy Main Amateurs	26	10	5	11	59	49	35
Gosforth Bohemian	26	8	5	13	56	83	29
Hexham Swinton	26	8	2	16	54	81	26
Procter & Gamble	26	6	3	17	37	74	21
Longbenton	26	4	3	19	45	95	15
Ashington Hirst Progressive	26	3	3	20	40	90	12
Swalwell	26	3	3	20	31	158	9

Heddon Institute, Newbiggin Central Welfare and Swalwell each had 3 points deducted.
Longbenton and Swalwell left the league.

Division Two

Coxlodge Social	28	22	3	3	116	30	69
Morpeth Town "A"	28	19	4	5	84	42	61
Shieldfield Social Club	28	18	3	7	81	39	57
Highfields United Berwick	28	16	2	10	69	41	50
Northern Social Club	28	13	4	11	76	51	43
Wallington	28	12	4	12	61	56	40
Newcastle B.T.	28	11	6	11	70	54	39
Stobhill Rangers	28	12	3	13	64	57	39
Wark	28	12	3	13	52	48	39
Otterburn	28	11	4	13	57	46	37
Hexham Border Counties	28	10	7	11	64	69	37
Gateshead Schooner	28	10	4	14	68	66	28
Rutherford Newcastle	28	7	7	14	41	64	28
Cullercoats	28	7	6	15	44	62	27
Whitley Bay Snooker	28	0	0	28	16	238	0

Gateshead Schooner had 6 points deducted.
Gateshead Schooner and Whitley Bay Snooker both left the league.
Amble Vikings, Chopwell Top Club and Shiremoor G.H. all joined. It is thought that Shieldfield Social Club changed their name to Newton Park after being promoted.

1998-99

Premier Division

West Allotment Celtic	28	21	4	3	75	31	67
Ponteland United	28	20	4	4	71	25	64
Ryton	28	17	5	6	63	35	56
Northbank	28	15	3	10	52	38	48
Hebburn Reyrolle	28	12	3	13	52	52	39
Newcastle Benfield Park	28	11	4	13	38	51	37
Shankhouse	28	11	6	11	41	36	36
Lemington United S&S	28	11	3	14	36	51	36
Seaton Delaval Amateurs	28	9	7	12	49	53	34
Carlisle City	28	10	4	14	44	51	34
Berwick Spittal Rovers	28	9	6	13	41	59	33
North Shields St. Columba's	28	8	7	13	46	56	31
Winlaton Hallgarth	28	8	4	16	50	68	28
Walker Central	28	8	4	16	33	56	28
Walker Ledwood Fosse	28	6	4	18	27	56	19

Shankhouse and Walker Ledwood Fosse each had 2 points deducted. Lemington United S&S changed their name to Cowgate Social Club and took voluntary relegation to Division Two. North Shields St. Columba's and Newcastle Benfield Park merged, continuing in the Premier Division as Newcastle Benfield Park. Hebburn Reyrolle changed their name to Hebburn S.K.L..

Division One

Percy Main Amateurs	**26**	**20**	**4**	**2**	**83**	**20**	**64**
Coxlodge Social	26	17	3	6	100	42	54
Newcastle University	26	15	7	4	90	35	52
Heaton Stannington	**26**	**11**	**9**	**6**	**68**	**49**	**42**
Newbiggin Central Welfare	**26**	**12**	**5**	**9**	**56**	**57**	**41**
Amble Town	26	13	3	10	58	55	39
Procter & Gamble	26	11	6	9	44	49	39
Heddon Institute	26	10	7	9	64	60	37
Morpeth Town "A"	26	9	5	12	45	50	32
Highfields United Berwick	26	9	3	14	56	72	30
Gosforth Bohemian	26	7	5	14	33	65	26
Ashington Hirst Progressive	26	6	4	16	41	68	22
Hexham Swinton	26	6	2	18	41	101	20
Newton Park	26	3	3	20	33	89	12

Amble Town had 3 points deducted.
Gosforth Bohemian and Newton Park both left the league. Hexham Swinton changed their name to Prudhoe Swinton. Highfields United Berwick changed their name to Highfields United.

Division Two

Amble Vikings	**22**	**16**	**6**	**0**	**62**	**23**	**54**
Cullercoats	**22**	**15**	**3**	**4**	**81**	**32**	**48**
Chopwell Top Club	**22**	**14**	**6**	**2**	**66**	**25**	**48**
Rutherford Newcastle	**22**	**12**	**6**	**4**	**52**	**26**	**42**
Wark	**22**	**9**	**7**	**6**	**43**	**34**	**34**
Northern Social Club	22	9	2	11	55	66	29
Wallington	22	8	6	8	39	47	27
Otterburn	22	6	5	11	44	44	20
Hexham Border Counties	22	4	5	13	41	78	17
Newcastle B.T.	22	5	3	14	32	49	15
Stobhill Rangers	22	5	3	14	32	72	15
Shiremoor G.H.	22	2	3	17	28	79	9

Newcastle B.T., Otterburn and Wallington each had 3 points deducted. Cowgate Social Club joined the league, having taken voluntary relegation from the Premier Division and having changed their name from Lemington United S&S. Hexham Border Counties and Shiremoor G.H. both left. Blyth Spartans "A", Forest Hall, Harraby Catholic Club, Haydon Bridge United, North Sunderland, Northumbria University, Walker Stack F.O.S. and Wallsend United all joined.

1999-2000

Premier Division

West Allotment Celtic	30	20	8	2	73	34	68
Shankhouse	30	20	5	5	62	22	65
Northbank	30	17	7	6	74	43	58
Ponteland United	30	16	7	7	81	37	55
Ryton	30	15	6	9	65	49	51
Carlisle City	30	14	8	8	63	36	50
Percy Main Amateurs	30	13	9	8	55	46	48
Newcastle Benfield Park	30	13	5	12	52	44	44
Walker Central	30	12	6	12	61	58	42
Seaton Delaval Amateurs	30	11	8	11	49	58	41
Winlaton Hallgarth	30	8	8	14	48	63	32
Berwick Spittal Rovers	30	7	6	17	40	68	27
Heaton Stannington	30	7	4	19	52	100	25
Hebburn S.K.L.	30	7	3	20	40	89	24
Newbiggin Central Welfare	**30**	**5**	**8**	**17**	**43**	**79**	**20**
Walker Ledwood Fosse	**30**	**3**	**6**	**21**	**33**	**65**	**12**

Newbiggin Central Welfare and Walker Ledwood Fosse each had 3 points deducted.
Newcastle Benfield Park changed their name to Newcastle Benfield Saints, Walker Ledwood Fosse changed their name to Walker Fosse, Hebburn S.K.L. changed their name to Hebburn Reyrolle and Northbank changed their name to Northbank Carlisle.

Division One

Coxlodge Social	26	23	2	1	80	28	71
Newcastle University	26	20	4	2	77	19	61
Amble Vikings	26	18	4	4	63	28	58
Amble Town	26	12	7	7	59	40	43
Cullercoats	26	12	5	9	62	50	41
Wark	26	11	6	9	52	56	39
Procter & Gamble	26	8	9	9	48	45	33
Chopwell Top Club	26	9	5	12	51	59	29
Heddon Institute	26	7	7	12	49	57	28
Morpeth Town "A"	26	8	4	14	37	45	25
Highfields United	26	7	3	16	50	84	24
Ashington Hirst Progressive	26	4	5	17	28	59	17
Prudhoe Swinton	26	4	5	17	41	90	17
Rutherford Newcastle	26	4	4	18	24	61	16

Chopwell Top Club, Morpeth Town "A" and Newcastle University each had 3 points deducted.
Ashington Hirst Progressive left the league. Morpeth Town "A" became Bedlington Terriers "A" while Prudhoe Swinton changed their name to Prudhoe RTH.

Division Two

Harraby Catholic Club	26	22	1	3	97	29	64
Cowgate Social Club	26	19	4	3	75	30	61
Northern Social Club	26	17	5	4	84	38	53
Northumbria University	26	15	3	8	59	39	48
North Sunderland	26	12	4	10	47	45	40
Wallsend United	26	9	5	12	70	68	32
Forest Hall	26	8	6	12	51	65	30
Wallington	26	8	4	14	41	57	28
Walker Stack	26	10	3	13	55	69	27
Blyth Spartans "A"	26	8	3	15	55	89	27
Haydon Bridge United	26	7	8	11	42	56	26
Newcastle B.T.	26	7	4	15	47	69	25
Otterburn	26	7	3	16	49	67	24
Stobhill Rangers	26	4	5	17	36	87	14

Walker Stack had 6 points deducted.
Harraby Catholic Club, Haydon Bridge United, Northern Social Club and Stobhill Rangers all had 3 points deducted.
North Sunderland left the league. Shankhouse Black Watch joined from the South-East Northumberland League, TFG Benwell Blues joined from the Newcastle & District Welfare League while Ashington Colliers and Horden Colliery Welfare Athletic both joined as newly formed clubs. Wallsend United merged with Wallsend Town of the Wearside League, continuing in Division Two as Wallsend.

2000-01
Premier Division

Walker Central	30	23	5	2	83	27	74
West Allotment Celtic	30	21	5	4	91	36	68
Shankhouse	30	18	3	9	64	32	57
Northbank Carlisle	30	17	4	9	84	58	55
Seaton Delaval Amateurs	30	14	7	9	56	46	49
Ponteland United	30	14	6	10	56	46	48
Newcastle Benfield Saints	30	14	4	12	69	59	43
Carlisle City	30	11	6	13	47	51	39
Coxlodge Social	30	12	2	16	53	75	38
Percy Main Amateurs	30	9	10	11	39	51	37
Newcastle University	30	12	3	15	70	67	36
Berwick Spittal Rovers	30	10	4	16	60	71	34
Winlaton Hallgarth	30	11	1	18	41	62	34
Ryton	30	9	4	17	39	59	31
Heaton Stannington	**30**	**8**	**4**	**18**	**34**	**82**	**28**
Hebburn Reyrolle	**30**	**2**	**2**	**26**	**34**	**98**	**8**

Newcastle Benfield Saints and Newcastle University each had 3 points deducted.
Coxlodge Social left the league. Following their promotion from Division One, Amble Vikings merged with Amble Town and joined the Premier Division as Amble United.

Division One

Amble Vikings	30	25	4	1	104	28	79
Harraby Catholic Club	30	24	3	3	83	23	75
Newbiggin Central Welfare	30	17	3	10	78	53	54
Procter & Gamble	30	18	0	12	65	44	54
Chopwell Top Club	30	16	4	10	71	51	52
Wark	30	16	4	10	69	57	49
Cowgate Social Club	30	14	3	13	83	71	45
Walker Fosse	30	15	4	11	64	41	43
Cullercoats	30	12	3	15	57	67	39
Bedlington Terriers "A"	30	10	5	15	71	68	35
Amble Town	30	8	8	14	41	59	32
Heddon Institute	30	8	4	18	54	85	28
Rutherford Newcastle	30	7	7	16	52	91	28
Prudhoe RTH	30	7	4	19	28	75	22
Northern Social Club	30	5	4	21	31	79	19
Highfields United	**30**	**6**	**4**	**20**	**43**	**102**	**19**

Highfields United, Prudhoe RTH and Wark each had 3 points deducted. Walker Fosse had 6 points deducted.
Amble Vikings and Amble Town merged and were promoted to the Premier Division as Amble United. Heddon Institute left. Shankhouse Black Watch changed their name after promotion from Division Two and joined Division One as Cramlington Town.

Division Two

Wallington	22	14	5	3	52	20	47
Shankhouse Black Watch	**22**	**13**	**5**	**4**	**71**	**37**	**44**
Walker Stack FOS	22	8	11	3	52	36	35
Newcastle B.T.	22	8	7	7	41	40	31
Wallsend Town	22	9	3	10	55	44	30
TFG Benwell Blues	22	8	5	9	53	55	29
Blyth Spartans "A"	22	9	4	9	64	49	28
Northumbria University	22	12	1	9	46	40	25
Ashington Colliers	22	7	3	12	43	39	24
Forest Hall	22	6	5	11	48	70	20
Stobhill Rangers	22	6	2	14	52	78	20
Horden Colliery Welfare Athletic	22	5	3	14	35	104	18

Haydon Bridge United and Otterburn were both forced to resign during the season because of travel difficulties caused by a major outbreak of Foot and Mouth Disease. Their records were deleted.

Haydon Bridge United's record: 14 5 1 8 30 39 16
Otterburn's record: 14 7 2 5 28 28 23
Both clubs rejoined the league for the 2001-02 season.

Shankhouse Black Watch changed their name to Cramlington Town after their promotion to Division One. Blyth Spartans "A" and Stobhill Rangers

both left the league. New Birtley joined from the Durham Alliance and Newcastle East End Railway joined from South-East Northumberland League. TFG Benwell Blues changed their name to Benwell.

2001-02
Premier Division

West Allotment Celtic	28	19	5	4	65	29	62
Shankhouse	28	18	7	3	57	16	61
Newcastle Benfield Saints	28	19	2	7	69	34	59
Carlisle City	28	14	6	8	49	33	48
Amble United	28	13	8	7	48	36	47
Walker Central	28	12	8	8	62	39	41
Ponteland United	28	12	5	11	55	48	41
Harraby Catholic Club	28	12	8	8	45	38	41
Northbank Carlisle	28	12	5	11	48	41	35
Winlaton Hallgarth	28	8	7	13	36	47	31
Spittal Rovers	28	8	4	16	30	67	28
Newcastle University	28	8	4	16	30	39	25
Ryton	28	5	8	15	39	56	23
Percy Main Amateurs	28	6	2	20	30	76	20
Seaton Delaval Amateurs	28	3	3	22	24	88	9

Harraby Catholic Club, Newcastle University, Seaton Delaval Amateurs and Walker Central all had 3 points deducted.
Northbank Carlisle had 6 points deducted.

Division One

Bedlington Terriers "A"	**26**	**20**	**3**	**3**	**87**	**14**	**63**
Procter & Gamble	26	16	8	2	68	23	56
Cullercoats	26	16	2	8	64	29	50
Heaton Stannington	26	13	6	7	61	38	45
Chopwell Top Club	26	13	4	9	45	46	43
Wallington	26	10	5	11	42	46	35
Walker Fosse	26	10	5	11	47	62	35
Wark	26	10	7	9	57	53	34
Newbiggin Central Welfare	26	10	4	12	57	56	34
Rutherford Newcastle	26	10	2	14	46	65	32
Hebburn Reyrolle	26	9	2	15	50	64	29
Cramlington Town	26	8	1	17	42	69	25
Cowgate Social Club	26	5	7	14	38	65	22
Prudhoe RTH	26	3	2	21	29	103	11

Wark had 3 points deducted.
Northern Social Club resigned during the season and their record was deleted when it stood as follows: 21 6 3 12 30 52 21
Prudhoe RTH left the league. Procter & Gamble changed their name to Procter & Gamble Heddon.

Division Two

Haydon Bridge United	**22**	**15**	**7**	**0**	**94**	**28**	**52**
Northumbria University	**22**	**16**	**3**	**3**	**60**	**21**	**51**
Walker Stack FOS	22	12	3	7	59	49	39
Newcastle East End Railway	22	11	5	6	61	43	38
Ashington Colliers	22	10	4	8	49	35	34
Otterburn	22	9	5	8	52	45	32
New Birtley	22	10	4	8	66	48	31
Benwell	22	8	5	9	53	57	26
Newcastle B.T.	22	6	2	14	38	58	20
Forest Hall	22	6	2	14	47	69	20
Wallsend Town	22	5	3	14	39	91	18
Highfields United	22	1	3	18	20	94	3

Benwell, Highfields United and New Birtley all had 3 points deducted. Horden Colliery Welfare Athletic resigned during the season and their record was deleted: 4 1 0 3 9 8 3
Benwell left the league. Walker Wincomblee joined from the Newcastle & District Welfare League while Blyth Town and Stobhill Rangers both joined as newly formed clubs. New Birtley changed their name to Birtley and Walker Stack FOS changed their name to Walker Birds Nest FOS.

2002-03
Premier Division

Newcastle Benfield Saints	30	23	3	4	81	35	72
Carlisle City	30	20	6	4	64	29	66
West Allotment Celtic	30	19	8	3	71	25	65
Shankhouse	30	17	7	6	61	41	58
Northbank Carlisle	30	16	3	11	64	40	51
Ponteland United	30	12	6	12	65	52	42
Winlaton Hallgarth	30	10	9	11	45	50	39
Harraby Catholic Club	30	11	10	9	38	47	37
Ryton	30	10	6	14	56	67	36
Walker Central	30	9	8	13	38	45	32
Amble United	30	8	8	14	30	54	32
Bedlington Terriers "A"	30	8	7	15	41	51	31
Newcastle University	30	9	6	15	50	52	30
Spittal Rovers	30	8	3	19	47	72	24
Percy Main Amateurs	30	4	10	16	29	61	22
Seaton Delaval Amateurs	30	3	6	21	23	82	15

Newcastle Benfield Saints moved to the Northern League while Amble United and Bedlington Terriers "A" also left the league. Eppleton Colliery Welfare joined from the Northern League. Northumbria University changed their name after promotion from Division One and joined the Premier Division as Team Northumbria.

Division One

Chopwell Top Club	26	19	2	5	71	41	59
Northumbria University	26	17	3	6	86	25	54
Walker Fosse	26	15	6	5	75	45	51
Procter & Gamble Heddon	26	14	6	6	55	39	48
Heaton Stannington	26	12	5	9	75	48	41
Cramlington Town	26	13	2	11	55	47	41
Haydon Bridge United	26	11	5	10	69	52	38
Cullercoats	26	12	3	11	42	57	36
Wark	26	9	3	14	66	92	30
Newbiggin Central Welfare	26	6	9	11	49	79	27
Wallington	26	7	5	14	30	59	26
Cowgate Sports Club	26	8	5	13	51	60	23
Rutherford Newcastle	26	4	4	18	42	85	16
Hebburn Reyrolle	26	4	4	18	25	62	13

Cullercoats and Hebburn Reyrolle each had 3 points deducted.
Cowgate Sports Club had 6 points deducted.
Cowgate Sports Club left the league.
Procter & Gamble Heddon changed their name to Heddon.

Division Two

Blyth Town	22	18	2	2	68	26	56
Newcastle East End Railway	22	15	2	5	60	31	47
Wallsend Town	22	13	4	5	54	38	43
Newcastle B.T.	22	11	3	8	64	46	36
Forest Hall	22	10	6	6	50	51	36
Ashington Colliers	22	10	5	7	48	28	35
Stobhill Rangers	22	7	5	10	33	39	26
Highfields United	22	8	5	9	38	58	26
Birtley	22	6	4	12	48	53	19
Walker Birds Nest FOS	22	3	3	16	38	76	12
Otterburn	22	6	4	12	38	57	9
Walker Wincomblee	22	1	5	16	42	78	8

Birtley and Highfields United each had 3 points deducted.
Otterburn had 13 points deducted.
Birtley and Walker Wincomblee both left the league. Alnmouth joined from the North Northumberland League, Felling Willows joined from the Tyneside Amateur League having changed their name from The Willows Leam Lane, Gosforth Bohemian Garnett joined from the Corinthians League while Daisy Hill Turbinia, Prudhoe RTH and Swarland also joined. Stobhill Rangers became Morpeth Town "A".

2003-04
Premier Division

West Allotment Celtic	30	24	2	4	115	33	74
Team Northumbria	30	18	7	5	78	35	61
Ryton	30	17	7	6	87	53	58
Percy Main Amateurs	30	17	6	7	76	40	57
Shankhouse	30	15	7	8	54	35	52
Harraby Catholic Club	30	15	5	10	66	44	50
Northbank Carlisle	30	15	4	11	68	50	49
Carlisle City	30	15	2	13	53	48	47
Walker Central	30	13	6	11	45	48	45
Ponteland United	30	11	6	13	56	60	39
Newcastle University	30	8	6	16	36	55	30
Winlaton Hallgarth	30	8	6	16	41	84	30
Seaton Delaval Amateurs	30	7	4	19	37	85	25
Spittal Rovers	30	7	3	20	40	90	24
Chopwell Top Club	**30**	**7**	**2**	**21**	**43**	**86**	**23**
Eppleton Colliery Welfare	**30**	**5**	**3**	**22**	**37**	**86**	**18**

West Allotment Celtic moved to the Northern League and Murton joined from the Northern League.

Division One

Heddon	24	19	3	2	63	16	60
Heaton Stannington	24	19	1	4	71	33	58
Walker Fosse	24	15	5	4	81	23	50
Blyth Town	24	16	1	7	73	35	49
Hebburn Reyrolle	24	11	4	9	71	55	37
Newbiggin Central Welfare	24	12	1	11	51	59	37
Wark	24	11	3	10	51	48	36
Haydon Bridge United	24	8	6	10	55	56	30
Cramlington Town	24	8	3	13	44	56	27
Newcastle East End Railway	24	8	3	13	54	66	27
Rutherford Newcastle	24	3	4	17	28	70	13
Cullercoats	24	3	3	18	32	94	12
Wallington	24	2	5	17	21	84	11

After their promotion from Division Two, Gosforth Bohemian Garnett changed their name and joined Division One as Garnett Bohemian.
Cullercoats changed their name to Wallsend.

Division Two

Alnmouth	22	16	2	4	67	32	50
Gosforth Bohemian Garnett	22	14	5	3	66	22	47
Felling Willows	22	13	6	3	67	22	45
Morpeth Town "A"	22	11	7	4	49	28	40
Ashington Colliers	22	11	5	6	64	38	38
Forest Hall	22	11	3	8	45	41	36
Highfields United	22	9	4	9	43	51	31
Newcastle B.T.	22	8	4	10	41	46	28
Prudhoe Town RTH	22	5	5	12	51	76	20
Swarland	22	4	2	16	31	75	11
Wallsend Town	22	3	3	16	32	58	8
Daisy Hill Turbinia	22	3	2	17	30	97	8

Swarland and Daisy Hill Turbinia each had 3 points deducted.
Wallsend Town had 4 points deducted.
Otterburn resigned during the season and their record was deleted when it stood as follows:

	11	0	1	10	5	63	1

Walker Birds Nest FOS resigned during the season and their record was deleted when it stood as:

	7	0	1	6	3	31	1

Daisy Hill Turbinia disbanded and Morpeth Town "A" also left the league. Lowick joined from the North Northumberland League while Penrith United and Sport Benfield both joined as newly formed clubs. Whitley Bay "A" also joined.

Northern Alliance 2004-2006

2004-05

Premier Division

Shankhouse	30	22	4	4	74	33	70
Ryton	30	21	5	4	89	37	68
Team Northumbria	30	22	4	4	89	29	67
Walker Central	30	15	8	7	53	24	53
Carlisle City	30	13	7	10	68	49	46
Heddon	30	13	7	10	45	50	46
Heaton Stannington	30	13	7	10	52	47	43
Winlaton Hallgarth	30	10	8	12	40	54	38
Ponteland United	30	10	6	14	59	63	36
Northbank Carlisle	30	10	6	14	34	43	36
Seaton Delaval Amateurs	30	9	6	15	45	70	33
Harraby Catholic Club	30	10	8	12	39	42	32
Newcastle University	30	9	4	17	37	51	31
Percy Main Amateurs	30	10	4	16	52	69	31
Murton	30	3	6	21	25	78	9
Spittal Rovers	**30**	**2**	**6**	**22**	**30**	**92**	**9**

Team Northumbria, Heaton Stannington, Percy Main Amateurs and Spittal Rovers all had 3 points deducted.
Harraby Catholic Club and Murton both had 6 points deducted.
Ryton moved to the Northern League and Winlaton Hallgarth also left.
Easington Colliery joined from the Northern League.

Division One

Alnmouth	28	21	5	2	88	35	68
Blyth Town	**28**	**20**	**5**	**3**	**75**	**27**	**65**
Walker Fosse	28	17	5	6	76	39	56
Wallsend	28	17	4	7	61	36	55
Newbiggin Central Welfare	28	14	5	9	64	53	44
Garnett Bohemian	28	13	5	10	59	45	41
Chopwell Top Club	28	12	5	11	56	56	41
Hebburn Reyrolle	28	11	5	12	46	49	38
Cramlington Town	28	11	4	13	49	50	37
Wark	28	10	4	14	57	69	34
Eppleton Colliery Welfare	28	10	1	17	43	70	31
Rutherford Newcastle	28	7	2	19	34	55	23
Haydon Bridge United	28	8	1	19	43	79	22
Newcastle East End Railway	28	6	2	20	45	86	20
Wallington	28	4	5	19	38	85	17

Newbiggin Central Welfare, Garnett Bohemian and Haydon Bridge United each had 3 points deducted.
Eppleton Colliery Welfare and Newbiggin Central Welfare both left.
Garnett Bohemian changed their name to Gosforth Bohemian Garnett.

Division Two

Ashington Colliers	**22**	**16**	**4**	**2**	**64**	**23**	**52**
Penrith United	**22**	**16**	**2**	**4**	**62**	**29**	**50**
Lowick	22	14	0	8	50	39	42
Whitley Bay "A"	22	12	5	5	64	38	41
Sport Benfield	22	13	2	7	59	41	38
Newcastle B.T.	22	8	9	5	34	32	33
Felling Willows	22	10	5	7	55	33	32
Wallsend Town	22	7	3	12	40	64	24
Prudhoe Town RTH	22	6	1	15	36	58	19
Highfields United	22	5	2	15	34	59	17
Forest Hall	22	6	1	15	25	52	16
Swarland	22	1	2	19	14	69	5

Sport Benfield, Felling Willows and Forest Hall all had 3 points deducted.
Forest Hall moved to the Tyneside Amateur League and Prudhoe Town RTH also left. Red Row Welfare joined from the North Northumberland League and Chemfica joined from the Corinthians League. Addlestone Jesmond, Gilford Park Spartans, Seaton Burn, Stocksfield and Westerhope all joined as newly formed clubs. Felling Willows changed their name to Felling Fox.

2005-06

Premier Division

Team Northumbria	30	23	3	4	99	34	72
Shankhouse	30	18	8	4	57	21	62
Carlisle City	30	18	5	7	68	31	59
Heaton Stannington	30	18	4	8	53	36	55
Northbank Carlisle	30	15	4	11	67	48	49
Walker Central	30	15	4	11	60	43	49
Blyth Town	30	14	8	8	65	42	47
Seaton Delaval Amateurs	30	11	6	13	56	62	39
Ponteland United	30	12	3	15	52	63	39
Heddon	30	11	2	17	45	59	35
Harraby Catholic Club	30	8	9	13	47	59	33
Alnmouth	30	9	6	15	52	83	33
Newcastle University	30	9	11	10	45	44	32
Easington Colliery	30	7	3	20	41	76	24
Murton	**30**	**6**	**4**	**20**	**42**	**83**	**22**
Percy Main Amateurs	**30**	**4**	**4**	**22**	**29**	**94**	**16**

Heaton Stannington and Blyth Town each had 3 points deducted.
Newcastle University had 6 points deducted.
Team Northumbria moved to the Northern League and Alnmouth also left.
Peterlee Town joined from the Northern League, having changed their name from Peterlee Newtown.

Division One

Wallsend	24	17	4	3	64	26	52
Ashington Colliers	**24**	**14**	**3**	**7**	**46**	**26**	**45**
Penrith United	24	13	3	8	55	37	42
Rutherford Newcastle	24	12	6	6	51	34	42
Chopwell Top Club	24	13	3	8	52	43	42
Gosforth Bohemian Garnett	24	12	5	7	45	42	41
Wark	24	11	3	10	60	51	36
Wallington	24	9	9	6	50	44	36
Cramlington Town	24	7	6	11	32	39	27
Hebburn Reyrolle	24	7	5	12	34	57	26
Newcastle East End Railway	24	5	6	13	36	58	21
Spittal Rovers	24	4	2	18	24	55	14
Haydon Bridge United	24	3	3	18	29	66	12

Wallsend had 3 points deducted.
Walker Fosse resigned during the season and their record was deleted when it stood as follows: 13 11 1 1 49 15 34
Spittal Rovers merged with Highfields United of Division Two, continuing in Division One as Berwick United.

Division Two

Whitley Bay "A"	**28**	**20**	**4**	**4**	**66**	**29**	**64**
Gilford Park Spartans	**28**	**19**	**3**	**6**	**99**	**53**	**57**
Seaton Burn	**28**	**16**	**6**	**6**	**53**	**47**	**54**
Stocksfield	28	14	8	6	64	30	50
Lowick	28	12	8	8	51	44	41
Westerhope	28	11	7	10	61	51	40
Sport Benfield	28	11	7	10	65	73	40
Red Row Welfare	28	9	8	11	54	53	35
Addlestone Jesmond	28	11	7	10	45	45	34
Swarland	28	10	2	16	55	74	32
Chemfica	28	8	7	13	52	59	31
Felling Fox	28	9	4	15	42	62	31
Newcastle B.T.	28	7	4	17	43	72	25
Wallsend Town	28	7	3	18	46	71	24
Highfields United	28	4	6	18	46	79	18

Gilford Park Spartans and Lowick each had 3 points deducted.
Addlestone Jesmond had 6 points deducted.
Sport Benfield and Felling Fox both left the league. Highfields United merged with Spittal Rovers of Division One to form Berwick United who continued in Division One. Whitley Bay Town joined from the Tyneside Amateur League having changed their name from Whitley Bay Venture. Blaydon, Cullercoats, Hexham and North Shields Athletic all joined as newly formed clubs. Addlestone Jesmond changed their name to Jesmond, Chemfica changed their name to Newcastle Chemfica and Swarland changed their name to Amble.

2006-07
Premier Division

	P	W	D	L	F	A	Pts
Harraby Catholic Club	28	22	4	2	73	29	70
Wallsend	28	17	4	7	73	47	55
Ponteland United	28	14	8	6	59	35	50
Walker Central	28	13	7	8	47	42	46
Carlisle City	28	12	9	7	54	37	45
Newcastle University	28	11	10	7	40	30	43
Shankhouse	28	12	5	11	54	37	41
Easington Colliery	28	12	3	13	56	58	39
Ashington Colliers	28	11	4	13	45	56	37
Heaton Stannington	28	10	5	13	55	51	35
Seaton Delaval Amateurs	28	9	6	13	43	57	33
Blyth Town	28	7	8	13	38	43	29
Northbank Carlisle	28	6	5	17	33	66	23
Heddon	28	6	3	19	28	72	21
Peterlee Town	28	4	7	17	20	58	19

Easington Colliery moved to the Wearside League. Alnwick Town joined from the Northern League. Gilford Park Spartans changed their name after promotion from Division One and joined the Premier Division as Gilford Park. Wallsend changed their name to Gateshead Leam Rangers.

Division One

	P	W	D	L	F	A	Pts
Gillford Park Spartans	30	24	3	3	101	39	75
Cramlington Town	30	20	4	6	63	33	64
Penrith United	30	18	5	7	92	40	59
Rutherford Newcastle	30	17	3	10	73	53	54
Murton	30	17	2	11	74	43	53
Wallington	30	14	4	12	63	49	46
Newcastle East End Railway	30	12	7	11	57	51	43
Wark	30	13	2	15	72	74	41
Chopwell Top Club	30	11	8	11	53	64	41
Whitley Bay "A"	30	12	6	12	62	60	35
Gosforth Bohemian Garnett	30	10	4	16	57	61	34
Berwick United	30	10	4	16	53	84	34
Seaton Burn	30	10	2	18	32	61	32
Percy Main Amateurs	30	9	4	17	46	72	31
Hebburn Reyrolle	30	7	3	20	43	92	24
Haydon Bridge United	30	4	3	23	47	112	15

Whitley Bay "A" had 7 points deducted.
Chopwell Top Club changed their name to Chopwell Officials Club.
Following their promotion from Division Two, Westerhope changed their name and joined Division One as Westerhope JG.

Division Two

	P	W	D	L	F	A	Pts
Westerhope	26	19	2	5	81	31	59
Stocksfield	26	16	7	3	91	40	55
Red Row Welfare	26	17	3	6	69	30	54
Cullercoats	26	17	3	6	67	33	54
Wallsend Town	26	15	5	6	72	44	50
Jesmond	26	14	2	10	42	36	44
Whitley Bay Town	26	13	2	11	61	48	41
Amble	26	10	6	10	57	52	36
Lowick	26	9	5	12	49	51	29
Newcastle B.T.	26	7	3	16	47	67	24
Hexham	26	6	5	15	40	62	20
North Shields Athletic	26	6	3	17	39	94	18
Newcastle Chemfica	26	4	5	17	34	76	17
Blaydon	26	2	3	21	27	112	9

Lowick, Hexham and North Shields Athletic each had 3 points deducted.
Lowick and Blaydon both left the league. Killingworth YPC and Willington Quay Saints both joined from the Tyneside Amateur League, Amble United joined from the North Northumberland League while Shields United, Tynemouth United, Wallsend Boys Club and Wideopen & District all joined as newly formed clubs.

2007-08
Premier Division

	P	W	D	L	F	A	Pts
Walker Central	30	21	7	2	86	27	70
Harraby Catholic Club	30	19	6	5	73	29	63
Gillford Park	30	17	10	3	67	30	61
Heddon	30	14	9	7	47	42	51
Peterlee Town	30	16	2	12	66	67	50
Heaton Stannington	30	14	9	7	63	47	47
Shankhouse	30	13	4	13	58	57	43
Blyth Town	30	11	6	13	47	71	39
Cramlington Town	30	10	7	13	48	51	37
Seaton Delaval Amateurs	30	11	4	15	57	63	37
Ponteland United	30	11	3	16	66	63	36
Ashington Colliers	30	10	6	14	51	64	36
Carlisle City	30	8	7	15	50	60	31
Alnwick Town	30	10	3	17	55	59	30
Newcastle University	30	8	1	21	38	75	19
Northbank Carlisle	30	3	4	23	35	102	13

Alnwick Town had 3 points deducted, Heaton Stannington had 4 points deducted and Newcastle University had 6 points deducted.
Gateshead Leam Rangers were expelled from the league during the season and their record was deleted: 8 | 5 | 1 | 2 | 16 | 10 | 16

Division One

	P	W	D	L	F	A	Pts
Wark	30	26	2	2	123	42	74
Murton	30	21	4	5	83	38	67
Rutherford Newcastle	30	16	6	8	70	53	54
Wallington	30	16	6	8	76	61	54
Stocksfield	30	15	4	11	74	63	49
Westerhope JG	30	14	5	11	83	69	47
Whitley Bay "A"	30	13	3	14	95	82	42
Penrith United	30	15	1	14	79	73	40
Red Row Welfare	30	11	5	14	57	73	38
Gosforth Bohemian Garnett	30	9	9	12	64	72	36
Berwick United	30	10	5	15	56	68	35
Percy Main Amateurs	30	10	5	15	43	57	35
Chopwell Officials Club	30	10	5	15	50	78	35
Seaton Burn	30	6	6	18	38	68	24
Hebburn Reyrolle	30	5	5	20	39	88	20
Newcastle East End Railway	30	5	5	20	43	88	11

Wark and Penrith United each had 6 points deducted.
Newcastle East End Railway had 9 points deducted.
Haydon Bridge United failed to complete their fixtures and their record was deleted when it stood as: 19 | 2 | 1 | 16 | 18 | 75 | 7
They were relegated to Division Two but resigned before the start of the 2008-09 season. Rutherford Newcastle changed their name to Gateshead Rutherford and Penrith United became Penrith "A".

Division Two

	P	W	D	L	F	A	Pts
Killingworth YPC	30	25	4	1	92	37	79
Cullercoats	30	23	2	5	106	44	71
Amble United	30	22	2	6	109	41	68
Wallsend Town	30	19	2	9	79	54	56
Jesmond	30	15	7	8	73	55	52
Whitley Bay Town	30	16	1	13	74	84	49
Wallsend Boys Club	30	14	4	12	72	52	46
Shields United	30	12	9	9	49	51	45
Wideopen & District	30	14	4	12	72	63	40
Amble	30	12	4	14	58	60	40
Newcastle Chemfica	30	11	4	15	63	89	37
Hexham	30	8	5	17	48	73	29
Willington Quay Saints	30	7	3	20	47	75	24
Newcastle B.T.	30	6	3	21	63	115	21
North Shields Athletic	30	5	5	20	52	79	17
Tynemouth United	30	1	1	28	32	117	4

Wallsend Town and North Shields Athletic each had 3 points deducted.
Wideopen & District had 6 points deducted.
Jesmond left the league. Shields United changed their name to South Shields United and Newcastle Chemfica changed their name to Benfield Chemfica. Stobswood Welfare joined from the North Northumberland League and Forest Hall joined from the Tyneside Amateur League.

Northern Alliance 2008-2010

2008-09

Premier Division

	P	W	D	L	F	A	Pts
Walker Central	32	23	8	1	99	38	77
Gillford Park	32	19	10	3	61	32	67
Harraby Catholic Club	32	18	9	5	55	27	63
Seaton Delaval Amateurs	32	17	7	8	76	48	58
Alnwick Town	32	13	7	12	57	51	46
Carlisle City	32	11	13	8	65	61	46
Shankhouse	32	12	9	11	65	59	45
Heaton Stannington	32	13	9	10	65	59	45
Blyth Town	32	11	8	13	67	78	41
Ponteland United	32	9	11	12	56	60	38
Heddon	32	8	13	11	43	50	37
Wark	32	10	6	16	70	94	36
Cramlington Town	32	9	5	18	53	68	32
Newcastle University	32	9	5	18	52	72	32
Ashington Colliers	32	8	7	17	46	68	31
Murton	32	9	3	20	51	78	24
Peterlee Town	**32**	**6**	**4**	**22**	**50**	**88**	**22**

Heaton Stannington had 3 points deducted.
Murton had 6 points deducted.
Gillford Park moved to the Northern League. Following their promotion from Division one, Killingworth YPC changed their name and joined the Premier Division as Killingworth Sporting.

Division One

	P	W	D	L	F	A	Pts
Killingworth YPC	**28**	**19**	**2**	**7**	**72**	**44**	**59**
Stocksfield	**28**	**18**	**4**	**6**	**70**	**42**	**58**
Whitley Bay "A"	28	18	3	7	85	43	57
Cullercoats	28	17	4	7	96	43	55
Percy Main Amateurs	28	17	2	9	58	42	53
Newcastle East End Railway	28	14	3	11	64	49	45
Gateshead Rutherford	28	11	6	11	62	58	39
Chopwell Officials Club	28	13	3	12	50	52	39
Northbank Carlisle	28	9	8	11	58	58	35
Hebburn Reyrolle	28	10	5	13	46	53	32
Wallington	28	10	5	13	56	65	29
Gosforth Bohemian Garnett	28	9	6	13	51	64	27
Berwick United	28	6	5	17	31	79	23
Seaton Burn	28	4	4	20	29	66	16
Red Row Welfare	28	3	4	21	29	99	13

Chopwell Officials Club and Hebburn Reyrolle each had 3 points deducted.
Wallington and Gosforth Bohemian Garnett had 6 points deducted.
Penrith "A" resigned during the season and their record was deleted when it stood as follows: 3 1 0 2 9 11 3
Westerhope JG resigned during the season and their record was deleted when it stoof as follows: 7 1 1 5 13 24 4
Red Row Welfare changed their name to Morpeth Sporting Club and Gosforth Bohemian Garnett changed their name to Gosforth Bohemian.

Division Two

	P	W	D	L	F	A	Pts
Amble United	**28**	**22**	**3**	**3**	**90**	**19**	**69**
South Shields United	**28**	**19**	**4**	**5**	**59**	**36**	**61**
Stobswood Welfare	28	16	5	7	70	36	53
Forest Hall	28	14	5	9	55	40	47
Willington Quay Saints	28	12	8	8	74	58	44
Wideopen & District	28	13	5	10	60	56	44
North Shields Athletic	28	12	7	9	63	55	43
Benfield Chemfica	28	12	4	12	42	45	40
Wallsend Town	28	12	3	13	65	56	39
Wallsend Boys Club	28	10	8	10	50	47	38
Hexham	28	11	3	14	48	57	36
Amble	28	11	3	14	49	61	36
Whitley Bay Town	28	6	5	17	37	77	23
Newcastle B.T.	28	4	3	21	30	102	15
Tynemouth United	28	1	4	23	28	75	7

Cullercoats Custom Planet joined from the Tyneside Amateur League, Cramlington Blue Star joined from the North-East Amateur League and Swalwell joined from youth football. Benfield Chemfica changed their name to Newcastle Chemfica.

2009-10

Premier Division

	P	W	D	L	F	A	Pts
Harraby Catholic Club	32	20	4	8	77	36	64
Wark	32	17	8	7	90	52	59
Walker Central	32	16	8	8	68	40	56
Blyth Town	32	16	5	11	62	49	53
Ashington Colliers	32	15	8	9	48	42	52
Killingworth Sporting	32	14	8	10	51	50	50
Heaton Stannington	32	15	8	9	74	56	49
Ponteland United	32	14	6	12	51	50	48
Murton	32	13	6	13	53	61	45
Carlisle City	32	11	11	10	46	53	44
Alnwick Town	32	12	6	14	68	57	42
Seaton Delaval Amateurs	32	11	5	16	66	68	38
Shankhouse	32	10	8	14	59	70	38
Stocksfield	32	9	6	17	40	79	33
Cramlington Town	32	9	9	14	43	70	32
Heddon	**32**	**6**	**6**	**20**	**53**	**72**	**24**
Newcastle University	**32**	**4**	**8**	**20**	**39**	**83**	**20**

Heaton Stannington and Cramlington Town each had 4 points deducted.

Division One

	P	W	D	L	F	A	Pts
Gateshead Rutherford	**30**	**22**	**3**	**5**	**76**	**43**	**69**
Percy Main Amateurs	**30**	**21**	**5**	**4**	**69**	**35**	**68**
Amble United	30	20	5	5	73	30	65
Whitley Bay "A"	30	19	4	7	100	50	61
Morpeth Sporting Club	30	18	1	11	71	64	55
Hebburn Reyrolle	30	15	6	9	68	54	51
South Shields United	30	15	3	12	63	49	48
Cullercoats	30	14	3	13	75	55	45
Gosforth Bohemian	30	13	4	13	56	48	43
Peterlee Town	30	13	4	13	66	65	43
Chopwell Officials Club	30	10	3	17	51	71	33
Berwick United	30	8	3	19	45	96	27
Wallington	30	7	7	16	44	63	22
Newcastle East End Railway	30	7	3	20	50	88	21
Northbank Carlisle	**30**	**6**	**1**	**23**	**35**	**74**	**19**
Seaton Burn	**30**	**2**	**5**	**23**	**31**	**88**	**8**

Newcastle East End Railway and Seaton Burn each had 3 points deducted.
Wallington had 6 points deducted.
Berwick United changed their name to Berwick United Ultras.

Division Two

	P	W	D	L	F	A	Pts
North Shields Athletic	**30**	**21**	**6**	**3**	**81**	**33**	**69**
Stobswood Welfare	**30**	**20**	**4**	**6**	**84**	**51**	**64**
Forest Hall	**30**	**15**	**10**	**5**	**70**	**38**	**55**
Amble	30	16	7	7	69	38	55
Wallsend Town	30	16	4	10	72	42	52
Wideopen & District	30	15	4	11	64	59	49
Newcastle Chemfica	30	16	0	14	66	57	45
Hexham	30	10	10	10	51	43	40
Swalwell	30	11	7	12	63	61	40
Wallsend Boys Club	30	13	5	12	54	51	38
Tynemouth United	30	12	2	16	67	86	38
Newcastle B.T.	30	9	6	15	52	74	33
Willington Quay Saints	30	6	6	18	39	87	24
Cullercoats Custom Planet	30	7	3	20	54	76	21
Cramlington Blue Star	30	6	3	21	42	92	21
Whitley Bay Town	30	5	19	48	88	17

Newcastle Chemfica and Cullercoats Custom Planet each had 3 points deducted.
Wallsend Boys Club and Whitley Bay Town each had 6 points deducted.
Simonside Social Club joined from the Durham Alliance and Red House Farm joined from youth football. Cramlington Blue Star changed their name to Cramlington United.

2010-11
Premier Division

Ponteland United	32	22	5	5	72	31	71
Alnwick Town	32	21	7	4	74	39	70
Harraby Catholic Club	32	19	8	5	76	36	65
Seaton Delaval Amateurs	32	20	5	7	71	45	65
Heaton Stannington	32	15	9	8	67	54	54
Carlisle City	32	15	5	12	57	54	50
Shankhouse	32	14	6	12	68	64	48
Percy Main Amateurs	32	13	7	12	59	48	46
Blyth Town	32	13	6	13	73	58	45
Ashington Colliers	32	13	8	11	59	50	44
Killingworth Sporting	32	12	4	16	51	66	40
Walker Central	32	11	4	17	51	70	37
Stocksfield	32	9	4	19	55	77	31
Gateshead Rutherford	32	7	9	16	44	67	26
Murton	32	6	6	20	38	66	24
Wark	**32**	**5**	**6**	**21**	**48**	**92**	**21**
Cramlington Town	**32**	**7**	**1**	**24**	**45**	**91**	**19**

Ashington Colliers and Cramlington Town each had 3 points deducted.
Gateshead Rutherford had 4 points deducted.
Alnwick Town moved to the Northern League.

Division One

Hebburn Reyrolle	**30**	**26**	**2**	**2**	**110**	**31**	**80**
Whitley Bay "A"	**30**	**24**	**5**	**1**	**78**	**33**	**77**
Amble United	30	19	4	7	72	39	61
Newcastle University	30	15	6	9	53	40	51
South Shields United	30	14	6	10	78	47	47
Heddon	30	15	2	13	64	55	47
Wallington	30	14	3	13	68	58	45
Cullercoats	30	12	6	12	57	43	42
Gosforth Bohemian	30	9	9	12	36	55	36
Newcastle East End Railway	30	11	2	17	57	78	35
Morpeth Sporting Club	30	10	2	18	52	76	29
Peterlee Town	30	7	8	15	53	80	29
Berwick United Ultras	30	7	7	16	53	86	28
Stobswood Welfare	30	8	2	20	54	84	26
Forest Hall	30	8	1	21	51	67	25
North Shields Athletic	**30**	**7**	**3**	**20**	**33**	**97**	**24**

South Shields United had 1 point deducted.
Morpeth Sporting Club had 3 points deducted.
Chopwell Officials Club resigned during the season and their record was deleted. Berwick United Ultras resigned and their reserves, playing in the North Northumberland League, became the first team. Peterlee Town moved to the Wearside League while South Shields United and Stobswood Welfare also left.

Division Two

Newcastle Chemfica	**26**	**22**	**0**	**4**	**87**	**38**	**66**
Wallsend Town	**26**	**20**	**2**	**4**	**101**	**42**	**62**
Simonside Social Club	26	17	4	5	84	64	55
Tynemouth United	26	14	2	10	75	59	44
Swalwell	26	12	5	9	58	56	41
Wallsend Boys Club	26	12	4	10	54	40	40
Willington Quay Saints	26	13	1	12	69	78	40
Northbank Carlisle	26	11	5	10	51	43	38
Seaton Burn	26	12	1	13	45	54	37
Red House Farm	26	11	2	13	60	54	35
Hexham	26	7	6	13	42	47	27
Whitley Bay Town	26	6	2	18	34	71	20
Cramlington United	26	2	4	20	31	86	10
Wideopen & District	26	2	4	20	27	86	10

Amble, Cullercoats Custom Planet and Newcastle B.T. all resigned during the season and their records were deleted.
Tynemouth United and Whitley Bay Town both left. Alnwick Town Reserves and Bedlington Terriers Reserves both joined from the North Northumberland League, Alston Moor Social Club joined from the Westmorland League, Whickham Lang Jacks joined from the Tyneside Amateur League and New Fordley joined from Sunday football. Simonside Social Club changed their name to Harton & Westoe Colliery Welfare.

2011-12
Premier Division

Heaton Stannington	30	21	3	6	86	35	66
Hebburn Reyrolle	30	19	6	5	83	39	63
Whitley Bay "A"	30	18	5	7	68	41	59
Harraby Catholic Club	30	18	2	10	68	48	56
Carlisle City	30	16	4	10	64	37	52
Ashington Colliers	30	13	7	10	53	54	46
Shankhouse	30	14	3	13	49	54	45
Seaton Delaval Amateurs	30	13	5	12	68	59	44
Killingworth Sporting	30	12	7	11	47	45	43
Percy Main Amateurs	30	11	7	12	47	58	40
Blyth Town	30	11	4	15	51	56	37
Stocksfield	30	9	5	16	52	74	32
Gateshead Rutherford	30	9	6	15	49	70	30
Walker Central	30	8	3	19	40	62	27
Ponteland United	**30**	**6**	**5**	**19**	**45**	**88**	**23**
Murton	30	5	2	23	39	89	17

Gateshead Rutherford had 3 points deducted.
Murton moved to the Durham Alliance.
Harraby Catholic Club changed their name to Harraby United.

Division One

Amble United	**20**	**17**	**2**	**1**	**54**	**13**	**53**
Wallsend Town	**20**	**15**	**2**	**3**	**69**	**36**	**47**
Wallington	20	14	2	4	48	26	44
Heddon	20	11	2	7	38	36	35
Gosforth Bohemian	20	10	3	7	41	29	33
Cullercoats	20	8	4	8	43	46	28
Cramlington Town	20	5	3	12	29	65	18
Newcastle University	20	5	4	11	42	38	16
Newcastle Chemfica	20	3	4	13	26	51	13
Forest Hall	20	5	2	13	29	53	11
Morpeth Sporting Club	20	2	2	16	20	46	8

Newcastle University had 3 points deducted.
Forest Hall had 6 points deducted.
Newcastle East End Railway and Wark both resigned during the season and their records were deleted.
Whickham Lang Jacks changed their name after promotion from Division Two and joined Division One as Gateshead Redheugh 1957. Newcastle Chemfica changed their name to Newcastle Chemfica (Independent) and Morpeth Sporting Club became Morpeth Town "A".

Division Two

Hexham	30	19	8	3	78	40	65
Red House Farm	30	17	9	4	82	55	60
Northbank Carlisle	30	19	4	7	78	39	58
Harton & Westoe Colliery Welfare	30	15	8	7	94	55	53
Whickham Lang Jacks	**30**	**15**	**4**	**11**	**95**	**73**	**49**
Bedlington Terriers Reserves	**30**	**15**	**4**	**11**	**65**	**43**	**49**
Willington Quay Saints	**30**	**14**	**4**	**12**	**77**	**65**	**46**
Wallsend Boys Club	30	14	6	10	77	62	41
New Fordley	30	11	7	12	77	65	40
Alston	30	11	6	13	62	76	39
Wideopen & District	30	10	8	12	53	54	38
Alnwick Town Reserves	30	12	1	17	49	69	37
North Shields Athletic	30	6	14	10	61	79	36
Seaton Burn	30	6	9	15	60	75	27
Swalwell	30	6	4	20	43	88	22
Cramlington United	30	1	2	27	26	139	5

Northbank Carlisle had 3 points deducted.
Wallsend Boys Club had 7 points deducted.
Harton & Westoe Colliery Welfare moved to the Wearside League.
Blyth Isabella, Grainger Park Old Boys (having changed their name from Grainger Park Boys Club), High Howdon Social Club and Longbenton all joined from the Tyneside Amateur League, Birtley St. Josephs joined from the Durham Alliance and Wooler joined from the North Northumberland League. Newcastle Benfield Reserves also joined.

Northern Alliance 2012-2014

2012-13
Premier Division

Heaton Stannington	30	25	2	3	98	33	77
Blyth Town	30	21	8	1	92	38	71
Carlisle City	30	19	3	8	78	39	60
Amble United	30	18	2	10	81	43	56
Whitley Bay "A"	30	15	5	10	75	43	50
Ashington Colliers	30	15	5	10	65	50	50
Harraby United	30	17	3	10	72	54	45
Stocksfield	30	13	6	11	66	57	45
Seaton Delaval Amateurs	30	12	9	9	52	47	45
Walker Central	30	10	7	13	41	59	37
Percy Main Amateurs	30	10	5	15	53	80	35
Wallsend Town	30	8	4	18	58	83	28
Killingworth Sporting	30	6	8	16	50	65	26
Shankhouse	30	8	2	20	51	84	26
Hebburn Reyrolle	30	5	2	23	37	108	17
Gateshead Rutherford	30	2	1	27	27	113	7

Harraby United had 9 points deducted.
Heaton Stannington moved to the Northern League and Amble United disbanded. Harraby United also left the league.

Division One

Wallington	30	22	3	5	94	42	69
Red House Farm	30	21	5	4	94	42	68
Northbank Carlisle	30	20	1	9	76	48	61
Heddon	30	17	4	9	62	52	55
Cramlington Town	30	16	4	10	67	54	52
Bedlington Terriers Reserves	30	15	2	13	64	63	43
Gateshead Redheugh 1957	30	15	3	12	74	54	42
Hexham	30	13	4	13	71	51	40
Ponteland United	30	12	4	14	68	66	40
Gosforth Bohemian	30	9	9	12	56	54	36
Newcastle Chemfica (Independ't)	30	11	3	16	66	76	36
Newcastle University	30	11	5	14	56	67	27
Cullercoats	30	9	3	18	55	82	27
Forest Hall	30	8	5	17	51	81	26
Willington Quay Saints	30	7	4	19	46	76	25
Morpeth Town "A"	30	2	5	23	34	126	8

Hexham, Cullercoats, Forest Hall and Morpeth Town "A" each had 3 points deducted.
Bedlington Terriers Reserves had 4 points deducted.
Gateshead Redheugh 1957 had 6 points deducted.
Newcastle University had 11 points deducted.
Forest Hall and Morpeth Town "A" both left the league.

Division Two

North Shields Athletic	30	26	2	2	101	36	80
Birtley St. Josephs	30	22	3	5	119	47	69
New Fordley	30	21	3	6	96	61	66
Wooler	30	15	8	7	62	42	53
Wideopen & District	30	14	8	8	79	56	50
Blyth Isabella	30	15	2	13	90	70	47
Seaton Burn	30	13	4	13	65	80	43
Longbenton	30	10	5	15	69	73	35
High Howdon Social Club	30	8	7	15	56	68	31
Alnwick Town Reserves	30	10	6	14	62	64	30
Wallsend Boys Club	30	9	6	15	61	74	30
Grainger Park Old Boys	30	10	3	17	64	81	30
Newcastle Benfield Reserves	30	8	5	17	43	79	29
Swalwell	30	7	8	15	53	96	26
Alston	30	6	8	16	49	76	23
Cramlington United	30	3	8	19	33	99	17

Alnwick Town Reserves had 6 points deducted.
Wallsend Boys Club, Grainger Park Old Boys, Swalwell and Alston all had 3 points deducted.
Alston left the league. AFC Newbiggin joined from the North Northumberland League and Gateshead Leam Lane Rangers joined from the Durham Alliance. Whitburn Athletic joined from the Wearside Combination and West Allotment Celtic "A" also joined. Grainger Park Old Boys changed their name to Grainger Park Boys Club.

2013-14
Premier Division

Blyth Town	28	19	5	4	95	27	62
Carlisle City	28	16	6	6	57	33	54
Killingworth Sporting	28	17	2	9	61	57	53
Walker Central	28	15	6	7	54	38	51
Red House Farm	28	15	4	9	56	43	49
Stocksfield	28	15	4	9	62	51	49
Shankhouse	28	13	6	9	62	44	42
Whitley Bay "A"	28	13	4	11	65	38	40
Wallington	28	11	6	11	57	58	39
Northbank Carlisle	28	8	8	12	45	59	32
Seaton Delaval Amateurs	28	9	5	14	45	53	29
Ashington Colliers	28	8	3	17	36	55	27
Gateshead Rutherford	28	5	6	17	38	91	21
Hebburn Reyrolle	28	5	5	18	48	94	17
Percy Main Amateurs	**28**	**4**	**4**	**20**	**29**	**69**	**16**

Shankhouse, Whitley Bay "A", Seaton Delaval Amateurs and Hebburn Reyrolle all had 3 points deducted.
Wallsend Town resigned during the season and their record was deleted. Stocksfield left the league. Gateshead Redheugh 1957 changed their name following their promotion from Division One and joined the Premier Division as Whickham Sporting Club.

Division One

North Shields Athletic	28	20	4	4	93	43	64
Gateshead Redheugh 1957	28	19	1	8	94	47	55
Cramlington Town	28	17	3	8	67	48	54
Newcastle Chemfica (Independ't)	28	15	7	6	71	40	52
Birtley St. Josephs	28	13	7	8	73	56	46
Gosforth Bohemian	28	13	4	11	55	48	43
Newcastle University	28	12	6	10	71	52	39
Wooler	28	10	7	11	54	68	37
Ponteland United	28	9	8	11	45	66	35
Bedlington Terriers Reserves	28	9	5	14	55	61	32
Cullercoats	28	9	4	15	47	62	31
Hexham	28	9	3	16	47	71	30
New Fordley	28	8	5	15	56	82	29
Heddon	28	7	2	19	45	98	20
Willington Quay Saints	**28**	**5**	**4**	**19**	**39**	**70**	**19**

Gateshead Redheugh 1957, Newcastle University and Heddon all had 3 points deducted.
Heddon left the league.

Division Two

Blyth Isabella	28	21	3	4	112	49	66
AFC Newbiggin	28	20	4	4	89	35	64
Wallsend Boys Club	28	19	3	6	75	33	60
Longbenton	28	18	4	6	89	41	58
Grainger Park Boys Club	28	16	2	10	77	66	50
Gateshead Leam Lane Rangers	28	14	5	9	74	36	47
Alnwick Town Reserves	28	14	4	10	63	64	46
Whitburn Athletic	28	9	9	10	52	58	36
High Howdon Social Club	28	10	4	14	59	69	34
Newcastle Benfield Reserves	28	11	3	14	66	69	33
Seaton Burn	28	7	9	12	40	58	30
Wideopen & District	28	6	4	18	40	84	22
West Allotment Celtic "A"	28	7	1	20	47	93	22
Swalwell	28	5	4	19	38	91	16
Cramlington United	28	1	5	22	32	107	5

Newcastle Benfield Reserves, Swalwell and Cramlington United each had 3 points deducted.
Shilbottle Colliery Welfare joined from the North Northumberland League, Lindisfarne Custom Planet joined from the Tyneside Amateur League and Forest Hall also joined. High Howdon Social Club changed their name to Wallsend Labour Club.

2014-15

Premier Division

Blyth Town	28	24	1	3	104	30	73
Carlisle City	28	18	4	6	104	42	58
Whitley Bay "A"	28	16	4	8	71	40	52
North Shields Athletic	28	14	3	11	74	65	45
Red House Farm	28	14	2	12	63	60	44
Wallington	28	11	8	9	69	63	41
Killingworth Sporting	28	11	7	10	60	66	40
Whickham Sporting Club	28	12	4	12	52	58	40
Shankhouse	28	11	3	14	48	44	36
Gateshead Rutherford	28	10	6	12	53	62	36
Walker Central	28	10	5	13	51	67	35
Ashington Colliers	28	9	4	15	40	66	31
Northbank Carlisle	28	8	6	14	51	64	30
Seaton Delaval Amateurs	28	8	3	17	37	73	27
Hebburn Reyrolle	**28**	**3**	**2**	**23**	**32**	**109**	**11**

Killingworth Sporting changed their name to Killingworth Town.

Division One

Percy Main Amateurs	**28**	**21**	**2**	**3**	**79**	**34**	**65**
AFC Newbiggin	**28**	**18**	**4**	**6**	**76**	**40**	**58**
Birtley St. Josephs	28	15	6	7	66	46	51
Wallsend Boys Club	28	14	5	9	62	43	47
Cullercoats	28	12	8	8	70	61	44
Bedlington Terriers Reserves	28	14	2	12	63	52	44
Cramlington Town	28	11	10	7	59	53	43
Newcastle University	28	13	1	14	67	67	40
Ponteland United	28	12	3	13	49	48	39
Gosforth Bohemian	28	9	5	14	53	63	32
Newcastle Chemfica (Ind.)	28	9	7	12	57	47	31
Hexham	28	10	3	15	57	70	30
Blyth Isabella	28	8	3	17	49	80	27
New Fordley	28	7	5	16	50	91	26
Wooler	**28**	**4**	**2**	**22**	**32**	**84**	**11**

Newcastle Chemfica (Independent), Hexham and Wooler each had 3 points deducted.
Bedlington Terriers Reserves left the league. Gateshead Leam Lane Rangers changed their name after promotion from Division Two and joined Division One as Felling Magpies.

Division Two

Shilbottle Colliery Welfare	**30**	**25**	**2**	**3**	**142**	**36**	**77**
Gateshead Leam Lane Rangers	**30**	**24**	**2**	**4**	**96**	**25**	**74**
Lindisfarne Custom Planet	**30**	**17**	**3**	**10**	**72**	**63**	**54**
Longbenton	**30**	**17**	**5**	**8**	**84**	**67**	**53**
Wallsend Labour Club	30	15	6	9	68	53	51
Seaton Burn	30	15	6	9	47	35	51
Newcastle Benfield Reserves	30	17	2	11	89	66	50
Grainger Park Boys Club	30	15	3	12	98	84	48
Whitburn Athletic	30	12	7	11	60	62	40
Forest Hall	30	12	2	16	51	59	38
Willington Quay Saints	30	10	5	15	47	60	35
Swalwell	30	8	4	18	62	85	28
Cramlington United	30	7	4	19	51	98	25
Alnwick Town Reserves	30	7	5	18	59	86	20
West Allotment Celtic "A"	30	5	4	21	54	107	19
Wideopen & District	30	4	0	26	36	130	12

Newcastle Benfield Reserves and Alnwick Town Reserves left the league. Almouth United joined from the North Northumberland League, Hazlerigg Victory joined from the Tyneside Amateur League, Gateshead Redheugh 1957 joined as a newly re-formed club while Gateshead "A" and Prudhoe Youth Club Senior also joined.

2015-16

Premier Division

Blyth Town	28	22	4	2	95	19	70
Whitley Bay "A"	28	22	1	5	72	38	67
Carlisle City	28	16	3	9	56	39	51
Seaton Delaval Amateurs	28	16	3	9	55	50	51
Walker Central	28	14	3	11	51	51	45
Killingworth Town	28	13	6	9	63	52	42
Wallington	28	12	4	12	58	55	40
Percy Main Amateurs	28	9	6	13	61	68	33
AFC Newbiggin	28	9	6	13	38	56	33
Gateshead Rutherford	28	9	4	15	53	67	31
North Shields Athletic	28	8	4	16	54	70	28
Shankhouse	28	8	3	17	40	66	27
Ashington Colliers	28	7	6	15	43	72	27
Northbank Carlisle	28	6	7	15	40	60	25
Red House Farm	28	7	4	17	49	65	22

Killingworth Town and Red House Farm each had 3 points deducted. Whickham Sporting Club resigned and their record was deleted.
Blyth Town moved to the Northern League and Carlisle City moved to the North-West Counties League. Birtley Town joined from the Northern League.

Division One

Shilbottle Colliery Welfare	28	21	3	4	98	33	66
Newcastle University	**28**	**20**	**3**	**5**	**111**	**33**	**63**
Ponteland United	**28**	**17**	**3**	**8**	**88**	**55**	**54**
Birtley St. Josephs	28	14	5	9	63	52	47
Felling Magpies	28	14	3	11	56	50	45
New Fordley	28	14	3	11	57	59	45
Hexham	28	14	2	12	56	52	38
Wallsend Boys Club	28	10	10	8	63	55	37
Cramlington Town	28	13	1	14	52	53	37
Lindisfarne Custom Planet	28	11	4	13	49	70	37
Hebburn Reyrolle	28	9	3	16	50	95	27
Gosforth Bohemian	28	8	2	18	56	82	26
Newcastle Chemfica (Ind.)	28	7	3	18	44	76	24
Cullercoats	28	6	5	17	57	84	23
Blyth Isabella	28	6	2	20	35	86	20

Hexham had 6 points deducted. Wallsend Boys Club, Cramlington Town and Hebburn Reyrolle each had 3 points deducted.
Shilbottle Colliery Welfare resigned before taking their promotion place in the Premier Division. Birtley St. Josephs and Blyth Isabella also left. Lindisfarne Custom Planet changed their name to Monkseaton and Newcastle Chemfica (Independent) became Heaton Stannington "A".

Division Two

Gateshead "A"	**28**	**24**	**1**	**3**	**142**	**27**	**73**
Grainger Park Boys Club	**28**	**20**	**3**	**5**	**96**	**56**	**60**
Seaton Burn	**28**	**18**	**5**	**5**	**62**	**34**	**59**
Wallsend Labour Club	**28**	**14**	**7**	**7**	**65**	**49**	**49**
Alnmouth United	**28**	**15**	**3**	**10**	**68**	**49**	**48**
Gateshead Redheugh 1957	**28**	**14**	**5**	**9**	**53**	**55**	**47**
Hazlerigg Victory	28	12	6	10	72	54	42
Forest Hall	28	10	4	14	53	62	34
Prudhoe Youth Club Senior	28	8	8	12	68	78	32
Whitburn Athletic	28	8	7	13	55	72	31
Cramlington United	28	8	6	14	50	69	30
Wideopen & District	28	8	4	16	53	95	28
Swalwell	28	6	5	17	48	93	23
West Allotment Celtic "A"	28	5	4	19	35	85	19
Willington Quay Saints	28	2	8	18	48	90	14

Grainger Park Boys Club had 3 points deducted.
Wooler resigned during the season and their record was deleted.
West Allotment Celtic "A" changed their name to Whitley Bay Boys Club Seniors during the season.
Swalwell left the league. Red Row Welfare and Spittal Rovers both joined from the North Northumberland League, Killingworth Y.P.C. joined from the Durham Alliance, Ryton & Crawcrook Albion joined from the Tyneside Amateur League and Blyth joined from the Newcastle Corinthians League. Bedlington Town joined as a newly formed club and Blyth Town "A" joined as a newly formed team.

Northern Alliance 2016-2018

2016-17
Premier Division

Killingworth Town	28	20	4	4	63	27	64
Newcastle University	28	17	7	4	76	37	58
North Shields Athletic	28	16	4	8	76	49	52
Ponteland United	28	16	2	10	62	49	50
Walker Central	28	17	2	9	86	49	47
Whitley Bay "A"	28	14	5	9	69	54	47
Shankhouse	28	11	5	12	48	65	38
Birtley Town	28	11	4	13	64	69	37
Seaton Delaval Amateurs	28	8	10	10	51	53	34
Wallington	28	10	4	14	51	67	34
AFC Newbiggin	28	9	6	13	45	73	33
Percy Main Amateurs	28	8	5	15	49	67	29
Ashington Colliers	28	8	2	18	50	66	26
Gateshead Rutherford	28	6	7	15	47	55	25
Northbank Carlisle	28	4	3	21	28	85	12

Walker Central had 6 points deducted.
Northbank Carlisle had 3 points deducted.
Red House Farm resigned during the season and their record was deleted.
Walker Central also left the league. Grainger Park Boys Club changed their name after promotion from Division One and joined the Premier Division as FC United of Newcastle.

Division One

Gateshead "A"	30	26	2	2	126	28	80
Grainger Park Boys Club	30	23	2	5	101	45	71
Hexham	30	19	4	7	85	51	61
Cullercoats	30	19	4	7	85	57	58
Wallsend Labour Club	30	18	1	11	73	63	55
Monkseaton	30	15	5	10	68	53	50
Heaton Stannington "A"	30	15	1	14	82	79	46
Felling Magpies	30	13	6	11	69	49	45
Seaton Burn	30	12	4	14	56	62	40
Hebburn Reyrolle	30	11	2	17	63	95	35
Wallsend Boys Club	30	10	3	17	51	67	33
Cramlington Town	30	10	3	17	48	79	33
New Fordley	30	7	3	20	48	81	24
Gosforth Bohemian	30	6	4	20	42	74	22
Alnmouth United	30	8	1	21	34	80	22
Gateshead Redheugh 1957	30	4	3	23	34	102	15

Cullercoats and Alnmouth United each had 3 points deducted.
Alnmouth United were to be relegated to Division Two but resigned before the start of the 2017-18 season. Hebburn Reyrolle became Hebburn Town U23, Heaton Stannington "A" changed their name to Newcastle Chemfica and Wallsend Labour Club changed their name to Wallsend Community.

Division Two

Killingworth Y.P.C.	28	21	4	3	108	21	61
Forest Hall	28	19	1	8	99	31	58
Hazlerigg Victory	28	17	5	6	91	34	56
Red Row Welfare	28	18	3	7	91	41	54
Willington Quay Saints	28	14	6	8	61	57	48
Cramlington United	28	14	3	11	59	57	45
Blyth Town "A"	28	13	5	10	77	57	44
Prudhoe Youth Club Seniors	28	13	5	10	81	60	41
Spittal Rovers	28	13	1	14	54	53	40
Bedlington Town	28	12	4	12	62	64	40
Whitburn Athletic	28	8	8	12	57	75	32
Whitley Bay Boys Club Seniors	28	9	4	15	55	78	31
Blyth	28	6	1	21	24	109	16
Wideopen & District	28	2	4	22	32	132	10
Ryton & Crawcrook Albion	28	2	4	22	35	117	7

Killingworth Y.P.C. had 6 points deducted.
Red Row Welfare, Prudhoe Youth Club Seniors, Blyth and Ryton & Crawcrook Albion all had 3 points deducted.
Seghill joined from the Newcastle Corinthians League while Coundon & Leeholme joined as a newly formed club and Blyth Spartans Reserves joined as a newly formed team. Ryton & Crawcrook Albion changed their name to Winlaton Vulcans.

2017-18
Premier Division

Newcastle University	30	25	2	3	123	31	77
Birtley Town	30	22	3	5	91	42	69
Ponteland United	30	17	6	7	68	49	57
Whitley Bay "A"	30	17	3	10	86	63	54
Seaton Delaval Amateurs	30	18	2	10	100	63	53
Wallington	29	16	5	8	85	54	53
Killingworth Town	30	13	5	12	59	54	44
Shankhouse	30	13	5	12	52	48	44
Ashington Colliers	30	14	4	12	68	61	43
Gateshead Rutherford	30	11	5	14	52	62	38
Percy Main Amateurs	30	12	2	16	58	72	38
AFC Newbiggin	30	11	2	17	56	88	29
Gateshead "A"	30	8	3	19	67	72	27
Northbank Carlisle	29	8	4	17	57	71	22
North Shields Athletic	30	7	1	22	49	106	19
FC United of Newcastle	30	0	2	28	25	160	-1

Seaton Delaval Amateurs, Ashington Colliers, North Shields Athletic and FC United of Newcastle all had 3 points deducted.
AFC Newbiggin and Northbank Carlisle each had 6 points deducted.
Birtley Town moved to the Northern League and Northbank Carlisle disbanded. Ashington Colliers and AFC Newbiggin also left the league. Alnwick Town joined from the Northern League and Newcastle Blue Star joined as a newly formed club. Killingworth Town merged with Killingworth YPC (Division One champions) to form AFC Killingworth.

Division One

Killingworth YPC	30	27	2	1	144	29	83
Hazlerigg Victory	30	24	2	4	131	32	74
Newcastle Chemfica	30	18	6	6	115	50	60
Felling Magpies	30	16	3	11	88	67	51
Wallsend Community	30	15	6	9	89	66	48
Seaton Burn	30	14	5	11	73	65	47
Forest Hall	30	14	3	13	61	58	45
New Fordley	30	16	2	12	75	52	44
Hexham	30	14	2	14	77	65	44
Red Row Welfare	30	13	3	14	74	77	39
Wallsend Boys Club	30	11	5	14	66	62	35
Gosforth Bohemian	30	10	4	16	46	70	34
Hebburn Town U23	30	8	3	19	53	121	27
Cullercoats	30	8	4	18	49	79	25
Monkseaton	30	3	3	24	34	152	9
Cramlington Town	30	2	1	27	30	160	7

Wallsend Community, Red Row Welfare, Monkseaton, Wallsend Boys Club and Cullercoats all had 3 points deducted.
New Fordley had 6 points deducted.
Monkseaton changed their name to Newcastle East End during the season. Hazlerigg Victory left the league.

Division Two

Blyth Spartans Reserves	28	23	4	1	126	33	73
Prudhoe Youth Club Seniors	28	20	1	7	96	45	61
Winlaton Vulcans	28	16	6	6	93	50	54
Bedlington Town	28	16	4	8	91	55	52
Blyth Town "A"	28	15	7	6	83	51	52
Cramlington United	28	14	6	8	79	70	48
Blyth	28	14	1	13	68	79	43
Whitburn Athletic	28	11	4	13	51	57	37
Whitley Bay Boys Club Seniors	28	10	6	12	62	68	36
Coundon & Leeholme	28	9	7	12	54	63	34
Wideopen & District	28	7	4	17	42	70	25
Spittal Rovers	28	6	7	15	43	82	22
Willington Quay Saints	28	6	3	19	44	84	21
Seghill	28	4	7	17	37	70	19
Gateshead Redheugh 1957	28	4	3	21	39	137	15

Whitley Bay Boys Club Seniors changed their name to Whitley Bay Sporting Club during the season.
Burradon, Ellington, Jesmond, Rothbury and Stobswood Welfare all joined. Whitburn Athletic changed their name to Whitburn & Cleadon.

TYNESIDE LEAGUE 1891-1939

The first Tyneside League was formed on Saturday 9th May 1891 following a meeting at Lockhart's Cocoa Rooms, St. Nicholas' Square, Newcastle. The 12 clubs that formed the league's first incarnation were: Benwell Hill, Bill Quay Albion, Jarrow Rangers, Neptune, Newburn St. Michael's, Pelicans, Portland, Trafalgar, Wallsend North-Eastern Rangers, West Wylam Harriers, Westgate Athletic and Worswick Rovers.

1891-92

It seems that clubs were only required to meet once in the 1891-92 season but despite this, the league programme was still not completed. Very little information on that season has been found but Trafalgar (a Newcastle team) were declared champions, having won 10 and drawn 1 of their 11 games. Jarrow are known to have finished 3rd with 6 wins and 4 defeats in their 10 matches while Wallsend North-Eastern Rangers were bottom, having played just 7 matches, drawing 2 and losing 5.

1892-93

The league continued in 1892-93 when the membership included Gateshead Wesley, Godfrey, Hebburn Argyle, Jarrow Rangers, Jarrow St. Bede's, Walker and Worswick Rovers but again, no tables have been found and it is not known which club were declared champions.
Hebburn Argyle moved to the Northern Alliance for 1893-94.

1893-94

The league did not operate.

1894-95

The league was revived on 11th April 1894 following another meeting at Lockhart's, with 11 clubs chosen as members – Axwell Rovers, Bill Quay Albion, Gateshead Town, Godfrey, Heaton Rovers, Hobson Wanderers, Jarrow, Jarrow Presbyterian, Mickley, Wallsend Celtic and Wallsend Royal Oak. Hexham Excelsior and Leadgate Park were added later but whether they were added to the original 11 members or were replacements for clubs who had withdrawn has not been established.
Once again, no tables have been found but Leadgate Park were the champions while Axwell Rovers, Godfrey, Heaton Rovers, Hexham Excelsior, Hobson Wanderers, Jarrow Presbyterian, Mickley and Wallsend Celtic were also definitely members of the league. Of the original 11 members, Bill Quay Albion, Gateshead Town and Wallsend Royal Oak may not have taken part while Jarrow (a new club formed as a replacement for the recently disbanded Jarrow Rangers) joined the Northern Alliance in 1894-95 instead of the Tyneside League.
At the end of the season, Axwell Rovers moved to the Northern Alliance while Godfrey, Heaton Rovers and Jarrow Presbyterian also left. Gateshead Engineers, Gateshead St. Cuthbert's, Prudhoe, St. Peter's Albion and Wallsend Park Villa joined.

1895-96

Leadgate Park	16	11	2	3	51	16	24
Mickley	16	10	2	4	40	23	22
Wallsend Park Villa	16	9	2	5	52	37	20
Hexham Excelsior	16	9	2	5	35	27	20
St. Peter's Albion	16	7	4	5	44	35	18
Hobson Wanderers	16	7	3	6	28	34	17
Wallsend Celtic	16	4	5	7	27	32	13
Gateshead St. Cuthbert's	16	2	3	11	21	56	7
Prudhoe	16	1	1	14	11	49	3

Gateshead Engineers resigned during the season and their record was deleted when it stood as: 12 1 2 9 9 60 4
Leadgate Park moved to the Northern League and St. Peter's Albion moved to the Northern Alliance. Annfield Plain Celtic, Bill Quay Albion, Consett Town Swifts, Heaton Science & Art and Wardley Blue Star all joined.

1896-97

Annfield Plain Celtic	20	12	6	2	49	23	30
Hobson Wanderers	20	11	7	2	49	23	29
Mickley	20	12	4	4	34	19	28
Wallsend Park Villa	20	12	2	6	46	21	26
Wallsend Celtic	20	9	5	6	38	27	23
Wardley Blue Star	20	9	3	7	36	37	21
Hexham Excelsior	20	7	6	7	44	33	20
Consett Town Swifts	20	6	3	11	35	50	15
Bill Quay Albion	20	5	4	11	28	53	14
Prudhoe	20	3	3	14	21	56	9
Heaton Science & Art	20	2	0	18	12	50	4

Gateshead St. Cuthbert's resigned during the season and their record was deleted. Wallsend Park Villa moved to the Northern Alliance and Heaton Science & Art also left the league. Dipton Wanderers joined from the Tyneside League, Blaydon United joined from the Derwent Valley League and Walbottle also joined.

1897-98

The latest table found is shown and this includes results up to and including 9th April 1898

Hobson Wanderers	16	13	2	1	31	10	28
Prudhoe	18	10	5	3	29	15	25
Walbottle	15	9	4	2	26	16	22
Consett Town Swifts	15	6	5	4	21	19	17
Annfield Plain Celtic	18	5	4	9	29	36	14
Allendale Park	15	4	5	6	27	23	13
Bill Quay Albion	15	6	1	8	21	19	13
Mickley	16	4	5	7	17	19	13
Dipton Wanderers	18	5	2	11	21	36	12
Hexham Excelsior	15	4	2	9	19	27	10
Blaydon United	15	3	3	9	17	30	9

Wallsend Celtic resigned and disbanded during October 1897 and their record was deleted: 3 0 0 3 2 15 0
Allendale Park joined the league in their place and played a full programme of games.
Wardley Blue Star resigned during December 1897 and their record was deleted when it stood as: 8 4 1 3 17 15 9
Bill Quay Albion and Blaydon United left the league.
Throckley, Newburn and Spen all joined.

1898-99

The latest table found is shown and this includes results up to and including 26th November 1898.

Mickley	7	6	0	1	29	9	12
Prudhoe	8	5	2	1	20	9	12
Walbottle	7	5	1	1	22	6	11
Throckley	7	4	1	2	12	11	9
Annfield Plain Celtic	4	3	0	1	12	5	6
Consett Town Swifts	5	2	1	2	8	5	5
Allendale Park	5	2	1	2	11	15	5
Hobson Wanderers	4	2	0	2	7	5	4
Spen	6	0	0	6	3	31	0
Newburn	5	0	0	5	1	16	0
Dipton Wanderers	6	0	0	6	1	24	0

Hexham Excelsior had resigned by this date and their record was deleted. There were further resignations before the end of the season.
A Final table has not been found but it is known that Mickley were champions and Consett Town Swifts finished 5th.

1899-1900

No tables have been found. Prudhoe were champions and other members of the league included Consett Town Swifts, Hobson Wanderers and Mickley.

1900-05

No record has been found that the league operated again until 1905 when it was re-formed with the following 8 clubs: Dinnington Royal Oak, Hebburn Argyle Reserves, Kibblesworth Albion, North Shields Athletic Reserves, South Shields Adelaide (who joined from the Shields & District League), Sunniside United, Willington Athletic Reserves and Willington St. Aidan's.

1905-06

South Shields Adelaide	14	10	1	3	44	22	21
North Shields Athletic Reserves	14	10	0	4	37	19	20
Willington St. Aidan's	14	10	0	4	37	20	20
Hebburn Argyle Reserves	14	5	4	5	22	27	14
Kibblesworth Albion	14	5	3	6	29	30	13
Whitley Athletic Reserves	14	4	3	7	20	29	9
Dinnington Royal Oak	14	3	2	9	18	35	8
Sunniside United	14	2	1	11	13	38	5

Whitley Athletic Reserves took over the fixtures of Willington Athletic Reserves on 3rd February 1906 when Willington's record stood as follows (2 points having been deducted): 7 2 2 3 10 13 4
North Shields Athletic Reserves won the second-place play-off against Willington St. Aidan's with a 1-0 scoreline, after two 1-1 draws, all of which were actually played early in the 1906-07 season.

Dinnington Royal Oak and Kibblesworth Albion both left the league. Blaydon St. Joseph's, Felling E.R., Newcastle Banks, Shiremoor United, Wardley United, Willington North End and Windy Nook Albion all joined. Whitley Athletic joined from the Shields & District League, replacing their reserves.

1906-07

South Shields Adelaide	22	17	3	2	76	14	37
North Shields Athletic Reserves	22	14	4	4	58	26	32
Felling E.R.	22	14	4	4	55	28	32
Whitley Athletic	22	12	5	5	62	34	29
Windy Nook Albion	22	11	4	7	37	39	26
Hebburn Argyle Reserves	22	10	3	9	35	42	23
Willington North End	22	10	3	9	55	47	21
Willington St. Aidan's	22	8	3	11	40	46	19
Wardley United	22	7	3	12	55	67	17
Blaydon St. Joseph's	22	4	2	16	31	65	10
Sunniside United	22	3	4	15	31	62	10
Newcastle Banks	22	2	2	18	22	87	6

Shiremoor United resigned in January and their record was deleted when it stood as follows: 9 1 1 7 10 31 3
Willington North End had 2 points deducted.
North Shields Athletic Reserves beat Felling E.R. 2-0 in the second place play-off.
South Shields Adelaide moved to the Northern Alliance and Hebburn Argyle Reserves, Newcastle Banks and Sunniside United also left.
Hebburn R.N.V.R., New York United, Pelaw and Wallsend Slipway joined.

1907-08

Windy Nook Albion	20	13	4	3	39	14	30
Wallsend Slipway	20	12	5	3	45	24	29
North Shields Athletic Reserves	20	10	5	5	51	28	25
Willington North End	20	9	5	6	28	23	23
New York United	20	8	6	6	33	25	22
Pelaw	20	9	3	8	46	33	21
Felling E.R.	20	9	5	6	38	31	21
Whitley Athletic	20	8	3	9	32	30	19
Willington St. Aidan's	20	7	2	11	28	48	16
Blaydon St. Joseph's	20	2	2	16	20	69	6
Hebburn R.N.V.R.	20	2	2	16	18	53	4

Wardley United resigned in January and their record was deleted when it stood as follows: 7 0 1 6 8 26 1
Felling E.R. and Hebburn R.N.V.R. each had 2 points deducted.
Whitley Athletic ceased activity for a year as they could not find a ground.
Blaydon St. Joseph's and Hebburn R.N.V.R. also left the league.
Boldon Colliery, Jarrow Caledonians, Shields Albion, South Shields Adelaide Reserves, South Shields Parkside and Wallsend Elm Villa all joined.

1908-09

Windy Nook Albion	26	17	4	5	59	35	38
South Shields Parkside	26	15	5	6	53	38	35
Jarrow Caledonians	26	13	4	9	66	47	30
Pelaw	26	12	6	8	53	44	30
North Shields Athletic Reserves	26	13	3	10	78	49	29
Wallsend Slipway	26	11	6	9	49	49	28
Willington St. Aidan's	26	10	5	11	53	48	25
Felling E.R.	26	10	5	11	38	37	25
Wallsend Elm Villa	26	9	6	11	43	50	24
Shields Albion	26	8	7	11	47	52	23
Boldon Colliery	26	8	8	10	51	62	23
Willington North End	26	9	6	11	33	46	22
South Shields Adelaide Reserves	26	5	8	13	39	63	18
New York United	26	4	3	19	32	74	11

Boldon colliery had 1 point deducted.
Willington North End had 2 points deducted.
South Shields Adelaide Reserves moved to the Wearside League while North Shields Athletic reserve side was disbanded. Jarrow Caledonians moved to the Northern Alliance and fielded their reserve side in the Tyneside League. Having obtained a ground, Whitley Athletic rejoined after a year's inactivity.

1909-10

Windy Nook Albion	24	20	1	3	53	24	41
Pelaw	24	16	6	2	54	22	38
Boldon Colliery	24	16	3	5	57	26	35
Jarrow Caledonians Reserves	24	14	4	6	49	32	32
South Shields Parkside	24	14	2	8	72	38	30
Wallsend Slipway	24	12	3	9	51	29	27
Shields Albion	24	7	6	11	32	50	20
Wallsend Elm Villa	24	6	7	11	52	54	19
New York United	24	5	8	11	35	41	18
Felling E.R.	24	6	5	13	39	60	17
Willington St. Aidan's	24	5	2	17	22	70	12
Willington North End	24	4	4	16	26	58	12
Whitley Athletic	24	3	17	30	68	11	

South Shields Parkside moved to the Northern Alliance while Willington North End and Whitley Athletic also left the league. Boldon Villa, Hebburn Black Watch and Jarrow Blackett all joined from the Shields & District League while Gateshead Rodsley and Gosforth also joined.

1910-11

	P	W	D	L	F	A	Pts
Windy Nook Albion	28	21	4	3	76	27	46
Wallsend Slipway	28	19	3	6	63	36	41
Wallsend Elm Villa	28	16	4	8	50	33	36
Felling E.R.	28	14	8	6	51	35	36
Pelaw	28	13	8	7	62	36	34
Boldon Colliery	28	15	3	10	43	36	33
Gateshead Rodsley	28	11	6	11	45	37	28
New York United	28	12	4	12	44	49	28
Jarrow Blackett	28	11	6	11	38	49	28
Shields Albion	28	7	10	11	44	51	24
Gosforth	28	9	5	14	51	57	23
Boldon Villa	28	9	4	15	38	43	22
Hebburn Black Watch	28	7	6	15	32	49	20
Jarrow Caledonians Reserves	28	3	6	19	26	62	12
Willington St. Aidan's	28	4	1	23	21	84	9

Willington St. Aidan's left the league.
Coxlodge Villa and North Shields Athletic Reserves joined.

1911-12

	P	W	D	L	F	A	Pts
New York United	30	18	6	6	49	22	42
Wallsend Slipway	30	18	4	8	59	41	40
Jarrow Blackett	30	18	4	8	65	46	40
Gateshead Rodsley	30	15	8	7	74	34	38
Boldon Colliery	30	17	4	9	55	34	38
Boldon Villa	30	11	10	9	42	43	32
Shields Albion	30	12	7	11	57	46	31
Coxlodge Villa	30	12	7	11	49	53	31
Wallsend Elm Villa	30	14	1	15	51	60	29
Windy Nook Albion	30	13	3	14	51	61	29
Felling E.R.	30	10	8	12	56	51	28
North Shields Athletic Reserves	30	9	8	13	54	61	26
Jarrow Caledonians Reserves	30	12	0	18	50	51	24
Pelaw	30	8	6	16	48	67	22
Gosforth	30	9	3	18	37	58	21
Hebburn Black Watch	30	4	1	25	24	93	9

Wallsend Slipway beat Jarrow Blackett 4-1 in the second place play-off.
Hebburn Black Watch moved to the Gateshead & District League while North Shields Athletic Reserves also left. South Shields Reserves joined from the Wearside League and Walker Church Institute joined.

1912-13

	P	W	D	L	F	A	Pts
Wallsend Slipway	28	21	2	5	78	27	44
Boldon Colliery	28	18	6	4	53	19	42
Gateshead Rodsley	28	15	7	6	57	33	37
Felling E.R.	28	14	7	7	45	30	35
Shields Albion	28	14	5	9	67	41	33
Walker Church Institute	28	12	9	7	41	31	33
Gosforth	28	12	8	8	60	39	32
South Shields Reserves	28	11	7	10	59	51	29
Windy Nook Albion	28	10	9	9	56	56	29
Boldon Villa	28	9	9	10	43	48	27
New York United	28	9	5	14	45	51	23
Coxlodge Villa	28	5	7	16	43	61	17
Jarrow Caledonians Reserves	28	6	4	18	32	90	16
Jarrow Blackett	28	5	4	19	26	75	14
Wallsend Elm Villa	28	4	1	23	30	83	9

Pelaw resigned in late March and their record was deleted when it stood as follows:

| | | 19 | 4 | 4 | 11 | 25 | 44 | 12 |

Jarrow Caledonians disbanded while Felling E.R. and Shields Albion also left the league. Brighton West End, Heworth Colliery, Jarrow Reserves and Willington U.M. all joined.

1913-14

	P	W	D	L	F	A	Pts
South Shields Reserves	28	22	4	2	85	25	48
Gosforth	28	19	5	4	69	37	43
Boldon Colliery	27	15	8	4	61	35	38
Wallsend Slipway	27	13	7	7	46	33	33
Gateshead Rodsley	28	12	8	8	51	39	32
Coxlodge Villa	28	13	3	12	51	46	29
Jarrow Blackett	27	11	3	13	38	50	25
Windy Nook Albion	28	11	3	14	50	63	25
Jarrow Reserves	27	8	8	11	32	39	24
Wallsend Elm Villa	28	10	4	14	42	56	24
Willington U.M.	28	8	5	15	39	54	21
Boldon Villa	26	8	4	14	39	39	20
Brighton West End	28	7	6	15	57	66	20
Heworth Colliery	26	3	6	17	27	77	12
Walker Church Institute	20	3	4	13	29	57	10

New York United resigned and disbanded in the first week of January and their record was deleted:

| | | 10 | 2 | 1 | 7 | 6 | 17 | 5 |

Walker Church Institute resigned on 12th March with 8 games still to play but the League rejected the resignation. Those 8 games were not played.
Gateshead Rodsley and Windy Nook Albion both moved to the Northern Alliance and Gosforth ceased activity as they had lost their ground.
Heworth Colliery and Jarrow Reserves also left. South Shields Parkside joined from the Northern Alliance while Dunston Atlas Villa, Hebburn Black Watch, Wallsend Collieries and Washington United also joined.

1914-15

	P	W	D	L	F	A	Pts
South Shields Reserves	20	15	1	4	63	19	31
Boldon Colliery	20	14	3	3	56	17	31
Washington United	19	11	5	3	34	19	27
Brighton West End	20	12	1	7	80	41	25
Wallsend Slipway	20	10	4	6	31	37	24
Boldon Villa	20	10	0	10	50	45	20
Jarrow Blackett	20	6	3	11	31	52	15
Hebburn Black Watch	20	7	1	12	16	49	15
Wallsend Collieries	18	5	4	9	28	35	14
South Shields Parkside	20	4	1	15	16	38	9
Dunston Atlas Villa	19	2	1	16	17	70	5

Two games were not played.
Boldon Colliery and South Shields Reserves were declared joint champions.
Three clubs resigned during the season, chiefly because many players had joined the Armed Forces. All three had their records deleted. They were:

Wallsend Elm Villa		6	0	1	5	5	16	1
Willington U.M.		9	1	0	8	10	28	2
Coxlodge Villa		15	2	4	9	21	40	8

1915-19

The Tyneside League closed down because of the First World War and did not operate again until it was re-formed in 1919 with 14 clubs.
Only 4 of the pre-war clubs re-joined. They were Boldon Colliery, Boldon Villa, Brighton West End and Dunston Atlas Villa. South Shields Reserves moved to the North-Eastern League while Hebburn Black Watch, Jarrow Blackett, South Shields Parkside, Wallsend Collieries, Wallsend Slipway and Washington United also did not re-join.
There were 10 new clubs: Preston Colliery joined as a club newly formed in North Shields, while Allhusens Works, Palmer's (Jarrow) Reserves, Pandon Temperance, Scotswood Reserves, St. Peter's Albion, Teamby United, Usworth Colliery, Wardley Colliery and Washington Colliery all also joined.

Tyneside League 1919-1925

1919-20

Team	P	W	D	L	F	A	Pts
St. Peter's Albion	26	19	3	4	53	16	41
Usworth Colliery	26	15	7	4	50	25	37
Preston Colliery	26	14	5	7	45	28	33
Allhusens Works	26	11	5	10	34	30	27
Palmer's (Jarrow) Reserves	26	11	5	10	32	32	27
Pandon Temperance	26	11	5	10	39	42	27
Scotswood Reserves	26	9	7	10	44	35	25
Brighton West End	26	9	7	10	34	31	25
Boldon Villa	26	11	3	12	43	44	25
Boldon Colliery	26	9	6	11	36	31	24
Dunston Atlas Villa	26	10	4	12	40	42	24
Washington Colliery	26	10	4	12	39	55	22
Teamby United	26	5	6	15	24	56	16
Wardley Colliery	26	2	5	19	23	69	9

Washington Colliery had 2 points deducted.
Palmer's (Jarrow) changed their name to Jarrow during the season.
Preston Colliery moved to the Northern Alliance while Allhusens Works, Jarrow Reserves and Scotswood Reserves also left the league.
Marsden Rescue, Middle Docks, Scotswood Works, Simonside, St. Anthony's Institute and Wood-Skinners all joined.

1920-21

Team	P	W	D	L	F	A	Pts
St. Peter's Albion	30	22	2	6	81	24	46
Dunston Atlas Villa	30	20	4	6	69	36	44
Boldon Colliery	30	19	5	6	57	19	42
Usworth Colliery	30	20	2	8	61	30	42
Middle Docks	30	15	9	6	41	29	39
Simonside	30	16	3	11	58	59	35
Boldon Villa	30	14	5	11	54	42	33
St. Anthony's Institute	30	13	6	11	57	48	32
Washington Colliery	30	13	3	14	54	54	29
Pandon Temperance	30	9	6	15	38	51	24
Wood-Skinners	30	9	4	17	43	67	22
Teamby United	30	7	7	16	43	61	19
Marsden Rescue	30	6	7	17	42	64	19
Brighton West End	30	7	5	18	38	74	19
Wardley Colliery	30	6	5	19	37	65	17
Scotswood Works	30	6	3	21	36	86	15

Boldon Colliery had 1 point deducted.
Teamby United had 2 points deducted.
Brighton West End and Pandon Temperance left because they had lost their grounds and Scotswood Works and Wardley Colliery also left. Pelaw, Preston Colliery Reserves, Smith's Dock and Wallsend Reserves joined.

1921-22

Team	P	W	D	L	F	A	Pts
St. Peter's Albion	30	23	4	3	79	20	50
Usworth Colliery	30	20	4	6	83	46	42
Boldon Colliery	30	19	3	8	61	32	41
Dunston Atlas Villa	30	17	7	6	64	41	40
Wood-Skinners	30	17	5	8	55	43	39
St. Anthony's Institute	30	13	9	8	50	40	35
Wallsend Reserves	30	14	6	10	53	46	33
Washington Colliery	30	14	6	10	49	44	32
Pelaw	30	11	9	10	60	49	31
Middle Docks	30	12	5	13	42	47	29
Preston Colliery Reserves	30	7	7	16	50	61	21
Boldon Villa	30	7	6	17	47	54	20
Smith's Dock	30	5	7	18	34	68	17
Marsden Rescue	30	6	5	19	31	66	17
Simonside	30	7	2	21	38	78	14
Teamby United	30	3	5	22	31	92	9

Dunston Atlas Villa and Wallsend Reserves each had 1 point deducted. Simonside, Teamby United, Usworth Colliery and Washington Colliery all had 2 points deducted.
Simonside and Teamby United both left the league. Washington Chemical Works joined from the Palatine League and Greenesfield Locomotive Works also joined.

1922-23

Team	P	W	D	L	F	A	Pts
St. Peter's Albion	28	25	1	2	73	18	51
Usworth Colliery	28	18	4	6	58	30	40
Pelaw	28	17	3	8	67	39	37
Dunston Atlas Villa	28	15	4	9	64	42	34
Preston Colliery Reserves	28	11	7	10	48	49	29
Boldon Villa	28	12	4	12	55	51	28
Washington Colliery	28	12	3	13	46	46	27
Wood-Skinners	28	12	3	13	48	56	27
Washington Chemical Works	28	11	5	12	43	47	26
Boldon Colliery	28	7	10	11	38	46	24
Middle Docks	28	8	8	12	38	46	24
St. Anthony's Institute	28	7	10	11	38	50	24
Wallsend Reserves	28	4	10	14	41	80	18
Greenesfield Locomotive Works	28	6	5	17	33	58	17
Smith's Dock	28	3	7	16	35	67	13

Washington Chemical works had 1 point deducted.
Marsden Rescue resigned from the league in December and their record was deleted when it was: 12 1 0 11 6 35 2
Wallsend Reserves and Washington Colliery left the league.
Hebburn Leslies, Jarrow Reserves and Wardley Colliery joined.

1923-24

Team	P	W	D	L	F	A	Pts
St. Peter's Albion	28	22	2	4	79	22	46
Wardley Colliery	28	19	4	5	74	27	42
Dunston Atlas Villa	28	17	7	4	66	39	41
Wood-Skinners	28	17	4	7	76	40	38
Greenesfield Locomotive Works	28	13	6	9	49	46	32
Pelaw	28	12	6	10	55	49	30
Usworth Colliery	28	12	5	11	44	41	29
Boldon Colliery	28	11	6	11	69	59	28
Washington Chemical Works	28	10	6	12	42	57	26
Middle Docks	28	11	2	15	48	51	22
St. Anthony's Institute	28	8	6	14	38	52	22
Jarrow Reserves	28	7	4	17	40	75	16
Hebburn Leslies	28	6	4	18	29	71	14
Boldon Villa	28	6	3	19	39	65	13
Smith's Dock	28	3	7	18	35	89	13

Boldon Villa, Hebburn Leslies, Jarrow Reserves and Middle Docks each had 2 points deducted.
Preston Colliery disbanded their reserve side which resigned at the end of December. Their record was: 13 4 3 6 13 21 11
Boldon Villa, Jarrow Reserves, Smith's Dock and Washington Chemical Works left the league. Newcastle United formed a new third team called Newcastle United Swifts which joined the Tyneside League while Armstrong-Whitworth and Wallsend Reserves also joined.

1924-25

Team	P	W	D	L	F	A	Pts
Wood-Skinners	26	20	4	2	74	23	44
Usworth Colliery	26	18	5	3	55	28	39
Pelaw	26	16	6	4	80	39	38
Dunston Atlas Villa	26	14	3	9	67	37	31
Boldon Colliery	26	14	2	10	59	35	30
Newcastle United Swifts	26	12	6	8	56	36	30
Middle Docks	26	11	6	9	56	43	28
St. Peter's Albion	26	11	5	10	48	46	27
Wallsend Reserves	26	10	3	13	37	49	20
Hebburn Leslies	26	6	7	13	40	52	19
Wardley Colliery	26	6	7	13	33	54	19
St. Anthony's Institute	26	7	2	17	43	66	16
Greenesfield Locomotive Works	26	5	5	16	53	73	15
Armstrong-Whitworth	26	1	1	24	15	135	3

Usworth Colliery had 2 points deducted.
Wallsend Reserves had 3 points deducted.
Hebburn Leslies left the league.
Benwell Colliery, Jarrow Reserves and Saltwell Villa joined.

1925-26

	P	W	D	L	F	A	Pts
Usworth Colliery	30	23	2	5	85	36	48
Boldon Colliery	30	21	6	3	113	45	48
Newcastle United Swifts	30	18	6	6	81	49	42
Wood-Skinners	30	16	9	5	80	53	41
Jarrow Reserves	30	15	7	8	91	56	37
Dunston Atlas Villa	30	12	8	10	86	70	32
Wardley Colliery	30	14	4	12	53	46	32
St. Anthony's Institute	30	12	5	13	69	68	27
St. Peter's Albion	30	8	10	12	58	63	26
Saltwell Villa	30	11	4	15	67	92	26
Middle Docks	30	8	9	13	47	65	25
Greenesfield Locomotive Works	30	10	4	16	59	85	24
Pelaw	30	9	4	17	66	91	22
Benwell Colliery	30	9	3	18	57	89	21
Wallsend Reserves	30	6	2	22	45	100	14
Armstrong-Whitworth	30	5	3	22	40	89	13

St. Anthony's Institute had 2 points deducted.

Championship play-off

Usworth Colliery vs Boldon Colliery   2-1

Armstrong-Whitworth, Benwell Colliery, Newcastle United Swifts and Wallsend Reserves all left. Gosforth & Coxlodge British Legion joined.

1926-27

	P	W	D	L	F	A	Pts
Usworth Colliery	22	18	3	1	74	30	39
Boldon Colliery	22	16	2	4	72	37	34
St. Anthony's Institute	22	12	7	3	54	35	31
Jarrow Reserves	22	12	3	7	51	36	25
Gosforth & Coxlodge British Legion	22	9	3	10	53	55	21
St. Peter's Albion	22	7	5	10	44	52	19
Dunston Atlas Villa	22	8	4	10	53	50	18
Middle Docks	22	7	3	12	36	51	17
Pelaw	22	7	2	13	40	49	16
Wood-Skinners	22	5	4	13	38	57	14
Wardley Colliery	22	5	4	13	42	74	12
Greenesfield Locomotive Works	22	4	4	14	38	69	12

Dunston Atlas Villa, Jarrow Reserves and Wardley Colliery each had 2 points deducted.
Saltwell Villa resigned in January and their record was deleted when it stood as follows: 9   1   1   7   12   38   3
Usworth Colliery moved to the North-Eastern League, St. Peter's Albion moved to the Northern amateur league while Greenesfield Locomotive Works and Wood-Skinners also left. Fatfield Albion joined from the Wearside League while Bill Quay Hibernians, Felling Celtic, Hebburn Colliery, Hebburn Leslies, Reyrolles, Washington Chemical Works and Washington Trinity also joined. Wardley Colliery changed their name to Wardley Welfare.

1927-28

	P	W	D	L	F	A	Pts
Middle Docks	30	21	4	5	72	40	46
Fatfield Albion	30	22	1	7	94	50	45
Pelaw	30	19	4	7	85	46	42
Hebburn Colliery	30	18	5	7	107	55	41
Bill Quay Hibernians	30	16	6	8	58	51	36
Hebburn Leslies	30	14	5	11	82	62	33
Gosforth & Coxlodge B.L.	30	15	5	10	89	70	33
Jarrow Reserves	30	14	5	11	75	68	33
Reyrolles	30	13	5	12	75	62	31
Dunston Atlas Villa	30	14	3	13	69	71	31
Washington Trinity	30	9	6	15	53	56	24
Felling Celtic	30	9	5	16	58	78	23
Wardley Welfare	30	9	3	18	57	79	21
St. Anthony's Institute	30	6	3	21	33	104	15
Boldon Colliery	30	5	3	22	44	96	13
Washington Chemical Works	30	3	3	24	38	101	9

Bill Quay Hibernians and Gosforth & Coxlodge British Legion each had 2 points deducted.
Dunston Atlas Villa, Washington Chemical Works and Washington Trinity all left the league. Felling Colliery joined from the North-Eastern League, Walker Park joined from the Northern Amateur League while Newcastle C.W.S. also joined.

1928-29

	P	W	D	L	F	A	Pts
Hebburn Colliery	28	21	3	4	94	28	45
Wardley Welfare	28	19	3	6	80	48	41
Hebburn Leslies	28	18	3	7	82	48	39
Gosforth & Coxlodge British Legion	28	15	5	8	86	58	35
Reyrolles	28	13	5	10	72	56	31
Middle Docks	28	12	7	9	72	61	31
Pelaw	28	11	5	12	62	63	27
Bill Quay Hibernians	28	11	4	13	61	47	26
Boldon Colliery	28	11	4	13	61	85	26
Walker Park	28	10	5	13	64	67	25
Newcastle C.W.S.	28	10	2	16	62	93	22
Jarrow Reserves	28	9	2	17	55	81	20
Fatfield Albion	28	9	1	18	49	79	19
Felling Colliery	28	7	3	18	41	79	17
Felling Celtic	28	7	2	19	49	97	16

St. Anthony's Institute resigned on 22nd April 1929 and their record was deleted when it stood as: 25   3   3   19   34   83   9
Fatfield Albion, Felling Celtic and Newcastle C.W.S. left the league.
Howdon British Legion, North Shields Reserves, Percy Main Amateurs and Washington Colliery Reserves joined.

1929-30

	P	W	D	L	F	A	Pts
Hebburn Colliery	30	24	2	4	104	36	50
Howdon British Legion	30	19	4	7	95	50	42
Pelaw	30	17	3	10	83	54	37
Hebburn Leslies	30	17	2	11	101	55	36
Percy Main Amateurs	30	16	3	11	80	70	35
Gosforth & Coxlodge British Legion	30	15	4	11	86	62	34
Felling Colliery	30	16	2	12	61	59	34
Boldon Colliery	30	13	6	11	72	68	32
Reyrolles	30	14	4	12	67	68	32
Bill Quay Hibernians	30	13	4	13	72	84	30
Middle Docks	30	13	3	14	74	67	29
North Shields Reserves	30	11	6	13	72	82	28
Walker Park	30	7	5	18	52	82	19
Jarrow Reserves	30	7	2	21	56	93	16
Washington Colliery Reserves	30	5	4	21	46	116	13
Wardley Welfare	30	4	4	22	33	108	12

Washington Colliery Reserves had 1 point deducted.
Washington Colliery Reserves left the league and South Shields Corinthians joined.

1930-31

	P	W	D	L	F	A	Pts
Bill Quay Hibernians	30	18	6	6	93	59	42
Hebburn Leslies	30	17	7	6	86	56	41
Middle Docks	30	16	7	7	82	57	39
Boldon Colliery	30	16	6	8	76	52	38
Hebburn Colliery	30	15	7	8	93	71	37
Percy Main Amateurs	30	15	6	9	80	62	36
Gosforth & Coxlodge British Legion	30	13	6	11	81	64	32
South Shields Corinthians	30	11	8	11	69	60	30
Howdon British Legion	30	13	4	13	74	73	30
Reyrolles	30	11	7	12	91	82	29
North Shields Reserves	30	8	10	12	81	84	25
Walker Park	30	10	5	15	68	81	25
Wardley Welfare	30	10	5	15	51	76	25
Felling Colliery	30	9	4	17	65	103	22
Pelaw	30	6	6	18	55	87	18
Jarrow Reserves	30	4	2	24	40	118	10

North Shields Reserves had 1 point deducted.
Boldon Colliery and Felling Colliery both disbanded.
Rosehill and Walker Celtic Reserves both joined.

Tyneside League 1931-1937

1931-32

Hebburn Colliery	30	23	3	4	83	41	49
Wardley Welfare	30	20	3	7	86	50	43
Percy Main Amateurs	30	19	4	7	86	49	42
Middle Docks	30	16	7	7	75	63	39
Reyrolles	30	17	4	9	71	47	38
Gosforth & Coxlodge British Legion	30	13	8	9	57	41	34
Rosehill	30	10	10	10	75	66	30
Walker Celtic Reserves	30	13	4	13	69	77	30
Jarrow Reserves	30	10	9	11	63	65	29
North Shields Reserves	30	8	12	10	60	74	28
Walker Park	30	10	6	14	72	63	26
Howdon British Legion	30	8	9	13	68	76	25
Hebburn Leslies	30	7	8	15	57	78	22
South Shields Corinthians	30	6	6	18	49	83	18
Bill Quay Hibernians	30	4	8	18	40	77	16
Pelaw	30	2	7	21	42	103	11

North Shields and Jarrow both disbanded their reserve sides.
Hebburn St. Cuthbert's joined from the Tyne Valley League and North Walbottle also joined.

1932-33

Wardley Welfare	28	25	1	2	100	33	51
Percy Main Amateurs	28	20	2	6	74	41	42
Walker Park	28	17	7	4	71	44	41
Rosehill	28	15	7	6	81	40	37
Hebburn St. Cuthbert's	28	11	6	11	60	64	28
Howdon British Legion	28	10	6	12	55	57	26
Walker Celtic Reserves	28	10	6	12	57	73	26
Hebburn Colliery	28	9	7	12	60	66	25
Reyrolles	28	10	5	13	54	60	25
North Walbottle	28	9	6	13	40	49	24
Bill Quay Hibernians	28	8	7	13	42	56	23
Gosforth & Coxlodge British Legion	28	9	3	16	51	72	21
Pelaw	28	8	3	17	55	72	19
Middle Docks	28	7	5	16	47	69	19
Hebburn Leslies	28	6	1	21	39	90	11

South Shields Corinthians resigned in mid-November and their record was deleted when it stood as: 7 3 0 4 11 17 6
Hebburn Leslies had 2 points deducted.
Bill Quay Hibernians, Hebburn Leslies, North Walbottle and Walker Celtic Reserves all left the league. North Shields re-formed their reserve side who re-joined the league and Blyth Spartans Reserves joined from the North-East Combination. Newburn, Newcastle United "A" and Newcastle West End also joined.

1933-34

Wardley Welfare	30	21	4	5	103	42	46
Newcastle United "A"	30	20	5	5	77	45	45
Rosehill	30	19	4	7	80	47	42
Hebburn Colliery	30	19	1	10	88	61	39
Newburn	30	17	3	10	81	63	37
Blyth Spartans Reserves	30	14	7	9	57	50	35
Middle Docks	30	14	6	10	75	57	34
Walker Park	30	12	5	13	70	70	29
Hebburn St. Cuthbert's	30	12	4	14	69	65	28
Gosforth & Coxlodge British Legion	30	10	6	14	68	81	26
Percy Main Amateurs	30	11	3	16	57	78	25
Howdon British Legion	30	8	5	17	52	76	21
Newcastle West End	30	8	4	18	50	80	20
North Shields Reserves	30	8	3	19	58	73	19
Pelaw	30	8	5	17	53	83	19
Reyrolles	30	5	3	22	39	106	13

Pelaw had 2 points deducted.
Rosehill left the league. Crawcrook Albion joined from the North-Eastern League as did Newcastle East End who changed their name to St. Peter's Albion. Jarrow re-formed their reserve side and re-joined the league.

1934-35

North Shields Reserves	34	25	1	8	106	60	51
Wardley Welfare	34	21	6	7	107	62	48
Newcastle United "A"	34	21	3	10	101	56	45
Blyth Spartans Reserves	34	18	7	9	107	63	43
Newburn	34	19	4	11	102	76	42
Hebburn St. Cuthbert's	34	17	7	10	92	50	41
Crawcrook Albion	34	16	8	10	87	73	40
Reyrolles	34	16	3	15	88	80	35
Newcastle West End	34	14	7	13	91	88	35
Jarrow Reserves	34	13	6	15	65	86	32
Gosforth & Coxlodge British Legion	34	12	7	15	78	87	31
Middle Docks	34	13	4	17	79	101	30
Percy Main Amateurs	34	14	3	17	92	88	29
Hebburn Colliery	34	11	6	17	68	94	28
Howdon British Legion	34	10	3	21	80	115	23
Pelaw	34	10	2	22	60	92	22
Walker Park	34	7	7	20	66	106	21
St. Peter's Albion	34	3	8	23	67	159	14

Percy Main Amateurs had 2 points deducted.
Middle Docks and Wardley Welfare left the league.

1935-36

Newburn	28	23	3	2	128	35	49
Reyrolles	28	19	2	7	86	51	40
North Shields Reserves	28	14	6	8	83	71	34
Crawcrook Albion	28	14	4	10	80	60	32
Hebburn St. Cuthbert's	28	14	4	10	69	55	32
Hebburn Colliery	28	13	6	9	69	68	32
Newcastle United "A"	28	15	3	10	79	53	31
Blyth Spartans Reserves	28	11	5	12	71	72	27
Newcastle West End	28	12	3	13	55	66	27
Pelaw	28	8	8	14	64	70	24
Gosforth & Coxlodge British Legion	28	10	3	15	48	73	23
St. Peter's Albion	28	8	4	16	66	90	20
Howdon British Legion	28	6	6	16	46	75	18
Percy Main Amateurs	28	5	3	20	43	99	13
Jarrow Reserves	28	7	2	19	49	98	12

Walker Park resigned from the league in April and their record was deleted when it stood as: 24 3 1 20 26 103 7
Newcastle United "A" had 2 points deducted.
Jarrow Reserves had 4 points deducted.
Blyth Spartans Reserves moved to the Northern Alliance. South Shields were a newly formed club whose reserves joined the league. Felling Red Star, New Gateshead United and Walker Celtic Reserves also joined.

1936-37

South Shields Reserves	32	23	5	4	110	48	49
Newburn	32	21	6	5	117	52	48
Newcastle United "A"	32	17	8	7	109	38	42
Jarrow Reserves	32	17	1	14	71	84	35
Reyrolles	32	14	6	12	82	67	34
Crawcrook Albion	32	11	11	10	62	61	33
New Gateshead United	32	12	9	11	71	75	33
Felling Red Star	32	11	10	11	71	56	32
Hebburn Colliery	32	14	4	14	72	78	32
St. Peter's Albion	32	12	6	14	72	108	30
North Shields Reserves	32	15	1	16	91	85	29
Pelaw	32	9	9	14	64	97	27
Walker Celtic Reserves	32	10	7	15	52	81	27
Gosforth & Coxlodge British Legion	32	11	4	17	69	76	26
Newcastle West End	32	10	5	17	64	78	25
Hebburn St. Cuthbert's	32	6	7	19	65	101	19
Percy Main Amateurs	32	8	3	21	65	122	19

Howdon British Legion resigned in January and their record was deleted when it stood as: 17 4 3 10 18 60 11
South Shields Reserves and North Shields Reserves had 2 points deducted.
Newcastle United "A" and South Shields Reserves both moved to the Northern Alliance while Pelaw also left the league.
Bensham St. Hilda's, Boldon Villa, Middle Docks and Windy Nook all joined.

1937-38

North Shields Reserves	34	25	3	6	131	46	53
Reyrolles	34	23	6	5	113	54	52
Walker Celtic Reserves	34	24	3	7	111	52	51
Newburn	34	23	3	8	126	53	49
Windy Nook	34	18	7	9	107	77	43
Middle Docks	34	17	5	12	118	96	39
Newcastle West End	34	17	3	14	96	69	37
Crawcrook Albion	34	15	6	13	77	87	36
Hebburn Colliery	34	13	8	13	85	87	34
Percy Main Amateurs	34	14	5	15	81	83	33
St. Peter's Albion	34	13	6	15	89	90	32
Boldon Villa	34	13	4	17	113	107	30
Felling Red Star	34	13	3	18	72	117	29
Bensham St. Hilda's	34	10	5	19	71	121	25
Jarrow Reserves	34	10	4	20	67	126	24
Gosforth & Coxlodge British Legion	34	5	6	23	45	104	16
New Gateshead United	34	5	5	24	53	120	15
Hebburn St. Cuthbert's	34	3	8	23	46	112	14

Newburn and North Shields Reserves both moved to the Northern Alliance while New Gateshead United and Percy Main Amateurs also left the league. Heaton Stannington and Wardley Colliery joined.

Summer of 1939

Walker Celtic disbanded their reserve side and Jarrow disbanded altogether while Windy Nook and Hebburn Colliery both resigned as they had lost the use of their grounds. Boldon Villa and Reyrolles both moved to the Wearside League, Heaton Stannington moved to the Northern League while Crawcrook Albion and Newcastle West End both moved to the Northern Alliance.

The large number of resignations meant that the Tyneside League decided it was unable to operate during the 1939-40 season, leaving the remaining clubs having to find a new league. Bensham St. Hilda's joined the Northern Combination, Felling Red Star joined the Washington Amateur League, Gosforth & Coxlodge British Legion joined the Cramlington & District League and Hebburn St. Cuthbert's joined the South Tyne Alliance.

St. Peter's Albion were unable to find a suitable league and so they closed down and Parson's (Heaton) Athletic of the Northern Amateur League took over their ground on the Fossway in Byker. Middle Docks also appear to have closed down.

Within a few weeks of the Tyneside League's closure, war was declared and the Tyneside League was not revived when the war ended in 1945.

1938-39

Reyrolles	28	22	3	3	108	43	47
Heaton Stannington	28	20	2	6	114	58	42
Middle Docks	28	19	1	8	93	58	39
Boldon Villa	28	19	0	9	118	57	38
Newcastle West End	28	14	7	7	74	56	35
Felling Red Star	28	16	4	8	85	63	34
Hebburn Colliery	28	13	4	11	71	55	30
Crawcrook Albion	28	11	3	14	68	73	25
St. Peter's Albion	28	8	6	14	60	84	22
Walker Celtic Reserves	28	9	3	16	60	83	21
Gosforth & Coxlodge British Legion	28	6	8	14	44	70	20
Hebburn St. Cuthbert's	28	7	5	16	47	91	19
Windy Nook	28	8	3	17	64	100	17
Bensham St. Hilda's	28	6	2	20	61	112	14
Jarrow Reserves	28	4	5	19	49	113	13

Wardley Colliery resigned in early November after the closure of the nearby Follonsby Pit which employed 1,200 men. The club's record was deleted when it stood as follows: 8 2 2 4 19 19 6
Felling Red Star and Windy Nook each had 2 points deducted.

WEARSIDE LEAGUE 1892-2018

The Wearside League was formed in 1892 on the initiative of Charles Kirtley, secretary of Sunderland Swifts, who suggested the formation of the competition in letters written to the Sunderland Daily Post & Herald on 15th June and to the Sunderland Daily Echo a day later. No doubt the success of Sunderland A.F.C. in having become Football League champions just a few weeks earlier had played a significant part in raising the profile of football in the area.

A meeting was held at the Central Coffee Tavern in Sunderland High Street on 21st June at which the league was formed and there were 11 founder members:

Boldon Star, East End Black Watch (formed 1887), Monkwearmouth, Seaham Albion, Ryhope Colliery, Seaham Harbour, South Hylton, Sunderland Celtic, Sunderland Swifts, Sunderland West End and Wearmouth Swifts Athletic.

Note: The abbreviation C.W. stands for Colliery Welfare.

1892-93

Seaham Harbour	18	15	0	3	63	24	30
Monkwearmouth	18	13	3	2	73	26	29
Ryhope Colliery	18	10	2	6	52	46	22
Boldon Star	18	10	0	8	44	45	20
East End Black Watch	18	9	1	8	53	33	19
Sunderland Swifts	18	7	2	9	33	39	16
Seaham Albion	18	5	5	8	27	56	15
Wearmouth Swifts Athletic	18	5	3	10	24	35	13
Sunderland Celtic	18	3	6	9	25	47	12
Sunderland West End	18	1	2	15	21	64	4

South Hylton resigned and disbanded during November 1892 and their record at the time was deleted: 3 1 0 2 6 13 2
West House and Silksworth Church Institute joined the league.

1893-94

Monkwearmouth	18	16	1	1	61	14	33
Boldon Star	18	14	2	2	72	25	30
Seaham Harbour	18	11	2	5	41	30	24
East End Black Watch	18	10	1	7	58	35	21
Ryhope Colliery	18	7	3	8	49	41	17
Sunderland Celtic	18	5	6	7	38	42	16
Silksworth Church Institute	18	6	1	11	37	59	13
Seaham Albion	18	5	2	11	30	54	12
Sunderland Swifts	18	4	2	12	21	52	10
Sunderland West End	18	1	2	15	25	80	4

West House resigned and disbanded at the end of September 1893 as they were unable to find enough players. Their record was deleted when it stood as follows 2 0 1 1 4 5 1
Wearmouth Swifts Athletic changed their name to Wearmouth Swifts at the end of November and also resigned from the league but continued to play in junior football.
Sunderland West End disbanded and Silksworth Church Institute also left. Egypt Rangers joined from the Wearside Alliance and Seaham Athletic, Sunderland Forest and Whitburn also joined.

1894-95

Monkwearmouth	16	12	2	2	53	30	26
East End Black Watch	16	9	2	5	58	40	20
Ryhope Colliery	16	10	0	6	41	33	20
Seaham Harbour	16	7	2	7	36	37	16
Whitburn	16	6	4	6	28	29	16
Seaham Albion	16	5	4	7	47	45	14
Boldon Star	16	6	0	10	35	46	12
Egypt Rangers	16	6	0	10	30	47	12
Seaham Athletic	16	3	2	11	25	46	8

Sunderland Swifts resigned in September, Sunderland Forest resigned at the end of November and Sunderland Celtic were expelled at the end of February for breaking league rules. The records of all three clubs were deleted.
Egypt Rangers left the league. New Herrington and Silksworth C.W. both joined. Sunderland Grange and Southwick also joined but then resigned before the start of the season.

1895-96

East End Black Watch	18	12	4	2	54	22	28
Seaham Harbour	18	14	0	4	40	21	28
Whitburn	18	12	1	5	48	26	25
Ryhope Colliery	18	10	2	6	45	30	22
Silksworth C.W.	18	8	3	7	37	42	19
Seaham Albion	18	8	2	8	30	32	18
Boldon Star	18	6	2	10	31	41	14
New Herrington	18	5	2	11	26	35	12
Seaham Athletic	18	3	2	13	13	57	8
Monkwearmouth	18	2	2	14	11	29	6

Seaham Athletic failed to appear for the last game of the season away to Seaham Harbour and the game was not played. The league awarded 2 points and 1 goal to Seaham Harbour, which resulted in East End Black Watch becoming champions on goal average. Seaham Harbour had needed to win 13-0 to take the title.
Monkwearmouth and Seaham Athletic both left the league. Marsden Rescue, Selbourne, South Hylton and Sunderland Royal Rovers all joined.

1896-97

Whitburn	22	15	4	3	71	29	34
East End Black Watch	22	12	5	5	55	29	29
Sunderland Royal Rovers	22	13	2	7	53	49	28
Selbourne	22	12	3	7	50	41	27
Silksworth C.W.	22	10	5	7	61	32	25
New Herrington	22	9	4	9	45	45	22
Boldon Star	22	9	4	9	34	39	22
Seaham Harbour	22	8	4	10	36	48	20
Seaham Albion	22	8	3	11	38	42	17
South Hylton	22	8	1	13	37	66	17
Ryhope Colliery	22	6	4	12	35	51	16
Marsden Rescue	22	2	1	19	33	77	5

Seaham Albion had 2 points deducted.
Marsden Rescue left the league and Sunderland Nomads joined.

1897-98

East End Black Watch	18	12	3	3	45	18	27
South Hylton	18	12	2	4	68	27	26
Selbourne	18	11	3	4	46	38	25
Whitburn	17	9	3	5	50	32	19
Seaham Harbour	17	9	1	7	33	33	19
Sunderland Royal Rovers	18	7	3	8	28	28	17
Silksworth C.W.	18	6	3	9	28	37	15
Sunderland Nomads	18	4	4	10	26	39	12
Seaham Albion	18	3	4	11	25	48	10
New Herrington	18	2	2	14	21	70	6

Whitburn had 2 points deducted for fielding an ineligible player.
Boldon Star and Ryhope Colliery both withdrew from the league during January and their records were deleted.
Whitburn vs Seaham Harbour was abandoned at half time on 26th February because of 'stormy weather' and was not replayed.
Wearmouth Colliery and Ryhope Villa both joined from the Houghton League and Sunderland Swifts also joined. Grangetown successfully applied to join but then resigned before the start of the season, continuing in the Sunderland & District League. Sunderland Nomads moved to the Northern Alliance and fielded their reserve side in the Wearside League.

1898-99

East End Black Watch	24	21	2	1	70	17	44
South Hylton	24	16	5	3	68	25	37
Silksworth C.W.	24	13	4	7	55	36	30
Seaham Harbour	24	12	3	9	36	33	27
Whitburn	24	10	6	8	49	33	26
Sunderland Royal Rovers	24	12	1	11	47	41	25
Sunderland Swifts	24	11	2	11	45	42	24
Wearmouth Colliery	24	11	1	12	41	53	23
Seaham Albion	24	8	4	12	39	51	20
Selbourne	24	8	3	13	33	44	19
Ryhope Villa	24	7	5	12	35	52	19
New Herrington	24	7	4	13	37	60	18
Sunderland Nomads Reserves	24	0	0	24	9	77	0

Sunderland Nomads Reserves and Wearmouth Colliery both left.
3rd Durham Rifles joined.

1899-1900

South Hylton	18	15	0	3	58	24	30
Sunderland Royal Rovers	18	14	1	3	48	18	29
Selbourne	17	12	2	3	45	27	26
East End Black Watch	17	11	1	5	49	26	23
Seaham Albion	17	7	3	7	40	35	17
Silksworth C.W.	17	5	4	8	24	34	14
Ryhope Villa	18	4	3	11	24	53	11
Sunderland Swifts	18	3	4	11	32	52	10
Whitburn	17	3	3	11	23	41	9
3rd Durham Rifles	15	0	3	12	15	48	3

No record has been found that the 4 outstanding games were played.
Seaham Harbour resigned and disbanded in mid-November and New Herrington resigned in late January. Their records were deleted.
Sunderland Swifts and 3rd Durham Rifles both left the league.
Sunderland West End (formed in May 1900) and Kingston Villa joined.

1900-01

Sunderland Royal Rovers	18	15	0	3	64	17	30
East End Black Watch	18	12	4	2	41	15	28
Sunderland West End	18	9	5	4	38	26	23
South Hylton	18	6	6	6	26	30	18
Kingston Villa	18	7	3	8	29	29	17
Ryhope Villa	18	5	5	8	34	28	15
Silksworth C.W.	18	5	5	8	21	43	15
Seaham Albion	18	5	3	10	33	46	13
Selbourne	18	4	5	9	26	38	11
Whitburn	18	2	4	12	18	58	8

Selbourne had 2 points deducted for fielding an ineligible player.
Southwick joined from the Sunderland & District League and Bearpark United also joined.

1901-02

Sunderland Royal Rovers	22	18	2	2	62	17	38
Sunderland West End	22	18	1	3	72	15	37
East End Black Watch	22	15	3	4	55	24	33
Southwick	21	13	3	5	41	25	29
Ryhope Villa	22	11	4	7	60	36	26
Selbourne	22	11	2	9	32	34	24
Seaham Albion	21	5	8	8	26	41	18
Kingston Villa	22	5	3	14	38	54	13
South Hylton	20	3	5	12	24	44	11
Silksworth C.W.	20	3	4	13	19	62	10
Bearpark United	18	3	1	14	22	70	7
Whitburn	18	1	2	15	14	43	4

The results of the 8 outstanding games have not been found although it is known that Southwick finished with 31 points.
Bearpark United left the league. Seaham White Star joined from the Hetton & District League.

1902-03

Sunderland Royal Rovers	20	16	3	1	54	17	35
Southwick	20	16	3	1	47	18	35
Sunderland West End	20	13	4	3	47	22	30
Seaham White Star	20	8	5	7	33	24	21
Kingston Villa	20	8	5	7	33	33	21
Ryhope Villa	20	5	8	7	40	42	18
Seaham Albion	19	6	4	9	27	43	16
South Hylton	20	5	5	10	23	36	15
Selbourne	20	3	5	12	20	38	11
East End Black Watch	19	3	3	13	23	34	9
Whitburn	18	1	3	14	15	55	5

Title decider (Played at Roker Park, 30th April 1903)
Sunderland Royal Rovers vs Southwick   0-0

Replay (at Roker Park, 23rd September 1903)
Sunderland Royal Rovers vs Southwick   3-0

Whitburn played just one of their two outstanding games. They lost but neither the score nor opponents have been traced.
Silksworth C.W. resigned in mid-February but continued to play cup ties. Their league record was deleted.
South Hylton left the league, having lost their ground.
Roker Park and Seaham United both joined.

Wearside League 1903-1910

1903-04

Team	P	W	D	L	F	A	Pts
Sunderland Royal Rovers	20	15	4	1	61	23	34
Seaham White Star	20	13	3	4	39	20	29
Sunderland West End	20	11	6	3	47	18	28
Southwick	20	12	2	6	40	18	26
Kingston Villa	20	10	3	7	47	24	23
Ryhope Villa	20	9	2	9	43	32	20
Selbourne	20	8	3	9	35	37	19
Seaham Albion	20	7	4	9	27	32	18
East End Black Watch	20	6	4	10	22	37	16
Whitburn	20	2	2	16	20	83	6
Roker Park	20	0	1	19	17	74	1

Seaham United resigned early in December as they were unable to compete effectively and their record was deleted. They continued playing friendlies. Seaham Villa joined from the Old Boys League.

1904-05

Team	P	W	D	L	F	A	Pts
Seaham White Star	22	16	2	4	44	16	34
Southwick	22	14	4	4	48	23	32
Kingston Villa	22	12	4	6	42	27	28
Ryhope Villa	22	11	5	6	41	25	27
Sunderland West End	22	9	8	5	38	29	26
Sunderland Royal Rovers	22	8	7	7	33	24	23
Selbourne	22	8	6	8	42	37	22
Roker Park	22	8	4	10	33	38	20
Whitburn	22	8	2	12	28	39	18
Seaham Albion	22	4	8	10	27	45	16
East End Black Watch	22	6	2	14	22	47	14
Seaham Villa	22	1	2	19	18	66	4

Selbourne disbanded.
Murton Red Star joined from the Sherburn & District League.

1905-06

Team	P	W	D	L	F	A	Pts
Southwick	22	16	5	1	76	18	37
Sunderland Royal Rovers	22	15	6	1	50	17	36
Kingston Villa	22	10	8	4	53	27	28
Seaham White Star	22	13	0	9	52	31	26
Sunderland West End	22	10	3	9	27	26	23
Ryhope Villa	22	8	5	9	29	34	21
Whitburn	22	9	3	10	28	33	21
Murton Red Star	22	8	4	10	32	35	20
East End Black Watch	22	9	2	11	29	35	20
Seaham Albion	22	6	2	14	24	50	14
Roker Park	22	4	3	15	15	56	11
Seaham Villa	22	3	1	18	21	74	7

Sunderland Royal Rovers left to become founder members of the new North-Eastern League while Roker Park and East End Black Watch also left. Hylton Star, Osmond Star and Washington United all joined.

1906-07

Team	P	W	D	L	F	A	Pts
Southwick	22	18	3	1	58	25	39
Seaham Albion	22	13	3	6	35	30	29
Sunderland West End	22	13	2	7	32	19	28
Kingston Villa	22	11	5	6	43	36	27
Hylton Star	22	9	4	9	38	33	22
Washington United	22	9	4	9	35	31	22
Seaham White Star	22	8	5	9	32	25	21
Murton Red Star	22	10	1	11	38	35	21
Ryhope Villa	22	7	3	12	37	55	17
Whitburn	22	5	6	11	31	40	16
Osmond Star	22	4	4	14	23	54	12
Seaham Villa	22	3	4	15	26	45	10

Kingston Villa moved to the Northern Alliance and Hylton Star also left.
Wingate Albion joined from the Mid-Durham League and Horden Athletic also joined.

1907-08

Team	P	W	D	L	F	A	Pts
Seaham White Star	22	18	2	2	76	19	38
Wingate Albion	22	16	1	5	76	28	33
Sunderland West End	22	13	5	4	41	13	31
Southwick	22	10	4	8	39	27	24
Murton Red Star	21	10	2	9	39	34	22
Seaham Albion	22	9	4	9	41	51	22
Seaham Villa	22	9	1	12	39	43	19
Washington United	22	8	3	11	34	41	19
Horden Athletic	22	7	3	12	39	49	17
Ryhope Villa	22	5	4	13	33	70	14
Osmond Star	22	5	3	14	23	74	13
Whitburn	21	2	6	13	16	47	10

It is believed that the outstanding game was not played.
Seaham White Star moved to the North-Eastern League and Osmond Star also left. Sunderland Celtic and West Hartlepool Expansion both joined.

1908-09

Team	P	W	D	L	F	A	Pts
Wingate Albion	22	16	4	2	67	23	36
West Hartlepool Expansion	22	17	1	4	74	27	35
Washington United	22	13	4	5	54	30	30
Horden Athletic	22	11	5	6	40	26	27
Sunderland West End	22	11	5	6	28	20	27
Murton Red Star	22	9	6	7	47	43	22
Sunderland Celtic	22	10	2	10	33	35	22
Seaham Albion	22	7	5	10	33	36	19
Ryhope Villa	22	5	4	13	23	33	14
Seaham Villa	22	5	1	16	19	55	11
Whitburn	22	5	0	17	25	67	10
Southwick	22	2	5	15	19	67	7

Murton Red Star and Southwick each had 2 points deducted.
Wingate Albion moved to the North-Eastern League and Sunderland West End also left the league. South Shields Adelaide Reserves joined from the Tyneside League while Grangetown (Sunderland), Haswell Swifts and Shotton Albion also all joined.

1909-10

Team	P	W	D	L	F	A	Pts
Haswell Swifts	24	18	5	1	56	24	41
Ryhope Villa	24	18	3	3	62	20	39
West Hartlepool Expansion	24	16	2	6	63	36	34
South Shields Adelaide Res.	24	15	2	7	51	29	32
Murton Red Star	24	11	4	9	48	37	26
Sunderland Celtic	24	9	7	8	47	38	25
Shotton Albion	24	9	3	12	42	48	21
Washington United	24	6	7	11	36	57	19
Whitburn	23	8	2	13	36	53	18
Seaham Albion	23	8	1	14	29	47	17
Horden Athletic	24	6	3	15	40	48	15
Seaham Villa	24	4	5	15	23	45	13
Grangetown (Sunderland)	24	4	2	18	29	60	10

Whitburn vs Seaham Albion was not played, Whitburn failed to appear.
Southwick resigned in the second half of September before they had played any games.
West Hartlepool Expansion disbanded while Washington United and Murton Red Star both moved to the Sunderland & District League. Sunderland Celtic also left the league.
Hylton Colliery joined from the Houghton & District League, New Seaham Gymnasium joined from the Church Institute League and Hartlepool United Reserves, Thornley and Wingate Albion Reserves also joined.
South Shields Adelaide changed their name to South Shields.

1910-11

	P	W	D	L	F	A	Pts
Haswell Swifts	24	20	3	1	74	16	43
South Shields Reserves	24	16	4	4	61	22	34
Hartlepool United Reserves	24	15	2	7	49	31	32
New Seaham Gymnasium	23	12	3	8	37	30	27
Ryhope Villa	24	11	3	10	42	41	23
Horden Athletic	23	11	1	11	38	38	23
Grangetown (Sunderland)	24	8	6	10	36	46	22
Hylton Colliery	24	9	4	11	33	46	22
Shotton Albion	24	7	6	11	27	33	20
Thornley	23	6	6	11	39	42	18
Seaham Villa	24	6	5	13	28	52	17
Whitburn	23	5	3	15	21	40	13
Wingate Albion Reserves	24	5	0	19	18	66	10

South Shields Reserves and Ryhope Villa each had 2 points deducted.
The games between Whitburn and Horden Athletic and between Thornley and New Seaham Gymnasium were not played.
Seaham Albion resigned in March 1911 and their record was deleted.
Thornley and Wingate Albion Reserves left the league.
Deaf Hill United and Trimdon Grange joined.

1911-12

	P	W	D	L	F	A	Pts
Horden Athletic	24	17	6	1	62	19	40
Haswell Swifts	24	18	4	2	53	16	40
Hartlepool United Reserves	24	12	9	3	48	25	33
Trimdon Grange	24	13	5	6	41	30	31
Deaf Hill United	23	8	11	4	40	30	27
South Shields Reserves	24	10	5	9	48	32	25
Whitburn	24	10	5	9	43	43	25
Ryhope Villa	24	8	7	9	27	37	23
Shotton Albion	24	7	4	13	38	55	18
Grangetown (Sunderland)	24	6	3	15	32	52	15
New Seaham Gymnasium	24	5	3	16	28	46	13
Hylton Colliery	23	4	3	16	27	62	11
Seaham Villa	24	3	3	18	25	65	9

The game between Hylton Colliery and Deaf Hill United was not played.
Haswell Swifts were to meet Horden Athletic in September 1912 in a title decider but resigned from the league before the game was played and so Horden Athletic were declared champions.
South Shields Reserves moved to the Tyneside League while Hylton Colliery and Seaham Villa also left. Arcade Mission, Dawdon Colliery, South Shields St. Hilda's, Thornley and Wingate Albion Reserves all joined.

1912-13

	P	W	D	L	F	A	Pts
Horden Athletic	24	19	3	2	80	14	41
Ryhope Villa	24	13	7	4	42	21	33
Hartlepool United Reserves	24	12	7	5	52	25	31
Trimdon Grange	24	13	4	7	52	27	30
New Seaham Gymnasium	24	13	4	7	45	35	30
Dawdon Colliery	24	10	6	8	37	36	26
Deaf Hill United	24	8	7	9	37	37	23
Thornley	24	10	1	13	26	22	19
Whitburn	24	9	1	14	40	46	19
Grangetown (Sunderland)	24	8	3	13	25	48	19
Wingate Albion Reserves	24	7	0	17	28	88	14
South Shields St. Hilda's	24	5	1	18	18	43	11
Shotton Albion	24	4	2	18	22	62	10

Arcade Mission resigned early in February and their record was deleted when it stood as follows: 10 2 3 5 16 22 5
Arcade Mission had already had 2 points deducted and this is reflected in the record shown above.
Thornley and South Shields St. Hilda's both failed to complete their fixtures and 2 points were awarded to each of their opponents.
Wingate Albion joined from the North-Eastern League, replacing their reserves. Hartlepool United Reserves, South Shields St. Hilda's and Thornley all left. Murton Colliery (ex-Red Star) joined from the Sunderland & District League, Easington Colliery, Seaham Albion and South Hetton all joined from the Houghton & District League.

1913-14

	P	W	D	L	F	A	Pts
Horden Athletic	26	22	3	1	68	17	47
Wingate Albion	26	21	4	1	92	9	46
Easington Colliery	26	13	4	9	42	39	30
Dawdon Colliery	26	11	4	11	31	33	26
Murton Colliery	26	11	4	11	44	47	26
Trimdon Grange	26	10	7	9	39	37	25
Deaf Hill United	26	9	6	11	35	27	24
Whitburn	26	10	4	12	36	37	24
New Seaham Gymnasium	26	9	5	12	33	60	23
Ryhope Villa	26	9	4	13	27	37	22
Grangetown (Sunderland)	26	9	3	14	36	44	21
Seaham Albion	26	8	5	13	21	44	21
Shotton Albion	26	6	3	17	28	52	15
South Hetton	26	2	8	16	20	69	12

Trimdon Grange had 2 points deducted.
South Hetton moved to the newly formed North-East Durham League and New Seaham Gymnasium also left the league. Seaham Harbour joined from the North-Eastern League and Southwick also joined.

1914-15

	P	W	D	L	F	A	Pts
Southwick	14	10	2	2	47	9	22
Seaham Harbour	14	9	2	3	29	13	20
Horden Athletic	14	8	2	4	27	13	18
Dawdon Colliery	14	6	4	4	20	14	16
Murton Colliery	14	6	2	6	24	28	14
Seaham Albion	14	3	1	10	16	37	7
Deaf Hill United	12	3	2	7	12	36	6
Grangetown (Sunderland)	12	1	1	10	12	37	3

Deaf Hill United had 2 points deducted.
Deaf Hill United and Grangetown agreed to cancel their 2 fixtures.
Following the outbreak of war, many players enlisted in The Army and clubs often found themselves unable to field a team. As a consequence of this, Easington Colliery, Shotton Albion and Wingate Albion resigned in early January 1915 while Ryhope Villa, Trimdon Grange and Whitburn also resigned later in the season and so the league finished the season with just 8 clubs. The records of the 6 clubs who resigned were deleted.

Deaf Hill United, Grangetown (Sunderland) and Southwick left the league. Sunderland Rovers joined from the North-Eastern League so that the league had 6 members when the 1915-16 season began: Dawdon Colliery, Horden Athletic, Murton Colliery, Seaham Albion, Seaham Harbour and Sunderland Rovers.

However, other clubs later found that they were able to continue playing and at a meeting held on 2nd October, Easington Colliery, Ryhope Villa, Silksworth Colliery and Wearmouth Colliery were all admitted to the league, raising membership to 10. However, Ryhope Villa disbanded shortly afterwards and, on 6th November, Blackhall Colliery were elected to replace them.

1915-16

	P	W	D	L	F	A	Pts
Murton Colliery	14	11	2	1	43	13	24
Seaham Harbour	14	9	2	3	30	10	20
Horden Athletic	14	7	2	5	21	19	16
Sunderland Shipbuilding M.W.	14	4	6	4	17	16	14
Easington Colliery	14	5	3	6	25	19	13
Dawdon Colliery	14	4	3	7	15	25	11
Wearmouth Colliery	14	3	3	8	21	31	9
Blackhall Colliery	14	2	1	11	9	48	5

Sunderland Rovers resigned in mid-November and Seaham Albion resigned soon afterwards. Sunderland Shipbuilding Company Munition Workers joined the league in December while Silksworth Colliery resigned in the second half of the season and their record was deleted.
Murton Colliery, Sunderland Shipbuilding Company Munition Workers and Wearmouth Colliery left before the next season, while Blackhall Colliery United and Robert Thompson's Munition Workers joined. At the end of October, Carol Street (Sunderland) P.M., Murton Colliery and Sunderland West End also joined.

Wearside League 1916-1923

1916-17

Robert Thompson's Munitions W.	14	9	3	2	30	13	21
Sunderland West End	14	8	3	3	29	11	19
Seaham Harbour	14	8	3	3	28	18	19
Horden Athletic	14	7	3	4	33	16	17
Easington Colliery	14	6	5	3	24	18	17
Murton Colliery	14	3	4	7	21	22	10
Carol Street P.M. (Sunderland)	14	3	2	9	12	31	8
Blackhall Colliery	14	0	1	13	11	59	1

Dawdon Colliery resigned at the end of November 1916 and Blackhall Colliery United also resigned during the season. The record of both clubs were deleted.
Easington Colliery, Murton Colliery, Seaham Harbour and Carol Street P.M. (Sunderland) all left. Grangetown (Sunderland) and Sunderland Rovers joined. The league started the 1917-18 season with 6 clubs but at the start of October, Ryhope Villa and Southwick joined and Seaham Harbour rejoined.

1917-18

Robert Thompson's Munitions W.	16	13	2	1	54	10	28
Southwick	15	10	2	3	34	16	22
Sunderland West End	16	8	4	4	29	19	20
Seaham Harbour	16	8	3	5	31	22	19
Horden Athletic	16	6	4	6	30	22	16
Sunderland Rovers	14	3	4	7	17	22	10
Grangetown (Sunderland)	16	4	2	10	40	54	10
Ryhope Villa	16	3	3	10	13	42	9
Blackhall Colliery	13	1	2	10	10	51	4

No record has been found that the 3 outstanding games were played.
Blackhall Colliery, Grangetown (Sunderland), Ryhope Villa and Sunderland Rovers all left the league. Harton Colliery, Murton Colliery and Smith's Dock all joined. South Shields Wanderers also joined but resigned before playing a game as they were unable to find a ground.

1918-19

Robert Thompson's Munitions W.	12	9	1	2	23	11	19
Sunderland West End	12	7	3	2	22	10	17
Southwick	11	6	3	2	18	11	15
Horden Athletic	11	3	1	7	14	14	7
Smith's Dock	9	3	1	5	15	19	7
Harton Colliery	12	2	3	7	8	24	7
Murton Colliery	11	3	0	8	11	22	6

No record has been found that the 3 outstanding games were played.
Seaham Harbour resigned at the end of September as they were unable to find a ground.
With the war having ended, the league was able to return to normal operations. Of the 7 clubs who had completed the last war-time season, only Smith's Dock and Harton Colliery did not continue in the league which was made up to 14 members by the addition of Dawdon C.W., Easington C.W., Ryhope Comrades, Seaham C.W., Seaham Harbour, Silksworth C.W., Sunderland Celtic, Sunderland Comrades and Whitburn.

1919-20

Seaham Harbour	26	18	6	2	53	16	42
Murton	26	18	5	3	61	26	41
Horden Athletic	26	18	3	5	85	29	39
Sunderland West End	26	16	6	4	53	22	38
Southwick	26	13	4	9	50	33	30
Easington C.W.	26	12	4	10	51	50	28
Whitburn	25	12	5	8	44	29	27
Robert Thompson's Munitions W.	26	12	1	13	41	46	23
Silksworth C.W.	26	7	7	12	32	41	21
Dawdon C.W.	26	7	7	12	37	50	21
Sunderland Celtic	26	4	6	16	31	62	14
Ryhope Comrades	26	6	4	16	33	67	14
Seaham C.W.	26	5	3	18	40	70	13
Sunderland Comrades	25	2	1	22	14	84	5

No record has been found that the outstanding game was played.
Robert Thompson's Munitions Workers, Ryhope Villa and Whitburn each had 2 points deducted.

Sunderland Comrades left the league.
Gray's (West Hartlepool), Lambton Star and Murton Athletic all joined.

1920-21

Seaham Harbour	30	22	6	2	81	22	50
Sunderland West End	30	18	6	6	65	31	42
Horden Athletic	30	20	1	9	82	43	41
Whitburn	30	16	6	8	52	31	38
Easington C.W.	30	15	6	9	67	45	36
Lambton Star	30	14	8	8	52	39	36
Murton	30	13	6	11	45	33	32
Silksworth C.W.	30	11	8	11	39	50	30
Southwick	30	10	7	13	35	44	27
Sunderland Celtic	30	9	8	13	41	67	26
Dawdon C.W.	30	10	4	16	34	45	24
Seaham C.W.	30	11	2	17	32	46	24
Murton Athletic	30	10	4	16	41	57	22
Robert Thompson's Munitions W.	30	8	6	16	42	62	22
Gray's (West Hartlepool)	30	5	5	20	28	63	15
Ryhope Comrades	30	6	1	23	32	90	13

Murton Athletic had 2 points deducted.
Gray's (West Hartlepool) left the league and Herrington Swifts joined.
Murton Athletic changed their name to Murton Colliery.

1921-22

Lambton Star	28	19	4	5	57	30	42
Horden Athletic	28	18	4	6	69	26	40
Sunderland West End	28	16	4	8	50	33	36
Herrington Swifts	28	12	11	5	64	36	35
Dawdon C.W.	28	12	8	8	38	41	32
Murton	28	11	8	9	45	39	30
Robert Thompson's Munitions W.	28	12	5	11	50	41	29
Seaham Harbour	28	12	3	13	45	37	27
Southwick	28	10	7	11	36	50	27
Easington C.W.	28	9	8	11	49	42	26
Whitburn	28	10	6	12	36	48	26
Silksworth C.W.	28	10	7	11	39	35	25
Murton Colliery	28	8	7	13	32	38	23
Seaham C.W.	28	5	7	16	33	48	17
Sunderland Celtic	28	0	3	25	29	128	3

Silksworth C.W. had 2 points deducted.
Ryhope Comrades resigned and disbanded and their record was deleted when it stood as follows: 24   3   3   18   23   65   9
Houghton joined from the North-Eastern League and Murton changed their name to Murton Democratic.

1922-23

Robert Thompson's Munitions W.	28	21	4	3	72	24	46
Horden Athletic	28	19	7	2	60	15	45
Seaham Harbour	28	20	4	4	66	18	44
Sunderland West End	28	14	7	7	54	31	35
Herrington Swifts	28	16	3	9	47	43	35
Lambton Star	28	10	8	10	54	47	28
Houghton	28	12	4	12	36	34	28
Murton Democratic	28	12	2	14	48	57	26
Southwick	28	7	10	11	53	53	24
Dawdon C.W.	28	10	4	14	42	69	24
Whitburn	28	9	5	14	46	46	23
Easington C.W.	28	8	7	13	38	55	23
Seaham C.W.	28	6	6	16	36	64	18
Silksworth C.W.	28	5	2	21	38	71	12
Sunderland Celtic	28	4	1	23	20	83	9

Murton Colliery withdrew in December and their record was deleted when it stood as follows: 7   0   0   7   8   27   0
Sunderland Celtic left the league and Murton Democratic disbanded. Fatfield Albion and Hylton Colliery both joined from the Houghton & District League and Hetton United joined from the Palatine League.

1923-24

Team	P	W	D	L	F	A	Pts
Hetton United	30	25	3	2	83	18	53
Fatfield Albion	30	18	8	4	69	30	44
Horden Athletic	30	19	3	8	69	30	41
Sunderland West End	30	17	4	9	46	31	38
Dawdon C.W.	30	16	4	10	57	36	36
Silksworth C.W.	30	15	4	11	45	36	34
Whitburn	30	14	4	12	60	46	32
Southwick	30	11	7	12	44	44	29
Herrington Swifts	30	13	4	13	46	57	28
Seaham Harbour	30	10	6	14	37	54	26
Robert Thompson's Munitions W.	30	10	5	15	43	49	23
Hylton Colliery	30	8	6	16	38	49	22
Houghton	30	11	2	17	36	73	22
Easington C.W.	30	10	1	19	53	69	21
Lambton Star	30	6	3	21	24	75	11
Seaham C.W.	30	3	4	23	25	78	10

Herrington Swifts, Houghton and Robert Thompson's Munitions Workers each had 2 points deducted.
Lambton Star had 4 points deducted.
Houghton changed their name to Houghton Colliery.

1924-25

Team	P	W	D	L	F	A	Pts
Robert Thompson's Munitions W.	30	18	8	4	64	23	44
Seaham C.W.	30	18	7	5	44	25	43
Hetton United	30	19	4	7	64	41	42
Sunderland West End	30	16	5	9	60	35	37
Seaham Harbour	30	14	7	9	64	44	35
Fatfield Albion	30	16	3	11	51	38	35
Whitburn	30	16	1	13	56	43	33
Houghton Colliery	30	13	7	10	50	50	33
Horden Athletic	30	14	4	12	61	40	30
Hylton Colliery	30	11	8	11	42	45	30
Easington C.W.	30	11	5	14	52	54	27
Lambton Star	30	9	5	16	46	70	23
Herrington Swifts	30	7	6	17	55	65	20
Dawdon C.W.	30	6	4	20	19	64	16
Silksworth C.W.	30	7	1	22	48	90	15
Southwick	30	6	3	21	36	85	15

Horden Athletic had 2 points deducted.
Silksworth C.W. left the league and Shotton joined from the Houghton & District League.

1925-26

Team	P	W	D	L	F	A	Pts
Shotton	26	17	7	2	79	31	41
Hetton United	26	17	7	2	59	23	41
Horden Athletic	26	17	5	4	67	31	39
Houghton Colliery	26	14	7	5	66	32	35
Seaham Harbour	26	12	5	9	67	44	29
Sunderland West End	26	13	2	11	61	56	28
Hylton Colliery	26	11	4	11	55	49	26
Fatfield Albion	26	11	2	13	46	56	24
Southwick	26	7	6	13	44	46	20
Herrington Swifts	26	8	4	14	50	57	20
Robert Thompson's Munitions W.	26	8	3	15	50	66	19
Easington C.W.	26	6	3	17	41	92	15
Seaham C.W.	26	5	4	17	34	82	14
Whitburn	26	5	3	18	31	85	13

Dawdon Colliery resigned in December and their record was deleted when it stood as follows: 9 1 2 6 10 22 4
Lambton Star resigned in April and their record was deleted when it stood as follows: 23 2 2 19 20 101 6

Title decider (Played at Horden, 28th August 1926)
Shotton vs Hetton United 5-1

Seaham Harbour moved to the North-Eastern League.
Bank Head Albion, Silksworth C.W. and Ryhope C.W. all joined.

1926-27

Team	P	W	D	L	F	A	Pts
Silksworth C.W.	30	22	6	2	85	33	50
Hetton United	30	23	3	4	91	40	49
Shotton	30	19	2	9	102	47	40
Houghton Colliery	30	17	5	8	96	54	39
Horden Athletic	30	15	5	10	76	54	35
Hylton Colliery	30	16	3	11	70	51	35
Whitburn	30	13	3	14	68	69	29
Sunderland West End	30	11	6	13	51	55	28
Fatfield Albion	30	13	4	13	59	68	28
Bank Head Albion	30	11	4	15	63	69	26
Southwick	30	9	8	13	61	74	26
Herrington Swifts	30	9	4	17	55	83	22
Easington C.W.	30	8	6	16	46	77	22
Robert Thompson's Munitions W.	30	6	9	15	36	77	21
Seaham C.W.	30	7	2	21	55	121	16
Ryhope C.W.	30	4	4	22	54	96	10

Fatfield Albion and Ryhope C.W. each had 2 points deducted.
Fatfield Albion moved to the Tyneside League. Shiney Row Swifts joined from the Houghton & District League.

1927-28

Team	P	W	D	L	F	A	Pts
Ryhope C.W.	30	22	3	5	98	47	47
Shiney Row Swifts	30	21	3	6	70	49	45
Easington C.W.	30	19	2	9	80	48	40
Whitburn	30	18	4	8	93	60	40
Hetton United	30	18	3	9	92	51	39
Shotton	30	16	6	8	70	46	38
Houghton Colliery	30	16	6	8	65	50	38
Horden Athletic	30	12	5	13	71	80	29
Southwick	30	10	5	15	52	55	25
Bank Head Albion	30	11	3	16	62	69	25
Sunderland West End	30	9	6	15	42	56	24
Silksworth C.W.	30	10	4	16	47	68	24
Robert Thompson's Munitions W.	30	8	7	15	49	68	23
Hylton Colliery	30	6	4	20	39	75	16
Herrington Swifts	30	7	1	22	39	95	15
Seaham C.W.	30	5	2	23	40	92	12

Horden Athletic changed their name to Horden C.W..
Murton C.W. joined the league and Seaham C.W. left.

1928-29

Team	P	W	D	L	F	A	Pts
Murton C.W.	28	21	3	4	75	31	45
Easington C.W.	28	20	4	4	92	30	44
Hetton United	28	17	5	6	86	45	39
Horden C.W.	28	14	5	9	83	58	33
Shotton	28	12	4	12	54	39	28
Robert Thompson's Munitions W.	28	12	4	12	66	63	28
Shiney Row Swifts	28	13	2	13	55	64	28
Silksworth C.W.	28	10	6	12	47	57	26
Southwick	28	10	6	12	46	61	26
Bank Head Albion	28	9	7	12	60	80	25
Sunderland West End	28	8	8	12	52	61	24
Ryhope C.W.	28	8	7	13	51	68	21
Whitburn	28	6	7	15	46	76	19
Houghton Colliery	28	5	6	17	48	86	16
Herrington Swifts	28	6	4	18	35	77	16

Sunderland West End had 2 points deducted.
Hylton Colliery resigned at the start of February due to financial problems and their record was deleted. Houghton Colliery left the league.
South Hetton C.W. and Marsden C.W. both joined.

Wearside League 1929-1935

1929-30

Team	P	W	D	L	F	A	Pts
Easington C.W.	28	20	5	3	102	34	45
Hetton United	28	18	5	5	77	35	41
Murton C.W.	28	16	4	8	69	36	36
Silksworth C.W.	28	14	8	6	74	58	36
Horden C.W.	28	15	2	11	95	74	32
Whitburn	28	15	2	11	75	74	32
Robert Thompson's Munitions W	28	12	8	8	64	58	30
South Hetton C.W.	28	12	2	14	55	60	26
Herrington Swifts	28	11	2	15	73	76	24
Bank Head Albion	28	10	6	12	62	76	24
Shiney Row Swifts	28	11	2	15	66	86	22
Shotton	28	6	4	18	51	84	19
Marsden C.W.	28	6	4	18	47	81	16
Sunderland West End	28	6	4	18	47	83	16
Southwick	28	6	6	16	48	90	16

Robert Thompson's Munition Workers, Bank Head Albion, Shiney Row Swifts and Southwick each had 2 points deducted.
Ryhope Colliery withdrew during the season and their record was deleted.
Robert Thompson's Munition Workers, Southwick and Sunderland West End left. Thornley Albion joined from the Mid-Durham League while Blackhalls C.W., Dawdon Recreation and Seaham C.W. also joined.

1930-31

Team	P	W	D	L	F	A	Pts
Seaham C.W.	30	20	5	5	82	49	45
Horden C.W.	30	19	5	6	108	67	43
Murton C.W.	30	19	4	7	89	37	42
Blackhalls C.W.	30	19	4	7	128	67	42
Easington C.W.	30	18	1	11	86	55	37
Shiney Row Swifts	30	18	1	11	102	71	35
Hetton United	30	14	5	11	72	70	33
South Hetton C.W.	30	13	5	12	72	64	31
Dawdon Recreation	30	11	3	16	64	72	25
Thornley Albion	30	12	1	17	80	97	25
Silksworth C.W.	30	10	3	17	70	85	23
Whitburn	30	8	6	16	66	76	22
Bank Head Albion	30	8	6	16	63	88	22
Marsden C.W.	30	7	7	16	52	101	21
Herrington Swifts	30	6	4	30	48	112	16
Shotton	30	7	2	21	47	118	16

Shiney Row Swifts had 2 points deducted.
Herrington Swifts changed their name to Herrington C.W., Shotton changed their name to Shotton C.W. and Thornley Albion changed their name to Thornley C.W..

1931-32

Team	P	W	D	L	F	A	Pts
Easington C.W.	30	21	5	4	80	35	47
Murton C.W.	30	19	5	6	82	42	43
Blackhalls C.W.	30	15	8	7	106	54	38
Seaham C.W.	30	17	4	9	81	54	38
Horden C.W.	30	14	9	7	83	56	37
Shotton C.W.	30	13	8	9	67	55	34
Thornley C.W.	30	13	7	10	66	62	33
Hetton United	30	13	5	12	82	67	31
Silksworth C.W.	30	13	3	14	75	66	29
Shiney Row Swifts	30	12	5	13	68	68	29
South Hetton C.W.	30	11	7	12	56	69	29
Whitburn	30	12	5	13	60	79	29
Herrington C.W.	30	11	1	18	71	86	23
Dawdon Recreation	30	7	8	15	54	69	22
Bank Head Albion	30	3	6	21	42	119	10
Marsden C.W.	30	2	2	26	42	134	6

Bank Head Albion had 2 points deducted.
Marsden Colliery moved to the South Tyne Alliance, Whitburn disbanded and Bank Head Albion also left.

1932-33

Team	P	W	D	L	F	A	Pts
Easington C.W.	24	19	2	3	72	36	40
Blackhalls C.W.	24	18	0	6	78	35	36
Horden C.W.	24	10	7	7	66	61	27
Seaham C.W.	24	12	2	10	53	47	26
Shotton C.W.	24	12	2	10	54	54	26
Herrington C.W.	24	10	3	11	55	50	23
Dawdon Recreation	24	9	3	12	59	61	21
Murton C.W.	24	8	5	11	49	63	21
Silksworth C.W.	24	9	2	13	36	43	20
Shiney Row Swifts	24	8	3	13	43	65	19
South Hetton C.W.	24	7	4	13	47	56	18
Thornley C.W.	24	9	2	13	40	58	18
Hetton United	24	6	3	15	40	63	15

Thornley C.W. had 2 points deducted.
Shiney Row Swifts moved to the Houghton & District League.

1933-34

Team	P	W	D	L	F	A	Pts
Horden C.W.	22	18	3	1	78	36	39
Murton C.W.	22	16	1	5	62	39	33
Herrington C.W.	22	13	2	7	44	37	28
Easington C.W.	22	13	2	7	59	45	26
Dawdon Recreation	22	11	2	9	51	39	24
Blackhall C.W.	22	9	5	8	57	49	23
South Hetton C.W.	22	8	4	10	34	44	20
Seaham C.W.	22	7	2	13	45	53	16
Shotton C.W.	22	6	3	13	39	54	15
Thornley C.W.	22	5	4	13	51	65	14
Hetton United	22	5	3	14	45	62	13
Silksworth C.W.	22	5	1	16	33	75	11

Thornley C.W. resigned and instead of two teams, decided to field just one, which replaced their reserves in the Wingate & District League.
Silksworth C.W. disbanded after losing their ground. Washington Chemical Works joined from the Washington Amateur League and Lumley Sixth Pit Welfare also joined.

1934-35

Team	P	W	D	L	F	A	Pts
Blackhall C.W.	22	18	3	1	79	21	39
Horden C.W.	22	15	2	5	58	31	32
Easington C.W.	22	14	3	5	68	30	31
Murton C.W.	22	13	1	8	46	40	27
Shotton C.W.	22	10	4	8	41	35	24
South Hetton C.W.	22	8	3	11	42	58	19
Dawdon Recreation	22	8	4	10	52	50	18
Seaham C.W.	22	6	6	10	34	47	18
Washington Chemical Works	22	6	4	12	39	58	14
Hetton United	22	4	6	12	39	67	14
Lumley Sixth Pit Welfare	22	5	2	15	32	54	12
Herrington C.W.	22	4	4	14	34	73	12

Dawdon Recreation and Washington Chemical Works each had 2 points deducted.
Horden C.W. moved to the North-Eastern League and Herrington C.W. disbanded. Herrington Juniors were formed as a replacement and joined the Hetton & District Junior League. Birtley, Chester-le-Street, Usworth Colliery and Washington Colliery all joined from the North-Eastern League ñ Division Two, Thornley C.W. joined from the Wingate & District League and Houghton C.W. joined from the Houghton & District League.

1935-36

	P	W	D	L	F	A	Pts
Lumley Sixth Pit Welfare	28	19	4	5	70	34	42
Blackhall C.W.	28	19	3	6	97	41	41
Birtley	28	14	7	7	94	50	35
Hetton United	28	13	6	9	83	54	32
Shotton C.W.	28	14	4	10	62	59	32
Murton C.W.	28	14	3	11	71	43	31
Easington C.W.	28	13	5	10	69	70	31
Washington Colliery	28	14	2	12	57	52	30
Houghton C.W.	28	11	5	12	49	56	27
Dawdon Recreation	28	11	4	13	61	66	26
Usworth Colliery	28	9	7	12	42	52	25
Washington Chemical Works	28	10	4	14	60	82	24
Seaham C.W.	28	7	5	16	51	85	19
Thornley C.W.	28	7	2	19	39	85	16
Chester-le-Street	28	4	1	23	44	120	9

South Hetton C.W. resigned on 20th January and later disbanded. Their record at the time was: 10 3 1 6 20 38 7
Chester-le-Street disbanded at the end of the season. Ouston United joined as a newly formed club and Sunderland's newly formed third team, Sunderland "A", also joined.

1936-37

	P	W	D	L	F	A	Pts
Murton C.W.	28	22	2	4	82	27	46
Sunderland "A"	28	19	7	2	83	27	45
Blackhall C.W.	28	19	2	7	105	34	40
Birtley	28	15	2	11	91	56	32
Washington Colliery	28	9	12	7	55	55	30
Hetton United	28	12	5	11	73	53	29
Houghton C.W.	28	12	3	13	58	67	27
Lumley Sixth Pit Welfare	28	10	5	13	57	64	25
Shotton C.W.	28	11	3	14	58	80	25
Dawdon Recreation	28	10	4	14	66	69	24
Washington Chemical Works	28	8	6	14	57	75	22
Ouston United	28	9	3	16	57	100	21
Seaham C.W.	28	8	4	16	44	68	20
Usworth Colliery	28	8	4	16	50	98	20
Easington C.W.	28	5	4	19	50	113	14

Thornley C.W. resigned on 16th December and their record was deleted when it stood as follows: 10 1 1 8 13 57 3
Sunderland decided not to run an "A" team during 1937-38.
Spennymoor United joined from the North-Eastern League and Brandon Social Club joined from the Durham City & District League.

1937-38

	P	W	D	L	F	A	Pts
Blackhall C.W.	28	24	1	3	117	26	49
Spennymoor United	28	18	6	4	88	40	42
Hetton United	28	17	3	8	86	50	37
Brandon Social Club	28	17	3	8	63	41	37
Ouston United	28	15	5	8	72	58	35
Lumley Sixth Pit Welfare	28	11	7	10	58	44	29
Usworth Colliery	28	12	4	12	54	57	28
Dawdon Recreation	28	10	7	11	70	60	27
Washington Chemical Works	28	11	5	12	63	75	27
Murton C.W.	28	11	5	12	38	62	27
Seaham C.W.	28	11	2	15	45	77	24
Houghton C.W.	28	10	4	14	51	79	22
Birtley	28	6	4	18	69	76	16
Shotton C.W.	28	4	2	22	41	119	10
Washington Colliery	28	3	2	23	35	86	6

Houghton C.W. and Washington Colliery each had 2 points deducted.
Easington C.W. resigned and disbanded on 1st December and their record was deleted when it was: 4 1 0 3 4 8 2
Spennymoor United returned to the North-Eastern League and Dawdon Recreation resigned in July 1938 because of a ground dispute. The dispute was later resolved but too late to rejoin so they joined the Seaham League instead. City of Durham joined from the North-Eastern League.

1938-39

	P	W	D	L	F	A	Pts
Blackhall C.W.	24	19	3	2	111	30	41
Brandon Social Club	24	15	4	5	85	33	34
Seaham C.W.	24	14	5	5	62	39	33
Hetton United	24	13	4	7	67	43	30
Lumley Sixth Pit Welfare	24	12	5	7	55	39	27
Ouston United	24	11	5	8	73	55	27
Usworth Colliery	24	10	5	9	60	61	25
Murton C.W.	24	11	2	11	51	57	24
Washington Chemical Works	24	7	6	11	46	59	20
Birtley	24	7	5	12	61	86	19
Washington Colliery	24	4	5	15	44	71	13
Houghton C.W.	24	3	4	17	28	111	10
Shotton C.W.	24	2	3	19	33	92	7

Lumley Sixth Pit Welfare had 2 points deducted.
City of Durham resigned and disbanded on 28th November and their record was deleted: 8 1 3 4 14 21 5
Blackhall C.W. moved to the North-Eastern League, Brandon Social Club moved to the Northern League while both Hetton United and Shotton C.W. disbanded. Sunderland "A" team joined, having been reformed, while South Shields Reserves joined from the Northern Alliance, Dawdon C.W. joined from the Seaham & District League, Boldon Villa and Reyrolles both joined from the Tyneside League, Trimdon Grange Social joined as a newly formed club and Easington C.W. joined as a newly re-formed club making a membership of 16 clubs.

1939-40

The season began on 26th August with a full programme of 8 games but when war was declared on 3rd September, all Wearside League activity was suspended. The league resumed on 7th October but Lumley Sixth Pit Welfare were unable to continue as their ground was being used for military purposes and Washington Chemical Works were also unable to continue. Meanwhile, many pitches all across the country were being converted to agricultural use.

On 21st December, Houghton Colliery decided to cease activity for the duration of the war and Birtley also resigned just before Christmas. Boldon Villa withdrew at the end of January and Trimdon Grange Social withdrew at the end of February, reducing the league to 10 clubs. The records of all 6 clubs who resigned during the season were deleted.

Final table

	P	W	D	L	F	A	Pts
Usworth Colliery	18	14	2	2	62	24	30
Murton C.W.	18	13	2	3	58	23	28
Ouston United	18	12	3	3	55	26	27
Reyrolles	18	10	2	6	55	41	22
South Shields Reserves	18	8	3	7	46	45	19
Dawdon C.W.	18	6	3	9	38	50	15
Seaham C.W.	18	4	5	9	41	46	13
Easington C.W.	18	4	4	10	29	58	12
Sunderland "A"	18	5	0	13	35	57	10
Washington Colliery	18	1	2	15	17	66	4

Wearside League 1945-1950

1940-45

The difficulties of clubs being able to operate under war-time conditions meant that the league had insufficient members to allow it to operate in the 1940-41 season. It then closed down until the war ended in 1945 when it was able to resume with 14 clubs. Six of these clubs – Dawdon C.W., Easington C.W., Seaham C.W., Sunderland "A", Usworth Colliery and Washington Chemical Works were members when war broke out in 1939 and there were 8 new members.

Those 8 new members were: Birtley Town, who replaced pre-war members Birtley, while Felling Red Star were pre-war members of the Tyneside League, Seaham United were pre-war members of the Seaham & District League and Wearmouth C.W. were pre-war members of the South Tyne Alliance. The other 4 new members were Shotton C.W., who had been formed as Shotton C.W. Juniors in 1939 following the disbanding of the senior club of the same name and had been playing in the Hetton & District Junior League during the war; North Sands who had been playing in the Sunderland Non-Conformists League during the war while there were 2 new clubs, Dawdon Mechanics and Doxford's C.D.S..

Of the pre-war members who did not return to the league, Murton C.W. joined the North-Eastern League and Reyrolles joined the North-East Industrial Welfare League. Boldon Villa, Houghton Colliery, South Shields Reserves and Trimdon Grange Social did not play in a league in 1945-46 while Lumley Sixth Pit Welfare, Ouston United and Washington Colliery did not reform.

1945-46

Birtley Town	26	20	4	2	97	39	44
Shotton C.W.	26	17	5	4	75	50	39
Easington C.W.	26	16	5	5	91	43	37
Seaham C.W.	26	15	3	8	94	68	33
Washington Chemical Works	26	11	6	9	69	65	28
North Sands	26	10	8	8	59	59	28
Sunderland "A"	26	9	7	10	72	56	25
Felling Red Star	26	11	3	12	64	76	25
Dawdon Mechanics	26	8	6	12	55	73	22
Doxford's C.D.S.	26	6	7	13	50	82	19
Wearmouth C.W.	26	6	6	14	59	73	18
Usworth Colliery	26	6	4	16	57	85	16
Seaham United	26	5	5	16	50	79	15
Dawdon C.W.	26	6	3	17	57	101	15

North Sands resigned because of ground difficulties while Usworth Colliery moved to the Northern Combination and Dawdon Mechanics moved to the Seaham & District League. Boldon Villa and South Shields Reserves rejoined after not playing in a league in 1945-46. Silksworth C.W., South Hetton C.W. and Stockton Reserves also joined. Doxford's C.D.S. changed their name to Doxford's Rovers.

1946-47

Seaham C.W.	30	23	5	2	121	45	51
Easington C.W.	30	20	6	4	112	46	46
South Hetton C.W.	30	20	3	7	121	62	43
Sunderland "A"	30	18	4	8	111	51	40
South Shields Reserves	30	17	5	8	91	64	39
Silksworth C.W.	30	15	6	9	93	61	36
Dawdon C.W.	30	16	4	10	80	58	36
Birtley Town	30	16	4	10	98	78	36
Shotton C.W.	30	12	7	11	64	59	31
Seaham United	30	11	6	13	75	82	28
Wearmouth C.W.	30	11	5	14	61	75	27
Stockton Reserves	30	10	3	17	76	84	23
Boldon Villa	30	6	4	20	56	97	16
Felling Red Star	30	6	0	24	63	146	12
Washington Chemical Works	30	4	1	25	54	155	9
Doxford's Rovers	30	3	1	26	36	149	7

Doxford's Rovers and Washington Chemical Works both left the league. Philadelphia C.W. joined from the Fence Houses & District League and Middlesbrough "A" also joined.
Boldon Villa changed their name to Boldon C.W..

1947-48

Easington C.W.	30	23	3	4	82	32	49
Philadelphia C.W.	30	19	5	6	71	42	43
South Hetton C.W.	30	16	8	6	65	47	40
Sunderland "A"	30	16	6	8	79	54	38
South Shields Reserves	30	16	5	9	74	48	37
Seaham United	30	15	2	13	94	76	32
Shotton C.W.	30	13	4	13	73	82	30
Middlesbrough "A"	30	12	4	14	65	52	28
Stockton Reserves	30	11	5	14	60	77	27
Birtley Town	30	10	6	14	53	56	26
Silksworth C.W.	30	10	5	15	79	70	25
Seaham C.W.	30	9	7	14	71	73	25
Wearmouth C.W.	30	9	6	15	49	74	24
Boldon C.W.	30	8	6	16	52	73	22
Dawdon C.W.	30	7	4	19	51	94	18
Felling Red Star	30	5	6	19	55	123	16

Seaham United moved to the Seaham & District League after losing use of their ground and Stockton Reserves also left. Horden C.W. Reserves joined from the Seaham & District League and Houghton C.W. also joined.

1948-49

Easington C.W.	30	25	3	2	105	36	53
Silksworth C.W.	30	19	2	9	84	48	40
South Hetton C.W.	30	17	6	7	87	61	40
Dawdon C.W.	30	17	4	9	94	50	38
Sunderland "A"	30	17	4	9	75	51	38
South Shields Reserves	30	15	5	10	88	71	35
Seaham C.W.	30	13	5	12	71	59	31
Middlesbrough "A"	30	11	8	11	59	65	30
Philadelphia C.W.	30	14	2	14	71	82	30
Horden C.W. Reserves	30	12	5	13	69	57	29
Birtley Town	30	11	4	15	61	80	26
Felling Red Star	30	9	6	15	58	90	24
Shotton C.W.	30	7	8	15	56	77	22
Boldon C.W.	30	8	3	19	62	101	19
Houghton C.W.	30	6	3	21	42	97	15
Wearmouth C.W.	30	3	4	23	27	84	10

Felling Red Star left after losing their ground to building and Houghton C.W. also left. Seaham United joined from the Seaham & District League as associate members and Wingate C.W. also joined.

1949-50

South Hetton C.W.	30	19	6	5	65	35	44
Sunderland "A"	30	18	5	7	79	46	41
Seaham C.W.	30	18	5	7	75	49	41
Wingate C.W.	30	18	5	7	84	64	41
Silksworth C.W.	30	17	5	8	75	54	39
Boldon C.W.	30	17	3	10	102	76	37
Easington C.W.	30	15	5	10	68	48	35
Dawdon C.W.	30	15	4	11	80	60	34
Shotton C.W.	30	11	9	10	73	72	31
Seaham United	30	9	4	17	79	96	22
Horden C.W. Reserves	30	10	2	18	60	75	22
Middlesbrough "A"	30	9	4	17	59	82	22
Wearmouth C.W.	30	9	2	19	61	86	20
Philadelphia C.W.	30	8	2	20	57	98	18
South Shields Reserves	30	7	4	19	47	85	18
Birtley Town	30	6	3	21	57	95	15

As goal average was not used to determine positions, Sunderland "A" were declared runners-up after a series of 3 games were played early in the 1950-51 season between the 3 clubs who finished with 41 points.
Philadelphia C.W. ceased activity for a season because of ground difficulties. Horden C.W. Reserves and South Shields Reserves were forced to resign because they did not have "first claim on their grounds". Both had needed to rearrange several home games during the season because their first teams also had home games, inconveniencing visiting sides. Seaham United also had to resign because their associate membership was not converted to full membership. Trimdon Grange and Ushaw Moor both joined from the Durham Central League while Durham City and Whitburn both joined as a newly re-formed clubs.

Wearside League 1950-1956

1950-51

	P	W	D	L	F	A	Pts
Sunderland "A"	30	21	5	4	109	36	47
Wingate C.W.	30	21	4	5	107	46	46
Boldon C.W.	30	20	4	6	100	63	44
Easington C.W.	30	17	6	7	86	55	40
Durham City	30	15	9	6	86	52	39
Ushaw Moor	30	17	4	9	89	66	38
Trimdon Grange	30	17	4	9	76	64	38
Whitburn	30	13	7	10	60	71	33
Dawdon C.W.	30	14	0	16	64	76	28
Silksworth C.W.	30	10	6	14	76	67	26
Seaham C.W.	30	8	6	16	58	99	22
Middlesbrough "A"	30	7	5	18	64	77	19
South Hetton C.W.	30	7	3	20	50	99	17
Wearmouth C.W.	30	7	2	21	57	101	16
Shotton C.W.	30	6	4	20	52	117	16
Birtley Town	30	4	3	23	46	91	11

South Hetton C.W. left the league and Eppleton C.W. joined from the North-Eastern League.

1951-52

	P	W	D	L	F	A	Pts
Sunderland "A"	30	23	4	3	106	32	50
Wingate C.W.	30	20	4	6	120	57	44
Boldon C.W.	30	15	7	8	87	51	37
Silksworth C.W.	30	15	6	9	94	57	36
Dawdon C.W.	30	15	6	9	62	51	36
Whitburn	30	16	4	10	59	60	36
Ushaw Moor	30	16	3	11	73	59	35
Durham City	30	14	7	9	75	67	35
Middlesbrough "A"	30	14	3	13	74	62	31
Eppleton C.W.	30	12	7	11	52	71	31
Easington C.W.	30	9	9	12	52	61	27
Trimdon Grange	30	7	6	17	49	72	20
Wearmouth C.W.	30	7	5	18	59	86	19
Seaham C.W.	30	5	6	19	45	85	16
Shotton C.W.	30	4	6	20	47	109	14
Birtley Town	30	5	3	22	38	112	13

Durham City moved to the Northern League and Birtley Town left. Murton C.W. joined from the Houghton & District League. Trimdon Grange changed their name to Trimdon Grange C.W..

1952-53

	P	W	D	L	F	A	Pts
Boldon C.W.	28	19	3	6	102	53	41
Silksworth C.W.	28	16	6	6	83	63	38
Sunderland "A"	28	15	5	8	72	46	35
Wingate C.W.	28	15	4	9	78	53	34
Ushaw Moor	28	16	2	10	81	57	34
Middlesbrough "A"	28	13	3	12	69	62	29
Dawdon C.W.	28	11	7	10	52	55	29
Seaham C.W.	28	11	7	10	50	60	29
Easington C.W.	28	10	8	10	73	66	28
Murton C.W.	28	10	8	10	54	57	28
Eppleton C.W.	28	9	7	12	66	63	25
Wearmouth C.W.	28	7	5	16	44	79	19
Whitburn	28	8	2	18	33	62	18
Shotton C.W.	28	5	7	16	47	93	17
Trimdon Grange C.W.	28	5	6	17	44	79	16

There were no changes to the league's constitution.

1953-54

	P	W	D	L	F	A	Pts
Shotton C.W.	28	19	5	4	88	52	43
Silksworth C.W.	28	15	5	8	66	49	35
Middlesbrough "A"	28	14	6	8	75	44	34
Ushaw Moor	28	15	4	9	85	64	34
Murton C.W.	28	13	8	7	59	47	34
Boldon C.W.	28	12	8	8	85	71	32
Wingate C.W.	28	13	4	11	73	68	30
Whitburn	28	11	8	9	61	65	30
Sunderland "A"	28	12	5	11	79	67	29
Easington C.W.	28	12	4	12	65	55	28
Seaham C.W.	28	11	4	13	62	76	26
Trimdon Grange C.W.	28	10	5	13	68	85	25
Dawdon C.W.	28	9	4	15	76	89	22
Eppleton C.W.	28	4	3	21	52	108	11
Wearmouth C.W.	28	2	3	23	44	98	7

Wearmouth C.W. moved to the Sunderland & District League.

1954-55

	P	W	D	L	F	A	Pts
Boldon C.W.	26	21	2	3	88	37	44
Middlesbrough "A"	26	18	3	5	94	39	39
Shotton C.W.	26	16	4	6	77	47	36
Sunderland "A"	26	15	4	7	85	53	34
Whitburn	26	11	7	8	61	54	29
Easington C.W.	26	11	5	10	85	73	27
Eppleton C.W.	26	9	6	11	64	67	24
Silksworth C.W.	26	9	6	11	55	83	24
Dawdon C.W.	26	9	3	14	56	62	21
Ushaw Moor	26	9	3	14	50	88	21
Seaham C.W.	26	7	5	14	56	69	19
Murton C.W.	26	8	3	15	48	60	19
Trimdon Grange C.W.	26	5	4	17	46	93	14
Wingate C.W.	26	5	3	18	54	94	13

Middlesbrough "A" and Sunderland "A" both left. Blackhall C.W. joined from the North-Eastern League and Langley Park C.W. also joined.

1955-56

	P	W	D	L	F	A	Pts
Shotton C.W.	26	18	3	5	90	37	39
Murton C.W.	26	17	3	6	61	37	37
Wingate C.W.	26	16	5	5	94	57	35
Easington C.W.	26	15	5	6	59	46	35
Silksworth C.W.	26	14	4	8	72	57	32
Whitburn	26	14	3	9	73	49	31
Blackhall C.W.	26	9	4	13	52	55	22
Boldon C.W.	26	9	3	14	63	65	21
Trimdon Grange C.W.	26	8	5	13	58	83	21
Dawdon C.W.	26	9	2	15	74	94	20
Langley Park C.W.	26	6	7	13	55	84	19
Ushaw Moor	26	6	7	13	49	75	19
Eppleton C.W.	26	8	2	16	48	65	18
Seaham C.W.	26	5	3	18	33	77	13

Wingate C.W. had 2 points deducted.
Ushaw Moor moved to the Durham Junior League. Thornley C.W. joined from the Durham Central League and Ryhope C.W. joined from the Houghton & District League.

Wearside League 1956-1962

1956-57

Team	P	W	D	L	F	A	Pts
Shotton C.W.	28	20	5	3	109	48	45
Trimdon Grange C.W.	28	18	3	7	83	66	39
Thornley C.W.	28	16	4	8	71	66	36
Murton C.W.	28	13	4	11	78	73	30
Easington C.W.	28	12	6	10	81	76	30
Silksworth C.W.	28	11	7	10	86	81	29
Wingate C.W.	28	12	4	12	81	70	28
Whitburn	28	12	5	11	65	51	27
Ryhope C.W.	28	11	4	13	55	65	26
Langley Park C.W.	28	9	8	11	55	66	26
Boldon C.W.	28	8	10	10	45	56	26
Eppleton C.W.	28	10	5	13	65	67	25
Blackhall C.W.	28	10	2	16	69	79	22
Seaham C.W.	28	6	6	16	47	86	18
Dawdon C.W.	28	3	5	20	44	84	11

Whitburn had 2 points deducted.
Chilton Athletic joined from the Durham Central League.

1957-58

Team	P	W	D	L	F	A	Pts
Silksworth C.W.	30	20	6	4	88	50	46
Thornley C.W.	30	19	6	5	79	56	44
Eppleton C.W.	30	15	8	7	80	49	38
Whitburn	30	15	7	8	95	56	37
Blackhall C.W.	30	16	4	10	79	51	36
Murton C.W.	30	15	4	11	71	61	34
Boldon C.W.	30	15	2	13	70	62	32
Ryhope C.W.	30	11	9	10	72	64	31
Langley Park C.W.	30	13	5	12	78	73	31
Easington C.W.	30	13	4	13	79	73	30
Trimdon Grange C.W.	30	10	7	13	73	63	27
Dawdon C.W.	30	10	7	13	69	76	27
Shotton C.W.	30	11	4	15	64	76	26
Chilton Athletic	30	8	5	17	67	87	21
Seaham C.W.	30	6	5	19	51	93	17
Wingate C.W.	30	0	3	27	31	156	3

There were no changes to the league's constitution.

1958-59

Team	P	W	D	L	F	A	Pts
Langley Park C.W.	30	21	4	5	127	54	46
Murton C.W.	30	20	5	5	123	42	45
Thornley C.W.	30	19	6	5	112	65	44
Silksworth C.W.	30	20	3	7	95	57	43
Eppleton C.W.	30	19	1	10	89	57	39
Easington C.W.	30	16	4	10	114	83	36
Shotton C.W.	30	15	5	10	71	70	35
Whitburn	30	14	3	13	98	64	31
Dawdon C.W.	30	14	3	13	62	77	31
Ryhope C.W.	30	13	2	15	78	73	28
Boldon C.W.	30	11	4	15	56	88	26
Trimdon Grange C.W.	30	7	6	17	54	96	20
Wingate C.W.	30	9	0	21	55	118	18
Chilton Athletic	30	6	5	19	55	101	17
Blackhall C.W.	30	6	4	20	45	78	16
Seaham C.W.	30	1	3	26	31	142	5

Blackhall C.W., Chilton Athletic, Seaham C.W. and Trimdon Grange C.W. all left the league.

1959-60

Team	P	W	D	L	F	A	Pts
Murton C.W.	22	18	3	1	75	21	39
Langley Park C.W.	22	14	4	4	71	39	32
Shotton C.W.	22	11	6	5	70	54	28
Silksworth C.W.	22	8	7	7	57	48	23
Thornley C.W.	22	10	2	10	45	48	22
Ryhope C.W.	22	11	0	11	42	50	22
Eppleton C.W.	22	5	10	7	38	50	20
Dawdon C.W.	22	6	7	9	43	45	19
Whitburn	22	7	4	11	56	63	18
Easington C.W.	22	7	3	12	49	60	17
Boldon C.W.	22	6	3	13	47	65	15
Wingate C.W.	22	4	1	17	38	88	9

Bowburn C.W. and South Shields Reserves both joined from the North-Eastern League. Reyrolles and Seaham C.W. also joined.

1960-61

Team	P	W	D	L	F	A	Pts
Shotton C.W.	30	24	1	5	112	32	49
Murton C.W.	30	19	7	4	77	35	45
Ryhope C.W.	30	18	4	8	96	44	40
South Shields Reserves	30	19	0	11	78	46	38
Bowburn C.W.	30	16	3	11	83	61	35
Langley Park C.W.	30	16	3	11	88	77	35
Easington C.W.	30	14	6	10	87	65	34
Silksworth C.W.	30	15	3	12	74	64	33
Reyrolles	30	12	6	12	68	76	30
Wingate C.W.	30	11	6	13	92	97	28
Boldon C.W.	30	11	4	15	68	68	26
Eppleton C.W.	30	11	3	16	55	81	25
Whitburn	30	8	6	16	50	69	22
Thornley C.W.	30	8	6	16	58	86	22
Dawdon C.W.	30	5	2	23	41	116	12
Seaham C.W.	30	2	2	26	30	140	6

Seaham C.W. left the league and Handon Hold C.W. joined.

1961-62

Team	P	W	D	L	F	A	Pts
Ryhope C.W.	30	28	2	0	122	26	58
Langley Park C.W.	30	19	7	4	87	44	45
Eppleton C.W.	30	19	6	5	80	42	44
South Shields Reserves	30	14	5	11	58	51	33
Silksworth C.W.	30	14	2	14	89	86	30
Murton C.W.	30	13	4	13	81	79	30
Whitburn	30	11	7	12	62	61	29
Boldon C.W.	30	12	5	13	71	75	29
Shotton C.W.	30	13	2	15	80	93	28
Thornley C.W.	30	11	5	14	73	81	27
Easington C.W.	30	11	4	15	52	58	26
Bowburn C.W.	30	10	5	15	55	69	25
Reyrolles	30	11	3	16	74	95	25
Handon Hold C.W.	30	5	8	17	55	86	18
Wingate C.W.	30	7	3	20	56	116	17
Dawdon C.W.	30	6	4	20	63	96	16

Bowburn C.W., Dawdon C.W. and Shotton C.W. all left the league.
Silksworth C.W. disbanded before the start of the 1962-63 season and were replaced by Roker who were a newly formed club. Hylton C.W. also joined.

1962-63

It was not possible to complete the full programme of fixtures because of an exceptionally severe winter. An abbreviated programme of 22 games was played in which some pairs of clubs met only once.

Team	P	W	D	L	F	A	Pts
Ryhope C.W.	22	17	3	2	86	31	37
Murton C.W.	22	16	3	3	64	25	35
South Shields Reserves	22	14	5	3	71	44	33
Langley Park C.W.	22	12	6	4	68	42	30
Handon Hold C.W.	22	12	4	6	59	34	28
Wingate C.W.	22	11	4	7	52	40	26
Reyrolles	22	12	2	8	54	55	26
Boldon C.W.	22	11	3	8	62	42	25
Eppleton C.W.	22	7	3	12	48	62	17
Hylton C.W.	22	5	3	14	43	80	13
Easington C.W.	22	5	2	15	46	80	12
Whitburn	22	4	3	15	36	64	11
Roker	22	4	0	18	29	70	8
Thornley C.W.	22	3	1	18	41	90	7

Wingate C.W. left the league.
Blackhall Club and Pyrex Sports Club both joined.

1963-64

Team	P	W	D	L	F	A	Pts
Ryhope C.W.	28	24	1	3	126	39	49
Blackhall Club	28	18	4	6	78	40	40
Langley Park C.W.	28	18	2	8	83	42	38
Pyrex Sports Club	28	15	5	8	67	53	35
Murton C.W.	28	11	9	8	68	52	31
Reyrolles	28	14	3	11	73	61	31
South Shields Reserves	28	12	5	11	62	54	29
Easington C.W.	28	12	4	12	63	69	28
Boldon C.W.	28	13	2	13	60	73	28
Roker	28	9	5	14	52	67	23
Handon Hold C.W.	28	7	8	13	58	63	22
Hylton C.W.	28	8	5	15	49	81	21
Whitburn	28	7	5	16	45	69	19
Thornley C.W.	28	6	5	17	53	105	17
Eppleton C.W.	28	3	3	22	37	106	9

Easington C.W. disbanded. Annfield Plain, Ashington, Consett, Horden C.W. and Stockton all joined from the North-Eastern League. Herrington C.W. also joined.

1964-65

Team	P	W	D	L	F	A	Pts
Horden C.W.	38	31	4	3	122	22	66
Ashington	38	31	4	3	151	34	66
Consett	38	27	5	6	116	49	59
Ryhope C.W.	38	26	6	6	141	65	58
Blackhall Club	38	24	4	10	109	56	52
South Shields Reserves	38	21	7	10	107	65	49
Stockton	38	20	5	13	101	79	45
Murton C.W.	38	19	4	15	79	72	42
Hylton C.W.	38	15	6	17	86	101	36
Annfield Plain	38	13	9	16	92	90	35
Roker	38	13	8	17	81	98	34
Langley Park C.W.	38	12	6	20	69	113	30
Handon Hold C.W.	38	14	1	23	79	112	29
Pyrex Sports Club	38	11	6	21	57	77	28
Reyrolles	38	11	5	22	88	122	27
Whitburn	38	10	7	21	47	95	27
Herrington C.W.	38	11	3	24	61	104	25
Thornley C.W.	38	7	5	26	54	102	19
Boldon C.W.	38	7	5	26	54	116	19
Eppleton C.W.	38	5	4	29	58	180	14

Ashington moved to the North Regional League while Eppleton C.W. and Langley Park C.W. also left. 24th Signals Regiment (Catterick) and Sunderland Structural Steel both joined.

1965-66

Team	P	W	D	L	F	A	Pts
Ryhope C.W.	34	26	6	2	120	41	58
Horden C.W.	34	22	6	6	91	40	50
Consett	34	21	6	7	85	43	48
Stockton	34	20	7	7	96	44	47
Hylton C.W.	34	21	5	8	104	58	47
South Shields Reserves	34	18	9	7	93	51	45
Annfield Plain	34	17	4	13	86	75	38
Blackhall Club	34	15	8	11	82	73	38
Thornley C.W.	34	15	6	13	77	76	36
Reyrolles	34	15	5	14	99	92	35
Pyrex Sports Club	34	16	3	15	71	75	35
Murton C.W.	34	13	5	16	74	68	31
Roker	34	13	2	19	77	87	28
Whitburn	34	10	4	20	67	118	24
Boldon C.W.	34	9	4	21	64	96	22
24th Signals Regiment (Catterick)	34	9	3	22	75	92	21
Handon Hold C.W.	34	2	3	29	51	145	7
Sunderland Structural Steel	34	1	0	33	19	163	2

Herrington C.W. disbanded on 18th December and their record was deleted when it stood as: 14 2 2 10 19 44 6
24th Signals Regiment (Catterick) and Hylton C.W. both left the league. Hartlepool United Reserves joined from the North Regional League while Hetton C.W. and Silksworth Colliery also joined.

1966-67

Team	P	W	D	L	F	A	Pts
Reyrolles	36	27	5	4	147	55	59
Murton C.W.	36	23	8	5	98	58	54
Hartlepool United Reserves	36	23	6	7	90	41	52
Horden C.W.	35	21	8	6	88	46	50
South Shields Reserves	36	22	5	9	111	57	49
Consett	36	21	6	9	111	56	48
Blackhall Club	36	19	6	11	102	73	44
Ryhope C.W.	36	20	3	13	102	66	43
Hetton C.W.	35	19	2	14	92	71	40
Stockton	36	15	8	13	70	58	38
Whitburn	36	16	5	15	102	96	37
Annfield Plain	36	15	6	15	82	73	36
Roker	36	10	4	22	55	111	24
Pyrex Sports Club	36	7	9	20	62	111	23
Boldon C.W.	36	8	5	23	67	101	21
Silksworth Colliery	36	8	4	24	77	137	20
Sunderland Structural Steel	36	7	3	26	42	116	17
Thornley C.W.	36	5	4	27	48	130	14
Handon Hold C.W.	36	5	3	28	56	146	13

One game was not played.
Stockton moved to the North Regional League while Handon Hold C.W. and Hetton C.W. also left. Wingate St. Mary's joined from the Hartlepool & District League, Darlington Reserves joined from the North Regional League, Gateshead Reserves joined from the Northern Alliance and Hylton C.W. also joined.

Wearside League 1967-1972

1967-68

Horden C.W.	38	30	6	2	148	50	66
Hartlepool United Reserves	38	28	4	6	106	45	60
Ryhope C.W.	38	27	5	6	109	43	59
Consett	38	27	3	8	106	48	57
Reyrolles	38	21	6	11	111	79	48
Annfield Plain	38	19	10	9	90	76	48
Murton C.W.	38	16	10	12	90	61	42
Darlington Reserves	38	17	7	14	79	54	41
South Shields Reserves	38	14	12	12	106	67	40
Blackhall Club	38	18	4	16	100	83	40
Whitburn	38	18	4	16	105	94	40
Hylton C.W.	38	15	6	17	73	95	36
Wingate St. Mary's	38	12	7	19	90	119	31
Boldon C.W.	38	12	4	22	80	95	28
Pyrex Sports Club	38	10	8	20	56	96	28
Roker	38	10	4	24	65	108	24
Gateshead Reserves	38	10	4	24	66	122	24
Thornley C.W.	38	7	6	25	51	119	20
Sunderland Structural Steel	38	4	6	28	54	137	14
Silksworth Colliery	38	7	0	31	49	143	14

Pyrex Sports Club left the league. Stockton joined from the North Regional League while Washington and Morrison Busty C.W. both joined from the Northern Alliance, Washington having changed their name from Washington Mechanics. Wingate St. Mary's changed their name to Wingate and Blackhall Club changed their name to Blackhall C.W..

1968-69

Darlington Reserves	42	33	4	5	143	50	70
Consett	42	29	5	8	130	56	63
Wingate	42	28	7	7	108	58	63
South Shields Reserves	42	26	4	12	139	82	56
Ryhope C.W.	42	24	7	11	110	65	55
Stockton	42	24	7	11	109	83	55
Hartlepool United Reserves	42	25	5	12	93	80	55
Boldon C.W.	42	19	13	10	114	97	51
Morrison Busty C.W.	42	21	8	13	109	77	50
Murton C.W.	42	19	9	14	114	83	47
Washington	42	18	6	18	95	83	42
Horden C.W.	42	16	8	18	74	85	40
Annfield Plain	42	16	7	19	96	104	39
Reyrolles	42	14	8	20	112	112	36
Gateshead Reserves	42	14	6	22	85	123	34
Hylton C.W.	42	13	6	23	77	104	32
Silksworth Colliery	42	12	4	26	96	118	28
Whitburn	42	10	8	24	76	135	28
Blackhall C.W.	42	8	8	26	72	119	24
Roker	42	8	7	27	72	127	23
Thornley C.W.	42	8	4	30	67	133	20
Sunderland Structural Steel	42	5	3	34	60	177	13

Blackhall C.W. left the league.

1969-70

Horden C.W.	40	29	5	6	158	42	63
Consett	40	28	4	8	138	55	60
Darlington Reserves	40	25	3	12	100	65	53
Washington	40	22	8	10	108	68	52
Hartlepool United Reserves	40	22	7	11	118	72	51
Stockton	40	23	4	13	131	66	50
Reyrolles	40	23	4	13	124	82	50
Murton C.W.	40	20	9	11	88	77	49
Wingate	40	22	4	14	111	75	48
Ryhope C.W.	40	20	5	15	80	68	45
South Shields Reserves	40	18	8	14	105	73	44
Morrison Busty C.W.	40	19	5	16	91	97	43
Roker	40	14	7	19	73	94	35
Hylton C.W.	40	16	2	22	102	109	34
Boldon C.W.	40	13	8	19	83	96	34
Silksworth Colliery	40	13	6	21	82	119	32
Gateshead Reserves	40	13	5	22	89	142	31
Annfield Plain	40	8	8	24	78	126	24
Thornley C.W.	40	7	4	29	54	154	18
Whitburn	40	5	2	33	54	170	12
Sunderland Structural Steel	40	5	2	33	53	170	12

Consett moved to the Northern League. Gateshead joined from the Northern Premier League, replacing their reserve side.

1970-71

Horden C.W.	38	31	3	4	146	50	65
Gateshead	38	28	6	4	143	37	62
Stockton	38	21	10	7	120	61	52
South Shields Reserves	38	20	11	7	93	45	51
Washington	38	19	11	8	94	60	49
Roker	38	22	3	13	83	71	47
Wingate	38	20	5	13	94	72	45
Murton C.W.	38	18	7	13	113	85	43
Boldon C.W.	38	18	3	17	83	92	39
Darlington Reserves	38	14	9	15	70	62	37
Hartlepool United Reserves	38	16	4	18	85	82	36
Annfield Plain	38	14	8	16	87	88	36
Silksworth Colliery	38	13	9	16	85	81	35
Reyrolles	38	14	7	17	84	97	35
Hylton C.W.	38	13	6	19	88	108	32
Ryhope C.W.	38	13	6	19	63	91	32
Morrison Busty C.W.	38	9	8	21	59	96	26
Sunderland Structural Steel	38	5	4	29	47	155	14
Whitburn	38	4	5	29	39	143	13
Thornley C.W.	38	3	5	30	44	144	11

Gateshead moved to the Midland League while Morrison Busty C.W. and Thornley C.W. also left. Chilton C.W. joined.

1971-72

Horden C.W.	34	23	6	5	107	41	52
Stockton	34	22	8	4	85	36	52
Washington	34	21	6	7	95	58	48
Hartlepool United Reserves	34	18	6	10	89	52	42
Annfield Plain	34	17	6	11	87	58	40
Wingate	34	17	5	12	82	50	39
Boldon C.W.	34	17	2	15	86	64	36
Ryhope C.W.	34	15	6	13	66	60	36
Murton C.W.	34	14	7	13	66	60	35
Silksworth Colliery	34	14	6	14	60	66	34
Roker	34	13	7	14	60	68	33
South Shields Reserves	34	12	8	14	77	72	32
Darlington Reserves	34	11	7	16	45	54	29
Sunderland Structural Steel	34	12	3	19	66	89	27
Reyrolles	34	11	4	19	69	100	26
Whitburn	34	10	4	20	54	112	24
Hylton C.W.	34	7	6	21	65	108	20
Chilton C.W.	34	1	5	28	33	144	7

Stockton moved to the Midland League and Darlington Reserves also left. Heaton Stannington and Seaham U.D.C. both joined.

1972-73

Team	P	W	D	L	F	A	Pts
Horden C.W.	34	27	4	3	112	37	58
Murton C.W.	34	27	3	4	114	42	57
Reyrolles	34	21	3	10	100	56	45
Boldon C.W.	34	21	3	10	111	78	45
Heaton Stannington	34	16	8	10	55	42	40
Seaham U.D.C.	34	16	7	11	82	56	39
Wingate	34	16	7	11	77	59	39
Annfield Plain	34	16	5	13	70	58	37
Hartlepool United Reserves	34	17	3	14	79	66	37
Washington	34	14	8	12	66	51	36
Hylton C.W.	34	12	7	15	57	74	31
Roker	34	10	10	14	58	61	30
Silksworth Colliery	34	10	7	17	57	92	27
# Steels Social Club	34	8	9	17	60	76	25
South Shields Reserves	34	10	4	20	53	83	24
Whitburn	34	7	7	20	47	101	19
Ryhope C.W.	34	6	2	26	32	79	14
Chilton C.W.	34	2	3	29	25	144	7

Sunderland Structural Steel resigned at the end of August after playing one game (a 5-0 defeat) and Steels Social Club took over their record and fixtures, starting on 23rd September.
Whitburn had 2 points deducted.
Whitburn left the league. Blue Star joined from the Northern Combination while Easington C.W. joined as a newly re-formed club and Wallsend Town also joined.

1973-74

Team	P	W	D	L	F	A	Pts
Blue Star	36	26	5	5	108	51	57
Easington C.W.	36	25	7	4	103	59	57
Horden C.W.	36	24	7	5	85	40	55
Washington	36	22	4	10	73	40	48
Steels Social Club	36	21	3	12	88	56	45
Wingate	36	19	6	11	78	72	44
Murton C.W.	36	18	7	11	97	68	43
Wallsend Town	36	17	8	11	89	63	42
Reyrolles	36	12	11	13	60	78	35
Boldon C.W.	36	14	5	17	88	89	33
Silksworth Colliery	36	15	3	18	87	92	33
South Shields Reserves	36	11	10	15	71	72	32
Hartlepool United Reserves	36	13	5	18	69	63	31
Seaham U.D.C.	36	11	4	21	53	82	26
Annfield Plain	36	9	7	20	66	89	25
Roker	36	9	7	20	53	72	25
Heaton Stannington	36	8	9	19	51	73	25
Ryhope C.W.	36	7	6	23	49	110	20
Chilton C.W.	36	2	4	30	39	138	8

Hylton C.W. resigned in November and their record was deleted when it stood as follows: 9 1 0 8 9 31 2
Chilton C.W. left the league. Whickham joined from the Northern Combination and Eppleton C.W. joined from the Houghton & District League. At the end of the season, South Shields moved to Gateshead and changed their name to Gateshead United.

1974-75

Team	P	W	D	L	F	A	Pts
Boldon C.W.	38	28	6	4	99	36	62
Blue Star	38	24	10	4	98	42	58
Wallsend Town	38	24	5	9	83	43	53
Horden C.W.	38	19	11	8	76	42	49
Eppleton C.W.	38	17	15	6	90	53	49
Easington C.W.	38	20	4	14	96	75	44
Steels Social Club	38	18	7	13	73	68	43
Whickham	38	17	7	14	77	71	41
Washington	38	13	13	12	59	57	39
Heaton Stannington	38	18	4	16	75	70	38
Hartlepool United Reserves	38	15	7	16	76	66	37
Gateshead United Reserves	38	15	7	16	76	79	37
Roker	38	15	6	17	50	69	36
Wingate	38	15	2	21	67	78	32
Annfield Plain	38	13	5	20	72	75	31
Silksworth Colliery	38	11	9	18	72	78	31
Reyrolles	38	9	9	20	58	88	27
Murton C.W.	38	10	6	22	49	87	26
Ryhope C.W.	38	6	8	24	52	101	20
Seaham U.D.C.	38	1	3	34	37	157	5

Heaton Stannington had 2 points deducted.
Horden C.W. moved to the Northern League and Steels Social Club also left.

1975-76

Team	P	W	D	L	F	A	Pts
Blue Star	34	26	5	3	99	29	57
Boldon C.W.	34	25	6	3	86	30	56
Seaham U.D.C.	34	16	14	4	67	37	46
Gateshead United Reserves	34	22	2	10	84	60	46
Heaton Stannington	34	19	6	9	74	46	44
Eppleton C.W.	34	14	12	8	59	34	40
Wallsend Town	34	15	8	11	67	46	38
Easington C.W.	34	14	8	12	79	53	36
Washington	34	14	8	12	59	57	36
Whickham	34	13	7	14	61	58	33
Roker	34	11	7	16	57	69	29
Silksworth Colliery	34	9	9	16	62	95	27
Annfield Plain	34	10	5	19	58	70	25
Wingate	34	7	9	18	52	99	23
Hartlepool United Reserves	34	7	8	19	45	79	22
Reyrolles	34	9	3	22	45	99	21
Murton C.W.	34	7	5	22	35	70	19
Ryhope C.W.	34	5	4	25	30	88	14

Gateshead United Reserves resigned and Silksworth Colliery were expelled. South Shields joined from the Northern Alliance. Boldon C.W. changed their name to Boldon Community Association and Easington C.W. changed their name to Easington Colliery.

1976-77

Team	P	W	D	L	F	A	Pts
South Shields	32	23	8	1	109	34	54
Blue Star	32	22	7	3	92	35	51
Boldon Community Association	32	19	10	3	71	30	48
Washington	32	18	4	10	86	53	40
Easington Colliery	32	17	5	10	75	59	39
Wallsend Town	32	14	10	8	62	36	38
Wingate	32	16	6	10	73	54	38
Whickham	32	15	8	9	62	47	38
Roker	32	14	5	13	45	57	33
Heaton Stannington	32	12	4	16	56	76	28
Murton C.W.	32	11	6	15	51	78	28
Eppleton C.W.	32	7	12	13	49	56	26
Ryhope C.W.	32	7	6	19	38	81	20
Seaham U.D.C.	32	5	8	19	37	85	18
Reyrolles	32	5	6	21	43	81	16
Hartlepool United Reserves	32	6	3	23	45	93	15
Annfield Plain	32	5	4	23	52	91	14

Seaham U.D.C. left the league and Garden Farm joined.

Wearside League 1977-1982

1977-78

	P	W	D	L	F	A	Pts
Whickham	32	22	6	4	66	24	50
Blue Star	32	21	4	7	93	40	46
Boldon Community Association	32	18	5	9	65	39	41
Eppleton C.W.	32	17	7	8	53	30	41
South Shields	32	16	8	8	51	39	40
Hartlepool United Reserves	32	16	6	10	65	49	38
Wallsend Town	32	16	5	11	62	43	37
Washington	32	13	10	9	64	57	36
Easington Colliery	32	14	8	10	65	59	36
Ryhope C.W.	32	13	8	11	59	47	34
Wingate	32	13	5	14	54	52	31
Garden Farm	32	10	8	14	48	56	28
Reyrolles	32	9	4	19	37	63	22
Roker	32	6	8	18	42	76	20
Annfield Plain	32	8	3	21	40	79	19
Heaton Stannington	32	4	6	22	33	89	14
Murton C.W.	32	4	3	25	32	87	11

Garden Farm changed their name to Chester-le-Street Town.

1978-79

	P	W	D	L	F	A	Pts
Wallsend Town	32	21	5	6	88	42	47
Wingate	32	21	4	7	81	46	46
Whickham	32	17	10	5	66	36	44
Boldon Community Association	32	18	7	7	77	43	43
South Shields	32	16	11	5	80	50	43
Hartlepool United Reserves	32	16	5	11	61	52	37
Chester-le-Street Town	32	13	10	9	55	48	36
Blue Star	32	20	5	7	90	42	35
Annfield Plain	32	13	6	13	67	69	32
Easington Colliery	32	11	8	13	50	73	30
Ryhope C.W.	32	8	11	13	49	50	27
Eppleton C.W.	32	8	6	18	52	71	22
Washington	32	7	8	17	32	59	20
Reyrolles	32	8	4	20	52	90	20
Roker	32	5	8	19	38	79	18
Heaton Stannington	32	6	5	21	43	86	17
Murton C.W.	32	4	9	19	27	75	17

Blue Star had 10 points deducted.
Washington had 2 points deducted.
Note: This table is as published but contains errors as the wins and losses and goals for and against records do not balance.
Peterlee Newtown and Seaham C.W. Red Star both joined from the Northern Alliance while Sunderland Reserves also joined. Murton C.W. changed their name to Murton.

1979-80

	P	W	D	L	F	A	Pts
Hartlepool United Reserves	38	27	5	6	92	36	59
Blue Star	38	26	5	7	102	47	57
Seaham C.W. Red Star	38	25	6	7	101	40	56
Whickham	38	25	4	9	89	44	54
Sunderland Reserves	38	22	8	8	71	35	50
Peterlee Newtown	38	17	12	9	67	57	46
Heaton Stannington	38	17	11	10	54	56	45
Boldon Community Association	38	14	10	14	67	58	38
Chester-le-Street Town	38	14	10	14	66	63	38
South Shields	38	14	9	15	58	62	37
Ryhope C.W.	38	11	14	13	51	56	36
Reyrolles	38	11	14	13	58	64	36
Wallsend Town	38	10	13	15	52	66	33
Annfield Plain	38	11	7	20	57	73	29
Easington Colliery	38	11	7	20	56	82	29
Wingate	38	8	11	19	59	78	27
Eppleton C.W.	38	9	9	20	47	78	27
Washington	38	7	10	21	41	73	22
Murton	38	8	4	26	32	103	18
Roker	38	5	7	26	48	97	17

Murton, Sunderland Reserves and Washington had 2 points deducted.
Sunderland Reserves left the league. Stockton joined as a newly re-formed club. Roker changed their name to Roker Zanussi.

1980-81

	P	W	D	L	F	A	Pts
Chester-le-Street Town	38	28	9	1	79	13	65
Whickham	38	29	6	3	95	33	64
Blue Star	38	25	8	5	94	40	58
Reyrolles	38	22	7	9	83	49	51
Peterlee Newtown	38	20	10	8	59	34	50
South Shields	38	17	9	12	97	58	43
Hartlepool United Reserves	38	15	13	10	54	45	43
Seaham C.W. Red Star	38	17	6	15	61	48	40
Heaton Stannington	38	14	8	16	64	64	36
Wallsend Town	38	11	10	17	63	73	32
Ryhope C.W.	38	12	8	18	47	68	32
Roker Zanussi	38	12	7	19	56	64	31
Annfield Plain	38	13	5	20	53	83	31
Wingate	38	10	10	18	49	73	30
Eppleton C.W.	38	9	10	19	37	58	28
Stockton	38	11	6	21	39	84	28
Murton	38	11	5	22	55	79	27
Boldon Community Association	38	8	11	19	39	65	27
Washington	38	6	13	19	38	86	25
Easington Colliery	38	8	3	27	41	85	19

Wallsend Town moved to the Northern Alliance. Brandon United joined from the Northern Amateur League. Roker Zanussi changed their name back to Roker. Reyrolles changed their name to Hebburn Reyrolle.

1981-82

	P	W	D	L	F	A	Pts
Seaham C.W. Red Star	38	27	5	6	67	27	59
Peterlee Newtown	38	24	8	6	81	31	56
Chester-le-Street Town	38	24	7	7	69	34	55
Hebburn Reyrolle	38	23	7	8	82	50	53
Blue Star	38	21	9	8	88	40	51
Brandon United	38	21	8	9	73	48	50
Whickham	38	19	11	8	81	46	49
South Shields	38	21	7	10	66	48	49
Hartlepool United Reserves	38	18	8	12	69	50	44
Easington Colliery	38	17	9	12	66	53	43
Roker	38	13	13	12	63	68	39
Washington	38	12	9	17	50	56	33
Heaton Stannington	38	13	5	20	53	76	31
Eppleton C.W.	38	8	9	21	42	58	25
Annfield Plain	38	7	9	22	50	84	23
Wingate	38	9	4	25	49	75	22
Murton	38	6	9	23	29	79	21
Stockton	38	8	5	25	46	100	21
Ryhope C.W.	38	6	7	25	44	89	19
Boldon Community Association	38	4	9	25	38	94	17

Hartlepool United Reserves and Peterlee Newtown moved to the Northern League and Heaton Stannington dropped into junior football because of ground problems. Coundon TT joined from the Durham & District League. (Note: The club was formed in 1976 as a pub team called Three Tuns, hence the TT in the name).

1982-83

Team	P	W	D	L	F	A	Pts
Blue Star	34	27	3	4	100	30	57
Chester-le-Street Town	34	23	5	6	84	29	51
Brandon United	34	25	0	9	84	45	50
Easington Colliery	34	21	5	8	71	38	47
Coundon TT	34	20	4	10	65	47	44
Stockton	34	14	12	8	67	46	40
Ryhope C.W.	34	14	8	12	51	41	36
Whickham	34	14	8	12	45	44	36
Seaham C.W. Red Star	34	14	7	13	57	50	35
South Shields	34	13	8	13	53	58	34
Eppleton C.W.	34	11	7	16	59	65	29
Murton	34	10	6	18	35	46	26
Washington	34	10	6	18	42	54	26
Boldon Community Association	34	10	5	19	36	70	25
Annfield Plain	34	7	9	18	48	79	23
Wingate	34	6	7	21	56	95	19
Hebburn Reyrolle	34	6	7	21	40	82	19
Roker	34	5	5	24	53	127	15

Brandon United, Chester-le-Street Town and Seaham C.W. Red Star all moved to the Northern League. Dawdon C.W. joined from the SavaCentre Washington League and South Hetton joined from the Tyne-Wear League. Gateshead Reserves also joined.

1983-84

Team	P	W	D	L	F	A	Pts
Blue Star	34	27	3	4	94	24	57
Coundon TT	34	27	2	5	93	29	56
Easington Colliery	34	24	7	3	79	34	55
Wingate	34	19	5	10	66	37	43
Whickham	34	18	6	10	66	44	42
South Shields	34	17	7	10	61	41	41
Annfield Plain	34	16	8	10	50	42	40
Washington	34	16	7	11	53	44	39
Boldon Community Association	34	11	12	11	55	54	34
Eppleton C.W.	34	13	5	16	66	50	31
Stockton	34	12	6	16	54	61	30
Dawdon C.W.	34	8	10	16	42	64	26
Murton	34	6	10	18	35	67	22
Ryhope C.W.	34	6	10	18	33	66	22
Gateshead Reserves	34	8	6	20	50	83	22
Hebburn Reyrolle	34	5	8	21	42	88	18
Roker	34	6	6	22	41	105	18
South Hetton	34	5	6	23	28	75	16

Newton Aycliffe joined from the Teesside League and Gateshead Clarke Chapman joined from the Northern Amateur League. South Hetton changed their name to Sporting Club Vaux.

1984-85

Team	P	W	D	L	F	A	Pts
Blue Star	38	29	7	2	124	28	65
Whickham	38	28	7	3	81	30	63
Coundon TT	38	27	5	6	106	44	59
South Shields	38	25	7	6	105	36	57
Eppleton C.W.	38	19	6	13	70	59	44
Ryhope C.W.	38	18	7	13	71	56	43
Wingate	38	16	10	12	68	56	42
Easington Colliery	38	15	7	16	75	69	37
Annfield Plain	38	13	10	15	61	58	36
Washington	38	14	7	17	66	75	35
Sporting Club Vaux	38	15	4	19	65	87	34
Murton	38	14	4	20	48	93	32
Boldon Community Association	38	11	9	18	66	79	31
Gateshead Reserves	38	12	4	22	55	93	28
Roker	38	11	5	22	71	95	27
Gateshead Clarke Chapman	38	12	3	23	66	96	27
Newton Aycliffe	38	12	3	23	55	92	27
Dawdon C.W.	38	11	4	23	64	85	26
Hebburn Reyrolle	38	11	4	23	50	99	26
Stockton	38	7	7	24	43	80	21

Blue Star, Easington Colliery and Stockton all moved to the Northern League. Marske United joined from the Teesside League.

1985-86

Team	P	W	D	L	F	A	Pts
Coundon TT	34	25	7	2	72	24	57
Murton	34	25	4	5	70	18	54
Whickham	34	22	7	5	68	23	51
Annfield Plain	34	17	9	8	71	49	43
Sporting Club Vaux	34	19	4	11	68	49	42
Gateshead Reserves	34	18	4	12	80	49	40
Washington	34	16	8	10	54	44	40
Marske United	34	18	3	13	70	44	39
Wingate	34	15	8	11	55	49	38
Eppleton C.W.	34	16	2	16	71	54	34
Newton Aycliffe	34	12	5	17	46	67	29
South Shields	34	9	8	17	46	60	26
Hebburn Reyrolle	34	10	6	18	51	76	26
Roker	34	9	6	19	48	72	24
Gateshead Clarke Chapman	34	7	8	19	39	62	22
Boldon Community Association	34	8	5	21	34	67	21
Dawdon C.W.	34	7	7	20	48	94	21
Ryhope C.W.	34	1	3	30	21	111	5

Hartlepool Boys Welfare Old Boys joined from the Teesside League and Herrington C.W. also joined.

Three points were awarded for a win from the next season.

1986-87

Team	P	W	D	L	F	A	Pts
Annfield Plain	38	27	5	6	104	38	86
Murton	38	27	4	7	71	35	85
Sporting Club Vaux	38	24	6	8	82	39	78
Whickham	38	22	7	9	76	39	73
Hartlepool Boys Welfare Old Boys	38	21	9	8	75	42	72
Eppleton C.W.	38	21	5	12	79	47	68
Marske United	38	18	9	11	67	47	63
Coundon TT	38	15	14	9	67	46	59
South Shields	38	17	8	13	66	50	59
Dawdon C.W.	38	16	9	13	59	50	57
Washington	38	10	14	14	56	54	44
Roker	38	13	5	20	55	70	44
Boldon Community Association	38	10	12	16	47	61	42
Ryhope C.W.	38	12	4	22	49	80	40
Hebburn Reyrolle	38	10	9	19	65	91	39
Newton Aycliffe	38	10	8	20	52	70	38
Herrington C.W.	38	8	13	17	52	82	37
Gateshead Clarke Chapman	38	5	11	22	40	87	26
Wingate	38	5	7	26	34	101	22
Gateshead Reserves	38	8	3	27	49	116	21

Gateshead Reserves had 6 points deducted.
Wingate moved to the Auckland & District League and Gateshead Reserves also left. Dunston Federation Breweries joined from the Northern Combination and Blackhall C.W. joined from the SavaCentre Washington League.

Wearside League 1987-1990

1987-88

Whickham	38	26	9	3	82	30	87
Coundon TT	38	22	5	11	71	46	71
Eppleton C.W.	38	19	13	6	79	47	70
Murton	38	17	14	7	63	36	65
South Shields	38	17	11	10	78	57	62
Marske United	38	18	8	12	72	62	62
Hebburn Reyrolle	38	18	7	13	77	49	61
Dawdon C.W.	38	18	6	14	85	61	60
Dunston Federation Breweries	38	16	10	12	59	50	58
Sporting Club Vaux	38	18	6	14	76	69	57
Washington	38	14	9	15	59	58	51
Blackhall C.W.	38	13	9	16	60	73	48
Newton Aycliffe	38	13	6	19	57	69	45
Roker	38	12	9	17	47	70	45
Boldon Community Association	38	11	10	17	54	58	43
Gateshead Clarke Chapman	38	11	6	21	52	68	39
Hartlepool Boys Welfare Old Boys	38	10	9	19	54	71	39
Annfield Plain	38	11	3	24	42	89	36
Herrington C.W.	38	6	14	18	41	66	32
Ryhope C.W.	38	6	4	28	29	108	22

Sporting Club Vaux had 3 points deducted.
Murton, Washington and Whickham all moved to the Northern League. Cleator Moor Celtic joined from the Carlisle & District League. Ryhope C.W. and Sporting Club Vaux merged to form Sunderland Vaux Ryhope, playing at the former ground of Ryhope C.W., Ryhope Recreation Park. Hebburn Reyrolle changed their name to Hebburn.

A Second Division containing 12 clubs was formed: Greatham and Wolviston both joined from the Teesside League, Lambton Street joined from the SavaCentre Washington League, Felling Leam Lane joined from the Northern Amateur League, N.E.I. Parsons Athletic joined from the Northern Combination, Stanley United joined from the Durham & District League, Wingate joined from the Auckland & District League, Winlaton Youngs Descaling joined from the Tyneside Amateur League while Washington Nissan and Silksworth both joined as newly formed clubs. Stockton E.D.C. and Thornley W.M.C. also joined.

Promoted clubs are shown in bold, relegated clubs in bold italics.

1988-89

Division One

Dunston Federation Breweries	32	23	7	2	70	23	76
Eppleton C.W.	32	24	3	5	76	25	75
Sunderland Vaux Ryhope	32	22	2	8	74	33	68
South Shields	32	19	5	8	67	46	62
Hebburn	32	18	6	8	68	44	60
Marske United	32	15	7	10	60	49	52
Newton Aycliffe	32	14	4	14	49	60	46
Boldon Community Association	32	12	7	13	47	47	43
Herrington C.W.	32	11	8	13	41	55	41
Hartlepool Boys Welfare O.B.	32	12	6	14	66	59	39
Cleator Moor Celtic	32	11	6	15	44	60	39
Roker	32	9	7	16	32	46	34
Annfield Plain	32	9	5	18	46	66	32
Dawdon C.W.	32	7	9	16	38	47	30
Coundon TT	32	8	5	19	38	69	29
Gateshead Clarke Chapman	32	7	5	20	45	77	26
Blackhall C.W.	32	3	4	25	23	78	13

Hartlepool Boys Welfare Old Boys had 3 points deducted.
Hebburn moved to the Northern League.

Division Two

N.E.I. Parsons Athletic	22	17	4	1	49	17	55
Stockton E.D.C.	22	13	6	3	45	25	45
Lambton Street	22	13	3	6	39	32	42
Stanley United	22	11	2	9	56	48	35
Greatham	22	8	7	7	42	34	31
Wolviston	22	9	4	9	41	38	31
Silksworth	22	7	6	9	29	35	27
Thornley W.M.C.	22	8	1	13	38	50	25
Winlaton Youngs Descaling	22	6	5	11	40	49	23
Washington Nissan	22	7	2	13	37	52	23
Wingate	22	6	3	13	36	51	21
Felling Leam Lane	22	4	3	15	25	46	15

Wingate Parish joined the league.

1989-90

Division One

Dunston Federation Breweries	28	21	5	2	60	14	68
Eppleton C.W.	28	18	8	2	77	25	62
Newton Aycliffe	28	14	9	5	59	32	51
Boldon Community Association	28	13	9	6	46	38	45
South Shields	28	11	10	7	68	46	43
Coundon TT	28	12	4	12	61	60	40
Annfield Plain	28	12	4	12	42	51	40
Marske United	28	11	5	12	50	57	38
Hartlepool Boys Welfare Old Boys	28	8	9	11	52	50	33
Roker	28	10	2	16	45	61	32
Sunderland Vaux Ryhope	28	8	6	14	43	54	30
Cleator Moor Celtic	28	7	8	13	36	53	29
Dawdon C.W.	28	8	7	13	39	43	28
Herrington C.W.	28	8	1	19	37	89	25
N.E.I. Parsons Athletic	28	3	5	20	30	72	14

Stockton E.D.C. resigned in December and their record was deleted. Boldon Community Association and Dawdon C.W. each had 3 points deducted.
N.E.I. Parsons Athletic changed their name to N.E.I. Bohemians.

Division Two

Wolviston	22	16	4	2	54	22	52
Washington Nissan	22	12	4	6	48	31	40
Greatham	22	10	8	4	45	25	38
Wingate	22	11	4	7	45	34	37
Thornley W.M.C.	22	10	4	8	48	42	34
Silksworth	22	9	5	8	42	32	32
Lambton Street	22	7	9	6	36	31	30
Stanley United	22	9	2	11	51	47	29
Felling Leam Lane	22	7	5	10	41	47	26
Blackhall C.W.	22	7	3	12	33	40	24
Winlaton Youngs Descaling	22	5	5	12	37	63	20
Wingate Parish	22	1	3	18	18	84	6

Gateshead Clarke Chapman resigned just before the season started. Winlaton Youngs Descaling left because of inadequate ground facilities while Felling Leam Lane and Wingate Parish also left. South Shields Cleadon S.C. and Usworth Village both joined from Washington League, Darlington Railway Athletic joined from the Teesside League, Esh Winning Pineapple joined from the Crook League, Marchon joined from the Cumberland County League and Windscale joined from the Furness Senior League. Greatham changed their name to Greatham Mayfair Centre.

1990-91
Division One

Eppleton C.W.	34	30	1	3	129	31	70
Dunston Federation Breweries	34	21	7	6	99	45	70
Annfield Plain	34	20	6	8	81	42	66
Boldon Community Association	34	20	6	8	84	47	66
South Shields	34	18	5	11	80	51	59
Marske United	34	16	5	13	82	58	53
Roker	34	15	8	11	65	47	53
Cleator Moor Celtic	34	17	2	15	61	73	53
Newton Aycliffe	34	14	10	10	65	51	52
Dawdon C.W.	34	13	8	13	64	65	47
Sunderland Vaux Ryhope	34	14	5	15	79	82	47
Greatham Mayfair Centre	34	14	2	18	48	55	41
N.E.I. Bohemians	34	11	3	20	40	76	36
Coundon TT	34	9	5	20	47	80	32
Wolviston	34	9	2	23	55	90	29
Herrington C.W.	34	8	4	22	48	104	28
Hartlepool Boys Welfare O.B.	**34**	**9**	**3**	**22**	**62**	**142**	**24**
Washington Nissan	**34**	**4**	**6**	**24**	**40**	**90**	**18**

Greatham Mayfair Centre had 3 points deducted.
Hartlepool Boys Welfare Old Boys had 6 points deducted.
Dunston Federation Breweries moved to the Northern League while Coundon TT and Dawdon C.W. also left. Greatham Mayfair Centre changed their name to Hartlepool Town, N.E.I. Bohemians changed their name to Newcastle Bohemians and Roker changed their name to Sunderland I.F.G. Roker.

Division Two (Clubs played each other 3 times)

South Shields Cleadon S.C.	**33**	**20**	**7**	**6**	**70**	**33**	**67**
Usworth Village	**33**	**18**	**8**	**7**	**53**	**33**	**62**
Darlington Railway Athletic	**33**	**17**	**9**	**7**	**70**	**38**	**60**
Windscale	33	16	8	9	89	51	56
Blackhall C.W.	33	14	9	10	55	72	51
Stanley United	33	14	8	11	59	48	50
Thornley W.M.C.	33	15	5	13	67	60	50
Silksworth	33	11	7	15	48	52	40
Marchon	33	10	9	14	52	56	39
Lambton Street	33	8	7	18	51	64	28
Wingate	33	7	6	20	50	83	27
Esh Winning Pineapple	33	2	9	22	24	98	15

Lambton Street had 3 points deducted.
Lambton Street and Thornley W.M.C. both left the league.
Jarrow joined from the Washington League, Jarrow Roofing Boldon Community Association joined from the Tyneside Amateur League, having changed their name from Jarrow Roofing. Sunderland Flo Gas joined from the Wearside Combination while Hebburn Colliery also joined. Esh Winning Pineapple changed their name to Esh Winning Albion.

1991-92
Division 1

Eppleton C.W.	30	22	3	5	79	34	69
Hartlepool Town	30	20	7	3	60	30	67
South Shields	30	21	3	6	90	34	66
Marske United	30	20	4	6	85	37	58
Annfield Plain	30	17	3	10	57	48	54
Boldon Community Association	30	12	9	9	48	41	45
Wolviston	30	13	5	12	59	55	44
South Shields Cleadon S.C.	30	12	7	11	45	43	43
Newton Aycliffe	30	13	3	14	44	45	42
Sunderland Vaux Ryhope	30	11	8	11	56	65	41
Sunderland I.F.G. Roker	30	12	4	14	43	46	40
Cleator Moor Celtic	30	8	6	16	43	64	30
Herrington C.W.	30	7	3	20	32	65	24
Darlington Railway Athletic	30	4	9	17	36	66	18
Usworth Village	**30**	**4**	**5**	**21**	**22**	**72**	**17**
Newcastle Bohemians	30	3	3	24	27	81	12

Marske United had 6 points deducted.
Darlington Railway Athletic had 3 points deducted.

Eppleton Colliery Welfare moved to the Northern League. Darlington Railway Athletic and Newcastle Bohemians also left. Sunderland Vaux Ryhope changed their name to Ryhope C.W..

Division Two

Silksworth	**22**	**15**	**3**	**4**	**70**	**35**	**48**
Jarrow Roofing Boldon C.A.	**22**	**15**	**3**	**4**	**53**	**29**	**48**
Windscale	**22**	**15**	**0**	**7**	**45**	**39**	**45**
Hebburn Colliery	22	13	2	7	45	31	41
Hartlepool Boys Welfare Old Boys	22	12	1	9	46	29	37
Stanley United	22	9	3	10	29	37	30
Marchon	22	8	4	10	37	41	28
Washington Nissan	22	7	7	8	32	43	28
Esh Winning Albion	22	7	3	12	33	46	24
Wingate	22	6	5	11	28	32	23
Jarrow	22	5	1	16	32	53	16
Sunderland Flo Gas	22	3	2	17	26	61	11

Blackhall C.W. resigned during the season and their record was deleted.
Birtley Town, Murton International, North Shields, Northallerton Town Supporters and Washington Glebe all joined. Sunderland Flo Gas changed their name to Fulwell Flo Gas.

1992-93
Division One

South Shields	28	20	5	3	84	35	65
Hartlepool Town	28	19	6	3	70	30	63
Silksworth	28	18	5	5	59	29	59
Jarrow Roofing Boldon C.A.	28	16	5	7	51	39	53
Marske United	28	12	11	5	55	37	47
Annfield Plain	28	11	7	10	57	58	40
Sunderland I.F.G. Roker	28	12	3	13	54	42	39
Boldon Community Association	28	12	3	13	42	50	39
South Shields Cleadon S.C.	28	9	7	12	51	49	34
Wolviston	28	9	5	14	47	50	32
Ryhope C.W.	28	8	6	14	50	64	30
Newton Aycliffe	28	6	9	13	31	63	27
Cleator Moor Celtic	28	6	5	17	41	59	23
Herrington C.W.	28	5	6	17	36	76	21
Windscale	28	5	1	22	35	82	16

Sunderland IFG Roker changed their name to Kennek Roker.

Division Two

Hartlepool Boys Welfare O.B.	**28**	**19**	**6**	**3**	**72**	**34**	**63**
North Shields	**28**	**18**	**5**	**5**	**79**	**36**	**59**
Jarrow	**28**	**16**	**5**	**7**	**73**	**41**	**53**
Washington Glebe	28	16	4	8	56	41	52
Washington Nissan	28	14	6	8	55	39	48
Wingate	28	12	10	6	58	46	46
Hebburn Colliery	28	10	8	10	51	51	38
Esh Winning Albion	28	11	4	13	47	73	37
Birtley Town	28	8	10	10	40	44	34
Stanley United	28	8	6	14	50	50	30
Northallerton Town Supporters	28	9	4	15	58	65	28
Marchon	28	7	5	16	42	57	26
Usworth Village	28	4	10	14	17	47	22
Murton International	28	5	7	16	35	75	22
Fulwell Flo Gas	28	5	6	17	36	70	21

South Shields County Kitchens joined from the Northern Alliance, Tradelink joined from the Washington League while Newcastle City and North Ormesby Sports joined as newly formed clubs. Guisborough Town Reserves joined as a newly formed team called Guisborough Priory. Wingate merged with Billingham Cassel Mall to form Wingate Mall. Hebburn Colliery changed their name to Hebburn D.T. and Fulwell Flo Gas changed their name to Fulwell Myers.

Wearside League 1993-1995

1993-94
Division One

Hartlepool Town	32	23	6	3	93	27	75
Marske United	32	25	2	5	97	25	74
Jarrow Roofing Boldon C.A.	32	20	7	5	79	34	67
South Shields	32	18	7	7	79	44	61
Silksworth	32	16	3	13	53	50	51
Kennek Roker	32	14	8	10	55	49	50
Ryhope C.W.	32	12	6	14	55	74	42
Windscale	32	11	8	13	74	73	41
South Shields Cleadon S.C.	32	11	7	14	47	68	40
Herrington C.W.	32	11	5	16	68	72	38
Hartlepool Boys Welfare Old Boys	32	11	5	16	57	64	38
Annfield Plain	32	10	8	14	47	57	38
North Shields	32	11	5	16	61	80	38
Cleator Moor Celtic	32	10	4	18	49	85	34
Boldon Community Association	32	8	6	18	43	70	30
Wolviston	32	6	8	18	46	82	26
Jarrow	32	5	5	22	38	87	20

Marske United had 3 points deducted.
Newton Aycliffe resigned during the season and their record was deleted when it stood as follows: 20 0 2 18 24 78 2
Hartlepool Town moved to the Northern League.

Division Two

Washington Nissan	32	27	2	3	88	34	83
North Ormesby Sports	32	25	6	1	102	15	81
Hebburn D.T.	32	21	4	7	78	37	67
Birtley Town	32	19	6	7	74	34	63
Washington Glebe	32	19	6	7	85	50	63
Stanley United	32	18	5	9	66	46	59
South Shields County Kitchens	32	16	5	11	70	53	53
Northallerton Town Supporters	32	16	3	13	69	61	51
Marchon	32	15	5	12	73	42	50
Guisborough Priory	32	12	4	16	68	63	37
Murton International	32	10	6	16	54	71	36
Fulwell Myers	32	9	4	19	41	71	31
Wingate Mall	32	7	6	19	46	76	27
Tradelink	32	7	4	21	48	95	25
Newcastle City	32	6	7	19	40	91	25
Usworth Village	32	2	6	24	24	94	12
Esh Winning Albion	32	1	5	26	29	122	8

Guisborough Priory had 3 points deducted.
Marchon disbanded and Whitehaven Amateurs were formed as a replacement, taking Marchon's place in the Wearside League. Esh Winning Albion, Hebburn D.T. and Tradelink also left. Hartlepool United Reserves joined from the Midland Senior League, Prudhoe Town Reserves joined as a newly formed team called Prudhoe Swinton and South Shields Harton & Westoe also joined. Fulwell Myers changed their name to Sunderland Sporting Club Fulwell, South Shields County Kitchens changed their name to South Shields Brinkburn C.A., Usworth Village changed their name to Chilton Moor and Wingate Mall changed their name to Wingate.

1994-95
Division One

South Shields	34	28	2	4	116	44	86
Marske United	34	24	8	2	109	44	80
Jarrow Roofing Boldon C.A.	34	21	5	8	104	40	68
Washington Nissan	34	20	6	8	84	36	66
Annfield Plain	34	20	6	8	81	63	66
Windscale	34	17	8	9	89	58	59
Kennek Roker	34	19	4	11	71	52	58
Ryhope C.W.	34	15	7	12	67	56	52
Boldon Community Association	34	15	5	14	66	53	50
North Shields	34	14	6	14	52	60	48
South Shields Cleadon S.C.	34	14	5	15	53	52	47
Jarrow	34	13	4	17	66	71	40
Wolviston	34	10	6	18	65	90	36
Herrington C.W.	34	8	8	18	44	76	32
Hartlepool Boys Welfare O.B.	34	7	6	21	48	70	24
North Ormesby Sports	34	6	4	24	47	99	22
Cleator Moor Celtic	34	4	7	23	28	118	19
Silksworth	34	0	5	29	31	139	5

Kennek Roker, Jarrow and Hartlepool Boys Welfare O.B. all had 3 points deducted.
South Shields moved to the Northern League. Cleator Moor Celtic, Herrington C.W., North Ormesby Sports and Silksworth also left.
North Shields changed their name to North Shields Athletic.
Following their promotion, South Shields Brinkburn C.A. changed their name to South Tyneside United.

Division Two

Birtley Town	24	18	2	4	84	29	56
South Shields Brinkburn C.A.	24	14	4	6	71	40	46
Sunderland Sporting Club Fulwell	24	12	9	3	47	22	45
Murton International	24	13	5	6	61	42	44
Whitehaven Amateurs	24	13	6	5	69	43	42
South Shields Harton & Westoe	24	12	4	8	56	47	40
Stanley United	24	10	8	6	65	44	38
Wingate	24	7	7	10	53	48	28
Guisborough Priory	24	7	7	10	42	49	28
Chilton Moor	24	8	2	14	41	64	26
Northallerton Town Supporters	24	5	4	15	37	76	16
Washington Glebe	24	3	5	16	33	83	14
Prudhoe Swinton	24	1	3	20	24	96	6

Whitehaven Amateurs had 3 points deducted.
Hartlepool United Reserves resigned during the season and their record was deleted when it was: 4 3 1 0 14 1 10
Newcastle City resigned during the season and their record was deleted when it stood as follows: 21 1 2 18 29 106 5
Guisborough Priory joined the Teesside League as Guisborough Town Reserves while Murton International, Prudhoe Swinton and Wingate also all left. South Bank joined, having re-formed after two years' inactivity. Northallerton Town Supporters changed their name to Northallerton Ainderby.

1995-96

Division One

Marske United	30	22	3	5	97	29	69
Jarrow Roofing Boldon C.A.	30	22	4	4	93	40	67
South Tyneside United	30	15	9	6	41	32	54
Birtley Town	30	15	6	9	60	49	51
Ryhope C.W.	30	14	8	8	53	31	50
Windscale	30	13	7	10	69	54	46
Boldon Community Association	30	12	6	12	59	50	42
Kennek Roker	30	12	5	13	56	55	41
Washington Nissan	30	11	7	12	44	40	40
Annfield Plain	30	12	4	14	50	47	40
Hartlepool Boys Welfare Old Boys	30	11	2	17	46	66	35
Wolviston	30	10	4	16	48	60	34
South Shields Cleadon S.C.	30	8	9	13	43	60	33
Jarrow	30	10	3	17	45	71	33
North Shields Athletic	30	7	5	18	34	74	26
Sunderland Sporting Club Fulwell	30	5	0	25	36	116	15

Jarrow Roofing Boldon C.A. had 3 points deducted.
Jarrow Roofing Boldon C.A. moved to the Northern League and Sunderland Sporting Club Fulwell also left the league.

Division Two (Clubs played each other 3 times)

Whitehaven Amateurs	18	12	1	5	54	27	37
Stanley United	18	10	1	7	56	25	31
South Shields Harton & Westoe	18	8	3	7	39	34	27
Washington Glebe	18	8	2	8	39	30	26
Chilton Moor	18	6	3	9	22	47	21
Northallerton Ainderby	18	6	3	9	22	48	21
South Bank	18	4	5	9	15	36	17

Chilton Moor and Northallerton Ainderby both left the league.

Division Two closed down and all remaining clubs joined the new single division.

1996-97

Boldon Community Association	34	25	6	3	105	33	81
Marske United	34	25	5	4	97	24	80
Birtley Town	34	21	9	4	74	33	72
Annfield Plain	34	19	8	7	83	52	62
Washington Nissan	34	17	10	7	63	41	61
Windscale	34	17	8	9	65	40	59
South Tyneside United	34	17	7	10	69	37	58
Kennek Roker	34	15	6	13	66	53	51
Wolviston	34	12	5	17	59	65	41
South Shields Harton & Westoe	34	11	5	18	63	66	38
Whitehaven Amateurs	34	10	8	16	50	81	38
Stanley United	34	10	6	18	58	88	36
South Shields Cleadon S.C.	34	9	6	19	47	72	33
North Shields Athletic	34	8	9	17	44	70	33
Hartlepool Boys Welfare Old Boys	34	10	2	22	46	97	32
Ryhope C.W.	34	9	3	22	35	68	30
South Bank	34	5	9	20	34	90	24
Jarrow	34	6	8	20	36	84	23

Washington Glebe left during the season and their record was deleted.
Marske United moved to the Northern League. Gateshead Reserves and Horden Athletic joined.

1997-98

Annfield Plain	36	26	3	7	121	43	81
Kennek Roker	36	23	8	5	103	44	77
Birtley Town	36	25	3	8	103	49	75
Gateshead Reserves	36	22	5	9	106	53	71
Ryhope C.W.	36	19	6	11	80	47	63
Washington Nissan	36	17	11	8	80	54	62
Boldon Community Association	36	19	5	12	90	79	62
South Shields Cleadon S.C.	36	18	7	11	71	49	61
Windscale	36	17	5	14	98	56	56
South Tyneside United	36	14	9	13	90	76	51
North Shields Athletic	36	14	7	15	67	71	49
Stanley United	36	14	6	16	98	91	48
Hartlepool Boys Welfare Old Boys	36	13	9	14	67	70	48
Wolviston	36	14	4	18	71	77	46
South Shields Harton & Westoe	36	11	8	17	67	95	41
Jarrow	36	6	7	23	56	95	25
Whitehaven Amateurs	36	7	4	25	55	133	25
South Bank	36	7	2	27	42	118	23
Horden Athletic	36	1	1	34	26	191	4

Birtley Town had 3 points deducted.
Gateshead Reserves and South Tyneside United left the league.

Division Two was re-formed with 13 clubs, with the bottom 2 clubs being relegated and 11 new clubs joining. New Marske S.C. joined from the Teesside League, Sunderland Red House W.M.C. joined from Sunday football while Ferryhill Athletic, Herrington C.W., Redcar Town, Silksworth Community, Simonside Social Club, South Shields Reserves, Wallsend Town, Whitburn and Workington Reserves also joined.

1998-99

Division One

North Shields Athletic	28	24	3	1	92	24	75
Wolviston	28	19	4	5	75	31	61
Washington Nissan	28	20	5	3	88	36	59
Hartlepool Boys Welfare Old Boys	28	16	5	7	56	35	53
Kennek Roker	28	15	6	7	65	40	51
Birtley Town	28	16	2	10	57	50	50
Windscale	28	15	4	9	52	35	46
Boldon Community Association	28	14	4	10	63	47	46
South Shields Cleadon S.C.	28	10	3	15	45	60	33
Annfield Plain	28	9	4	15	64	82	31
South Shields Harton & Westoe	28	7	2	19	48	79	23
Jarrow	28	6	3	19	36	62	21
Stanley United	28	4	2	22	33	88	14
Whitehaven Amateurs	28	4	4	20	39	105	13
Ryhope C.W.	28	4	3	21	30	69	12

Washington Nissan had 6 points deducted. Windscale, Whitehaven Amateurs and Ryhope C.W. each had 3 points deducted.
Hartlepool Boys Welfare Old Boys left the league. North Shields Athletic changed their name to North Shields. Kennek Roker merged with Ryhope C.A. of the Northern League and continued in that league as Kennek Ryhope C.A..

Division Two

Sunderland Red House W.M.C.	**24**	**19**	**1**	**4**	**125**	**40**	**58**
New Marske S.C.	**24**	**16**	**6**	**2**	**86**	**29**	**54**
Workington Reserves	**24**	**17**	**2**	**5**	**89**	**28**	**53**
Redcar Town	24	14	5	5	85	37	47
Herrington C.W.	24	13	3	8	67	48	42
Simonside S.C.	24	12	4	8	73	51	40
Silksworth Community	24	11	5	8	70	45	38
Ferryhill Athletic	24	10	4	10	50	56	34
South Shields Reserves	24	7	4	13	45	65	25
Horden Athletic	24	6	3	15	44	101	21
South Bank	24	5	2	17	51	96	17
Whitburn	24	5	2	17	44	102	17
Wallsend Town	24	0	1	23	12	143	1

South Bank disbanded while Horden Athletic, Silksworth Community and South Shields Reserves also left. Stokesley Sports Club joined from the Teesside League and Thornaby-on-Tees Reserves also joined.

Wearside League 1999-2004

1999-2000

Division One

Team	P	W	D	L	F	A	Pts
Washington Nissan	30	24	0	6	86	35	69
New Marske S.C.	30	21	5	4	95	36	65
Windscale	30	18	7	5	75	40	61
North Shields	30	17	6	7	76	43	54
Sunderland Red House W.M.C.	30	17	3	10	67	51	54
South Shields Harton & Westoe	30	14	4	12	59	63	46
Boldon Community Association	30	13	6	11	58	48	45
Wolviston	30	12	5	13	69	68	38
Birtley Town	30	9	9	12	52	59	36
Ryhope C.W.	30	10	6	14	46	68	36
Workington Reserves	30	10	5	15	51	54	35
Whitehaven Amateurs	30	7	10	13	38	67	31
Annfield Plain	30	8	4	18	65	92	28
South Shields Cleadon S.C.	30	6	7	17	45	76	25
Stanley United	30	6	5	19	46	86	23
Jarrow	30	6	2	22	40	82	20

New Marske S.C., North Shields, Washington Nissan and Wolviston all had 3 points deducted.
Sunderland Red House W.M.C. returned to Sunday football and Workington Reserves also left the league.

Division Two (Clubs played each other 3 times)

Team	P	W	D	L	F	A	Pts
Redcar Town	21	14	4	3	80	32	46
Stokesley Sports Club	21	15	1	5	68	41	46
Simonside S.C.	21	10	4	7	69	51	31
Thornaby-on-Tees Reserves	21	7	10	4	50	41	31
Ferryhill Athletic	21	8	5	8	69	45	29
Herrington C.W.	21	7	4	10	41	63	25
Whitburn	21	5	3	13	52	77	18
Wallsend Town	21	2	1	18	27	106	7

Simonside S.C. had 3 points deducted.
Wallsend Town merged with Wallsend United of the Northern Alliance and continued in that league as Wallsend. Herrington C.W. also left.
Thornaby-on-Tees changed their name to Thornaby.

Divisions One and Two merged into a new single division.

2000-01

Team	P	W	D	L	F	A	Pts
Washington Nissan	38	31	3	4	120	29	96
North Shields	38	29	6	3	143	24	93
Wolviston	38	24	6	8	107	58	78
Windscale	38	23	6	9	102	49	75
South Shields Harton & Westoe	38	23	4	11	118	67	73
Boldon Community Association	38	24	4	10	104	63	73
Redcar Town	38	21	8	9	103	61	68
New Marske S.C.	38	19	7	12	90	58	64
Stokesley Sports Club	38	19	6	13	116	67	63
Whitehaven Amateurs	38	19	5	14	82	78	62
Ferryhill Athletic	38	16	4	18	92	89	52
Stanley United	38	12	12	14	77	76	48
Thornaby Reserves	38	14	6	18	86	101	48
Birtley Town	38	15	4	19	79	101	43
Annfield Plain	38	13	3	22	87	96	39
South Shields Cleadon S.C.	38	7	4	27	49	113	25
Ryhope C.W.	38	6	5	27	46	102	23
Simonside S.C.	38	7	2	29	33	195	23
Jarrow	38	5	6	27	50	117	21
Whitburn	38	2	1	35	38	178	7

Boldon Community Association, Redcar Town and Annfield Plain each had 3 points deducted.
Birtley Town had 6 points deducted.
Washington Nissan moved to the Northern League. Thornaby Reserves moved to the Teesside League while Simonside S.C. and Whitburn also left.
Darlington Railway Athletic joined from the Auckland & District League.

2001-02

Team	P	W	D	L	F	A	Pts
North Shields	32	25	3	4	94	31	78
New Marske S.C.	32	21	7	4	81	37	70
Darlington Railway Athletic	32	21	4	7	75	43	67
Windscale	32	18	9	5	74	44	63
Redcar Town	32	19	5	8	88	45	59
Birtley Town	32	16	9	7	86	58	57
Wolviston	32	14	6	12	66	59	48
Stokesley Sports Club	32	13	7	12	69	61	46
South Shields Harton & Westoe	32	11	9	12	72	61	42
Boldon Community Association	32	11	3	18	57	82	36
South Shields Cleadon S.C.	32	9	7	16	50	63	34
Ryhope C.W.	32	9	6	17	47	70	33
Jarrow	32	8	9	15	41	70	33
Annfield Plain	32	7	5	20	47	84	26
Whitehaven Amateurs	32	6	8	18	48	86	26
Stanley United	32	4	8	20	49	77	20
Ferryhill Athletic	32	6	3	23	41	114	18

Redcar Town had 3 points deducted.
Barnard Castle Glaxo Sports & Social Club joined.

2002-03

Team	P	W	D	L	F	A	Pts
Birtley Town	34	26	4	4	120	39	82
Wolviston	34	25	4	5	96	43	79
Stokesley Sports Club	34	25	2	7	110	49	77
New Marske S.C.	34	19	4	11	85	53	61
Boldon Community Association	34	18	6	10	80	55	60
Windscale	34	17	7	10	63	37	58
Darlington Railway Athletic	34	15	10	9	75	40	55
North Shields	34	15	6	13	74	47	51
Whitehaven Amateurs	34	13	4	17	49	67	43
Annfield Plain	34	12	6	16	53	83	42
Ryhope C.W.	34	11	5	18	60	75	38
South Shields Harton & Westoe	34	13	7	14	71	76	37
South Shields Cleadon S.C.	34	11	4	19	37	90	37
Stanley United	34	10	6	18	74	94	36
Jarrow	34	10	4	20	56	92	34
Redcar Town	34	8	7	19	54	96	31
Barnard Castle Glaxo Sports & S.C.	34	8	4	22	71	98	28
Ferryhill Athletic	34	4	2	28	44	138	14

South Shields Harton & Westoe had 9 points deducted.
Stanley United disbanded. Redcar Town resigned during the season, then changed their minds and were reinstated but left at the end of the season.
Gateshead Reserves joined after being re-formed and Nissan U.K. joined having previously been playing in the Wearside Combination as Washington Nissan Reserves.

2003-04

Team	P	W	D	L	F	A	Pts
North Shields	34	28	5	1	113	23	89
Birtley Town	34	23	7	4	107	68	76
Stokesley Sports Club	34	24	3	7	121	35	75
South Shields Cleadon S.C.	34	17	9	8	67	58	60
Darlington Railway Athletic	34	16	9	9	75	44	57
Wolviston	34	18	3	13	79	63	57
Boldon Community Association	34	15	9	10	88	63	54
Ryhope C.W.	34	15	9	10	66	65	54
Gateshead Reserves	34	16	4	14	84	65	52
New Marske S.C.	34	13	8	13	65	64	47
Whitehaven Amateurs	34	13	6	15	59	70	45
Jarrow	34	11	10	13	60	61	43
Windscale	34	12	6	16	55	58	42
South Shields Harton & Westoe	34	10	9	15	45	54	39
Annfield Plain	34	8	5	21	44	74	29
Barnard Castle Glaxo Sports & S.C.	34	4	6	24	53	127	18
Ferryhill Athletic	34	3	3	28	39	119	12
Nissan U.K.	34	3	3	28	44	153	9

Nissan U.K. had 3 points deducted.
North Shields joined the Northern League and Barnard Castle Glaxo Sports & Social Club also left. Coxhoe Athletic joined from the Durham Alliance, Shotton Comrades joined from the Northern League, Cleator Moor Celtic joined from the Cumberland League and Sport Catterick joined as a newly formed club. Nissan U.K. changed their name to Washington Nissan U.K..

2004-05

Darlington Railway Athletic	36	28	4	4	111	28	88
Birtley Town	36	24	6	6	95	45	78
Stokesley Sports Club	36	24	5	7	99	31	77
Coxhoe Athletic	36	24	3	9	100	42	75
Jarrow	36	20	7	9	60	41	67
Annfield Plain	36	18	8	10	74	58	62
Boldon Community Association	36	17	8	11	77	62	59
Cleator Moor Celtic	36	17	5	14	81	56	56
South Shields Cleadon S.C.	36	16	7	13	70	55	55
South Shields Harton & Westoe	36	16	5	15	55	55	53
Windscale	36	15	4	17	52	53	49
Ryhope C.W.	36	14	5	17	70	69	47
New Marske Sports Club	36	13	6	17	53	63	45
Whitehaven Amateurs	36	12	6	18	62	69	42
Wolviston	36	9	9	18	47	81	36
Shotton Comrades	36	6	7	23	68	102	25
Gateshead Reserves	36	5	9	22	50	96	24
Washington Nissan U.K.	36	5	7	24	43	130	22
Ferryhill Athletic	36	3	1	32	30	161	10

Sport Catterick resigned during the season and their record was deleted when it stood as follows: 18 7 3 8 46 55 24
Darlington Railway Athletic moved to the Northern League and Gateshead Reserves were replaced by Gateshead Low Fell. Washington Nissan U.K. changed their name to Nissan S.S.C. Sunderland. Willington joined from the Northern League and Teesside Athletic joined from the Teesside League.

2006-07

Birtley Town	32	26	5	1	81	13	83
Whitehaven Amateurs	32	23	6	3	95	35	75
Wolviston	32	18	5	9	65	32	59
Guisborough Black Swan	32	17	6	9	83	52	57
Boldon Community Association	32	16	3	13	62	56	51
Ryhope C.W.	32	14	8	10	53	36	50
South Shields Cleadon	32	15	4	13	54	57	49
Teesside Athletic	32	15	6	11	68	54	48
Jarrow	32	14	5	13	64	46	47
Cleator Moor Celtic	32	13	5	14	72	61	44
Windscale	32	13	3	16	43	51	42
Hartlepool	32	13	2	17	54	71	38
Coxhoe Athletic	32	11	5	16	45	70	38
Annfield Plain	32	8	3	21	48	94	27
South Shields Harton & Westoe	32	5	7	20	44	92	22
Willington	32	6	3	23	34	88	21
New Marske Sports Club	32	5	4	23	30	87	16

Teesside Athletic, Hartlepool and New Marske Sports Club each had 3 points deducted.
Nissan S.S.C. Sunderland resigned and disbanded during the season and their record was deleted: 7 0 0 7 4 47 0
Birtley Town moved to the Northern League. Ashbrooke Belford joined from the Durham Alliance and changed their name to Ashbrooke Belford House while Silksworth C.C. also joined from the Durham Alliance. Easington Colliery joined from the Northern Alliance and East Durham United joined as a newly formed club. New Marske Sports Club merged with Carlin How W.M.C. of the Teesside League, staying in the Wearside League with the same name and ground.

2005-06

Whitehaven Amateurs	34	26	4	4	118	27	82
Stokesley Sports Club	34	23	7	4	70	30	76
Birtley Town	34	20	9	5	67	32	69
South Shields Cleadon S.C.	34	21	4	9	64	48	67
Teesside Athletic	34	21	3	10	64	34	66
Cleator Moor Celtic	34	20	5	9	71	25	65
Windscale	34	19	4	11	69	36	61
Boldon Community Association	34	18	3	13	50	47	54
Annfield Plain	34	17	2	15	63	67	53
Jarrow	34	12	6	16	52	58	42
Willington	34	12	2	20	48	68	38
Ryhope C.W.	34	11	4	19	48	73	37
Wolviston	34	9	5	20	47	69	32
South Shields Harton & Westoe	34	7	11	16	40	90	32
New Marske Sports Club	34	9	6	19	53	74	30
Gateshead Low Fell	34	7	8	19	41	69	29
Coxhoe Athletic	34	7	3	24	36	81	24
Nissan S.S.C. Sunderland	34	2	4	28	28	101	10

Boldon Community Association and New Marske Sports Club each had 3 points deducted.
Shotton Comrades resigned and disbanded during the season and their record was deleted: 4 0 1 3 3 9 1
Ferryhill Athletic resigned during the season and their record was deleted when it stood as follows: 29 3 3 23 33 111 12
They subsequently joined the Durham Alliance for the 2006-07 season. Stokesley Sports Club moved to the Northern League and Gateshead Low Fell also left the league. Guisborough Black Swan and Hartlepool both joined from the Teesside League.

2007-08

New Marske Sports Club	36	28	6	2	120	31	90
Jarrow	36	23	7	6	93	54	76
Whitehaven Amateurs	36	25	3	8	96	40	75
Wolviston	36	20	10	6	76	41	70
Ryhope C.W.	36	19	9	8	66	50	66
Hartlepool	36	19	5	12	80	54	62
Easington Colliery	36	17	10	9	84	57	61
Annfield Plain	36	18	9	9	62	43	60
Boldon Community Association	36	15	8	13	70	60	53
Cleator Moor Celtic	36	16	5	15	76	72	53
Teesside Athletic	36	13	8	15	50	53	47
Ashbrooke Belford House	36	13	7	16	63	77	46
South Shields Harton & Westoe	36	9	6	21	49	81	33
Guisborough Black Swan	36	9	5	22	59	84	32
Coxhoe Athletic	36	10	2	24	54	94	32
Willington	36	8	7	21	51	86	31
East Durham United	36	7	6	23	44	97	27
Windscale	36	6	7	23	37	74	25
Silksworth C.C.	36	4	6	26	28	110	18

Whitehaven Amateurs and Annfield Plain each had 3 points deducted.
South Shields Cleadon S.C. resigned and disbanded during the season and their record was deleted: 24 10 3 11 52 44 33
Whitehaven Amateurs moved to the Northern League, Kirkbymoorside joined from the Teesside League and Newton Aycliffe joined from the Durham Alliance. Guisborough Black Swan changed their name to Guisborough Town H.C..

Wearside League 2008-2012

2008-09

Team	P	W	D	L	F	A	Pts
Newton Aycliffe	36	28	4	4	121	31	88
New Marske Sports Club	36	26	7	3	93	43	85
Easington Colliery	36	22	8	6	82	43	74
Teesside Athletic	36	21	11	4	77	40	74
Jarrow	36	21	5	10	72	38	68
Coxhoe Athletic	36	18	6	12	79	61	60
Annfield Plain	36	15	8	13	78	70	53
Ryhope C.W.	36	15	8	13	49	44	53
Ashbrooke Belford House	36	15	5	16	71	76	50
Kirkbymoorside	36	15	4	17	61	59	49
Cleator Moor Celtic	36	14	4	18	68	63	46
Hartlepool	36	14	4	18	54	61	46
Wolviston	36	10	10	16	55	69	40
Silksworth C.C.	36	11	6	19	50	75	39
Boldon Community Association	36	11	6	19	49	94	39
Windscale	36	10	6	20	44	71	36
Guisborough Town H.C.	36	7	2	27	46	97	23
East Durham United	36	6	5	25	39	93	23
Willington	36	6	5	25	51	111	23

South Shields Harton & Westoe resigned and disbanded during the season and their record was deleted: 5 1 1 3 6 10 4

Newton Aycliffe moved to the Northern League and East Durham United disbanded. Sunderland South joined from the Durham Alliance, changing name to Houghton Town. Scarborough Town joined from the Teesside League.

2009-10

Team	P	W	D	L	F	A	Pts
Scarborough Town	36	29	5	2	140	31	92
Ryhope C.W.	36	27	5	4	97	29	86
Teesside Athletic	36	22	6	7	83	40	75
New Marske S.C.	36	21	8	7	108	64	71
Cleator Moor Celtic	36	22	3	11	101	65	69
Annfield Plain	36	20	8	8	65	48	68
Easington Colliery	36	18	7	11	84	52	61
Ashbrooke Belford House	36	17	5	14	78	74	56
Kirkbymoorside	36	13	12	11	73	59	51
Jarrow	36	15	5	15	79	64	50
Windscale	36	14	9	13	71	59	48
Boldon Community Association	36	14	4	18	77	82	46
Wolviston	36	12	8	16	55	65	44
Silksworth C.C.	36	11	5	20	45	90	38
Houghton Town	36	11	5	20	54	95	38
Hartlepool	36	6	5	25	50	98	23
Guisborough Town H.C.	36	6	3	27	46	133	21
Coxhoe Athletic	36	4	6	26	42	112	18
Willington	36	4	1	31	33	121	10

Windscale and Willington each had 3 points deducted.

Scarborough Town resigned to join the Northern Counties (East) League for which they needed floodlights but planning permission was not granted in time and the club was forced to cease activity for 2010-11. Guisborough Town H.C. moved to the Teesside League as Guisborough Town Reserves. Darlington Cleveland Bridge and Stockton Town both joined from the Teesside League and Prudhoe Town joined as a newly formed club. Teesside Athletic changed their name to Redcar Athletic, New Marske S.C. changed their name to New Marske and Silksworth C.C. changed their name to Silksworth.

2010-11

Team	P	W	D	L	F	A	Pts
Ryhope C.W.	38	28	5	5	104	29	89
Easington Colliery	38	26	5	7	99	39	83
New Marske	38	24	5	9	96	59	77
Redcar Athletic	38	22	8	8	78	34	74
Jarrow	38	22	6	10	97	52	72
Kirkbymoorside	38	23	2	13	92	65	71
Windscale	38	18	11	9	84	44	65
Hartlepool	38	18	9	11	70	52	63
Darlington Cleveland Bridge	38	18	4	16	63	70	58
Stockton Town	38	16	8	14	59	56	56
Ashbrooke Belford House	38	17	5	16	59	64	56
Annfield Plain	38	16	6	16	61	74	54
Wolviston	38	16	5	17	66	64	53
Willington	38	14	2	22	49	78	44
Cleator Moor Celtic	38	10	7	21	56	79	37
Boldon Community Association	38	11	3	24	74	98	36
Silksworth	38	9	6	23	51	83	33
Prudhoe Town	38	6	5	27	50	114	23
Houghton Town	38	7	2	29	37	127	23
Coxhoe Athletic	38	5	4	29	39	103	19

Easington Colliery joined the Northern League. Houghton Town merged with Sunderland West End of the Wearside Combination, continuing in the Wearside League as Sunderland West End and playing at Sunderland West End's ground. New Marske moved to the Teesside League and Windscale disbanded. Gateshead Leam Rangers joined from the Durham Alliance and Peterlee Town joined from the Northern Alliance. Silksworth merged with Herrington Grindon Rangers, continuing in the Wearside League as Silksworth Rangers.

2011-12

Team	P	W	D	L	F	A	Pts
Ryhope C.W.	36	30	5	1	136	30	95
Redcar Athletic	36	29	3	4	104	32	90
Stockton Town	36	22	6	8	74	46	72
Sunderland West End	36	23	2	11	81	56	71
Willington	36	20	5	11	72	63	65
Jarrow	36	17	9	10	83	62	60
Cleator Moor Celtic	36	16	6	13	76	55	57
Darlington Cleveland Bridge	36	15	8	13	65	69	53
Boldon Community Association	36	16	4	16	78	74	52
Peterlee Town	36	15	6	15	71	90	51
Ashbrooke Belford House	36	13	10	13	61	63	49
Hartlepool	36	15	2	19	69	80	47
Prudhoe Town	36	13	7	16	78	89	46
Wolviston	36	10	10	16	57	61	40
Annfield Plain	36	9	7	20	56	80	34
Gateshead Leam Rangers	36	8	3	25	46	91	27
Kirkbymoorside	36	7	4	25	50	100	25
Silksworth Rangers	36	6	4	26	38	98	22
Coxhoe Athletic	36	4	5	27	34	90	17

Ryhope C.W. moved to the Northern League. Easington Colliery joined from the Northern League, Richmond Town joined from the Teesside League. Harton & Westoe Colliery Welfare joined from the Northern Alliance and Seaton Carew also joined.

2012-13

Stockton Town	42	34	1	7	112	33	103
Willington	42	32	5	5	89	40	101
Richmond Town	42	28	10	4	122	47	94
Cleator Moor Celtic	42	26	5	11	105	68	83
Redcar Athletic	42	21	8	13	71	59	71
Ashbrooke Belford House	42	22	5	15	84	74	71
Prudhoe Town	42	20	10	12	81	58	70
Sunderland West End	42	20	9	13	75	61	69
Jarrow	42	19	10	13	87	56	67
Seaton Carew	42	18	7	17	90	92	61
Peterlee Town	42	19	3	20	88	74	60
Harton & Westoe C.W.	42	16	5	21	79	110	53
Gateshead Leam Rangers	42	13	10	19	67	88	49
Hartlepool	42	13	8	21	84	95	47
Darlington Cleveland Bridge	42	14	4	24	79	118	46
Boldon Community Association	42	14	3	25	71	102	45
Wolviston	42	11	9	22	61	78	42
Annfield Plain	42	13	2	27	53	103	41
Coxhoe Athletic	42	12	4	26	67	88	40
Kirkbymoorside	42	12	4	26	64	91	40
Easington Colliery	42	12	3	27	55	87	39
Silksworth Rangers	42	9	3	30	51	113	30

Willington moved to the Northern League and Darlington Cleveland Bridge, Kirkbymoorside and Peterlee Town also left. Horden C.W. and Ryhope C.W. both joined from the Northern League. Silksworth Rangers changed their name to Silksworth Colliery Welfare.

2013-14

Stockton Town	38	34	2	2	129	28	104
Ryhope C.W.	38	30	5	3	132	26	95
Redcar Athletic	38	27	3	8	103	54	84
Cleator Moor Celtic	38	25	4	9	100	47	79
Richmond Town	38	22	8	8	108	55	74
Easington Colliery	38	19	3	16	104	76	60
Seaton Carew	38	17	6	15	90	78	57
Silksworth Colliery Welfare	38	16	7	15	64	64	55
Sunderland West End	38	16	7	15	71	82	55
Jarrow	38	15	7	16	75	82	52
Horden C.W.	38	16	4	18	78	90	52
Ashbrooke Belford House	38	14	7	17	94	98	49
Annfield Plain	38	13	7	18	73	92	46
Wolviston	38	12	9	17	67	70	45
Harton & Westoe C.W.	38	10	9	19	67	111	39
Prudhoe Town	38	9	7	22	60	109	34
Hartlepool	38	8	4	26	58	109	28
Coxhoe Athletic	38	6	7	25	47	118	25
Boldon Community Association	38	7	3	28	35	120	24
Gateshead Leam Rangers	38	4	11	23	48	94	23

Ryhope C.W. moved to the Northern League and Coxhoe Athletic also left. Whitehaven joined from the Northern League and Spennymoor Town Reserves joined from the Durham Alliance.

2014-15

Stockton Town	38	35	2	1	140	19	107
Easington Colliery	38	31	2	5	139	42	95
Cleator Moor Celtic	38	28	5	5	97	44	89
Redcar Athletic	38	23	5	10	98	65	74
Spennymoor Town Reserves	38	22	6	10	86	51	72
Horden C.W.	38	22	4	12	103	64	70
Whitehaven	38	19	5	14	103	59	62
Sunderland West End	38	19	5	14	72	57	62
Silksworth Colliery Welfare	38	17	7	14	91	51	58
Hartlepool	38	16	9	13	81	79	57
Ashbrooke Belford House	38	13	7	18	71	85	46
Jarrow	38	11	8	19	53	86	41
Richmond Town	38	11	6	21	69	92	39
Boldon Community Association	38	10	6	22	52	105	36
Prudhoe Town	38	9	8	21	56	91	35
Harton & Westoe C.W.	38	9	6	23	42	112	33
Wolviston	38	7	9	22	54	88	30
Gateshead Leam Rangers	38	7	9	22	40	95	30
Seaton Carew	38	8	2	28	63	153	26
Annfield Plain	38	3	9	26	48	120	18

Easington Colliery moved to the Northern League and Seaton Carew also left the league. Murton joined from the Durham Alliance and Seaham Red Star Reserves also joined.

2015-16

Stockton Town	38	33	2	3	164	26	101
Redcar Athletic	38	29	4	5	169	46	91
Sunderland West End	38	29	3	6	97	37	90
Cleator Moor Celtic	38	24	4	10	114	46	76
Hartlepool	38	21	1	16	106	76	64
Horden C.W.	38	20	4	14	84	85	64
Richmond Town	38	19	4	15	107	62	61
Jarrow	38	18	7	13	84	79	61
Spennymoor Town Reserves	38	16	11	11	93	63	59
Ashbrooke Belford House	38	17	6	15	90	108	54
Boldon Community Association	38	15	7	16	85	87	52
Whitehaven	38	14	7	17	80	87	49
Silksworth Colliery Welfare	38	13	7	18	71	79	46
Prudhoe Town	38	12	9	17	81	101	45
Harton & Westoe C.W.	38	12	5	21	68	110	41
Gateshead Leam Rangers	38	11	6	21	50	98	39
Wolviston	38	8	8	22	57	91	32
Annfield Plain	38	8	4	26	57	143	28
Seaham Red Star Reserves	38	8	2	28	56	134	26
Murton	38	1	3	34	28	183	6

Ashbrooke Belford House had 3 points deducted.
Stockton Town moved to the Northern League, Whitehaven moved to the West Lancashire League while Horden C.W. and Murton also left. Stokesley Sports Club joined from the Northern League while Darlington Reserves, Windscale and South Shields Reserves joined as newly formed clubs. Spennymoor Town Reserves changed their name to Coxhoe Athletic.

Wearside League 2016-2018

2016-17

Jarrow	38	29	4	5	94	36	91
Redcar Athletic	38	27	6	5	125	46	87
Cleator Moor Celtic	38	25	5	8	104	48	80
Richmond Town	38	24	5	9	112	51	77
Boldon Community Association	38	22	8	8	71	47	74
Silksworth Colliery Welfare	38	22	6	10	92	45	72
Hartlepool	38	18	7	13	95	76	61
Coxhoe Athletic	38	19	3	16	87	80	60
South Shields Reserves	38	17	6	15	63	67	57
Sunderland West End	38	17	4	17	78	84	55
Darlington Reserves	38	16	3	19	80	91	51
Gateshead Leam Rangers	38	14	3	21	82	94	45
Prudhoe Town	38	12	9	17	66	78	45
Stokesley Sports Club	38	13	5	20	73	89	44
Ashbrooke Belford House	38	13	1	24	63	116	40
Annfield Plain	38	10	8	20	66	114	38
Wolviston	38	9	8	21	59	93	35
Windscale	38	8	5	25	61	93	29
Harton & Westoe C.W.	38	7	4	27	55	115	25
Seaham Red Star Reserves	38	6	4	28	41	104	22

Jarrow moved to the Northern League. Ashbrooke Belford House and Seaham Red Star Reserves both disbanded. Hebburn Town Reserves joined.

2017-18

Redcar Athletic	32	25	5	2	98	32	80
Cleator Moor Celtic	32	25	4	3	112	26	79
Sunderland West End	32	20	6	6	105	42	66
Hebburn Town Reserves	32	20	4	8	74	38	64
Boldon Community Association	32	19	7	6	68	43	64
Richmond Town	32	16	5	11	73	49	53
Silksworth Colliery Welfare	32	15	5	12	70	54	50
Wolviston	32	16	2	14	73	64	50
Hartlepool	32	14	5	13	80	55	47
Gateshead Leam Rangers	32	12	5	15	46	64	41
Darlington Reserves	32	12	4	16	76	63	40
Harton & Westoe C.W.	32	8	7	17	49	83	31
Annfield Plain	32	8	2	22	38	102	26
Stokesley Sports Club	32	7	4	21	56	112	25
South Shields Reserves	32	8	0	24	50	106	24
Windscale	32	6	5	21	46	107	23
Coxhoe Athletic	32	4	4	24	42	116	16

Prudhoe Town resigned and disbanded on 14th March 2018 and their record was deleted.
Redcar Athletic moved to the Northern League, Cleator Moor Celtic moved to the North West Counties League and Stokesley Sports Club moved to the North Riding league. South Shields Reserves also left. Darlington Railway Athletic joined from the Northern League while Horden C.W. and West Auckland Tuns both joined from the Durham Alliance.

NORTH-EASTERN LEAGUE 1906-1964

The North-Eastern League was formed when the chairman of Newcastle United, Mr. John Cameron, decided that a better class of football was needed for the second XI's of the region's Football League clubs.

A meeting took place in the Newcastle United boardroom on 5th May 1906 at which 10 clubs agreed to form the new league. The 10 consisted of 6 Football League clubs – Bradford City, Hull City, Leeds City, Middlesbrough, Newcastle United and Sunderland – plus Carlisle United, West Hartlepool, West Stanley and Workington.

However, Hull City placed their reserves in the Midland League instead and West Hartlepool chose to stay in the Northern League. These two were replaced in the North-Eastern League by Royal Rovers (from Sunderland) and Hebburn Argyle.

Middlesbrough Reserves, Newcastle United Reserves and Sunderland Reserves had played in the Northern League in 1905-06 although these sides were referred to as "A" teams at the time. Carlisle United and Workington had been playing in Division Two of the Lancashire Combination in 1905-06 and continued in that league as well. Officially both clubs fielded their first team in both leagues but as this would have meant 56 league fixtures, whether this actually happened must be open to doubt and the Lancashire Combination seems to have taken precedence.

Of the other 5 founder members, Bradford City's reserve side had been playing in the West Yorkshire League during 1905-06 but for 1906-07 they fielded teams in both the Midland League and the North-Eastern League as well as the Football League. Their North-Eastern League side was described as the "A" team but although the North-Eastern League was supposedly the club's third priority, as it turned out they frequently fielded their first team. Nearby Leeds City also fielded teams in the Football League and Midland League as well as the North-Eastern League.

Hebburn Argyle had previously been playing in the Northern Alliance as had West Stanley where they were known as Stanley while Royal Rovers moved from the Wearside League.

1906-07

Newcastle United Reserves	18	12	2	4	35	20	26
Sunderland Reserves	18	12	1	5	44	22	25
West Stanley	18	10	4	4	37	23	24
Leeds City "A"	18	9	4	5	33	20	22
Workington	18	6	6	6	34	33	18
Royal Rovers	18	4	9	5	23	30	17
Middlesbrough Reserves	18	5	6	7	34	34	16
Carlisle United	18	4	5	9	24	38	13
Bradford City "A"	18	5	1	12	26	34	11
Hebburn Argyle	18	2	4	12	16	52	8

Penrith joined from the Cumberland League and Shildon Athletic joined from the Northern League while the reserves of the newly formed Bradford Park Avenue also joined. Carlisle United and Workington officially fielded reserve sides rather than first teams.

1907-08

Newcastle United Reserves	24	16	2	6	90	28	34
Sunderland Reserves	24	14	6	4	72	31	34
Shildon Athletic	24	14	3	7	43	35	31
Leeds City "A"	24	13	3	8	64	46	29
Sunderland Royal Rovers	24	11	4	9	44	47	26
Middlesbrough Reserves	24	9	6	9	43	53	24
West Stanley	24	9	4	11	53	52	22
Hebburn Argyle	24	9	4	11	37	65	22
Bradford Park Avenue Reserves	24	9	3	12	43	55	21
Bradford City "A"	24	7	6	11	47	56	20
Workington Reserves	24	7	6	11	40	57	20
Carlisle United Reserves	24	7	3	14	48	58	17
Penrith	24	4	4	16	34	65	12

Penrith, Leeds City "A" and Bradford City "A" all left the league. Darlington and Spennymoor United both joined from the Northern League, North Shields Athletic, South Shield Adelaide and Wallsend Park Villa all joined from the Northern Alliance and Seaham White Star joined from the Wearside League. Hartlepools United and Huddersfield Town joined as newly formed clubs.

North-Eastern League 1908-1914

1908-09

Team	P	W	D	L	F	A	Pts
Newcastle United Reserves	34	26	4	4	106	48	56
South Shields Adelaide	34	22	4	8	80	41	48
Bradford Park Avenue Reserves	34	19	5	10	84	49	43
Hartlepools United	34	16	9	9	79	51	41
Middlesbrough Reserves	34	17	6	11	82	45	40
Sunderland Reserves	34	18	3	13	81	54	39
West Stanley	34	18	3	13	73	56	39
Darlington	34	15	8	11	76	73	38
North Shields Athletic	34	14	6	14	63	48	34
Spennymoor United	34	13	7	14	55	63	33
Wallsend Park Villa	34	13	6	15	55	66	32
Workington Reserves	34	12	5	17	50	80	29
Seaham White Star	34	10	7	17	55	64	27
Hebburn Argyle	34	10	6	18	55	91	26
Carlisle United Reserves	34	10	4	20	61	84	24
Huddersfield Town	34	10	4	20	47	78	24
Shildon Athletic	34	7	6	21	51	101	20
Sunderland Royal Rovers	34	7	5	22	39	100	19

Huddersfield Town and Bradford Park Avenue Reserves both moved to the Midland League. Wingate Albion joined from the Wearside League. Seaham White Star changed their name to Seaham Harbour.

1909-10

Team	P	W	D	L	F	A	Pts
Spennymoor United	32	24	3	5	75	39	51
Newcastle United Reserves	32	21	6	5	134	31	48
Middlesbrough Reserves	32	21	5	6	90	51	47
Hartlepools United	32	17	11	4	82	27	45
Darlington	32	16	5	11	60	55	37
Sunderland Reserves	32	15	6	11	65	43	36
Shildon Athletic	32	13	8	11	61	61	34
South Shields Adelaide	32	14	5	13	77	63	33
North Shields Athletic	32	12	8	12	60	61	32
Seaham Harbour	32	14	3	15	56	57	31
Wallsend Park Villa	32	12	6	14	56	67	30
Carlisle United Reserves	32	11	4	17	52	62	26
Wingate Albion	32	8	8	16	43	80	24
West Stanley	32	9	5	18	56	85	23
Hebburn Argyle	32	8	4	20	33	103	20
Workington Reserves	32	7	4	21	41	98	18
Sunderland Royal Rovers	32	2	5	25	25	83	9

Jarrow Croft joined from the Newcastle & District Amateur League. Carlisle United and Workington were barred from the Lancashire Combination for geographical reasons and so their first teams replaced their reserves in the North-Eastern League. South Shields Adelaide changed their name to South Shields and Sunderland Royal Rovers changed their name to Sunderland Rovers.

1910-11

Team	P	W	D	L	F	A	Pts
Newcastle United Reserves	34	25	4	5	88	25	54
Sunderland Reserves	34	20	6	8	81	38	46
Hartlepools United	34	18	8	8	71	40	44
Darlington	34	19	5	10	79	39	43
South Shields	33	18	5	10	56	33	41
North Shields Athletic	34	19	3	12	57	56	41
Middlesbrough Reserves	34	16	6	12	83	54	38
Wingate Albion	34	14	7	13	48	39	35
Wallsend Park Villa	34	15	3	16	49	59	33
Hebburn Argyle	34	13	6	15	38	62	32
Seaham Harbour	34	13	5	16	44	63	31
Spennymoor United	32	12	5	15	52	54	29
Workington	34	12	3	19	47	72	27
Shildon Athletic	34	11	3	20	50	64	25
Carlisle United	34	8	8	18	45	52	24
Jarrow Croft	34	11	2	21	34	70	24
West Stanley	33	10	3	20	39	84	23
Sunderland Rovers	34	8	2	24	37	94	18

Two games involving Spennymoor United were left unplayed. Workington disbanded at the end of June 1911. Newcastle City joined from the Northern Alliance and Gateshead Town joined as a newly formed club. North Shields Athletic changed their name to North Shields.

1911-12

Team	P	W	D	L	F	A	Pts
Middlesbrough Reserves	36	28	5	3	122	33	61
Newcastle United Reserves	36	28	2	6	113	33	58
Darlington	36	23	8	5	84	34	54
Sunderland Reserves	36	21	5	10	99	52	47
South Shields	36	21	4	11	73	43	46
Spennymoor United	36	18	6	12	62	57	42
Newcastle City	36	16	9	11	62	43	41
Gateshead Town	36	16	6	14	64	66	38
Hartlepools United	36	14	8	14	62	50	36
West Stanley	36	13	10	13	61	58	36
North Shields	36	13	9	14	59	72	35
Seaham Harbour	36	15	2	19	52	67	32
Hebburn Argyle	36	11	9	16	56	54	31
Wingate Albion	36	9	11	16	41	84	29
Jarrow Croft	36	10	7	19	52	87	27
Shildon Athletic	36	9	6	21	62	97	24
Carlisle United	36	7	6	23	27	98	20
Wallsend Park Villa	36	8	3	25	43	93	19
Sunderland Rovers	36	2	4	30	42	125	8

Houghton Rovers joined from the Sunderland & District League. Jarrow Croft changed their name to Jarrow and Wallsend Park Villa changed their name to Wallsend.

1912-13

Team	P	W	D	L	F	A	Pts
Darlington	38	31	4	3	116	23	66
South Shields	38	27	7	4	103	30	61
Middlesbrough Reserves	38	26	6	6	102	40	58
Sunderland Reserves	38	26	5	7	100	48	57
Newcastle United Reserves	38	24	5	9	109	47	53
Spennymoor United	38	19	6	13	80	61	44
Shildon Athletic	38	17	9	12	79	69	43
Houghton Rovers	38	15	9	14	53	64	39
Wallsend	38	14	10	14	83	71	38
North Shields	38	15	7	16	72	78	37
Newcastle City	38	15	7	16	48	62	37
Hartlepools United	38	15	6	17	69	66	36
Hebburn Argyle	38	12	6	20	49	75	30
Carlisle United	38	12	5	21	61	98	29
Seaham Harbour	38	10	7	21	48	77	27
Jarrow	38	10	5	23	52	86	25
West Stanley	38	7	10	21	54	94	24
Sunderland Rovers	38	7	8	23	39	79	22
Gateshead Town	38	8	6	24	49	112	22
Wingate Albion	38	5	2	31	28	114	12

Wingate Albion moved to the Wearside League. Blyth Spartans joined from the Northern Alliance.

1913-14

Team	P	W	D	L	F	A	Pts
South Shields	38	32	5	1	133	29	69
Middlesbrough Reserves	38	23	8	7	99	37	54
Newcastle United Reserves	38	24	5	9	91	40	53
Darlington	38	20	10	8	72	43	50
Sunderland Reserves	38	20	8	10	83	55	48
Blyth Spartans	38	19	7	12	71	51	45
Hartlepools United	38	17	10	11	68	37	44
Hebburn Argyle	38	14	11	13	55	50	39
Shildon Athletic	38	18	3	17	54	60	39
Gateshead Town	38	17	5	16	58	76	39
Jarrow	38	12	10	16	55	63	34
North Shields	38	11	10	17	57	81	32
Carlisle United	38	11	10	17	48	84	32
Spennymoor United	38	10	11	17	60	63	31
Sunderland Rovers	38	10	10	18	46	67	30
Newcastle City	38	7	16	15	34	57	30
West Stanley	38	13	3	22	54	87	29
Houghton Rovers	38	11	2	25	38	81	24
Seaham Harbour	38	7	8	23	30	73	22
Wallsend	38	5	6	27	44	115	16

Seaham Harbour moved to the Wearside League. Ashington joined from the Northern Alliance.

1914-15

South Shields	38	31	4	3	160	34	66
Middlesbrough Reserves	38	28	5	5	151	34	61
Newcastle United Reserves	38	26	6	6	132	43	58
Darlington	38	25	4	9	109	37	54
West Stanley	38	24	4	10	79	44	52
Sunderland Reserves	38	18	9	11	86	50	45
Hartlepools United	38	16	11	11	74	57	43
North Shields	38	19	5	14	67	63	43
Ashington	38	15	11	12	60	63	41
Sunderland Rovers	38	17	4	17	74	79	38
Spennymoor United	38	12	9	17	40	82	33
Shildon Athletic	38	11	9	18	70	61	31
Blyth Spartans	38	11	9	18	49	72	31
Hebburn Argyle	38	12	6	20	49	73	30
Jarrow	38	10	10	18	45	95	30
Houghton Rovers	38	11	4	23	43	125	26
Carlisle United	38	8	7	23	51	120	23
Newcastle City	38	8	5	25	42	87	21
Gateshead Town	38	8	3	27	51	121	19
Wallsend	38	6	3	29	44	136	15

At the league's Annual General Meeting, held in Newcastle on 24th July 1915, it was decided to suspend the North-Eastern League for the duration of the war. However, a temporary competition was set up called the "North-Eastern League – Tyneside Combination". There were 8 clubs competing in this league, 7 of which were members of the North-Eastern League – Hebburn Argyle, Houghton Rovers, Jarrow, North Shields, South Shields, Sunderland Rovers and Wallsend. The 8th club was Scotswood who were members of the Northern Alliance.

NORTH-EASTERN LEAGUE – TYNESIDE COMBINATION

1915-16

South Shields	14	10	1	3	37	18	21
Scotswood	14	7	5	2	22	17	19
Wallsend	14	7	1	6	25	25	15
Sunderland Rovers	14	4	4	6	25	24	12
Houghton Rovers	13	5	2	6	15	18	12
Hebburn Argyle	14	5	2	7	18	22	12
Jarrow	14	3	4	7	17	28	10
North Shields	13	1	7	5	19	26	9

One match was not played.
Note: This was the "first series" of games. A second series was played but no final table has been found.

1916-17

Hebburn Argyle and North Shields were both unable to take part in the 1916-17 competition which began in September with the remaining 6 clubs. At the start of October, Tyne Electrical Engineers joined the competition, replacing Houghton Rovers.
Once again, two series of games were played with those 6 clubs competing in both, but no final tables have been found.

1917-19

At the end of the 1916-17 season, it was decided to suspend the competition entirely until such time as the war ended.

1919

When the war ended on 11th November, 1918, a temporary competition was formed called the Northern Victory League. The clubs that took part were Darlington Forge Albion (a club that included Darlington F.C. players as Darlington themselves did not yet have use of their own ground), Durham City (a newly formed club), Hartlepools United, Middlesbrough, Newcastle United, Scotswood, South Shields and Sunderland.
The competition began on 11th January, 1919.

Note: The full-time professional players employed by Newcastle United, Sunderland, Middlesbrough, etc. were by now, no longer under contract and full-time contracts were only just beginning to be offered. The teams these clubs put out therefore would have been a mixture of players who were hoping for a full-time contract when normal football returned.

NORTHERN VICTORY LEAGUE

Middlesbrough	14	10	1	3	29	12	21
Sunderland	14	8	2	4	32	20	18
South Shields	14	5	5	4	27	25	15
Scotswood	14	5	4	5	29	24	14
Newcastle United	14	5	4	5	21	23	14
Darlington Forge Albion	14	5	2	7	15	27	12
Hartlepools United	14	5	1	8	34	34	11
Durham City	14	2	3	9	8	30	7

1919

The league was revived at the end of the war and the constitution of the competition for the 1919-20 season was decided at the Annual Meeting held in Newcastle on 28th June 1919.
South Shields had been elected to the Football League but retained membership of the North-Eastern League by moving their reserves from the Tyneside League. Gateshead Town, Hebburn Argyle, Newcastle City and Sunderland Rovers did not resume activity after the war. Jarrow also did not re-appear but they were replaced in the North-Eastern League by Palmer's (Jarrow) who were pre-war members of the Newcastle & District League. Palmer's (Jarrow) subsequently changed their name to Jarrow during the 1919-20 season. North Shields also did not reappear but a new club called Preston Colliery was formed in North Shields that joined the Tyneside League.
The remaining 13 pre-war members all rejoined. They were: Ashington, Blyth Spartans, Carlisle United, Darlington, Hartlepools United, Houghton (who had changed their name from Houghton Rovers), Middlesbrough Reserves, Newcastle United Reserves, Shildon Athletic, Spennymoor United, Sunderland Reserves, Wallsend and West Stanley. The league was made up to 18 clubs by the election of Scotswood from the Northern Alliance, Leadgate Park from the Northern League and Durham City who were a new club.

NORTH-EASTERN LEAGUE

1919-20

Middlesbrough Reserves	34	22	7	5	86	30	51
Darlington	34	24	1	9	91	44	49
Newcastle United Reserves	34	22	5	7	82	41	49
Blyth Spartans	34	18	8	8	62	42	44
Durham City	34	17	6	11	52	41	40
Jarrow	34	16	6	12	55	52	38
Ashington	34	14	8	12	51	51	36
South Shields Reserves	34	14	7	13	67	57	35
Sunderland Reserves	34	15	4	15	67	49	34
Hartlepools United	34	12	10	12	45	36	34
Scotswood	34	13	6	15	47	55	32
West Stanley	34	12	7	15	45	63	31
Carlisle United	34	12	3	19	47	76	27
Shildon Athletic	34	10	6	18	50	75	26
Houghton	34	8	8	18	28	60	24
Spennymoor United	34	10	2	22	52	78	22
Leadgate Park	34	8	6	20	51	83	22
Wallsend	34	6	6	22	26	71	18

Bedlington United joined from the Northern Alliance and Chester-le-Street joined as a newly formed club.

North-Eastern League 1920-1925

1920-21

Darlington	38	28	4	6	75	29	60
Middlesbrough Reserves	38	27	5	6	93	35	59
Newcastle United Reserves	38	23	7	8	96	39	53
Sunderland Reserves	38	21	10	7	73	49	52
Blyth Spartans	38	19	11	8	69	34	49
Carlisle United	38	18	10	10	79	46	46
West Stanley	38	14	14	10	54	42	42
Hartlepools United	38	18	6	14	64	50	42
Ashington	38	14	13	11	66	52	41
Jarrow	38	14	11	13	46	44	39
Durham City	38	16	5	17	31	60	37
Chester-le-Street	38	13	11	14	50	58	37
Leadgate Park	38	13	10	15	57	58	36
South Shields Reserves	38	12	11	15	51	66	35
Spennymoor United	38	10	10	18	51	79	30
Houghton	38	7	10	21	38	69	24
Shildon Athletic	38	8	7	23	41	75	23
Scotswood	38	8	5	25	35	76	21
Wallsend	38	6	8	24	39	98	20
Bedlington United	38	4	6	28	32	104	14

The Football League formed its new Division Three (North) and Ashington, Darlington, Durham City and Hartlepools United all became founder members. Blyth Spartans and West Stanley also applied to the Football League but were not elected. Darlington maintained their membership of the North-Eastern League by moving their reserves from the Palatine League while Preston Colliery and Seaton Delaval both joined from the Northern Alliance and Workington joined as a newly re-formed club.

1921-22

Carlisle United	38	24	8	6	85	39	56
Newcastle United Reserves	38	24	7	7	80	30	55
Blyth Spartans	38	16	16	6	55	31	48
Chester-le-Street	38	20	7	11	53	35	47
South Shields Reserves	38	16	13	9	60	31	45
Shildon Athletic	38	20	5	13	65	44	45
Middlesbrough Reserves	38	18	8	12	61	45	44
Sunderland Reserves	38	16	11	11	66	43	43
Workington	38	17	8	13	52	49	42
Darlington Reserves	38	15	9	14	67	68	39
Jarrow	38	16	5	17	51	59	37
Leadgate Park	38	14	9	15	56	66	37
West Stanley	38	10	15	13	55	65	35
Spennymoor United	38	14	5	19	59	65	33
Wallsend	38	11	11	16	49	62	33
Preston Colliery	38	7	15	16	38	58	29
Bedlington United	38	8	11	19	32	56	27
Seaton Delaval	38	6	14	18	36	69	26
Scotswood	38	5	10	23	43	90	20
Houghton	38	4	11	23	27	85	19

Houghton moved to the Wearside League. Hartlepools United Reserves joined from the Palatine League.

1922-23

Newcastle United Reserves	38	30	8	0	109	24	68
Blyth Spartans	38	23	7	8	78	43	53
Sunderland Reserves	38	23	3	12	74	35	49
Middlesbrough Reserves	38	20	8	10	76	45	48
South Shields Reserves	38	21	5	12	74	44	47
Carlisle United	38	19	8	11	56	43	46
Workington	38	20	4	14	85	57	44
Shildon Athletic	38	17	10	11	74	55	44
Jarrow	38	17	6	15	56	63	40
Preston Colliery	38	16	7	15	48	47	39
Hartlepools United Reserves	38	14	9	15	64	56	37
Bedlington United	38	14	5	19	50	61	33
West Stanley	38	10	12	16	43	60	32
Darlington Reserves	38	13	5	20	46	57	31
Chester-le-Street	38	12	6	20	47	71	30
Seaton Delaval	38	10	7	21	40	68	27
Wallsend	38	8	9	21	43	89	25
Leadgate Park	38	8	8	22	38	82	24
Scotswood	38	6	10	22	40	91	22
Spennymoor United	38	6	9	23	42	92	21

Shildon Athletic changed their name to Shildon.

1923-24

South Shields Reserves	38	29	5	4	106	32	63
Newcastle United Reserves	38	26	9	3	99	44	61
Middlesbrough Reserves	38	26	6	6	95	34	58
Sunderland Reserves	38	24	5	9	90	40	53
Workington	38	21	10	7	87	43	52
Blyth Spartans	38	21	7	10	68	35	49
West Stanley	38	18	11	9	66	43	47
Seaton Delaval	38	14	8	16	61	61	36
Hartlepools United Reserves	38	13	10	15	60	62	36
Shildon	38	15	4	19	60	63	34
Carlisle United	38	13	8	17	46	61	34
Darlington Reserves	38	13	6	19	55	64	32
Spennymoor United	38	10	10	18	41	65	30
Bedlington United	38	12	4	22	52	94	28
Scotswood	38	8	10	20	46	81	26
Leadgate Park	38	10	6	22	50	92	26
Preston Colliery	38	9	7	22	37	64	25
Chester-le-Street	38	9	6	23	36	80	24
Wallsend	38	6	11	21	44	91	23
Jarrow	38	10	3	25	46	96	23

1924-25

Sunderland Reserves	38	27	7	4	98	29	61
Darlington Reserves	38	25	7	6	97	40	57
Newcastle United Reserves	38	24	5	9	93	35	53
Middlesbrough Reserves	38	22	7	9	81	40	51
South Shields Reserves	38	19	11	8	79	55	49
Shildon	38	19	9	10	88	58	47
Workington	38	20	6	12	80	57	46
Blyth Spartans	38	17	9	12	69	46	43
West Stanley	38	14	14	10	51	53	42
Hartlepools United Reserves	38	16	7	15	63	54	39
Carlisle United	38	16	6	16	67	63	38
Jarrow	38	13	11	14	51	56	37
Spennymoor United	38	11	11	16	54	69	33
Seaton Delaval	38	12	3	23	39	79	27
Scotswood	38	9	9	20	36	78	27
Preston Colliery	38	10	6	22	41	73	26
Chester-le-Street	38	10	6	22	35	75	26
Leadgate Park	38	9	5	24	52	103	23
Bedlington United	38	6	8	24	41	84	20
Wallsend	38	5	5	28	33	101	15

Wallsend moved to the Northern Alliance and Leadgate Park disbanded. Annfield Plain and Durham City Reserves both joined from the Northern Alliance.

1925-26

Team	P	W	D	L	F	A	Pts
Newcastle United Reserves	38	31	4	3	147	43	66
Sunderland Reserves	38	26	6	6	133	50	58
South Shields Reserves	38	22	6	10	113	71	50
Workington	38	21	6	11	84	59	48
Carlisle United	38	19	9	10	83	70	47
Darlington Reserves	38	20	6	12	107	57	46
Middlesbrough Reserves	38	21	3	14	107	71	45
West Stanley	38	18	7	13	92	73	43
Jarrow	38	18	4	16	62	72	40
Preston Colliery	38	16	7	15	71	66	39
Shildon	38	16	5	17	93	86	37
Annfield Plain	38	15	7	16	77	78	37
Hartlepools United Reserves	38	16	5	17	77	108	37
Blyth Spartans	38	13	6	19	77	105	32
Chester-le-Street	38	14	1	23	68	97	29
Bedlington United	38	13	3	22	75	113	29
Scotswood	38	9	5	24	70	121	23
Durham City Reserves	38	11	1	26	58	109	23
Spennymoor United	38	6	8	24	76	134	20
Seaton Delaval	38	5	1	32	51	138	11

The league expanded to two divisions. The 20 existing members formed Division One, while Division Two was formed by an amalgamation with the Northern Alliance, all 16 of its clubs joining the new division which was made up to 18 by the addition of Seaham Harbour from the Wearside League and Dipton United from the Northern Combination, both of whom had been elected to the Northern Alliance for 1926-27 prior to the amalgamation.

Promoted clubs are shown in bold, relegated clubs in bold italics

1926-27
Division One

Team	P	W	D	L	F	A	Pts
Sunderland Reserves	38	27	2	9	115	54	56
Newcastle United Reserves	38	24	6	8	99	43	54
South Shields Reserves	38	24	6	8	103	65	54
Middlesbrough Reserves	38	22	7	9	133	69	51
Carlisle United	38	23	3	12	106	75	49
Jarrow	38	16	9	13	80	66	41
Hartlepools United Reserves	38	16	9	13	91	79	41
Darlington Reserves	38	15	11	12	86	82	41
Blyth Spartans	38	17	6	15	78	72	40
Annfield Plain	38	15	9	14	83	81	39
Shildon	38	13	10	15	83	87	36
Bedlington United	38	14	8	16	84	94	36
Durham City Reserves	38	15	5	18	72	91	35
Preston Colliery	38	14	6	18	89	101	34
Spennymoor United	38	11	10	17	82	89	32
Workington	38	12	8	18	60	76	32
Scotswood	38	9	10	19	77	106	28
West Stanley	38	10	8	20	66	113	28
Chester-le-Street	38	9	5	24	55	105	23
Seaton Delaval	38	4	2	32	40	134	10

Division Two

Team	P	W	D	L	F	A	Pts
Consett	34	25	1	8	114	64	51
Ashington Reserves	34	22	6	6	129	53	50
Wallsend	34	21	4	9	92	65	46
Walker Celtic	34	20	6	8	93	67	46
Chilton Colliery Recreation Athletic	34	19	6	9	96	52	44
Chopwell Institute	34	16	9	9	98	81	41
Dipton United	34	16	6	12	92	62	38
Seaham Harbour	34	17	2	15	97	86	36
Craghead United	34	13	7	14	88	86	33
Washington Colliery	34	12	8	14	63	64	32
Spen Black & White	34	13	3	18	66	85	29
Birtley	34	11	7	16	66	95	29
High Fell	34	12	3	19	72	92	27
Ouston Rovers	34	10	7	17	65	90	27
Crawcrook Albion	34	11	5	18	54	81	27
Mickley	34	9	4	21	60	85	22
Felling Colliery	34	8	6	20	59	109	22
Newburn	34	6	0	28	54	141	12

Chilton Colliery Recreation Athletic moved to the Northern League and Newburn also left the league. It is thought that Newburn disbanded following the depression in the steel trade. Usworth Colliery joined from the Tyneside League.

1927-28
Division One

Team	P	W	D	L	F	A	Pts
Sunderland Reserves	38	31	3	4	128	30	65
Carlisle United	38	25	5	8	111	61	55
Middlesbrough Reserves	38	22	8	8	126	59	52
West Stanley	38	22	6	10	106	82	50
Annfield Plain	38	21	5	12	96	61	47
Newcastle United Reserves	38	21	4	13	101	61	46
South Shields Reserves	38	20	4	14	98	74	44
Bedlington United	38	18	5	15	78	97	41
Workington	38	18	4	16	99	80	40
Spennymoor United	38	16	8	14	71	73	40
Hartlepools United Reserves	38	16	4	18	98	113	36
Darlington Reserves	38	16	2	20	92	90	34
Blyth Spartans	38	14	4	20	56	77	32
Ashington Reserves	38	12	6	20	71	106	30
Jarrow	38	12	5	21	76	122	29
Shildon	38	10	8	20	56	73	28
Consett	38	10	8	20	76	117	28
Scotswood	38	8	9	21	61	97	25
Preston Colliery	38	7	6	25	60	130	20
Durham City Reserves	38	7	4	27	48	105	18

Carlisle United left after being elected to Division Three (North) of the Football League where they replaced Durham City. Durham City dropped into the North-Eastern League where they replaced their reserves, who left the league. Following their relegation, Preston Colliery changed their name to North Shields.

Division Two

Team	P	W	D	L	F	A	Pts
Washington Colliery	32	22	5	5	108	45	49
Wallsend	32	21	6	5	100	47	48
Dipton United	32	20	4	8	119	64	44
Usworth Colliery	32	18	6	8	73	49	42
Birtley	32	18	2	12	90	64	38
Seaham Harbour	32	16	6	10	68	50	38
Chopwell Institute	32	16	4	12	90	69	36
Spen Black & White	32	16	4	12	87	73	36
Walker Celtic	32	16	3	13	89	65	35
Seaton Delaval	32	15	3	14	72	77	33
Chester-le-Street	32	11	7	14	70	79	29
Mickley	32	12	2	18	61	103	26
Craghead United	32	7	11	14	77	96	25
Crawcrook Albion	32	11	2	19	59	75	24
Ouston Rovers	32	9	4	19	72	107	22
High Fell	32	4	4	24	51	128	12
Felling Colliery	32	3	1	28	44	139	7

North-Eastern League 1928-1931

Felling Colliery moved to the Tyneside League. St. Peters Albion joined from the Northern Amateur League while Carlisle United Reserves and White-le-Head Rangers also joined.

1928-29

Division One

Sunderland Reserves	38	30	3	5	127	41	63
South Shields Reserves	38	23	8	7	110	49	54
Middlesbrough Reserves	38	21	7	10	113	66	49
Workington	38	19	8	11	100	74	46
Newcastle United Reserves	38	20	4	14	99	67	44
Spennymoor United	38	18	8	12	79	66	44
Annfield Plain	38	18	6	14	75	66	42
Hartlepools United Reserves	38	16	6	16	77	97	38
Jarrow	38	16	5	17	67	77	37
Wallsend	38	16	4	18	75	80	36
Blyth Spartans	38	13	10	15	66	75	36
Bedlington United	38	16	3	19	72	80	35
Shildon	38	12	10	16	74	77	34
Consett	38	14	6	18	65	91	34
Washington Colliery	38	14	5	19	81	103	33
Darlington Reserves	38	13	6	19	74	97	32
Scotswood	38	11	7	20	64	94	29
West Stanley	38	7	11	20	55	91	25
Ashington Reserves	*38*	*9*	*7*	*22*	*47*	*89*	*25*
Durham City	*38*	*8*	*8*	*22*	*51*	*91*	*24*

Ashington failed to gain re-election to the Football League and so joined the league, with their first team replacing the reserves in Division Two. Durham City disbanded but a new club with the same name was quickly formed and took the previous club's place in Division Two.

Division Two

North Shields	34	26	6	2	120	44	58
Carlisle United Reserves	34	26	0	8	130	40	52
Spen Black & White	34	19	9	6	105	61	47
Walker Celtic	34	16	10	8	84	56	42
White-le-Head Rangers	34	17	8	9	94	66	42
Usworth Colliery	34	16	8	10	78	53	40
Dipton United	34	16	7	11	85	76	39
St. Peters Albion	34	15	6	13	78	63	36
Chopwell Institute	34	15	6	13	83	88	36
Crawcrook Albion	34	16	3	15	73	85	35
Birtley	34	10	9	15	61	72	29
High Fell	34	9	9	16	62	83	27
Mickley	34	10	5	19	79	127	25
Seaham Harbour	34	10	5	19	58	103	25
Craghead United	34	9	5	20	73	96	23
Chester-le-Street	34	7	7	20	62	115	21
Ouston Rovers	34	6	6	22	61	99	18
Seaton Delaval	34	5	7	22	61	120	17

Seaham Harbour, High Fell and Ouston Rovers all left the league.

1929-30

Division One

Sunderland Reserves	38	26	6	6	157	58	58
Newcastle United Reserves	38	27	2	9	111	46	56
Darlington Reserves	38	21	8	9	103	79	50
Middlesbrough Reserves	38	22	4	12	118	53	48
West Stanley	38	20	6	12	89	79	46
Hartlepools United Reserves	38	20	5	13	97	80	45
North Shields	38	18	8	12	89	69	44
Jarrow	38	17	6	15	74	68	40
Workington	38	18	3	17	96	89	39
South Shields Reserves	38	16	4	18	80	85	36
Wallsend	38	14	8	16	73	88	36
Carlisle United Reserves	38	15	5	18	83	97	35
Spennymoor United	38	13	8	17	85	99	34
Annfield Plain	38	11	11	16	84	93	33
Consett	38	13	4	21	73	113	30
Scotswood	38	13	2	23	75	110	28
Shildon	38	11	6	21	65	101	28
Washington Colliery	38	11	4	23	79	126	26
Blyth Spartans	38	10	6	22	58	95	26
Bedlington United	**38**	**9**	**4**	**25**	**65**	**126**	**22**

South Shields moved to Gateshead so South Shields Reserves changed their name to Gateshead Reserves.
Crook Town joined from the Northern League.

Division Two

Walker Celtic	**28**	**20**	**3**	**5**	**99**	**36**	**43**
White-le-Head Rangers	28	21	0	7	85	50	42
Ashington	**28**	**20**	**1**	**7**	**96**	**40**	**41**
Spen Black & White	28	18	1	9	79	65	37
Usworth Colliery	28	15	3	10	85	61	33
Crawcrook Albion	28	13	3	12	83	70	29
Durham City	28	14	1	13	77	66	29
St. Peters Albion	28	11	7	10	57	65	29
Chopwell Institute	28	12	4	12	64	74	28
Birtley	28	10	4	14	83	78	24
Dipton United	28	10	2	16	51	74	22
Craghead United	28	8	3	17	66	82	19
Mickley	28	7	4	17	40	78	18
Seaton Delaval	28	6	2	20	34	92	14
Chester-le-Street	28	4	4	20	38	106	12

1930-31

Division One

Middlesbrough Reserves	42	33	7	2	159	40	73
Newcastle United Reserves	42	33	6	3	159	39	72
Sunderland Reserves	42	28	5	9	130	65	61
Workington	42	23	9	10	105	57	55
Jarrow	42	23	6	13	111	69	52
Washington Colliery	42	20	11	11	82	62	51
Blyth Spartans	42	22	6	14	95	78	50
Walker Celtic	42	16	13	13	97	92	45
Hartlepools United Reserves	42	20	4	18	102	92	44
North Shields	42	17	9	16	102	87	43
Carlisle United Reserves	42	17	8	17	90	94	42
Wallsend	42	17	3	22	88	103	37
Darlington Reserves	42	13	10	19	97	116	36
Spennymoor United	42	15	5	22	85	84	35
Gateshead Reserves	42	12	10	20	59	74	34
Crook Town	42	14	6	22	85	114	34
West Stanley	42	14	6	22	65	106	34
Ashington	42	12	6	24	65	101	30
Annfield Plain	42	12	5	25	65	108	29
Shildon	42	12	5	25	65	128	29
Consett	*42*	*10*	*8*	*24*	*58*	*126*	*28*
Scotswood	*42*	*3*	*4*	*35*	*45*	*161*	*10*

Division Two

Team	P	W	D	L	F	A	Pts
Chopwell Institute	26	19	4	3	81	30	42
Durham City	26	18	4	4	77	38	40
Spen Black & White	26	12	7	7	64	36	31
Usworth Colliery	26	14	3	9	70	48	31
Dipton United	26	13	4	9	67	60	30
St. Peters Albion	26	10	8	8	58	47	28
Crawcrook Albion	26	11	6	9	52	48	28
White-le-Head Rangers	26	11	5	10	68	58	27
Craghead United	26	9	4	13	80	85	22
Mickley	26	10	2	14	55	77	22
Bedlington United	26	8	5	13	52	67	21
Birtley	26	7	4	15	47	69	18
Seaton Delaval	26	6	2	18	34	91	14
Chester-le-Street	26	4	2	20	44	95	10

White-le-Head Rangers and Seaton Delaval left. Eden Colliery Welfare joined from the Northern League and Throckley Welfare also joined.

1931-32

Division One

Team	P	W	D	L	F	A	Pts
Middlesbrough Reserves	42	29	7	6	128	45	65
Newcastle United Reserves	42	29	6	7	139	48	64
Sunderland Reserves	42	26	9	7	106	47	61
Workington	42	27	7	8	119	63	61
Blyth Spartans	42	24	9	9	129	75	57
Crook Town	42	23	6	13	100	63	52
Darlington Reserves	42	22	7	13	84	72	51
Spennymoor United	42	20	6	16	106	88	46
Hartlepools United Reserves	42	21	4	17	103	93	46
Jarrow	42	19	5	18	82	81	43
Wallsend	42	17	6	19	53	91	40
West Stanley	42	16	7	19	96	98	39
Gateshead Reserves	42	16	6	20	73	104	38
Chopwell Institute	42	14	9	19	80	104	37
Ashington	42	17	2	23	91	104	36
Carlisle United Reserves	42	13	8	21	65	80	34
North Shields	42	10	11	21	73	89	31
Durham City	42	13	5	24	56	89	31
Annfield Plain	42	12	5	25	72	123	29
Walker Celtic	42	11	6	25	82	109	28
Shildon	42	8	5	29	43	120	21
Washington Colliery	*42*	*5*	*4*	*33*	*41*	*135*	*14*

Shildon moved to the Northern League.

Division Two

Team	P	W	D	L	F	A	Pts
Crawcrook Albion	26	16	3	7	65	48	35
Dipton United	26	14	4	8	70	47	32
St. Peters Albion	26	14	3	9	73	51	31
Eden Colliery Welfare	26	14	3	9	67	56	31
Usworth Colliery	26	12	5	9	44	46	29
Throckley Welfare	26	11	6	9	49	42	28
Chester-le-Street	26	10	6	10	52	49	26
Spen Black & White	26	10	6	10	47	50	26
Consett	26	10	5	11	70	61	25
Mickley	26	9	6	11	56	58	24
Birtley	26	10	3	13	63	62	23
Scotswood	26	7	7	12	46	75	21
Bedlington United	26	6	5	15	46	77	17
Craghead United	26	7	2	17	43	69	16

Craghead United left the league.
Pegswood United and West Wylam Colliery Welfare joined.
St. Peters Albion changed their name to Newcastle East End.

1932-33

Division One

Team	P	W	D	L	F	A	Pts
Middlesbrough Reserves	38	32	0	6	146	55	64
Newcastle United Reserves	38	24	7	7	91	52	55
North Shields	38	23	7	8	107	59	53
Sunderland Reserves	38	23	4	11	87	56	50
Workington	38	22	5	11	101	53	49
Spennymoor United	38	22	4	12	71	43	48
Darlington Reserves	38	18	5	15	85	84	41
Carlisle United Reserves	38	17	6	15	80	72	40
Walker Celtic	38	14	7	17	70	85	35
Blyth Spartans	38	15	4	19	79	84	34
Crook Town	38	15	4	19	67	73	34
Chopwell Institute	38	14	6	18	83	91	34
Hartlepools United Reserves	38	14	6	18	63	87	34
Ashington	38	12	9	17	87	92	33
Annfield Plain	38	13	6	19	84	97	32
Gateshead Reserves	38	10	10	18	68	85	30
Durham City	38	10	10	18	63	86	30
West Stanley	38	11	5	22	62	118	27
Jarrow	38	10	3	25	65	121	23
Wallsend	*38*	*6*	*2*	*30*	*43*	*109*	*14*

Durham City changed their name to City of Durham.
Newcastle United Reserves moved to the Central League.
Wallsend changed their name to Wallsend Town.

Division Two

Team	P	W	D	L	F	A	Pts
Eden Colliery Welfare	**30**	**19**	**4**	**7**	**97**	**50**	**42**
Consett	30	20	2	8	87	50	42
Throckley Welfare	30	19	3	8	91	63	41
Scotswood	30	18	3	9	83	66	39
Usworth Colliery	30	17	3	10	82	55	37
Crawcrook Albion	30	13	9	8	53	46	35
Bedlington United	30	16	2	12	71	58	34
Birtley	30	15	4	11	76	65	34
Mickley	30	12	6	12	62	63	30
Pegswood United	30	10	8	12	80	71	28
Washington Colliery	30	10	4	16	52	68	24
West Wylam Colliery Welfare	30	8	6	16	55	84	22
Dipton United	30	6	8	16	52	86	20
Spen Black & White	30	7	5	18	46	85	19
Newcastle East End	30	7	4	19	41	80	18
Chester-le-Street	30	5	5	20	60	98	15

Spen Black & White left the league. Stakeford Albion joined as a newly formed club and Newbiggin West End also joined.

1933-34

Division One

Team	P	W	D	L	F	A	Pts
Sunderland Reserves	38	28	5	5	119	37	61
Jarrow	38	24	7	7	105	42	55
Spennymoor United	38	22	8	8	114	42	52
Blyth Spartans	38	23	5	10	81	58	51
Workington	38	24	2	12	147	68	50
Middlesbrough Reserves	38	17	8	13	89	59	42
North Shields	38	18	6	14	85	65	42
Gateshead Reserves	38	19	4	15	81	81	42
Hartlepools United Reserves	38	16	5	17	73	77	37
Crook Town	38	15	7	16	62	68	37
Carlisle United Reserves	38	14	5	19	81	64	33
Darlington Reserves	38	12	8	18	76	101	32
Ashington	38	13	5	20	58	100	31
Annfield Plain	38	13	5	20	55	110	31
Chopwell Institute	38	12	6	20	77	126	30
West Stanley	38	13	3	22	55	87	29
Consett	38	12	5	21	45	84	29
City of Durham	38	11	7	20	47	89	29
Eden Colliery Welfare	38	10	8	20	76	107	28
Walker Celtic	38	7	5	26	54	115	19

North-Eastern League 1934-1937

Chopwell Institute were expelled following irregularities in their game at Workington on 5th May 1934. The club initially joined the North-West Durham League but disbanded before the start of the 1934-35 season.

Division Two

Throckley Welfare	30	21	7	2	94	35	49
Bedlington United	30	21	2	7	99	57	44
Wallsend Town	30	18	7	5	94	49	43
Stakeford Albion	30	17	5	8	82	56	39
Mickley	30	16	5	9	89	70	37
Birtley	30	14	4	12	73	57	32
Newbiggin West End	30	13	3	14	72	64	29
Pegswood United	30	12	5	13	78	73	29
Usworth Colliery	30	12	5	13	61	71	29
Washington Colliery	30	10	7	13	61	82	27
Chester-le-Street	30	12	1	17	84	88	25
Scotswood	30	10	5	15	63	81	25
West Wylam Colliery Welfare	30	9	5	16	58	79	23
Dipton United	30	8	5	17	58	99	21
Crawcrook Albion	30	4	10	16	44	82	18
Newcastle East End	30	3	4	23	43	110	10

Crawcrook Albion and Newcastle East End both moved to the Tyneside League. After leaving, Newcastle East End changed their name to St. Peters Albion. Dipton United moved to the North-West Durham League. Hexham joined as a newly formed club.

1934-35

Division One

Middlesbrough Reserves	38	26	9	3	129	51	61
Sunderland Reserves	38	28	3	7	126	37	59
Walker Celtic	38	27	3	8	109	53	57
Jarrow	38	24	5	9	93	60	53
Blyth Spartans	38	23	4	11	95	55	50
Eden Colliery Welfare	38	19	10	9	92	62	48
Spennymoor United	38	18	9	11	84	59	45
Workington	38	18	5	15	76	81	41
North Shields	38	17	6	15	90	69	40
Gateshead Reserves	38	17	4	17	67	72	38
Hartlepools United Reserves	38	15	6	17	91	86	36
Darlington Reserves	38	15	5	18	95	90	35
Throckley Welfare	38	13	5	20	75	94	31
Carlisle United Reserves	38	13	4	21	73	83	30
Crook Town	38	12	5	21	84	111	29
Ashington	38	10	7	21	57	96	27
Annfield Plain	38	10	6	22	74	117	26
City of Durham	38	10	2	26	56	142	22
Consett	38	5	7	26	44	118	17
West Stanley	38	6	3	29	58	132	15

Consett moved to the Northern Alliance.
Horden Colliery Welfare joined from the Wearside League.

Division Two

Newbiggin West End	24	20	2	2	79	28	42
Bedlington United	24	13	4	7	58	45	30
West Wylam Colliery Welfare	24	13	3	8	70	61	29
Hexham	24	11	5	8	53	49	27
Stakeford Albion	24	10	5	9	65	50	25
Scotswood	24	11	3	10	53	48	25
Wallsend Town	24	10	4	10	49	50	24
Usworth Colliery	24	10	3	11	59	59	23
Pegswood United	24	9	4	11	56	65	22
Birtley	24	8	5	11	56	48	21
Washington Colliery	24	7	6	11	51	75	20
Mickley	24	5	5	14	38	56	15
Chester-le-Street	24	3	3	18	33	86	9

Division Two closed down and the league reverted to a single division. Birtley, Chester-le-Street, Usworth Colliery and Washington Colliery moved to the Wearside League. Bedlington United, Hexham, Mickley, Newbiggin West End, Pegswood United, Scotswood, Stakeford Albion, Wallsend Town and West Wylam Colliery Welfare joined the newly re-formed Northern Alliance.

1935-36

Blyth Spartans	38	26	4	8	104	60	56
Walker Celtic	38	23	8	7	87	45	54
North Shields	38	22	8	8	95	52	52
Sunderland Reserves	38	22	4	12	115	65	48
Workington	38	20	5	13	87	53	45
Middlesbrough Reserves	38	21	2	15	123	78	44
Gateshead Reserves	38	18	7	13	86	73	43
Horden Colliery Welfare	38	18	6	14	84	64	42
Spennymoor United	38	19	4	15	83	81	42
Jarrow	38	17	7	14	78	68	41
Darlington Reserves	38	18	4	16	93	86	40
Throckley Welfare	38	16	5	17	80	78	37
Annfield Plain	38	16	5	17	86	96	37
Hartlepools United Reserves	38	14	6	18	77	81	34
Carlisle United Reserves	38	13	6	19	65	104	32
West Stanley	38	12	4	22	73	127	28
Eden Colliery Welfare	38	12	3	23	59	89	27
Ashington	38	10	6	22	48	74	26
City of Durham	38	8	3	27	57	115	19
Crook Town	38	5	3	30	50	141	13

Crook Town moved to the Northern League. Hexham joined from the Northern Alliance and South Shields joined as a newly formed club.

1936-37

Sunderland Reserves	38	29	5	4	155	55	63
Spennymoor United	38	23	8	7	107	55	54
Middlesbrough Reserves	38	21	9	8	117	48	51
Workington	38	22	7	9	114	54	51
Blyth Spartans	38	21	7	10	103	68	49
North Shields	38	21	5	12	115	56	47
Ashington	38	21	4	13	93	72	46
Annfield Plain	38	18	9	11	99	84	45
Throckley Welfare	38	19	7	12	99	90	45
Darlington Reserves	38	19	6	13	88	83	44
Horden Colliery Welfare	38	17	5	16	88	79	39
South Shields	38	16	7	15	88	97	39
Hartlepools United Reserves	38	15	7	16	65	81	37
Carlisle United Reserves	38	11	7	20	79	93	29
Walker Celtic	38	12	5	21	74	102	29
Jarrow	38	10	6	22	55	115	26
Hexham	38	9	6	23	64	99	24
City of Durham	38	6	6	26	67	131	18
Gateshead Reserves	38	7	3	28	67	122	17
West Stanley	38	2	3	33	37	189	7

Eden Colliery Welfare resigned and disbanded following a 19-0 defeat at Spennymoor on 6th February 1937. Their record was deleted when it stood as follows:

	23	2	2	19	32	117	6

Spennymoor United moved to the Wearside League.
Consett joined from the Northern Alliance.

1937-38

	P	W	D	L	F	A	Pts
Horden Colliery Welfare	38	24	8	6	99	39	56
Sunderland Reserves	38	26	3	9	106	39	55
South Shields	38	26	3	9	119	54	55
Blyth Spartans	38	21	6	11	113	70	48
Carlisle United Reserves	38	19	8	11	112	73	46
Ashington	38	19	8	11	87	63	46
Workington	38	20	6	12	111	86	46
Gateshead Reserves	38	19	6	13	87	74	44
Middlesbrough Reserves	38	18	4	16	97	63	40
North Shields	38	14	9	15	81	81	37
Annfield Plain	38	16	5	17	76	77	37
Walker Celtic	38	11	13	14	68	75	35
Darlington Reserves	38	13	8	17	67	91	34
Throckley Welfare	38	16	1	21	86	93	33
Hartlepools United Reserves	38	13	6	19	73	81	32
West Stanley	38	11	9	18	60	91	31
Hexham	38	13	2	23	73	130	28
Jarrow	38	10	5	23	71	105	25
Consett	38	8	7	23	64	118	23
City of Durham	38	3	3	32	43	189	9

City of Durham moved to the Wearside League.
Spennymoor United joined from the Wearside League.

1938-39

	P	W	D	L	F	A	Pts
South Shields	38	28	4	6	141	50	60
Workington	38	26	5	7	121	59	57
North Shields	38	25	7	6	111	62	57
Sunderland Reserves	38	23	5	10	121	55	51
Middlesbrough Reserves	38	21	5	12	128	76	47
Gateshead Reserves	38	21	5	12	109	71	47
Ashington	38	20	6	12	107	87	46
Horden Colliery Welfare	38	16	11	11	69	43	43
Blyth Spartans	38	15	9	14	82	97	39
Darlington Reserves	38	14	8	16	95	92	36
Consett	38	12	11	15	84	113	35
Spennymoor United	38	12	7	19	91	104	31
Hartlepools United Reserves	38	12	6	20	77	92	30
Carlisle United Reserves	38	12	4	22	98	101	28
West Stanley	38	11	6	21	75	104	28
Jarrow	38	11	5	22	56	103	27
Walker Celtic	38	11	5	22	56	103	27
Throckley Welfare	38	10	7	21	63	133	27
Hexham	38	8	8	22	66	143	24
Annfield Plain	38	7	6	25	55	130	20

Jarrow resigned from the league and disbanded. Walker Celtic moved to the Northern Alliance after being expelled for refusing to travel to Middlesbrough and Workington unless those clubs lent them money for their travel costs. Stockton joined from the Northern League and Blackhall Colliery Welfare joined from the Wearside League.

1939-40

The season started on 26th August with all 20 clubs playing their opening games but when war was declared on 3rd September, the government announced that sporting activities that would attract crowds must cease immediately and the competition was suspended.

North-Eastern League
3rd September 1939

	P	W	D	L	F	A	Pts
Sunderland Reserves	4	3	0	1	11	5	6
South Shields	3	3	0	0	8	4	6
Gateshead Reserves	3	2	1	0	10	3	5
Blackhall Colliery Welfare	3	2	1	0	10	5	5
Stockton	3	1	2	0	6	2	4
Consett	3	2	0	1	8	4	4
Blyth Spartans	3	2	0	1	6	4	4
Middlesbrough Reserves	2	1	1	0	5	1	3
Horden Colliery Welfare	2	1	0	1	4	3	2
West Stanley	2	1	0	1	7	6	2
Throckley Welfare	2	1	0	1	6	6	2
Ashington	2	0	2	0	4	4	2
Hartlepools United Reserves	2	1	0	1	3	3	2
Spennymoor United	3	1	0	2	7	9	2
Carlisle United Reserves	3	1	0	2	2	4	2
North Shields	3	0	1	2	4	8	1
Workington	3	0	1	2	4	10	1
Annfield Plain	2	0	1	1	2	5	1
Darlington Reserves	3	0	0	3	3	13	0
Hexham	3	0	0	3	0	11	0

The government soon relaxed its restrictions and the league decided to form a war-time competition which started on 21st October with 14 clubs: Annfield Plain, Ashington, Blackhall Colliery Welfare, Blyth Spartans, Consett, Gateshead Reserves, Hexham, Horden Colliery Welfare, North Shields, South Shields, Spennymoor United, Stockton, Throckley Welfare and West Stanley.

However, Hexham resigned at the end of October, citing poor support and at the end of November, both Blyth Spartans and Annfield Plain also resigned because support was far too small to meet costs. West Stanley resigned on 21st February, leaving 10 clubs to complete the season.

North-Eastern League
War-time competition

	P	W	D	L	F	A	Pts
Consett	18	11	5	2	49	29	27
Blackhall Colliery Welfare	18	10	5	3	44	35	25
North Shields	18	10	4	4	57	33	24
Stockton	18	9	5	4	56	31	23
Gateshead Reserves	18	8	2	8	50	49	18
South Shields	18	6	4	8	38	43	16
Ashington	18	6	4	8	49	56	16
Horden Colliery Welfare	18	5	3	10	33	51	13
Spennymoor United	18	5	2	11	43	59	12
Throckley Welfare	18	2	2	14	27	60	6

1940-44

Only five members of the league – Ashington, Blackhall Colliery Welfare, Consett, Darlington and Gateshead – confirmed that they would be able to field a team in the league in 1940-41 and, although clubs from outside the league were invited to take up war-time membership, only three more – Chopwell Colliery, Holiday Sports Club and Newcastle United – responded. The Management Committee deemed this insufficient and so the league closed down.

Most of those 8 clubs did though get together with a few lower status clubs in the region to form a new competition called the Northumberland & Durham War League. This was won in 1940-41 by Gateshead Reserves but even this competition could attract only 5 members for 1941-42 and so, like the North-Eastern League, it then closed down.

North-Eastern League 1944-1949

The North-Eastern League remained closed until 1944 when 9 clubs – Blackhall Colliery Welfare, Consett, Darlington Reserves, Gateshead Reserves, Hartlepools United Reserves, Horden Colliery Welfare, North Shields, Spennymoor United and Sunderland Reserves – were able to resume activity and these were joined by 3 other clubs – Murton Colliery Welfare and Reyrolles who were both pre-war members of the Wearside League, and Eppleton Colliery Welfare who were not playing at a senior level before the war but did compete in local war-time cup competitions.

1944-45

Spennymoor United	22	12	7	3	76	44	31
Blackhall Colliery Welfare	21	13	2	6	57	37	28
North Shields	22	9	8	5	62	45	26
Murton Colliery Welfare	21	11	3	7	55	43	25
Gateshead Reserves	20	10	2	8	57	44	22
Darlington Reserves	21	8	4	9	54	54	20
Horden Colliery Welfare	20	7	5	8	59	62	19
Reyrolles	21	8	2	11	48	62	18
Eppleton Colliery Welfare	20	6	5	9	45	44	17
Consett	19	7	2	10	33	37	16
Sunderland Reserves	20	5	5	10	31	51	15
Hartlepools United Reserves	21	5	1	15	46	100	11

The table above is the latest found and includes games played on 13th January 1945, when Spennymoor United were declared champions. There were still 8 games to be played but the clubs immediately began on a second series of games that continued into May. However, this second series do not appear to have counted towards any championship and no published tables have been found. It also appears that as soon as the championship was decided, the first series of games was considered complete, despite there being 8 outstanding games.

1945

After the war had ended, the league was able to resume normally for the 1945-46 season. However, both Blyth Spartans and Hexham had disbanded during the war and so Eppleton Colliery Welfare and Murton Colliery Welfare, both of whom had played in the league's war-time competition in 1944-45, were elected to replace them.

Meanwhile, new clubs were being formed in both Jarrow and Hexham as replacements for the pre-war clubs that had disbanded. Both Jarrow and Hexham Hearts joined the Northern Alliance in 1946. However there was no replacement for the other two disbanded pre-war members, Walker Celtic and Blyth Spartans.

1945-46

Spennymoor United	38	24	3	11	146	74	51
Murton Colliery Welfare	38	24	6	8	105	59	50
Ashington	38	23	4	11	116	89	50
North Shields	38	21	7	10	97	67	49
Annfield Plain	38	23	2	13	97	68	48
Consett	38	18	8	12	92	62	44
South Shields	38	19	6	13	107	87	44
Gateshead Reserves	38	17	3	18	83	90	37
Eppleton Colliery Welfare	38	15	7	16	66	92	37
Middlesbrough Reserves	38	15	6	17	76	82	36
Sunderland Reserves	38	14	7	17	84	79	35
Stockton	38	15	5	18	88	105	35
West Stanley	38	15	4	19	97	106	34
Horden Colliery Welfare	38	15	4	19	93	105	34
Darlington Reserves	38	14	6	18	76	88	34
Blackhall Colliery Welfare	38	13	6	19	76	101	32
Workington	38	12	6	20	71	75	30
Hartlepools United Reserves	38	12	4	22	62	116	28
Carlisle United Reserves	38	10	5	23	77	117	25
Throckley Welfare	38	7	9	22	60	109	23

Murton Colliery Welfare had 4 points deducted.

1946-47

Middlesbrough Reserves	38	23	6	9	104	56	52
Sunderland Reserves	38	23	5	10	111	61	51
South Shields	38	19	10	9	103	79	48
Ashington	38	19	6	13	98	93	44
Darlington Reserves	38	19	5	14	81	64	43
Gateshead Reserves	38	18	6	14	105	87	42
Consett	38	18	5	15	97	83	41
Carlisle United Reserves	38	18	5	15	101	87	41
Stockton	38	18	5	15	75	73	41
Annfield Plain	38	17	7	14	90	88	41
West Stanley	38	17	6	15	112	99	40
North Shields	38	17	4	17	97	91	38
Workington	38	14	9	15	80	69	37
Hartlepools United Reserves	38	15	7	16	70	75	37
Blackhall Colliery Welfare	38	13	10	15	57	76	36
Eppleton Colliery Welfare	38	12	7	19	63	98	31
Spennymoor United	38	11	6	21	70	81	28
Horden Colliery Welfare	38	11	6	21	71	101	28
Throckley Welfare	38	13	2	23	78	132	28
Murton Colliery Welfare	38	4	5	29	43	113	13

Throckley Welfare moved to the Northern Combination.
Blyth Spartans joined from the Northern Alliance.

1947-48

Sunderland Reserves	38	24	9	5	102	51	57
Gateshead Reserves	38	25	6	7	105	48	56
Middlesbrough Reserves	38	24	6	8	91	46	54
North Shields	38	21	7	10	89	65	49
Hartlepools United Reserves	38	17	9	12	62	62	43
West Stanley	38	18	5	15	87	74	41
Consett	38	18	4	16	87	75	40
Blyth Spartans	38	15	10	13	62	60	40
Ashington	38	16	7	15	81	70	39
Horden Colliery Welfare	38	17	3	18	60	66	37
Stockton	38	13	10	15	57	59	36
Spennymoor United	38	14	7	17	70	69	35
Darlington Reserves	38	15	5	18	65	68	35
Carlisle United Reserves	38	14	7	17	61	65	35
South Shields	38	17	1	20	65	79	35
Workington	38	14	6	18	80	98	34
Murton Colliery Welfare	38	12	7	19	65	85	31
Annfield Plain	38	11	9	18	72	96	31
Blackhall Colliery Welfare	38	7	6	25	70	115	20
Eppleton Colliery Welfare	38	3	6	29	41	121	12

1948-49

Middlesbrough Reserves	38	26	6	6	126	47	58
South Shields	38	18	13	7	80	60	49
Gateshead Reserves	38	20	7	11	77	62	47
Spennymoor United	38	19	8	11	88	66	46
Sunderland Reserves	38	18	9	11	90	53	45
Consett	38	18	9	11	80	72	45
Ashington	38	18	8	12	96	83	44
Blyth Spartans	38	18	7	13	71	56	43
Carlisle United Reserves	38	19	5	14	62	68	43
Hartlepools United Reserves	38	16	7	15	85	97	39
West Stanley	38	15	8	15	82	79	38
Horden Colliery Welfare	38	14	9	15	67	54	37
Annfield Plain	38	15	7	16	74	65	37
Stockton	38	12	10	16	67	75	34
North Shields	38	15	4	19	74	94	34
Eppleton Colliery Welfare	38	11	9	18	64	101	31
Darlington Reserves	38	11	5	22	67	83	27
Workington	38	12	3	23	84	105	27
Murton Colliery Welfare	38	8	3	27	55	106	19
Blackhall Colliery Welfare	38	4	9	25	39	102	17

1949-50

North Shields	38	24	6	8	95	60	54
West Stanley	38	23	6	9	65	45	52
Middlesbrough Reserves	38	22	7	9	124	53	51
Stockton	38	21	7	10	69	52	49
Sunderland Reserves	38	20	5	13	90	54	45
Blyth Spartans	38	18	8	12	87	69	44
Carlisle United Reserves	38	16	10	12	59	49	42
Horden Colliery Welfare	38	16	9	13	75	64	41
Workington	38	16	8	14	84	83	40
Spennymoor United	38	15	9	14	73	53	39
Hartlepools United Reserves	38	15	9	14	85	77	39
Consett	38	14	10	14	65	86	38
Murton Colliery Welfare	38	14	6	18	72	95	34
South Shields	38	11	11	16	61	78	33
Ashington	38	13	5	20	74	93	31
Gateshead Reserves	38	11	8	19	77	79	30
Annfield Plain	38	9	10	19	69	91	28
Darlington Reserves	38	11	5	22	63	91	27
Blackhall Colliery Welfare	38	9	5	24	63	115	23
Eppleton Colliery Welfare	38	8	4	26	51	114	20

1950-51

Stockton	38	25	6	7	79	37	56
Middlesbrough Reserves	38	25	5	8	100	51	55
Carlisle United Reserves	38	21	4	13	105	60	46
Horden Colliery Welfare	38	21	4	13	78	53	46
Workington	38	18	9	11	79	68	45
Sunderland Reserves	38	16	12	10	80	49	44
North Shields	38	16	12	10	80	64	44
Ashington	38	16	11	11	83	67	43
Spennymoor United	38	18	7	13	80	65	43
Blyth Spartans	38	15	9	14	67	76	39
Darlington Reserves	38	15	8	15	69	64	38
Blackhall Colliery Welfare	38	16	3	19	63	81	35
Consett	38	14	6	18	76	84	34
Hartlepools United Reserves	38	14	5	19	74	91	33
West Stanley	38	12	9	17	55	68	33
South Shields	38	12	8	18	48	81	32
Gateshead Reserves	38	10	6	22	60	82	26
Annfield Plain	38	11	4	23	64	95	26
Eppleton Colliery Welfare	38	6	11	21	51	95	23
Murton Colliery Welfare	38	5	9	24	49	109	19

Workington were elected to the Football League but maintained membership of the North-Eastern League by fielding their reserve side. Eppleton Colliery Welfare moved to the Wearside League and Murton Colliery Welfare moved to the Houghton & District League.

1951-52

Middlesbrough Reserves	34	23	4	7	96	38	50
North Shields	34	21	3	10	95	43	45
Sunderland Reserves	34	18	8	8	82	50	44
Gateshead Reserves	34	17	6	11	86	64	40
Ashington	34	15	8	11	84	78	38
Blackhall Colliery Welfare	34	14	8	12	67	51	36
Hartlepools United Reserves	34	16	4	14	69	66	36
West Stanley	34	16	3	15	74	72	35
Spennymoor United	34	14	6	14	78	70	34
Blyth Spartans	34	11	10	13	53	68	32
Stockton	34	11	8	15	60	77	30
Horden Colliery Welfare	34	13	4	17	54	80	30
Carlisle United Reserves	34	11	6	17	66	63	28
South Shields	34	9	10	15	53	74	28
Consett	34	11	6	17	70	101	28
Annfield Plain	34	10	8	16	59	90	28
Darlington Reserves	34	9	9	16	58	84	27
Workington Reserves	34	7	9	18	69	104	23

1952-53

Sunderland Reserves	34	28	2	4	102	27	58
Middlesbrough Reserves	34	23	4	7	95	46	50
Carlisle United Reserves	34	19	7	8	88	55	45
Blyth Spartans	34	20	5	9	93	61	45
Darlington Reserves	34	16	8	10	76	64	40
Spennymoor United	34	10	14	10	68	71	34
Workington Reserves	34	13	7	14	74	68	33
North Shields	34	14	3	17	81	85	31
Gateshead Reserves	34	12	6	16	68	68	30
Ashington	34	12	6	16	71	76	30
Stockton	34	13	4	17	48	66	30
Consett	34	10	9	15	45	66	29
South Shields	34	10	8	16	41	55	28
West Stanley	34	9	10	15	54	85	28
Hartlepools United Reserves	34	9	9	16	61	85	27
Blackhall Colliery Welfare	34	9	8	17	50	80	26
Horden Colliery Welfare	34	9	6	19	55	80	24
Annfield Plain	34	9	6	19	56	88	24

1953-54

Middlesbrough Reserves	34	20	7	7	92	45	47
Sunderland Reserves	34	21	5	8	92	50	47
Spennymoor United	34	20	4	10	80	45	44
Horden Colliery Welfare	34	18	7	9	66	52	43
Hartlepools United Reserves	34	18	6	10	84	74	42
Gateshead Reserves	34	17	4	13	85	69	38
Annfield Plain	34	16	4	14	71	71	36
Consett	34	17	2	15	63	75	36
Carlisle United Reserves	34	17	1	16	100	78	35
South Shields	34	12	7	15	66	68	31
Darlington Reserves	34	12	5	17	76	78	29
Workington Reserves	34	12	5	17	63	69	29
Blackhall Colliery Welfare	34	12	5	17	50	66	29
Blyth Spartans	34	11	6	17	48	82	28
Ashington	34	11	5	18	61	79	27
North Shields	34	10	5	19	65	100	25
Stockton	34	10	4	20	56	86	24
West Stanley	34	8	6	20	59	90	22

1954-55

Middlesbrough Reserves	34	25	5	4	97	27	55
Sunderland Reserves	34	23	3	8	112	42	49
Spennymoor United	34	20	7	7	80	48	47
Workington Reserves	34	19	5	10	76	42	43
Horden Colliery Welfare	34	17	5	12	72	61	39
North Shields	34	14	9	11	76	73	37
South Shields	34	13	10	11	74	67	36
Darlington Reserves	34	14	7	13	81	64	35
Blyth Spartans	34	13	7	14	64	78	33
Gateshead Reserves	34	14	4	16	71	74	32
Carlisle United Reserves	34	14	3	17	85	70	31
Annfield Plain	34	11	9	14	67	86	31
Ashington	34	10	9	15	61	74	29
Hartlepools United Reserves	34	11	5	18	65	82	27
Consett	34	12	3	19	57	98	27
Stockton	34	8	7	19	48	77	23
Blackhall Colliery Welfare	34	8	4	22	33	95	20
West Stanley	34	6	6	22	45	106	18

Blackhall Colliery Welfare moved to the Wearside League.
Whitley Bay Athletic joined from the Northern Alliance.

1955-56

Team	P	W	D	L	F	A	Pts
Middlesbrough Reserves	34	28	3	3	112	34	59
South Shields	34	20	7	7	96	51	47
Ashington	34	19	7	8	92	59	45
Workington Reserves	34	18	8	8	81	42	44
Sunderland Reserves	34	20	3	11	87	54	43
Gateshead Reserves	34	13	11	10	69	65	37
Blyth Spartans	34	17	3	14	68	80	37
Stockton	34	15	5	14	68	65	35
Carlisle United Reserves	34	14	6	14	74	56	34
Darlington Reserves	34	13	7	14	76	71	33
Annfield Plain	34	12	8	14	54	65	32
Spennymoor United	34	12	5	17	59	63	29
Consett	34	11	6	17	58	88	28
North Shields	34	10	6	18	54	78	26
Hartlepools United Reserves	34	10	6	18	48	78	26
Whitley Bay Athletic	34	8	8	18	62	92	24
Horden Colliery Welfare	34	8	5	21	50	94	21
West Stanley	34	4	4	26	34	107	12

1956-57

Team	P	W	D	L	F	A	Pts
Spennymoor United	34	22	7	5	79	42	51
South Shields	34	22	5	7	88	39	49
North Shields	34	21	6	7	92	39	48
Ashington	34	20	8	6	117	55	48
Middlesbrough Reserves	34	20	7	7	92	43	47
Sunderland Reserves	34	20	5	9	97	46	45
Workington Reserves	34	16	7	11	74	57	39
Blyth Spartans	34	17	5	12	90	71	39
Hartlepools United Reserves	34	18	3	13	80	71	39
Darlington Reserves	34	14	6	14	78	75	34
Gateshead Reserves	34	13	6	15	62	79	32
Annfield Plain	34	10	7	17	66	86	27
Horden Colliery Welfare	34	11	4	19	54	84	26
Consett	34	8	4	22	51	86	20
Stockton	34	10	0	24	59	107	20
Carlisle United Reserves	34	5	8	21	35	83	18
West Stanley	34	6	4	24	32	100	16
Whitley Bay Athletic	34	6	2	26	44	127	14

1957-58

Team	P	W	D	L	F	A	Pts
South Shields	34	27	3	4	107	42	57
Middlesbrough Reserves	34	22	5	7	92	33	49
Ashington	34	22	5	7	79	48	49
North Shields	34	16	9	9	66	44	41
Workington Reserves	34	17	5	12	73	59	39
Sunderland Reserves	34	17	4	13	84	50	38
Gateshead Reserves	34	15	8	11	82	72	38
Carlisle United Reserves	34	16	4	14	66	57	36
Blyth Spartans	34	14	7	13	66	66	35
Horden Colliery Welfare	34	13	9	12	58	59	35
Hartlepools United Reserves	34	15	4	15	72	61	34
Spennymoor United	34	13	8	13	70	72	34
Consett	34	13	6	15	68	63	32
Annfield Plain	34	9	7	18	57	96	25
Darlington Reserves	34	7	8	19	56	92	22
Stockton	34	7	5	22	60	107	19
West Stanley	34	8	2	24	47	97	18
Whitley Bay Athletic	34	3	5	26	35	120	11

The North-Eastern League (NEL) was thrown into turmoil in February 1958 following the announcement of the intention to form a new league in the north that would cater specifically for Football League reserve sides. The idea of the new league came jointly from Sunderland and Middlesbrough but 4 more NEL reserve sides – Carlisle United, Darlington, Hartlepools United and Workington – also decided to join the new league, initially known as the North Central League. The NEL lost another club at the end of April when Whitley Bay Athletic resigned to join the Northern League.

The NEL was thus reduced to 11 clubs and there was just one potential replacement, Redcar Albion of the Teesside League. Others were sought and Middlesbrough, Newcastle United and Sunderland applied for entry for their 3rd teams. These applications were eventually agreed by the NEL Management Committee, but were unacceptable to the 4 strongest non-League sides – Ashington, Blyth Spartans, North Shields and South Shields – who believed it would significantly reduce the strength of the league.

These 4 therefore also resigned and joined the Midland League which itself had lost 8 Football League reserve sides to the new league. Consett, Horden Colliery Welfare and Stockton joined the exodus from the NEL to the Midland League a few days later, as did Spennymoor United after withdrawing a hurriedly made application to the Northern League.

This left just 3 members of the NEL. Of these, West Stanley joined the Northern Alliance and so did Annfield Plain after an unsuccessful attempt to join the Northern League. Gateshead Reserves joined the new North Central League, having initially rejected the idea. Redcar Albion stayed in the Teesside League where they captured their third successive league title in 1958-59.

The NEL was then "put into abeyance" with its remaining funds intact, and with the hope that it might be re-formed in a year's time.

MIDLAND LEAGUE

In addition to the 8 clubs who moved from the North-Eastern League in 1958, there were 11 other clubs who were members of the Midland League (ML) in 1958-59, as listed here. The record of each club in 1957-58 is given in brackets. They were: Denaby United (23rd in ML), Frickley Colliery (10th in ML), Gainsborough Trinity (12th in ML), Goole Town (17th in ML), Grantham (18th in ML), Peterborough United (ML champions in each of the previous 3 seasons), Scarborough (7th in ML), Scunthorpe United Reserves (11th in ML), Skegness Town (newcomers to the league, champions of the Central Alliance, Division One – South), Sutton Town (newcomers to the league, 2nd in Central Alliance, Division One – North) and Worksop Town (24th in ML).

1958-59

Team	P	W	D	L	F	A	Pts
Peterborough United	36	32	4	0	137	26	68
Ashington	36	28	4	4	125	40	60
North Shields	36	21	6	9	82	49	48
South Shields	36	19	8	9	79	45	46
Blyth Spartans	36	18	10	8	79	52	46
Skegness Town	36	17	7	12	73	71	41
Horden Colliery Welfare	36	15	10	11	68	73	40
Consett	36	16	4	16	72	72	36
Scarborough	36	13	9	14	63	79	35
Frickley Colliery	36	12	9	15	70	75	33
Goole Town	36	12	7	17	72	90	31
Gainsborough Trinity	36	10	10	16	70	77	30
Sutton Town	36	10	9	17	69	98	29
Spennymoor United	36	8	12	16	55	92	28
Scunthorpe United Reserves	36	8	10	18	58	70	26
Denaby United	36	10	3	23	57	107	23
Stockton	36	7	8	21	65	106	22
Grantham	36	7	7	22	66	90	21
Worksop Town	36	10	1	25	50	98	21

Scunthorpe United Reserves moved to the North Regional League and Grantham moved to the Central Alliance.

Midland League / Northern Counties League / North-Eastern League 1959-64

1959-60

Peterborough United	32	23	6	3	108	37	52
North Shields	32	22	5	5	76	27	49
Ashington	32	19	7	6	90	40	45
South Shields	32	16	8	8	65	41	40
Blyth Spartans	32	13	10	9	74	51	36
Stockton	32	12	8	12	53	66	32
Goole Town	32	13	5	14	62	78	31
Consett	32	13	4	15	54	65	30
Spennymoor United	32	12	6	14	47	57	30
Horden Colliery Welfare	32	12	5	15	46	62	29
Gainsborough Trinity	32	7	14	11	41	60	28
Skegness Town	32	9	9	14	50	64	27
Scarborough	32	9	8	15	48	65	26
Worksop Town	32	10	4	18	41	70	24
Sutton Town	32	6	11	15	44	76	23
Denaby United	32	8	6	18	44	68	22
Frickley Colliery	32	7	6	19	54	70	20

The cost of travel in the Midland League was too high for the former NEL clubs and in early March, first Stockton and then Spennymoor United resigned to join the Northern League. At the end of the month, Ashington, Blyth Spartans, Consett, Horden Colliery Welfare, North Shields and South Shields all resigned to form a new competition, the Northern Counties League. Scarborough, who had been members of the Midland League since 1927, resigned at the same time to join the new league.

The number of clubs in the Northern Counties League (NCL) was raised to 10 as Stockton joined, having withdrawn their application to the Northern League, Annfield Plain joined from the Northern Alliance and Gateshead joined after failing to be re-elected to the Football League. Spennymoor United did join the Northern League instead.

Of the other Midland League clubs, Peterborough United were elected to the Football League while Goole Town, Gainsborough Trinity, Skegness Town, Worksop Town, Sutton Town and Denaby United all joined the Central Alliance and Frickley Colliery joined the Cheshire League. The Midland League then closed down.

NORTH-EASTERN LEAGUE 1959-60

After a season in abeyance, the NEL was re-formed at a meeting in Newcastle on 9th May, 1959. There were 11 clubs in the re-formed league but of a far lower standard than those who were members in 1957-58.

The local Football League clubs fielded their 3rd teams instead of their reserves and South Shields fielded their reserves instead of their first team. The 11 clubs were Bowburn C.W., Cockfield, Gateshead "A", Heaton Stannington, Kibblesworth C.W., Middlesbrough "A", Redcar Albion, Reyrolle, South Shields Reserves, Sunderland "A" and West View Albion.

Redcar Albion	20	16	2	2	34
South Shields Reserves	20	15	1	4	31
Sunderland "A"	20	14	2	4	30
Heaton Stannington	20	8	5	7	21
Kibblesworth Colliery Welfare	20	8	4	8	20
Bowburn Colliery Welfare	20	8	3	9	19
Middlesbrough "A"	20	7	2	11	16
Gateshead "A"	20	5	4	11	14
Cockfield	20	6	2	12	14
West View Albion	20	5	3	12	13
Reyrolle	20	4	0	16	8

Note: No goal record has been found.

At the end of the season, Sunderland and Middlesbrough were amongst several clubs who resigned and the NEL again went into abeyance.

NORTHERN COUNTIES LEAGUE 1960-61

North Shields	18	11	5	2	59	28	27
Ashington	18	12	2	4	50	22	26
Blyth Spartans	18	8	6	4	29	22	22
Gateshead	18	8	4	6	35	26	20
Consett	18	9	1	8	46	42	19
Scarborough	18	9	1	8	32	30	19
South Shields	18	7	4	7	31	32	18
Stockton	18	5	4	9	39	55	14
Horden Colliery Welfare	18	6	2	10	25	43	14
Annfield Plain	18	0	1	17	15	61	1

Carlisle United Reserves, Darlington Reserves and Workington Reserves all joined from the North Regional League.

1961-62

Consett	24	16	3	5	77	44	35
South Shields	24	16	2	6	67	30	34
Ashington	24	14	5	5	63	36	33
Horden Colliery Welfare	24	13	4	7	57	50	30
Gateshead	24	13	3	8	42	34	29
Scarborough	24	11	5	8	48	31	27
North Shields	24	10	5	9	61	42	25
Darlington Reserves	24	8	5	11	55	57	21
Blyth Spartans	24	7	6	11	52	61	20
Carlisle United Reserves	24	6	7	11	31	43	19
Stockton	24	6	3	15	41	82	15
Annfield Plain	24	5	3	16	34	72	13
Workington Reserves	24	5	1	18	36	82	11

The Northern Counties League was struggling financially but the dormant NEL had £1,700 in its bank account. At the end of the season, the decision was therefore taken to close the Northern Counties League and for all of its members to join the North-Eastern League. However, Gateshead decided to join the North Regional League instead. Redcar Albion joined after a season's inactivity because of ground problems.

NORTH-EASTERN LEAGUE 1962-63

Scarborough	22	14	4	4	71	34	32
South Shields	22	13	5	4	48	27	31
North Shields	22	11	4	7	54	43	26
Blyth Spartans	22	11	3	8	49	39	25
Ashington	22	7	7	8	47	46	21
Darlington Reserves	22	10	1	11	35	37	21
Horden Colliery Welfare	22	8	5	9	33	36	21
Stockton	22	8	3	11	39	57	19
Consett	22	7	4	11	40	49	18
Workington Reserves	22	8	2	12	32	49	18
Annfield Plain	22	7	3	12	27	46	17
Carlisle United Reserves	22	6	3	13	35	47	15

Redcar Albion resigned on 11th February 1963 because they could not afford the rent for their ground and their record was deleted.

The reserves sides of Carlisle United, Darlington and Workington returned to the North Regional League and Scarborough returned to the Midland League.

1963-64

Horden Colliery Welfare	14	10	2	2	34	11	22
South Shields	14	11	0	3	37	20	22
Ashington	14	7	2	5	33	19	16
Blyth Spartans	14	7	2	5	43	33	16
Stockton	14	4	4	6	32	35	12
Annfield Plain	14	4	2	8	22	37	10
North Shields	14	2	3	9	25	40	7
Consett	14	2	3	9	14	45	7

Annfield Plain, Ashington, Consett, Horden Colliery Welfare and Stockton all joined the Wearside League, Blyth Spartans and North Shields joined the Northern League and South Shields joined the North Regional League. The North-Eastern League disbanded at the end of the season.

PALATINE LEAGUE 1920-1926

The Palatine League was a semi-professional competition founded on 6th May 1920 with 10 clubs. Its principal aim was to provide fixtures for the reserve sides of 4 North-Eastern League clubs – Darlington, Durham City, Shildon Athletic and Spennymoor United.

The other 6 founder members were: Coundon United, Darlington Rise Carr, Haverton Hill, Washington Chemical Works, West Auckland (who had moved from the Northern League and changed their name from Auckland St. Helen's United) and West Hartlepool St. Joseph's (who had also moved from the Northern League).

1920-21

A Final table has not been found.

Darlington Reserves were champions and the other competing sides were Coundon United, Darlington Rise Carr, Durham City Reserves, Haverton Hill, Shildon Athletic Reserves, Spennymoor United Reserves, Washington Chemical Works, West Auckland and West Hartlepool St. Joseph's (who finished 4th).

At the end of the season, Darlington Reserves moved to the North-Eastern League and Durham City Reserves moved to the Northern Alliance. Haverton Hill and West Auckland also left. Chester-le-Street Reserves, Chilton Colliery Recreation Athletic, Ferryhill Athletic, Hartlepools United Reserves, Hetton United, Leasingthorne E.R., Trimdon Grange and West Stanley Reserves all joined.

1921-22

Ferryhill Athletic	26	18	3	5	83	25	39
Hartlepools United Reserves	26	18	2	6	71	28	38
Trimdon Grange	26	17	3	6	70	38	37
Shildon Athletic Reserves	26	15	5	6	63	41	35
Coundon United	26	12	10	4	52	34	34
West Stanley Reserves	26	11	8	7	59	49	30
Chilton Colliery Recreation Athletic	26	11	6	9	46	38	28
West Hartlepool St. Joseph's	26	11	3	12	33	42	25
Spennymoor United Reserves	26	8	7	11	32	61	23
Leasingthorne E.R.	26	7	7	12	40	58	21
Darlington Rise Carr	26	6	5	15	45	64	17
Hetton United	26	6	4	16	25	65	16
Chester-le-Street Reserves	26	3	5	18	22	56	11
Washington Chemical Works	26	4	2	20	36	75	10

Hartlepools United Reserves moved to the North-Eastern League and Washington Chemical Works moved to the Tyneside League.
West Hartlepool St. Joseph's, Leasingthorne E.R. and Darlington Rise Carr also all left the league. Wheatley Hill Colliery and Thornley Albion joined.

1922-23

Ferryhill Athletic	20	18	2	0	76	16	38
Chilton Colliery Recreation Athletic	20	13	1	6	64	24	27
Trimdon Grange	20	11	4	5	44	19	26
Coundon United	20	9	2	9	39	49	20
Wheatley Hill Colliery	20	8	3	9	38	39	19
West Stanley Reserves	20	7	5	8	32	38	19
Thornley Albion	20	7	4	9	34	32	18
Spennymoor United Reserves	20	6	4	10	39	52	16
Shildon Athletic Reserves	20	6	3	11	38	59	15
Chester-le-Street Reserves	20	5	1	14	26	60	11
Hetton United	20	5	1	14	24	56	11

Ferryhill Athletic moved to the Northern League and Hetton United moved to the Wearside League. Chester-le-Street Reserves and West Stanley Reserves also left the league. Coxhoe United, Kelloe Colliery, West Auckland and Wingate Albion Comrades all joined.
Shildon Athletic changed their name to Shildon.

1923-24

Chilton Colliery Recreation Athletic	20	13	3	4	49	17	29
Thornley Albion	20	10	6	4	49	28	26
Coundon United	20	11	3	6	35	34	25
Coxhoe United	20	9	3	8	38	29	21
Trimdon Grange	20	8	4	8	31	30	20
Spennymoor United Reserves	20	7	5	8	36	37	19
Kelloe Colliery	20	7	4	9	40	46	18
Wingate Albion Comrades	20	6	5	9	30	35	17
West Auckland	20	6	5	9	24	31	17
Wheatley Hill Colliery	20	8	1	11	26	51	17
Shildon Reserves	20	4	3	13	27	47	11

Coxhoe United, Spennymoor United Reserves and West Auckland all left the league and Deaf Hill United joined.

1924-25

Chilton Colliery Recreation Athletic	16	15	1	0	54	13	31
Trimdon Grange	16	11	1	4	46	28	23
Wheatley Hill Colliery	16	6	6	4	35	25	18
Thornley Albion	16	6	6	4	33	25	18
Shildon Reserves	16	5	4	7	27	27	14
Coundon United	16	3	8	5	39	40	14
Kelloe Colliery	16	5	2	9	31	53	12
Wingate Albion Comrades	16	3	5	8	22	30	11
Deaf Hill United	16	1	1	14	17	61	3

Kelloe Colliery resigned from the league and disbanded.
Chilton Colliery Recreation Athletic moved to the Northern Alliance but are recorded as having continued to play in the Palatine League, possibly fielding a reserve side. Shildon Reserves and Coundon United also left. Sunnybrow Olympic and Butterknowle W.C. both joined.

1925-26

A Final table has not been found.

The 8 competing clubs were Butterknowle W.C., Chilton Colliery Recreation Athletic, Deaf Hill United, Sunnybrow Olympic, Thornley Albion, Trimdon Grange, Wheatley Hill Colliery and Wingate Albion Comrades but Trimdon Grange did not complete the season, having resigned and disbanded at the end of September, 1925.

The Palatine League closed down at the end of the 1925-26 season.

NORTH REGIONAL LEAGUE 1958-1969

The North Regional League was the result of an initiative led by Sunderland and Middlesbrough who wanted to form a competition composed entirely of Football League reserve teams as they felt this would better aid the development of their younger players. They therefore organised a meeting, held in York on 10th February 1958, to discuss the idea.

Sunderland and Middlesbrough both had their reserve sides playing in the North-Eastern League where there were 5 other FL reserve sides. Darlington and Hartlepools United both attended the meeting while Carlisle United, Gateshead and Workington gave written support for the idea, although Gateshead later withdrew that support.

In addition, 10 other reserve sides were represented at the meeting, 9 of them from the Midland League – Bradford (Park Avenue), Bradford City, Grimsby Town, Hull City, Lincoln City, Mansfield Town, Notts County, Rotherham United and York City – plus Halifax Town from the Yorkshire League. Applications to join were later received from Accrington Stanley of the Lancashire Combination, Stockport County of the Cheshire League and Barrow of the Lancashire League. Notts County and Mansfield Town later withdrew their support but Doncaster Rovers joined and with 18 clubs confirming membership, the new league was able to go ahead.

The league was originally to be called the North Central League but that was perhaps too similar a name to the existing Central League, so a new title was required. After a brief dalliance with Combined Counties League, the title North Regional League was decided upon.

The departure of so many clubs hit both the North-Eastern League and the Midland League very hard. The North-Eastern League was unable to find adequate replacements and so its remaining clubs moved to a variety of other leagues, 8 of them joining the Midland League, thus filling the gaps created there by the new league. The North-Eastern League was unable to operate in 1958-59 and so Gateshead, its one remaining reserve side, made a late application to become the 19th founder member of the North Regional League, which was accepted.

1958-59

Middlesbrough Reserves	36	23	7	6	88	37	53
Sunderland Reserves	36	24	3	9	104	46	51
Hull City Reserves	36	21	6	9	89	61	48
Rotherham United Reserves	36	18	7	11	94	65	43
York City Reserves	36	18	6	12	70	56	42
Lincoln City Reserves	36	15	10	11	75	67	40
Stockport County Reserves	36	14	9	13	75	61	37
Hartlepools United Reserves	36	15	7	14	78	84	37
Carlisle United Reserves	36	14	9	13	49	55	37
Bradford City Reserves	36	13	10	13	64	71	36
Grimsby Town Reserves	36	12	10	14	58	58	34
Workington Reserves	36	14	5	17	78	75	33
Accrington Stanley Reserves	36	12	7	17	54	62	31
Doncaster Rovers Reserves	36	11	9	16	59	81	31
Darlington Reserves	36	10	9	17	51	66	29
Halifax Town Reserves	36	10	9	17	55	78	29
Bradford (Park Avenue) Reserves	36	9	9	18	49	73	27
Barrow Reserves	36	10	4	22	46	95	24
Gateshead Reserves	36	7	8	21	54	99	22

Crewe Alexandra Reserves and Port Vale Reserves both joined from the Cheshire League and Scunthorpe United Reserves joined from the Midland League.

1959-60

Middlesbrough Reserves	42	28	6	8	115	46	62
Sunderland Reserves	42	23	8	11	103	60	54
Port Vale Reserves	42	25	4	13	101	70	54
Workington Reserves	42	22	8	12	112	76	52
Scunthorpe United Reserves	42	22	7	13	79	58	51
Hull City Reserves	42	22	6	14	85	69	50
York City Reserves	42	19	6	17	91	78	44
Darlington Reserves	42	16	11	15	75	79	43
Carlisle United Reserves	42	18	6	18	78	67	42
Rotherham United Reserves	42	16	10	16	79	69	42
Bradford (Park Avenue) Reserves	42	19	4	19	83	86	42
Gateshead Reserves	42	19	3	20	85	80	41
Halifax Town Reserves	42	15	10	17	73	89	40
Lincoln City Reserves	42	17	5	20	77	72	39
Crewe Alexandra Reserves	42	15	9	18	65	67	39
Bradford City Reserves	42	16	7	19	67	72	39
Doncaster Rovers Reserves	42	17	4	21	81	99	38
Accrington Stanley Reserves	42	16	5	21	60	95	37
Grimsby Town Reserves	42	13	8	21	58	67	34
Hartlepools United Reserves	42	11	10	21	82	125	32
Stockport County Reserves	42	10	8	24	56	103	28
Barrow Reserves	42	6	9	27	50	126	21

Gateshead Reserves moved to the Northern Alliance.

North Regional League 1960-1964

1960-61

Team	P	W	D	L	F	A	Pts
Middlesbrough Reserves	40	28	8	4	126	46	64
Port Vale Reserves	40	30	2	8	132	63	62
Sunderland Reserves	40	23	7	10	100	60	53
Scunthorpe United Reserves	40	21	8	11	89	52	50
Hartlepools United Reserves	40	21	7	12	91	79	49
Hull City Reserves	40	20	7	13	92	66	47
Darlington Reserves	40	21	4	15	85	82	46
Lincoln City Reserves	40	19	6	15	84	79	44
Bradford (Park Avenue) Reserves	40	17	8	15	100	67	42
Rotherham United Reserves	40	19	4	17	98	77	42
Doncaster Rovers Reserves	40	16	10	14	67	75	42
Crewe Alexandra Reserves	40	16	6	18	83	81	38
Carlisle United Reserves	40	13	10	17	64	77	36
Grimsby Town Reserves	40	14	8	18	62	81	36
Bradford City Reserves	40	12	8	20	73	97	32
Halifax Town Reserves	40	12	8	20	66	88	32
York City Reserves	40	12	6	22	69	85	30
Workington Reserves	40	9	9	22	60	96	27
Accrington Stanley Reserves	40	11	3	26	55	106	25
Stockport County Reserves	40	9	6	25	46	122	24
Barrow Reserves	40	7	5	28	48	110	19

Carlisle United Reserves, Darlington Reserves and Workington Reserves all moved to the Northern Counties League, Barrow Reserves moved to the Lancashire Combination and Doncaster Rovers disbanded their reserve team.

1961-62

Team	P	W	D	L	F	A	Pts
Middlesbrough Reserves	28	18	4	6	79	36	40
Scunthorpe United Reserves	28	17	6	5	61	39	40
Sunderland Reserves	28	16	2	10	67	50	34
Bradford City Reserves	28	15	4	9	56	43	34
Lincoln City Reserves	28	13	7	8	57	40	33
Grimsby Town Reserves	28	14	3	11	70	50	31
Crewe Alexandra Reserves	28	12	4	12	42	49	28
Port Vale Reserves	28	9	9	10	56	58	27
Bradford (Park Avenue) Reserves	28	11	4	13	52	49	26
Rotherham United Reserves	28	9	7	12	50	60	25
Hartlepools United Reserves	28	11	3	14	48	60	25
York City Reserves	28	8	4	16	40	58	20
Stockport County Reserves	28	7	6	15	42	82	20
Hull City Reserves	28	7	5	16	33	51	19
Halifax Town Reserves	28	7	4	17	32	59	18

Accrington Stanley Reserves resigned during the season and their record was deleted. Port Vale moved their reserve side to the Midland Intermediate League. Oldham Athletic Reserves joined from the Lancashire Combination and Doncaster Rovers joined, the reserve side having been re-formed. Gateshead became the first club to field their first team in the North Regional League after joining from the Northern Counties League.

1962-63

Team	P	W	D	L	F	A	Pts
Rotherham United Reserves	32	23	5	4	89	32	51
Middlesbrough Reserves	32	20	4	8	80	49	44
Crewe Alexandra Reserves	32	16	9	7	69	45	41
Bradford (Park Avenue) Reserves	32	17	6	9	88	52	40
Scunthorpe United Reserves	32	16	8	8	58	43	40
Sunderland Reserves	32	17	6	9	65	54	40
Doncaster Rovers Reserves	32	16	5	11	62	55	37
Grimsby Town Reserves	32	16	3	13	68	53	35
Lincoln City Reserves	32	14	7	11	54	58	35
Oldham Athletic Reserves	32	12	6	14	49	60	30
Gateshead	32	10	9	13	60	55	29
Hull City Reserves	32	11	7	14	57	61	29
Hartlepools United Reserves	32	10	8	14	53	62	28
York City Reserves	32	6	6	20	35	80	18
Stockport County Reserves	32	6	5	21	33	64	17
Halifax Town Reserves	32	4	9	19	34	67	17
Bradford City Reserves	32	3	7	22	45	109	13

Carlisle United Reserves, Darlington Reserves and Workington Reserves joined from the North-Eastern League and Port Vale Reserves joined from the Midland Intermediate League.

1963-64

Team	P	W	D	L	F	A	Pts
Gateshead	32	21	3	8	79	47	45
Middlesbrough Reserves	32	19	6	7	74	37	44
Rotherham United Reserves	32	18	8	6	76	47	44
Hull City Reserves	32	20	4	8	67	43	44
Scunthorpe United Reserves	32	19	4	9	85	53	42
Grimsby Town Reserves	32	15	9	8	67	49	39
Lincoln City Reserves	32	15	7	10	77	69	37
Sunderland Reserves	32	12	11	9	69	62	35
Crewe Alexandra Reserves	32	16	3	13	51	51	35
Port Vale Reserves	32	13	7	12	63	65	33
Carlisle United Reserves	32	12	8	12	49	53	32
Oldham Athletic Reserves	32	12	5	15	85	65	29
Doncaster Rovers Reserves	32	11	7	14	50	63	29
Darlington Reserves	32	10	7	15	60	59	27
Bradford (Park Avenue) Reserves	32	11	5	16	63	74	27
Halifax Town Reserves	32	9	8	15	57	72	26
York City Reserves	32	8	10	14	38	59	26
Bradford City Reserves	32	8	7	17	63	88	23
Workington Reserves	32	8	6	18	53	76	22
Stockport County Reserves	32	4	10	18	34	79	18
Hartlepools United Reserves	32	3	9	20	44	93	15

Stockport County Reserves left the league.
South Shields (first team) joined from the North-Eastern League.

1964-65

Hull City Reserves	32	24	4	4	95	26	52
Sunderland Reserves	32	23	5	4	105	33	51
Middlesbrough Reserves	32	19	8	5	102	45	46
Gateshead	32	17	7	8	80	43	41
South Shields	32	18	4	10	79	61	40
Port Vale Reserves	31	15	8	8	60	39	38
Rotherham United Reserves	32	15	8	9	72	54	38
Lincoln City Reserves	32	15	6	11	61	54	36
Carlisle United Reserves	32	15	5	12	68	43	35
Scunthorpe United Reserves	32	14	7	11	65	58	35
Oldham Athletic Reserves	32	15	5	12	75	72	35
Grimsby Town Reserves	30	14	4	12	60	63	32
Doncaster Rovers Reserves	32	11	9	12	59	59	31
Bradford City Reserves	32	11	5	16	65	76	27
Workington Reserves	32	11	5	16	56	90	27
York City Reserves	32	8	6	18	48	69	22
Bradford (Park Avenue) Reserves	32	9	4	19	46	74	22
Crewe Alexandra Reserves	31	8	4	19	37	78	20
Darlington Reserves	32	5	6	21	45	99	16
Hartlepools United Reserves	32	4	7	21	32	95	15
Halifax Town Reserves	32	3	3	26	32	111	9

Two games were not played.
Lincoln City Reserves and Scunthorpe United Reserves both moved to the Midland League, Port Vale Reserves moved to the West Midlands League, Crewe Alexandra Reserves moved to the Lancashire League and Grimsby Town disbanded their reserve side. Ashington (first team) joined from the Wearside League.

1965-66

Hull City Reserves	32	23	4	5	89	30	50
Middlesbrough Reserves	32	21	5	6	79	41	47
Carlisle United Reserves	32	22	3	7	75	39	47
South Shields	32	21	4	7	115	46	46
Sunderland Reserves	32	20	2	10	99	64	42
Ashington	32	15	8	9	70	55	38
Rotherham United Reserves	32	14	5	13	59	54	33
Oldham Athletic Reserves	32	10	7	15	50	66	27
Workington Reserves	32	10	7	15	66	92	27
Gateshead	32	10	6	16	48	67	26
Darlington Reserves	32	11	4	17	57	82	26
Doncaster Rovers Reserves	32	8	9	15	51	65	25
Hartlepools United Reserves	32	9	7	16	56	76	25
York City Res	32	9	6	17	58	78	24
Bradford City Reserves	32	10	4	18	36	68	24
Bradford (Park Avenue) Reserves	32	7	5	20	45	90	19
Halifax Town Reserves	32	6	6	20	37	77	18

Bradford City Reserves and York City Reserves both moved to the Yorkshire League, Oldham Athletic Reserves moved to the Lancashire Combination, Hartlepools United Reserves moved to the Wearside League and Halifax Town Reserves and Workington Reserves also left.

1966-67

South Shields	20	13	3	4	53	29	29
Hull City Reserves	20	11	6	3	37	22	28
Sunderland Reserves	20	11	2	7	57	33	24
Ashington	20	9	6	5	53	34	24
Rotherham United Reserves	20	11	2	7	44	38	24
Middlesbrough Reserves	20	8	3	9	45	42	19
Carlisle United Reserves	20	8	3	9	27	44	19
Doncaster Rovers Reserves	20	6	4	10	31	36	16
Gateshead	20	6	3	11	29	41	15
Bradford (Park Avenue) Reserves	20	5	4	11	22	43	14
Darlington Reserves	20	3	2	15	30	66	8

Darlington Reserves moved to the Wearside League while Rotherham United, Doncaster Rovers and Bradford (Park Avenue) moved their reserves to the Northern Intermediate League. Stockton (first team) joined from the Wearside League and Workington Reserves also joined.

1967-68

Hull City Reserves	15	11	3	1	42	17	25
Middlesbrough Reserves	16	10	3	3	47	27	23
Sunderland Reserves	16	9	4	3	45	27	22
South Shields	16	9	3	4	39	18	21
Ashington	16	6	4	6	28	26	16
Gateshead	16	5	6	5	26	37	16
Carlisle United Reserves	15	2	4	9	18	30	8
Stockton	16	1	4	11	21	44	6
Workington Reserves	16	1	3	12	17	46	5

One game was not played.
South Shields, Ashington and Gateshead moved to the new Northern Premier League, Stockton moved to the Wearside League and Hull City moved their reserves to the Northern Intermediate League.

1968-69

Sunderland Reserves	6	4	2	0	17	8	10
Middlesbrough Reserves	6	4	1	1	20	5	9
Carlisle United Reserves	6	2	1	3	13	10	5
Workington Reserves	6	0	0	6	5	32	0

The North Regional League closed down. Carlisle United disbanded their reserve side and Sunderland Reserves played just friendlies in 1969-70.